More praise for

Our Savage Neighbors

Winner of the Bancroft Prize and the Mark Lynton History Prize

"I know of no other book like this fascinating, disturbing meditation on the ways in which the terrors of Indian war shaped American culture. *Our Savage Neighbors* will compel historians to rethink the origins of American pluralism, and lay readers will find that it transforms the ways in which they understand the origins of the United States. It is not too much to call this book a masterpiece."

—Fred Anderson, University of Colorado,
author of *The War That Made America*

"With elegant, vivid prose, Peter Silver guides us through a world where American leaders, often aided and abetted by the press, engaged in fear mongering in order to advance their own agendas, stirring up (or conjuring up) anti-Indian feeling among the populace. *Our Savage Neighbors* sheds startling new light on everything from the American frontier and the Seven Years' War to the American Revolution and the toxic well-springs of Indian-hating."

—James Merrell, Vassar College, author of *Into the American Woods*

"With vivid prose and in evocative detail, Peter Silver plunges readers into a colonial heart of darkness: the fear and loathing of Indians along the frontier of British America. This powerful book illuminates the rise of the American republic from the ashes of native villages and settler cabins in a borderland of terror and violence, both real and imagined."

—Alan Taylor, University of California, Davis,
author of *The Divided Ground*

"Takes us deep into the terror of violent interactions. . . . Silver's superb analysis and stunning prose create unsettling implications for other times of war . . . both historically specific and frighteningly timeless."

—Kathleen DuVal, *Common-place*

... Fascinating ... on the role of frontier violence in forging a uniquely American psyche."   —Mark Burch, *Library Journal*

"Shows how the logic and grammar of hatred worked. . . . As a study of a vital strain of . . . colonial culture, Silver's book is little short of monumental."   —Peter C. Mancall, *Reviews in American History*

OUR SAVAGE NEIGHBORS

*How Indian War
Transformed Early America*

PETER SILVER

W. W. NORTON & COMPANY · NEW YORK LONDON

For my mother and father
with love and gratitude

For information about permission to reproduce selections from this book,
write to Permissions, W. W. Norton & Company, Inc., 500 Fifth Avenue,
New York, NY 10110

For information about special discounts for bulk purchases, please contact
W. W. Norton Special Sales at specialsales@wwnorton.com or 800-233-4830

Manufacturing by RR Donnelley, Bloomsburg
Book design by Lovedog Studio
Production manager: Anna Oler

Library of Congress Cataloging-in-Publication Data

Silver, Peter Rhoads.
Our savage neighbors : how Indian war transformed early America /
Peter Silver. — 1st ed.
p. cm.
Included bibliographical references and index.
ISBN 978-0-393-06248-9 (hardcover)
1. Indians of North America—History—Colonial period, ca. 1600–1775. 2. Indians of
North America—First contact with Europeans. 3. Indians of North America—Wars.
4. Frontier and pioneer life—United States—History. 5. United States—History—
Colonial period, ca. 1600–1775. 6. United States—Race relations. I. Title.
E77.S573 2008
973.2—dc22   2007025279

ISBN 978-0-393-33490-6 pbk.

W. W. Norton & Company, Inc.
500 Fifth Avenue, New York, N.Y. 10110
www.wwnorton.com

W. W. Norton & Company Ltd.
Castle House, 75/76 Wells Street, London W1T 3QT

1 2 3 4 5 6 7 8 9 0

[H]ere is about a hundred families Setteled upon our Land and what they are their Setteled for we knowe not the Reason of it. . . . we cannot injoy our Birth-Right in Peace and Quietness, but we are abused as if we were Enemies, and not Friends, for we dare not speake for our Rights but there is an Uprore, and in Danger of being cut in Peices and distroyed . . . .

—Petition of Delaware Indians near
Upper Smithfield, Pennsylvania (1741)

[I]n as much as we Dwell upon the Frontiers our case at present is Lamentably Dangerous, we being in such imminent Peril of being inhumanly Butchered by our Savage neighbours, whose tender Mercies are Cruelty, and if they should come upon us now we are naked and Defenceless . . . .

—Petition of European residents of
Lurgan, Pennsylvania (1755)

This account . . . [is] only for this necessary purpose, that the dreadful experience of former times, may be, as instructive cautions in our future transactions with our Indian neighbours, in the several settlements now likely to be made on lands belonging to them . . . .

—Anthony Benezet, *Some Observations on
the Situation, Disposition, and Character of the
Indian Natives of This Continent* (1784)

CONTENTS

FIGURES

3.1: Blood streams from the dead man's and woman's chest injuries, whose head markings may be meant for scalping wounds; the woman's eyes have been gouged out, and a child's body is at center. *Detail of [James Claypoole Jr.], "The German bleeds & bears the Furs / Of Quaker Lords & Savage Curs . . ." (Philadelphia, 1764). Courtesy of the Library Company of Philadelphia.* 93

3.2: "The Colonies Reduced." Franklin first had this hugely popular image printed for distribution on small cards to members of Parliament during debates over repeal of the Stamp Act (*London, late 1765 or early 1766; reproduced from frontispiece to Dec. 1768* Political Register and Impartial Review of New Books). *Courtesy of the Lewis Walpole Library, Yale University.* 93

6.1: An Indian delegation is proudly shown the sights of Philadelphia by the state assembly speaker—Heinrich Melchior Mühlenberg's son, Frederick—in about 1793. *Detail of William Birch, "New Lutheran Church, in Fourth Street Philadelphia" (1799), in* The City of Philadelphia . . . *(Philadelphia, 1800), pl. 21. Courtesy of the Library Company of Philadelphia.* 173

7.1: A pastiche of highlights from the Paxton crisis. Watchmen pound on doors, the Friends meetinghouse is filled with volunteers, one unit nearly fires on another, and the governor dismisses the crowd. *Henry Dawkins, "The Paxton Expedition, Inscribed to the Author of the Farce . . . ," illustrating* The Paxton Boys: A Farce *(both Philadelphia, 1764). Courtesy of the Library Company of Philadelphia.* 206

7.2: Quaker mischief. *Left:* A view of the *King Wampum* fantasy, with Israel Pemberton "embracing BARBARIANS" at a 1762 treaty conference. *Center:* More of the same. *Right:* Friendly Association clerk Abel James hands out tomahawks for use on non-Quakers. *Detail of [James Claypoole Jr.], "An Indian Squaw King Wampum spies . . ."; two details of*

CHARTS

MAP

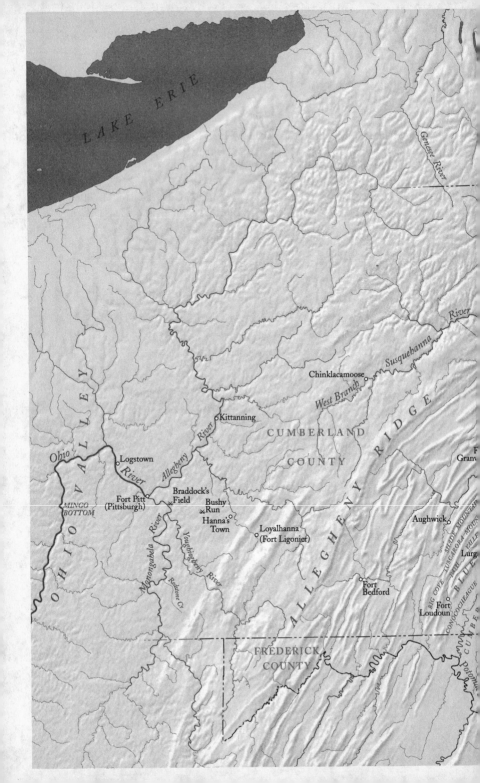

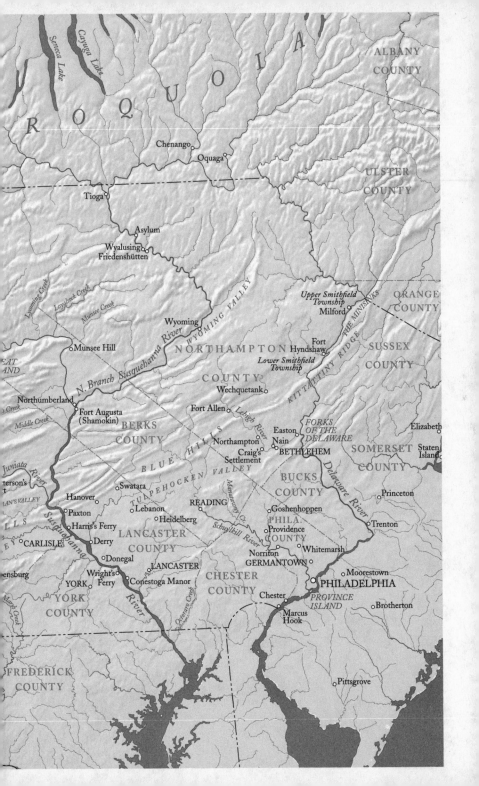

INTRODUCTION

IN MIDWINTER 1759, A TRADER NAMED JAMES KENNY PASSED up the Cumberland Valley from Maryland into Pennsylvania. After four seasons of Indian raids in the countryside, he found that many people thought the snow-covered landscape around them to be charged with the presence of the dead. Kenny had little sympathy for the "Slavish fears . . . those People are so much addicted to," but still could not help feeling a little anxious about the places through which he would travel. "Some of them here tells me of it being a very lonely or wild road to pass," he observed, "& especially as I must lie one night in the Woods & may happen to strike up my Fire near . . . where the murders was comitted as they talk of Several such places on the Road." It might have been hard for Kenny not to run over in his mind some of the attacks that had struck the valley's farmsteads, or to sometimes imagine before him the scalped and unclothed dead who, he knew, had lain sprawled across its roads. The summer before this journey north, a New Jersey poet wrote of seeing "empurpl'd fields" of bodies in the hinterland, and pictured the Monongahela as a stream

> On whose gore-moisten'd banks the num'rous slain,
> Spring up in vegetative life again:
> Whilst their wan ghosts, as night's dark glooms prevail,
> Murmur to whistling winds the mournful tale . . . .[1]

By midcentury, the story of war between Indians and Europeans in the mid-Atlantic colonies, and of the terrors that they inflicted on one another there, had been rooted and twined into the countryside itself.

THIS BOOK is about how fear and horror, with suitable repackaging, can remake whole societies and their political landscapes. The societies in question are the middle provinces of British North America—a collection of rural colonies strung along the center of the Atlantic seaboard, joining Indian country to the ocean—during a long generation of wars from the 1750s to the 1780s. The horror and fear flowed from the attacks that Indians and Europeans made on one another, and they ran by twisting paths toward some surprising things: a democratic revolution and the dignifying of ordinary people; a commitment to toleration, or at least a deep hostility to bigotry between Europeans; and, in time, most of the American republic's institutional beginnings.

I have hoped in writing this book to give a satisfactory account of how different sorts of people got along in the middle colonies—especially Pennsylvania, which is at its heart, but also to some extent New Jersey, Delaware, northern Maryland, and parts of New York—colonies that together made the eighteenth-century mid-Atlantic perhaps the most racially, ethnically, and religiously mixed place in the world. These little societies, whose human diversity makes them seem strangely modern, were in important ways simply accidents. They were the unintended by-products of a force that is now alien: early modern settler colonialism, in which huge numbers of Europeans and Africans were drawn across the ocean, in freedom or bondage, and replanted in new landscapes. The sheer heterogeneity of the people who could actually be coerced and cajoled into making this trip, combined with the heterogeneity of the native peoples they found there already, made the middle colonies a case study in early modern diversity. "[C]omposed," as one English tourist observed, "of people of different nations, different manners, different religions, and different languages," they were in fact plural societies before the ideal of pluralism had been fully imagined, and this was not a condition that most of the people in them found happy.[2]

The movement of large numbers of people into the middle colonies, from Europe and from other parts of Indian country, unsettled the region's human relations. It seems like common sense that everyday social contact between members of different groups should break down their shared stereotypes, improving not only individuals' views of one another but intergroup relations as a whole. But almost nothing about the history of the early modern middle colonies suggests that this hopeful view of contact between groups is true. With few exceptions, living together made the different sorts of people there feel frightened of one another's intentions. Forced proximity brought many groups to a fresh appreciation for their own distinctive ways, ways they thought of as "traditional" and fought to recover amid the disturbing novelties that came with diversity. Most strove both to make the other peoples around them act more like themselves and to keep, if they could, from coming to resemble those neighbors, making for a jittery, culturally competitive society. A series of revivals of different groups' religious identities began, revivals that drove the members of most groups into feeling more distant from one another than ever before. The resulting rifts were greatest among Europeans: among Indians the rise of charismatic revivalists more often worked to shape a pan-Indian ideology and identity. But it took much more than coming together on the face of the countryside to make most Europeans feel that they had anything meaningful in common.[3]

It took war, and the fear that it brought. In 1755, with the onset of the Seven Years' War between Britain and France—a conflict that soon spilled over much of the globe, from America to Europe to India— French-allied western Indians started to attack the middle colonies, fighting almost as a unified bloc. Before long there were signs that practically any Indian could inspire a contagious terror among the rural Europeans living under British rule. As they sensed this, some provincial leaders and publicists started to experiment with the fear that washed almost irresistibly over the countryside, trying to rebottle and employ it for ends of their own. The enraptured discourse of fear that they refined rapidly entrenched itself in political argument and became a vital means of forming public coalitions.

Being at war with Indians brought a new style to printed debates and even to literature. Pamphlets, sermons, petitions, newspaper accounts, private correspondence, poems and plays—all were transformed by a horror-filled rhetoric of victimization, intent on the damage that Indians had done to colonists' bodies and families. This rhetoric—in this book it is called the anti-Indian sublime—quickly proved all but unanswerable as political discourse. Anyone who professed not to see the dangers it decried, or who seemed not to care enough about the suffering it relentlessly described, was open to the charge of acting against the best interests of a new group, more and more often invoked in the middle colonies after midcentury: "the white people."

THE DISCOVERY of new identities played a central part in sorting out the middle colonies' complexity. As a concept, identity has been much abused. It is important to be clear that many of the new ways in which people learned to think of themselves were both fleeting and dependent on specific situations: the situation of being at war with Indians or the British empire, for example. Others do seem to have been durable once they first took shape, and to have allowed for the forming of coalitions that would otherwise have been impossible. In the face of contact with other populations, members of some groups came to suddenly see new kinships with one another—kinships that became easy to perceive only when they had a reason to imagine themselves as they must look through another group's unfriendly eyes.[4]

When the experience of Indian war engulfed the mid-Atlantic, some of the many dissatisfactions that European colonists had felt toward one another would be trumped, or at least put into a new context. But Indians may in fact have been the first North American population to discover a broad identity in this way. Encounters with Europeans in many regions had brought some of the hundreds of different native peoples of the continent to see that they shared more than they had realized before. In the eighteenth-century Southeast, many Indian groups even arrived at the idea of their being red, in contrast to differently colored Europeans and Africans. Indians in the very different colonial region studied here— the middle colonies and their hinterland—less often used the language of redness, but by the middle of the eighteenth century they could nonetheless be found invoking the idea that there had been completely distinct divine creations of Indians, Europeans, and Africans; calling for the abandonment of European goods and habits; trying to achieve the physical separation of Indian and European settlements; and working to weave together complicated Indian coalitions, some sprawling over half the continent, that could go to war against all the Europeans in the British colonies.5

Though a few American historians have had recourse to the slippery idea of "proto-racism," most scholars working on related subjects have found that racial thinking had no coherent existence, let alone any independent ability to determine people's beliefs and actions, before the scientific racialism of the nineteenth century. If the term "racism" is to have a specific meaning or explanatory value, more is lost than gained by applying it hazily to a great many early antagonisms between groups— groups that were never limited in their interactions to the nineteenth-century racial categories, and behind whose enmities lay far more than a spirit of racial animus.6 As an explanation, in other words, it is lazy, and one of the most interesting things about the whole tangled history of American intergroup relations turns out to be not how much they have stayed fundamentally the same, but how drastically they have changed. Despite the use of words and phrases like "Indian" and "white people," modern racial thinking played no part in most groups' views of each other for nearly all of the period studied in this book. At its very end, by the close of the American Revolution, the partisans of the United States would have found a new rhetoric for decrying Indians that was genuinely worth calling racist. But the surprising paths that the middle colonies' European inhabitants had to travel to reach that point are well worth retracing.

With Europeans so riven by their national divisions, the very name of "the white people" would be influenced by Indians' own ways of speaking and thinking. And it was to work less as a coherent coalition—let alone a racial self-identification that could powerfully color people's everyday lives—than as a convenient way, first, of embodying an overall opposition between Indian and European interests; second, of invoking the suffering of the great bulk of ordinary rural Europeans at Indians' hands; and, third and most crucially, of providing a standard of loyalty against which individuals' actions could be judged. If Europeans acted against the interests of the suffering white people who stood to be hurt by Indians—and white people in this period were nearly always depicted as suffering at Indians' hands rather than triumphing over them—then they certainly did not deserve to rule over them.

This seemingly simple test was used in the efforts to delegitimize first Quaker and then British rule in the middle colonies. And as officials and political insurgents made strident claims to be keeping the country people safe against Indian attack, and to be speaking for their interests, their rhetoric started to transform groups once seen as backwoods undesirables into something like the font of political legitimacy. This would be one important source for the fundamental revolutionary idea of a sovereign people.

THE AMERICAN REVOLUTION was to follow the Seven Years' War after little more than a decade, with more problems in want of solving. How could loyalty be determined? What did loyalty even mean, in a political order so inverted? Many of the answers were provided by Indians, as Britain's North American forces slowly succeeded in gaining native allies and the Revolutionary War became an Indian war, too. Here fear of Indian war—and the ennobling suffering that many revolutionaries assumed it brought—proved able to justify not only American rebellion but nearly anything else one could ask: an ostensibly preemptive invasion of French Canada, the pillaging of Indian villages in Iroquoia, new land claims, even the internment of Loyalists.

Europeans were strikingly concerned during these years not only with Indians but with how they themselves were being treated by other Europeans. Whenever anti-Indian rhetoric was not focused tightly on Indian victimization in the most literal and physical senses—carved-up, mutilated bodies, bleeding scalps—it was nearly always applied to people who were not Indian at all. For it is remarkable how many of the bitterest arguments between groups came to depend on tying enemies to Indians—a linkage by which even what had once been the bumbling, almost impossibly benign figure of the Pennsylvania Quaker could be remade as something ominous. The mid-Atlantic's Indians were nearly always cobogeymen: they were seldom discussed as having the initiative to do much harm apart from the aid, comfort, and direction that they were presumably provided by a European villain of the moment. And as new forms of popular organization took shape before and during the Revolution, the idea that some Europeans might be indifferent to or even complicit in ordinary country people's sufferings at Indian hands proved to carry explosive power. Quakers during the Seven Years' War, and Loyalists and British people during the Revolution, would bear the brunt of accusations of caring too much for Indians—or, in the Loyalists' case, at least, of being worse than Indians.

The closing years of the Revolution saw extraordinary anti-Indian violence. The outraged reaction against this violence by European reformers—and their selective understanding of its sources—ensured that the idea of color prejudice's being a fundamental problem in intergroup relations emerged out of these dark years as another of their legacies.

In all of these ways, the culture of the European mid-Atlantic twisted in upon and transformed itself during its age of Indian wars, arriving under stress at positions that no one could have predicted before the first attacks.7

SOMEHOW, OUT of such unpromising beginnings, one of history's most self-consciously tolerant societies was made. The idea of "the white people" may have helped some people to feel greater sympathetic identification with other Europeans—even as it made a few, like the Quakers, into cultural villains, and drove up negative feelings toward all Indians. This, to be sure, has the shape of a quintessential American paradox: increased toleration for one group can nearly always be found tangled together with increased intolerance toward another. There is a musical-chairs logic to this idea, in which taking a new group into your charmed circle requires shoving another one out.8

But that is not the whole story. When two antagonists fight over something they both think is very important, no matter how vicious their fight, they will nearly always end up strengthening its status in each other's minds. (This assumes, of course, that they are fighting over something immaterial or otherwise hard to destroy, like an idea or a patch of ground.) Conversely, the bitterest fights—this is most obviously true of civil wars—are often over things that people share, or to which both parties feel they have a legitimate claim.

So it becomes significant that every European group involved in the woes of the eighteenth-century mid-Atlantic should have strenuously accused its opponents of bigotry and intolerance—most damningly, of bigotry against other Europeans in favor of Indians. By this back-and-forth vituperation—and the sort of unwitting cooperation between antagonists I have been describing—they entrenched toleration of Europeans from other religions and ethnicities as an increasingly unchallengeable principle. At midcentury, publicists writing both for and against the Quakers freely denounced one another as bigots, who must believe themselves a chosen people and want to persecute, or even kill, people from other denominations. And with the passage of time, what the mid-Atlantic region's sparring partners had shouted out about toleration in the course of such debates came to matter as much as the specific, intolerant things they had done to each other at every opportunity.

The same perverse logic applies to what might seem a natural endpoint for this study: the growth of American nationalism. Neither the Europeans nor the Indians of the middle colonies were reliably united by the eighteenth-century wars, though militants in each population hoped they would be. And on the American side, at least, this period's changes were not so much about people's truly learning to get along with one another as about a few activists' learning how to manufacture authority and command assent, in an otherwise impossibly divided social setting. On the whole these events refractured already broken populations along new lines.

For the obvious problem with seeing the experiences of fighting with Indians and the British as having been politically unifying is that, though in the 1780s a new nation was born, there were few signs of a usable national identity's being born with it. The contentiously assembled states that made up the revolutionary Republic were constantly threatening to fall apart, and Americans in the 1780s often showed more excitement over the French dauphin's birthday than the fourth of July. Political life was splintered, especially in Pennsylvania, where partisans and opponents of the state constitution that had been written during the Revolution would square off even before their struggle was subsumed into the larger contests between Federalists and their adversaries that marked the century's close.

As with the earlier controversies over bigotry, though, these shared tussles, in which both antagonists publicly professed their faith in an aspect of the revolutionary cause, proved a nationalizing experience. By unendingly accusing their opponents of violating the Constitution, for instance, Americans steadily exalted it into their most important national symbol. And those scholars who have looked the hardest for American nationalism before the war of 1812 have rightly concluded that a hugely fractured and antagonistic politics lay squarely at its heart.9

At least in the middle colonies, the pattern for American public life— the framework of quarreling within which national symbols were to be produced and slowly hallowed—may first have been set in place by the divisiveness of Indian war. The bitterly riven nationalism that resulted would in time carry Americans to places even stranger and more distant than the Ohio country.

As with much history, this book has built into it a bias toward conflict and change, toward periods in which remarkable things happened. But if it could devote more time to describing the interwar period and the decades after the Revolution, it would become clear how much the animosities recounted here owed to wartime. Though they were pivotal parts of the culture, they shifted with peace.10

Then, too, many of the events we will explore—even mass refugeeism and large-scale rioting—were the unfolding results of actions taken by small numbers of people. When generalizing about the attitudes of the mid-Atlantic European population as a whole, it usually makes better sense to see its members as having been afraid of Indians than as having hated them. But amid the extraordinary events that marked this region's course through the later eighteenth century, a few individuals regularly set patterns and made choices for large numbers of other people.

The violence that tipped the countryside into chaos, for example, was not a product of very many people's preferences or personal convictions. The few hundred squatters who during the 1750s settled squarely on

Indian land, refused to leave, and incited Indian attack helped by their actions to create a new world of conflict within which everyone else in the countryside then had to manage as best they could. At times—as with the actions of Daniel Greathouse, Michael Cresap, and their small groups of friends, who by massacring Indians around Fort Pitt in 1774 brought on a full-scale war (Dunmore's War) between Virginia and Shawnees in the Ohio Valley—small numbers of extremists could succeed in committing whole societies to violence. The best example of all is probably the outbreak of the American Revolution itself, but that lies beyond the scope of this book.[11]

On both the Indian and European sides, if conditions were right, people who were dedicated to creating conflict could hijack and considerably worsen intergroup relations. This fact probably does not get its full due in most histories of large, important-seeming events. But it is crucial to solving the puzzles of human relations posed by the mid-Atlantic societies, which were wracked by such painful transformations. Because such groups as the border squatters or Greathouse's murder gang could have a wildly disproportionate impact, they were no less pivotal for being small. But they were not the bulk of people—and when we try to explain the full range of European responses to Indian war, that turns out to matter a great deal.[12]

OUR SAVAGE NEIGHBORS

Chapter 1

AN UNSETTLED COUNTRY

GOTTLIEB MITTELBERGER WAS A MUSIC TEACHER, AND HE noticed sounds. In 1750, at the end of a long voyage up the Rhine and across the Atlantic, he found himself living in Providence, Pennsylvania, a village at the heart of the American countryside. Here he heard a medley of new noises. He heard the clear-toned ping made by cedar shingles under rain; the way frogs in America gulped instead of croaking; and the hiss of hummingbird wings. In a way the nights were lovely, with a dark summer "full of glowworms flying so thick, that it seems to snow fire"— but an absent sound bothered Mittelberger, one he was used to hearing ripple through the air, ordering hours and marking out places. There were no bells. "In the countryside," he wrote, "no church has a tower built yet that is provided with a bell or clock, so that the whole year through you hear neither ringing nor striking; on this account, especially in the nighttime, it is very tedious for newly arrived people."[1]

This silence at night was one sign of a larger emptiness the young Lutheran could feel in the countryside. There was no established church or securely salaried clergy here, either. Instead, there was a teeming mass of sects, all equally tolerated and all, he feared, leading the unwary astray. He could give endless examples of "the lewd life of . . . people in this free country"—going without baptisms, serving as servants under English-speaking foreigners so long they forgot their mother tongue. It was a place palpably too mixed and ungoverned. There was a danger of coming unmoored. "The most exemplary preachers," Mittelberger noted with pain, "are often, especially in the countryside, . . . mocked, called 'thou,' and jeered to their faces like the Jews."

> Such unheard-of rudeness and spite arise from the country's excessive freedoms and the blind zeal of the numerous sects. Pennsylvanian freedom does many people's souls and bodies more harm than good. . . . on account of there being such a diversity of religious professions, [there is] great confusion . . . . by which the young people in particular grow up . . . the same as the aborigines or savages.

It was perhaps not a coincidence that the liquid calls of bobwhites in the fields seemed to Mittelberger's ears to be endlessly urging, "Get away!" and in 1754 he traveled back to Germany over the sea.[2]

But for about three decades before this, thousands of other Europeans had been showing up every year to settle for good in the middle provinces. Most came sailing either from Ireland or, like Mittelberger, from the German-speaking lands of central Europe. Once in Pennsylvania, they combined with other, older inhabitants to make an unhappily assorted new society—a place whose residents seemed determined to share less, not more, the longer they lived together.

AFTER SOME exploratory probes in New Jersey, in the 1680s William Penn and thousands of other English and Welsh Quakers had arrived on the lower Delaware River to found Pennsylvania. Penn made it a central part of his vision to tolerate all religious denominations, probably hoping both to encourage settlement and to make the position of Quakers safer. If many different groups came to live in the middle Atlantic, they were likelier to cancel one another out, and the religious impasse, or "Concord of Discords," that might result seemed to Penn "not . . . the infirmest *Basis* Government can rise or stand upon." Certainly none of the other groups would be able to impose an establishment of their church on Quakers: not the Anglicans, who had harried thousands of Friends from England and Wales, and not the Presbyterians, whose Puritan brethren in New England had actually hanged some Quakers in the desire to be shed of them. Nor would another group be able to force through laws that most Quakers could not in conscience obey, like acts demanding military service or the swearing of oaths in judicial proceedings.3

By the 1720s, Pennsylvania had gained a reputation as an asylum for religiously oppressed European peoples. This reputation—together with the availability of unrivaled farming land for freehold purchase, the lack of military service or church tithes, the desperate need for labor, and a series of economic crises in Europe—made the port of Philadelphia an astonishing place to be in the first half of the century. Ships came steadily swarming in, packed so dangerously full of people that many died in transit. Perhaps a hundred thousand immigrants from Ireland and a hundred thousand more from German-speaking Europe (give or take 20 percent) arrived in America between 1700 and 1775. Both sets of immigrants landed mostly at Philadelphia, and they came in heavier waves after the 1730s. Unrelenting immigration from the Rhineland and Ireland helped to make Pennsylvania by far the fastest-growing place in North America, and one of the most tumultuous.4

One contemporary thought the number of Irish people landing at Philadelphia in the 1730s and 1740s must have been little short of a quarter million. This overstated the size of their migration by a factor of ten, but accurately got across its frightening velocity. The new arrivals came disproportionately from Ireland's six northern counties of Ulster, which were about two-thirds Protestant and one-third Presbyterian. Despite what many Pennsylvanians assumed, this heavily commercialized province was seldom a place where one could find "infinite Numbers starving in every Ditch in the midst of Rags, Dirt and Nakedness." But most of the Ulster people did cross the sea for economic reasons. With thousands of cottagers weaving linen for the market instead of growing crops, ships—bringing food and flaxseed—had been set going between the middle colonies and eastern Ulster. During crises they proved easy to fill up with people. Soaring rents, bad harvests, and, above all, a magnetic attraction for Pennsylvania itself—all drove thousands of Ulstermen across the Atlantic nearly every year, until emigration seemed "a contagious distemper." From the late 1710s through the 1740s, with each crash in the boom-and-bust cycle of the linen industry there was a spike in the number of Irish ships that arrived at Philadelphia.5

The most religiously aware of these voyagers were heirs to a powerful idea: the idea not simply of Protestant–Catholic conflict, but of a self-reliant Irish Presbyterian community, which could survive the buffeting of a hostile surrounding population and the indifference of an unfriendly crown only by vigilance, reprisal, and the constant monitoring of its own bounds. At least in that sense, some Ulster emigrants had already gotten used to picturing themselves within a "plantation" or settlers' regime, against a forbidding background of unbelievers. Ulster was not some comfortable Old World milieu, but a religiously edgy set of overlapping societies that could teach those who left it—people used to living side by side with others in mental states of unremitting purity and separation—to define themselves against all comers. In the middle colonies they would find plenty of human material to work with.[6]

German-speaking immigration, especially from the traditionally war-torn southern Rhineland, also gathered strength continuously from the 1720s on. This stream of "Palatine" immigration to Pennsylvania—so called after the Rhenish Palatinate, the state from which many of the migrants came (after their arrival, most would simply be called "Dutch")—was the largest influx of non-English-speakers into the northern and middle colonies before the Revolution. (Farther south it was dwarfed by the forced importation of Africans.) Even more than with the Irish, German immigration centered on Philadelphia. A minimum of seventy thousand German-speakers arrived in Philadelphia during the fifty years before the Revolution, with a full half that total flooding in—as immigration surged to levels ten times those recorded only twenty-five years before—in one five-year span (1749–54) at mid-century, after which the outbreak of the Seven Years' War had the effect of turning off a tap.[7]

Many German-speaking immigrants were so-called redemptioners, voyaging free in exchange for sale into indentured servitude on arrival—which would actually take the form, with luck, of "redemption" through purchase by New World friends or relations. Such credit structures were needed because of the cost of the voyage up the Rhine and then over the sea, whose hardships far exceeded anything the Irish faced. On some long crossings hundreds of passengers died, as Mittelberger gloomily reported, amid "vapors, terror, vomiting, . . . diarrhea, . . . mouth-rot, and the like."

Other passages ended in starvation, or the eating of rats and mice; voyagers were often bilked, "beat and used as if we were Slaves" by English-speaking crews.[8]

By the early 1750s, as the business of shipping Germans for profit tapped ever more marginal pools of migrants, family groups traveling together started giving way to young, single people, whose labor contracts could be bought and sold in Philadelphia. But even as late as the 1770s, a majority of the Palatines still arrived in families, often with just enough property to set up independently. They would move into the countryside as soon as they could, for they had come in search of security, and security meant having farms for yourself and your children.[9]

Like Ulster, the corner of southwestern Germany nearest to Switzerland that most of these determined new colonists were leaving behind was hardly a bland background. From families that had been drawn to the depopulated southern Rhineland in the wake of the Thirty Years' War, many migrants, every bit as much as their Irish counterparts, could have told old stories full of the horror and power of religious violence. Their home region—a quarrelsome assortment of Reformed and Lutheran Protestants, Catholics, and countless scattered smaller churches and Pietist-spawned sects, with a significant number of Huguenots and Jews (as Mittelberger's casual reference to Jew-baiting suggested)—had the fractures of a mosaic without its overarching pattern. They were moving from one area of diversity in Europe to another in America—greater, and more divided, if for a while less violent.[10]

It was very bad luck that all of these newcomers started to press ashore at Philadelphia by the tens of thousands in the 1720s—an entire decade during which, as it happened, no one had clear legal authority to purchase, survey, or sell land in Pennsylvania at all. The death of William Penn in 1718 had set off a bitter fourteen-year battle for control of the colony between his second wife and various children, leaving title to the province up in the air.[11]

But even in more settled times it would prove hard to police the countryside. After ownership of the province was pinned down in the 1730s, and the Penns' agents tried to bring some profit or regularity to the burgeoning settlements, they still often had to take what they could get from squatters: a token quitrent, a promise to pay. In 1735, one observer sug-

gested a desperately innovative means, short of simple amnesty, of dealing with the growing backlog of squatting. With so "many Families . . . ,
through Inadvertency, settled on Lands to which they have no Right,"
why not hold a lottery for land titles totaling, say, a hundred thousand
acres or so?

But for thousands of rural people, with the rising volume and disorgani-
zation of settlement, squatting had already become a way of life. There
were simply "So many Idle worthless people flocking" into the countryside,
as an agent for the Penns observed, "Who Coming full of Expectation to
have Land for nothing Are Unwilling to be Disapointed."[12]

THE NEW ARRIVALS did not sink unnoticed into the landscape. Many
at once came into competition with Indians. In 1741, a group of Indians
living beyond the forks of the Delaware River, high above Philadelphia,
wrote angrily to Pennsylvania's governor to describe one burst of colonization. "[H]ere is about a hundred families Setteled upon our Land,"
the Delawares wrote through an interpreter, "and what they are their Setteled for we knowe not the Reason of it. . . . we Desire Thomas Penn
would take these people off from our Land . . . that we may not be at the
trouble to Drive them off."

As these Delawares made clear, the growth of colonial settlements was
not an abstract unfolding of demographic forces, best studied with maps.
Though sometimes it led to friendship, often it was sudden and violent,
taking the form of person-by-person confrontations. "[W]e cannot injoy
our Birth-Right in Peace and Quietness, but we are abused as if we were
Enemies, and not Friends," they wrote:

> for we dare not speake for our Rights but there is an Uprore, and in
> Danger of being cut in Peices and distroyed . . . . For they think that by
> this Uproare they will sceare us to be easy and let them alone in there
> wicked Ways to take our Land and never give us any thing for it.[13]

After 1740 or so, with the rapid spread of European households up to
the next watercourse west of the Delaware, the Susquehanna River, it
became a fallback boundary between Europeans and Indians—"few or

None of [whom]," as a resident of Donegal township, on the eastern bank, observed in 1740, "are Seen this side of the River at our house Now adays."[14]

Indeed, the eighteenth-century history of the Delawares could be summed up as one of westward slippage from river to river—Delaware, Susquehanna, Ohio, Muskingum—punctuated by wars. At the end of this passage toward the Ohio country, Delaware-speakers all thought of themselves as one people, but they had come from three different group-ings (the most distinctive of which spoke the harsh-sounding Munsee dialect) strung along the Delaware. By the time they got to the Susque-hanna, it was already filling up with other dislodged native nations. For here, a little before the European surge and almost certainly as a bulwark against it, the powerful Iroquois confederacy to the north—making self-serving claims to suzerainty over other mid-Atlantic Indians based on its conquests during the previous century—had set about planting villages of relocated Indians. The river was a corridor of peoples.[15]

Besides Delaware-speakers, there were Conestogas, the remnant of a group buffeted in the seventeenth century by Chesapeake Bay colonists; Tuscaroras, passing north from Carolina on their way to become a new Iroquois member nation; Tutelos, Nanticokes, and Conoys, from Virginia and the Chesapeake; and the fantastically wide-ranging Shawnees, long without a home territory, who often lived and migrated alongside Delawares. By the 1740s, all of these groups had arrived to live in some of the fifty or so Indian towns that the Iroquois sponsored along the Susquehanna. They would be joined in setting up new towns nearer the Ohio by many western Senecas—members of the Iroquois confederacy who were themselves hiving off (to become known as the Mingos, a new people) and drifting away from its claims of control.[16]

Some of these Indian towns had resident Iroquois "half-kings," or pro-consuls, and many more did not. Nearly all were uneasy, multiethnic jum-bles. The settlement of Shamokin, for instance, at the Susquehanna's forks, was like a human Venn diagram—settled "partly on the east, partly on the west side, of the river; and partly on a large Island in it: . . . con-tain[ing] upwards of fifty houses; & near three hundred souls; but of three different tribes of Indians; speaking, three languages; wholly unin-telligible to each other."[17]

But if the collection of native colonies on the Susquehanna was meant to make a fence between Indians and Europeans, that fence was ever more often hurdled. The Penn family launched expeditions to put to the torch the cabins of Irish and German "poor people" on the river's western side, but they were still to be found there, "Setling building & Improveing Daily." As squatters overran the Susquehanna, there were angry episodes of Indians' "opposing the peoples Setlings" themselves. More than once they had "thrown Down" or "Threatened to burn their Houses and Obliged Em to Quit their Setlemts & return back to th[e eastern] Side." Sometimes, though, the thwarted Europeans would simply troop "to another place . . . in Such a Body as to be able to Defend themselves."[18]

These spreading clumps were maddening to try to stop. Border settlement came in dribs and drabs, made up of such crude "Cabbins or Loghouses . . . as the Country People erect in a Day or two, . . . cost[ing] only the Charge of an Entertainment" for a few neighbors' help. Pulled down, they often reappeared a few months later or a few miles away. Children seethed around them. They tended to spring up just beyond the agreed-upon borders of provinces: the boundary-line limbo between Maryland and Pennsylvania was soon thickly freckled with shacks. To some observers it almost seemed "as if these People were only prompted by a Desire to make Mischief": there were better lands to squat on in parts of Pennsylvania that the Indians had inarguably sold.

One illegal spurt of colonization over the Susquehanna—which would end by being legitimized, in 1754, with a huge purchase from the Iroquois—had actually started in not the east but the west. Edging up carefully from the Maryland borderland, "taking Advantage of the Confusion" of Philadelphia's passing preoccupation with a threat of Spanish coastal raids, the squatters followed a series of valleys north as they "stole" into the so-called Little Cove and Big Cove in the mountains "by little and little." Thirty European families were planted there by 1744. Then more sneaked north into the Path Valley to hook eastward into Shearman's Valley, and farther north to Aughwick, and finally all the way up and east to the Juniata River, where by decade's end five households had defiantly emerged back at the Susquehanna itself, in "a Place much esteemed by the *Indians* for some of their best hunting Ground."[19]

Here, facing back across the river at the other settlements, with "the

Indians all th[e] while repeatedly complaining," the trespassers made an apt symbol, part mulish and part ruthless, of the conflicts colonization could bring before the Seven Years' War.[20]

THERE WERE not only sudden pockets of squatters springing up in the countryside. Summer by summer, whole European towns grew up from nothing. In 1750 Reading, Pennsylvania, had a single house. Two years later there were 130 (as well as forty-one stables). After the 1730s and 1740s, Europeans started to worry in earnest whether the new immigrants could all be digested into their culture and politics. "It now looks as if Irel[an]ᵈ or the Inhabitants of it were to be transplanted hither," James Logan, Pennsylvania's provincial secretary, wrote unhappily. "[W]e may easily believe there are some grounds for the common apprehensions of the people that if some speedy Method be not taken, they will soon make themselves Proprietors of the Province."[21]

As the flood of new arrivals streamed down the Allegheny ridge, it could feel as if their settlements threatened civilization itself. This might have been because there was something different, among Europeans, about the way the Irish cultivated a landscape—more casually, with less attention to looks and less permanence than their English or German counterparts. Or it might have been because of how tightly tied the idea of Irishness was, for most English-speakers, to slovenliness, disorder, and a kind of pre-Protestant savagery.[22]

Whatever the reasons, the Anglican missionary Charles Woodmason was not alone in finding the "Multitudes of New Imported Irish People" in the North Carolina borderland—and the part where he worked had been, it seemed to him, "all (or greatest Part) . . . settled within these 5 Years by Irish Presbyterians from Belfast, or Pennsylvania"—to be degenerated human rubbish. These "Ignorant, mean, worthless, beggarly Irish Presbyterians," he recorded with a disgust that verged on relish, were "the most lowest vilest Crew breathing." Loud, dirty, and indolent, they were a people who "delight[ed] in their . . . low, lazy, sluttish, heathenish, hellish Life." And, as he noted in a comparison that was becoming commonplace, by "'run[ning] wild" like "the Common Savages," these new settlers had become "hardly a degree removed from them."[23]

The equally great immigration of German-speakers aroused uneasiness as well. No one—not even previous generations of German migrants—thought well of the new arrivals. In the mid-1750s, there were legislative debates over how to save the public from "Palatine fever," the collection of infections thought to ooze ashore from overcrowded transports. In a bitter 1755 address to the governor, the English-speaking members of Pennsylvania's assembly linked the new Palatines, the "Refuse" of Germany, plucked out of its "very Goals," not only to epidemics but to sharply rising crime. In 1754, even a group of German-speakers complained that filth-drenched Palatine passengers were going through the city "a begging to the Terror & Danger of the Inhabitants, who from the smell of their Cloaths when brought near a Fire, & [their] infectious Disorder[s] . . . apprehend themselves in great Danger." When a reformer visited one of the horrifyingly befouled house lots where many redemptioners were kept confined and half-starving until they could be sold, he found it thick with blood and feces; neighbors could see naked Germans crawling weakly through the muck toward a latrine.[24]

But not even the healthiest Germans won favor in everyone's eyes. English-speakers outside Philadelphia were unnerved on New Year's Eve in 1750 by the shooting off at midnight of hundreds of guns. This was a frightening and "pernicious Custom . . . introduced . . . by the *Germans*," which seemed likely to bring all kinds of troubles (like "Maiming by the Bursting of overloaded Guns") onto the reputable farmers' heads. Philadelphia's Quakers had long noticed tensely that many of the Irish, for their part, were raucously shooting into the air and "Classing together Nationally . . . under Pretence of Keeping a day to their Saint called Saint Patrick."[25]

With foreigners bringing tumult and disease, it seemed possible that even the sanity of people in this convulsively growing place might be at risk. "[W]ith the Numbers of People," as one group of petitioners complained, "the Number of Lunatics . . . hath greatly encreased in this Province . . . [who] going at large, are a Terror to their Neighbours, who are daily apprehensive of the Violences they may commit."[26]

In short, Europeans thought and worried, amid the whirligig of colonization, about the simple growth of what we would call diversity. Even the members of little German sects like the Mennonites, Schwenkfelders, and Anabaptist Dunkards—religious idealists who tried harder than any-one else in the region to segregate themselves—had to experience it, as they found themselves forced to scatter amid new neighbors with whom they shared nothing.[27] For the time being, this mixture of groups in the countryside provoked more disgust than affection. "[T]here are so many different religions here in the countryside, that many times I have not known what I should think about it," a German character—named "Newcomer"—protested in one dialogue printed in an almanac for 1751. He went on to ask an old-timer how one could get proper bread amid the farmsteads; but his first concern was with this abrasive diversity—of which, he said, "[I] still do not know what to make."[28]

Many of the English returned the favor. Even to Benjamin Franklin the prospect that the Germans "will soon . . . out number us" was one full of alarm. Their children didn't seem to learn English; they read imported German books and a German newspaper; interpreters were now needed in some courts. The very "Signs in our Streets have inscriptions in both languages," he noted warily, "and in some places only German."[29]

Elections became flash points in this hodgepodge of peoples. Because crowds chose election inspectors by massing behind the candidates of their choice—and, in Philadelphia, then had to tread up the narrow steps of the courthouse to return their ballots—the province-wide elections each October could be wild affairs. In 1742, there was a riot in Philadel-phia's marketplace for possession of the voting steps so intense that two decades later the bare memory of it could be counted on to fire up Ger-man readers against "the Irish, who have long sought dominion over us." Large groups of Germans with clubs had tried to defend themselves against bat-wielding watermen who ran about the square, smashing in the heads of Quaker "Broad-brims and Dutch Dogs," and happily yelling out to each other to "knock those Dutch Sons of Bitches off the Steps."[30] In York County, Pennsylvania, eight years later, the sheriff, surrounded by "his Party, the [mostly Irish] *Marsh-Creek* People," again used clubs to beat German voters away from the election house. Rural voting was by "press[ing] and croud[ing] in a Body to deliver their Tickets . . . at the Ends of cloven Sticks"—with many in their excitement "vot[ing] repeat-edly, . . . three, four, five, and some ten Times"—and the outcome was a riotous scrum between national groups.[31]

Such fighting became part of would-be landlords' strategies for holding title to settlements on contested colonial boundaries. On the southern Susquehanna, where a group of Germans had settled under
Pennsylvania licenses, the Penns' efforts to defend their border against
incursions from Maryland were sometimes helped by ethnic rivalry and
sometimes hurt by it. It helped them when Germans on both sides of the
river readily clumped together for three days at the threat of an approaching eviction raid from the south. It hurt them, though, when Maryland's
governor went to the Eastern Shore and seemed on the point of successfully "procur[ing] Irish Newcomers or other Disaffected persons to Come
up and Remove the Dutch on the other Side." If this should happen, the
Penns' agent thought, the only remedy would be to find "Some Suitable
person their Country man" to try and persuade those Irishmen not to
come. Otherwise, the agent's preferred means of defense—calling on the
residents of Donegal township, who were Irish, too—would be made useless, for "Itt might be Dificult to get the Donegal people to go against
their Country men."32

Much of the mid-Atlantic countryside had been turned into a crazy
patchwork of overlapping linguistic, cultural, and religious zones. There
were no ethnic homelands here, and no one could doubt they lived in a
world that was being radically remade.

IN 1747, five Eskimos who lived two thousand miles north of all this,
near a Moravian mission station in West Greenland, said they wanted "to
see Christendom." So the missionaries put them on a ship for Europe.
They spent two years touring the German-speaking lands, with two
young men named Matthew Kajarnak and Johann Angusmak staying the
longest. By 1749, they "had travelled backwards and forwards through
Germany on foot, and nobody, that did not know it, could ever have
thought they were of the savages." When Kajarnak and Angusmak did
catch a ship home from the Continent, they stopped over first in London
(where they were presented to George II), and then in the middle
colonies, where they visited the largely Delaware and Mahican members
of Moravian mission communities in Pennsylvania and New York. When

as part of this grand tour they stayed at one such Indian town in Pennsylvania, a local man was persuaded to try on an Eskimo suit they had brought with them, and Kajarnak and Angusmak carried back to Greenland a packet of pen-pal letters from Indian converts.33

To shorten, as they said, the long winter nights, the Greenland missionaries often read aloud to the Inuit by guttering whale lamps about "their black and tawny [Moravian-converted] brethren and sisters" in the Caribbean, in Surinam, and in North America. In 1755, news came that one of the first attacks of the Seven Years' War had struck the same Pennsylvania mission the Inuit had visited. On hearing of these distant troubles, the Greenlanders found their pity was aroused. They "we[pt] heartily" and pledged whatever they could to the southerners. "One said: 'I have a fine rein-deer skin, which I will give.' Another: 'And I a pair of new rein-deer boots, which I will send.' 'And I, said a third, will send them a seal, that they may have something to eat and to burn.'"34

These tears shed amid the ice fields of Greenland for the woes of mid-Atlantic Indians were one small product of the eighteenth-century Moravians' fantastically ambitious efforts at spreading the light of Christ to peoples all over the world. Their missionary empire-building yoked wildly disparate cultures together. The easy sympathy between the "tawny" peoples of Greenland and northeastern America might suggest that they liked the sensation, as many surely did. But others hated it with a special passion.35

For after Moravians arrived in the mid-Atlantic hinterland in the 1740s, their proselytizing helped at least a little to set off another, less outward-looking set of religious changes among Indians. A collection of native reformers started trying to reshape their own lives into purer, more traditional forms, working consciously against the European influences they saw rising among them. The religious changes they set in motion are often described as "revitalization movements," using an anthropological model. A revitalization movement occurs whenever a charismatic leader uses a divinely revealed system of rituals to channel the dissatisfactions that come with cultural change—and its worrisome half-digestion of new ways—toward a reawakening of traditional ideas and customs. The promoters of revitalization movements can be aggressive nativists, since they may seek to stop their culture's being "distorted" and to recover the imagined past by simply getting rid not only of strange ways but of "alien persons."[36]

When Moravian missionaries and their converts came into contact with these change- and outsider-hating renewal movements, they all felt the force of anti-European feeling. In the late 1760s, for instance, some converts were simply abandoned by their families for having become "*Schwonnaks* (white people)"—from the insulting Delaware coinage *shuwánakw*, "sour (or white) people"—as with a Delaware man who cast aside his wife, saying "she was . . . no longer an Indian, for she believed the white people." It was probably as a defense against Indian nativists that the missionary David Zeisberger started claiming that his colleagues "should not be regarded . . . as *schwonnak* (white people)" at all, "but rather as . . . friends, who are there for the Indians' betterment."[37]

The missionaries were pitted against a powerful language of human boundaries. An array of preachers and prophets had started seizing not only on ways to undo European influence but on the distinctness, so basic it organized the world, of Indians and Europeans. One was a Nanticoke dreamer to whom God spoke in 1749, telling him "he had made brown and white people" separately, and on no account wanted them to "go the same way." Another was Wangomend, the Munsee holy man who by 1760 had a Bible-like "Book of Pickters he Maid him Self . . . [showing] Heaven and Hell and Rum and Swan hak [*shuwánakw*] and Indiens," from which "he would Read Like Mad . . . in the Morning and Sing to the Sune Rising" every day. In 1767, Wangomend was still drawing maps of wholly separate Indian and European paths to heaven, telling Delawares that God "has created them and us for different purposes," and describing how he had himself caught "a peep into the heavens of which there were three, one for the Indians, one for the negroes, and another for the white people"—with the Indian heaven much "the happiest of the three."[38]

But this story of Indian reformation hinges above all on Neolin, the Delaware prophet. By 1762, he was famous for preaching a gospel based on the rejection of European ways. After seven years of spiritual training, Neolin's followers were to "quit all Commerce with the White People and Clothe themselves with skins." In the meantime, they purged themselves of "White peoples ways & Nature," starting with liquor drinking and the use of guns, and moving on to the sale of furs, "run[ning] after the girls," and even—by sipping a so-called black, or bitter, drink and throwing up in ritualized bouts that made a huge impression on observers—of anything within their bodies that was not Indian enough. By hearkening faithfully to their ancestors' far-away voices, in time the Delawares could "drive the white people out of their country" again.[39]

Neolin's message of purity depended on God's having made Indians and Europeans two colors—he chided his listeners for "looking upon a people of a different colour from our own"—and his having meant for them to live unmixed, in different quarters of the world. The Indians' country was created only for them, and Neolin scolded Indians for "suffering [white people] to sit down by our side" against this plan. Indeed, as interpreted by Pontiac, the Ottawa headman who helped to inspire what is usually called Pontiac's War, this vision of segregation demanded cleansing through war, resulting in a wholesale campaign against Britain's western forts and settlements from 1763 to 1765. "[S]end them back to the lands which I have created for them," God told Neolin, "and let them stay there." Like Wangomend, Neolin could map the cosmos by human colors, with a separate Indian heaven.[40]

Such prophets' messages had in many ways been energized by contact with Christianity. Cultural friction could be creative: it did not always lead directly to anti-European feeling, and even the most strident traditionalists had obvious debts—a single God, a Bible, sin—to missionaries' ideas. But even among natives who shared in neither the prophets' grasp of Christianity nor their harsh-sounding programs, by the 1740s an assumption that Indians and Europeans had sprung up in separate corners of the earth, free of any common ancestry, was widespread.[41]

At a treaty conference between the Iroquois and Pennsylvania, Maryland, and Virginia in 1744, for instance, a Cayuga war chief named Gachradodon prefaced a speech by observing how "[t]he World at the first was made on the other Side of the Great Water different from what it is on this Side, as may be known from the different Colours of our Skin, and of our Flesh." It was obvious, Gachradodon continued, that God "did not approve" of the Europeans' coming over to swarm among the Indians, for if he had "he would not have placed the Sea where it is, as the Limits between us and you." In 1752, a group of Shawnees sent a similar message to Pennsylvania's governor, patiently relating how when the "one God that made all things . . . made you white and us black, he placed You on the Ground beyond the Great Sea, and us on the Ground on this side of that Sea." This clear, emphatic idea of separate creations by one maker of all mankind held sway among many mid-Atlantic Indians well before the wave of prophecy that would crest with Neolin, and after it as well.[42]

EUROPEANS HAD the same response to the bewildering changes that came with migration. Unlike Indians, though, when Europeans reacted against the chafing of diversity in revitalization movements of their own, they only sharpened their distaste toward each other as groups. German Lutherans, Irish Presbyterians, Quakers—all came to speak of special, divinely guided destinies for themselves as peoples, and to feel a fierce need to live up to their own imagined histories.

Like Indians, many Europeans responded most angrily to diversity when it came in the shape of proselytizing Moravians. The first Great Awakening—a remarkable run of religious revivals, starting in the 1740s, that anticipated and shadowed the movements of the great English evangelist George Whitefield and his imitators up and down the American seaboard—was just the sort of religious excitement that Moravians had hoped to inspire. But other Europeans soon viewed the United Brethren so suspiciously that they shoved them outside the revival network. (Soon after a nondenominational meetinghouse was built in Philadelphia at Whitefield's urging, for instance, the Moravians were physically barred from the building, and it became the Second Presbyterian Church instead.) In the early 1740s, Moravians actually sponsored a series of grand interdenominational conferences with the aim of ushering in a *"reunion of all the Religions and Sects in this Province."* But the relentlessly mild, hopeful inclusiveness that they showed in these meetings (which few other denominations could be persuaded to attend) only deepened opposition to them, especially among Presbyterian, Lutheran, and Reformed church leaders.[43]

For to unfriendly eyes, the Moravians' ecumenism itself seemed suspicious—more like self-serving spiritual shape-shifting than any kind of idealism. From almost the day that their charismatic leader, Count Niko-laus Ludwig von Zinzendorf, arrived in the middle colonies in 1741, Ger-man churchgoers panicked regularly at the idea of Moravian infiltration. As a minister noted in 1747, at the smallest sign of innovation—saying "unser Vater" instead of "Vater unser" in the Lord's prayer, for instance— "[t]he wild and untamed Lutherans become afraid that one is trying to make Moravians out of them . . . . and grasp their swords in both hands." The danger came, German observers agreed, from their being so artful at "metamorphiz[ing] themselves into *Lutherians*, sometimes into *Reformed*, nay sometimes into all Religions, by which Means they get their Prose-lytes, which they . . . employ to subvert . . . the rest."44

In 1742, the members of one of the Moravians' interdenominational conferences felt able to report that after asking God (via an elaborate sys-tem of casting lots) how he would describe the province they were in, he had answered very plainly: "*Pennsylvania* is a compleat *Babel*." Provincial groups often invoked this idea of the middle colonies as a Babel—a dan-gerously mixed landscape not only of tongues but of religious errors and differences. The Moravians were afire to undo the differences, or to find a holy pattern underneath them, but many other Europeans' response to living in Babel was to try to protect their defining traits. In this setting the Moravians' eagerness to embrace converts everywhere, instead of in a preselected band of the faithful, made them unsettling. So unsettling, in fact, that the Moravian church's most pivotal role may have been simply to rouse a frightened opposition to itself—like a magic lantern of the spirit that threw huge shadows across other Europeans' views of colonial life.45

Members of various churches that had been proudly national in Europe all worried about having their orthodoxy sapped by living amid the Moravians and the region's radical sects: Quakers, Mennonites, Schwenkfelders, Dunkards. And the sectarians, who had lived in Penn-sylvania before these waves of church people came, felt a parallel concern that they might lose their way. The familiar heading of the Great Awak-ening is not really wide enough to contain these events. At least in the mid-Atlantic, where they started, the Awakening's episodes of revival make most sense once they are seen as peaks in a much larger pattern of revitalizations—of redefinitions and sharpenings, of anxious cinchings up—that were all set off by an explosion of religious diversity.[46]

Indian reformers had been the first to see a way to reorder this new world of resentful social fragments. But Europeans, for now, showed no knack of their own for thinking in terms of separate creations. Nor were they inclined to draw on the shadow notion of European unity that lay like a seed in the pan-Indianists' message. They were too consumed by mutual distaste to care much about the things that, from Indians' perspective, they could be seen to share. Instead, when Europeans looked at one another—and especially when the best-established groups viewed disorderly new arrivals—they saw people they often described as being worse than Indians. Migration and revival can both be strongly nationalizing experiences: in the middle provinces they were combined. The result was a collection of peoples, all laboring to deepen the trenches between them.[47]

WHEN Heinrich Melchior Mühlenberg voyaged to Pennsylvania in 1742 to start his life's work of building up the Lutheran Church in the middle colonies—in time he would become their best-known German public figure—he could already speak some English. And as a resident of Hanover, the German state from which the British ruling house had been drawn since he was two, he had long had tenuous ties to Britain. His new environment did not have to come as a complete shock.[48]

But it still did. Even during the crossing on an English ship, Mühlenberg started measuring everything around him against what he knew to be sound and familiar—by what was most like home. By turns vomiting, listening miserably to the blasphemies of English-speaking passengers, and poring for consolation over the book of Exodus, he found himself restricting his regard and attention, more and more, to the small collection of emigrants from Salzburg who were also aboard. These "dear" Salzburgers, whom the other passengers made fun of and blamed when anything went wrong, seemed to Mühlenberg always eager to lap up God's word. By contrast, his interactions with the cacophonous English "children of unbelief," who were always boxing, drinking, or singing their nation's endless repertory of indecent songs, dwindled mainly to dressing them down and—unless he was begged—refusing them ministry. As he had already decided by the halfway point of the passage, "I would rather preach to the heathen and live among cattle than among them."[49]

When he debarked in Philadelphia, Mühlenberg found himself in a world so unsettled and overwhelmingly alien—with sects, cults, and bizarre religious splinter factions, many of which were there precisely because they had been scourged as subversives out of Europe—that at first it caused him, like many of his countrymen whose acts he recorded, to collapse back in on himself. And he was in the middle of nowhere. Preaching from an outdoor platform, Mühlenberg listened glumly to his own voice, observing how, "[s]ince the plantations here are totally surrounded by forests, there is a strong echo which moved me to think of the wilderness mentioned in several passages of the Prophets. The wilderness is great enough in all conscience, and the sheep, too, are lost."[50]

He was most isolated from the sources of orthodoxy. Even the smallest German-speaking state had some sort of establishment, but in Pennsylvania the structures underlying any church that relied on salaried ministers were chaotic and gappy. Surrounded by "disorderly groups . . . who call themselves Lutherans," Mühlenberg found other ministers' legitimacy maddeningly hard to establish. And sometimes he proved as vulnerable as they to the charge of not really being what practically everyone—whether self-ordained, a Moravian, or only a charlatan—claimed above all else to be, a "genuine Lutheran."[51]

Trying, like Mühlenberg, to find a safe corner in this confusing landscape, many of the German church people he met had regrouped around what seemed to them the core traits of their national religious tradition and started feverishly forming congregations. Well before they could pay ministers, rural Lutherans shaped themselves into preacherless little churches anywhere a few families were settled within range. As the members of one such unit told Mühlenberg in 1751, they gathered every Sunday to sing hymns and hear a printed sermon read aloud by someone (perhaps an elder or schoolmaster) who could play the part of pastor in these reassuring performances. "All sorts of small churches" popped up, sometimes even with "two churches . . . built, one right next to the other." The construction was a symptom of Lutherans' competitive anxiety: as Mühlenberg noted, St. Michael's Church in Philadelphia, begun in spring 1743, "would never have been started on such an ambitious scale if the Herrnhuters [or Moravians] and other sects had not driven us to it." These church buildings provided playing fields for debates over theology and identity. Contests for the buildings' control became another side of the search for orthodoxy, with rival groups of Lutherans who accused one another of crypto-Moravianism literally tussling for their possession. Sometimes they threw or locked one another out in massed flying wedges, armed with clubs and swords.[52]

In 1748, Mühlenberg had to modify the wording of his baptismal oath for godparents when a tiny modernization frightened congregants into "believ[ing] . . . we intended to lead them away from Lutheran doctrine." And over and over, as figureheads for his own fears of bastardization, Mühlenberg conjured up the awful example of good Lutheran servants who, sold into the service of heretics and foreigners, had lost their identities entirely—like the girl who "forgo[t] her German tongue" and went nine years without communion. In this place where unbaptized heretics "are the ones who have control, wealth, and worldly prestige," fears of falling into infidelity—embodied in this image of "grow[ing] up in darkness and ignorance among the Quakers"—made a tightening of Lutheran group discipline feel essential.[53]

Exposure to so much that was strange helped Lutherans to see the German church's fragility, and even their own chosenness as a people. The language of Israel was everywhere—Mühlenberg told favorite parishioners they were "true Israelite[s]"—and the clergy tied noteworthy events to Israel's experiences: preaching from Genesis, to "[p]oin[t] out the similarity between Jacob's circumstances and those of our German fellow-believers in this western wilderness," when building new churches; or from Amos, to explain when God punished "His covenant people," when there was no rain. Always they tried to marshal their immigrant parishioners into a proud people and teach them Jeremiah's lesson, which was "[h]ow covenant people in a strange land under strange rulers must conduct themselves."[54]

Many Lutherans conceived of cultural mixture as religious decay. Every day brought evidence that young people, in particular, would "gradually degenerat[e on] . . . mixing with other nationalities" (especially, as Mühlenberg noted, in Philadelphia, a place simply "teeming and swarming" with the young of all nations). In 1764, when some Lutheran boys made trouble at a Sunday school, they confirmed these perils by "clench[ing] their fists at th[e deacons] and pour[ing] out English curses such as *'Go to he . . l!' 'You son of a b . . ch!' 'God d . . mn you!'* etc." The printer Christoph Saur summed up German parents' uneasiness at the idea of interethnic charity schools, where "German children [would] learn to speak English, and have intercourse with others" (and, perhaps, come to "desire to be dressed according to English fashions"). When different nations' children mixed, people said, they would only "mutually learn . . . evil things from each other, rather than good." In 1760, the Presbyterian revivalist Gilbert Tennent complained he could not have any relation deeper than mutual resentment with the German minister of St. Michael's Church, because of "his judgment of the whole English people": Tennent had heard him flatly say "he believed . . . there was not a single truly pardoned and converted soul among them."55

New World conditions were leading not to ecumenism, but to its opposite: a demand for ultra-orthodoxy and the keeping up of a clear divide between Lutherans and less godly groups. Once when Mühlenberg preached in New Jersey, he wrote, "[s]everal guileless Reformed people were sure that I was not a Lutheran preacher because I had not reviled and run down other denominations." It was not that German church people all sheered away from anyone who was not a Lutheran, or not a speaker of German. That would have been impossible—which was itself the problem.56

Having to watch a stream of little adjustments and agreements—the taking up of foreign fashions, the intermarriages and language loss, the casualness some country people were said to show toward baptism—drove up the unhappiness of many religious and political opinion makers, together with that of their flocks. "Inasmuch as many parties dwell together, intermarry, and have business and social relations with each other, a dangerous indifferentism might easily develop, and it is therefore necessary," as Mühlenberg noted sharply, "to point out the differences."57

EVEN IN very remote parts of the countryside, the new Irish communities avidly set about building up congregations. When the Presbyterian ministers Charles Beatty and George Duffield made a preaching tour of the backwoods in 1766, at valley after valley they found themselves being led to clearings where the half-finished stumps of meetinghouses, slowly being built, rose up out of the grass. In the valley between the Tuscarora and Shade mountains, they gave their sermons at "the Place designed for a meeting House where they have Some Logs put up & expect soon to raise it & coverer it in." Twenty-five miles away, in the Juniata Valley, they preached "at a place in the woods . . . near to which a house for worship is intended to be built." Even in places where there was no building yet, in residents' minds a clear if invisible structure—where the minister's house would go, the exact families who would contribute—was nearly always in place.⁵⁸

In these housing starts and careful plans, what Beatty and Duffield were seeing was not religious formlessness, or milling masses in want of organization, but a series of pre-congregations that needed only the capstone of a settled minister to be complete—or, from the pleased perspective of these missionaries, preaching to "large and attentive" crowds at many stops, a series of empty sockets just waiting to be filled. And, of course, these sockets were not really even empty: in all the valleys they visited, families were already used to "meet[ing] together for worship" without a salaried minister.⁵⁹

Any informality in the buildings of the Irish went unreflected in their institutions. Far from being rough-hewn, their structures of presbyteries, synods, and congregations were dazzling in their intricacy and hairsbreadth differentiation. The Irish jostled and argued all the time, endlessly proposing tests of orthodoxy, disowning one another, splintering and reforming. But the overall direction of change was toward more Presbyterian unity before outside threats.

In 1745, so-called Old and New sides—one opposing and one favoring revival preaching—formally separated into two dueling synods. But by 1758, after a decade of near-misses at reunion, they merged again. The people who had helped the schism along repented it almost at once. One was Rev. Gilbert Tennent, a stylistically sensational but theologically orthodox young revivalist. In 1740, Tennent famously lashed out at his opponents in a sermon proclaiming *The Danger of an Unconverted Ministry*. But after the first, informal stage of the Presbyterian schism, Tennent was already apologizing for his "excessive heat of temper" and putting out feelers toward a reconciliation. "I would to God the breach were healed," he wrote. The reason was obvious. The appearance of the Moravians had

> given me a clear view of the danger of every thing which tends to enthu-siasm and division . . . . I think that while the enthusiastical Moravians, and Long-beards or Pietists, are uniting their bodies, (no doubt to increase their strength and render themselves more considerable,) it is a shame that the ministers who are in the main of sound principles in reli-gion should be divided and quarrelling.

Tennent's rapid about-face—brought on in large part by the menacing diversity of his religious environment—was at least as typical of Presby-terianism's course as his earlier dust-kicking.[60]

In comparison with Pennsylvania's sects, practically any kind of Pres-byterianism seemed good enough. Rev. Alexander Creaghead showed as much when he led extraordinary group re-swearings on Octoraro Creek of the Scottish National Covenant and the Solemn League and Covenant—two group vows of Presbyterian principles from one hundred years before, in which participants publicly renounced the reigning king. Amid naked, upraised swords, Creaghead's crowds chanted out declara-tions of war against the church's enemies and proclaimed that George I, George II, and any other members of the royal house of Hanover had no shadow of a

> legal Right to rule over this Realm . . . being . . . outlandish Lutheran[s] . . . sworn Prelaticks, the Head of Malignants and Protectors of sectar-ian Hereticks, and electory Princes . . . in chusing of new Emperors, which is there giving their Power to the Beast; and for their Confeder-acy with popish Princes . . . and for want of their scriptural and national Qualifications . . . .

All the same, compared with the heretics who could be found everywhere in the middle colonies, Rev. Samuel Finley—later to become the president of Princeton—judged that even these extravagant latter-day Covenanters "have infinitely the Preference, because they hold the Truths of Religion."[61]

Though their opponents mocked Creaghead and his Covenanters, their religious worries only overstated some of what many Presbyterians were feeling. By publicly renewing Presbyterians' old covenants with God, Creaghead's followers meant to be "lifting up a Testimony against the Abominations of the Age and Place in which we live." They wanted not simply to redo the acts of their ancestors but in a sense actually to *be* them once more: to dredge up out of the clear well of Presbyterian history "in its former Purity" their real nature as a church and a chosen people—that "unspeakable Dignity," with which Creaghead told them only the Jews and they had ever been honored.[62]

The covenant renewals were two-day outdoor events run by tag teams of ministers, ending in a group celebration of the Lord's Supper. Religious life for nearly all Irish Presbyterians was structured by such mass communions, with crowds clutching little leaden tokens that would entitle them to take bread and wine in multiple sittings at long outdoor tables, "covered with snowy linen," after they had heard "fencing" sermons that called on specific lists of sinners to "stand off upon your Peril." What Creaghead—like many ordinary Irish congregants—so valued about these communion festivals was how visibly they made salvation and community coincide. What he feared most was that they might be celebrated too indiscriminately. If this happened, as he claimed some revivalists would like, a gaping door would open to error, and for pious-seeming "Persons in the *Church of England*"—perhaps even Baptists!—to "creep into the Church." For Creaghead, it was important that all good Presbyterians, but only good Presbyterians, take the Lord's Supper, because without a sufficiently "national" basis for communion, an awful prospect loomed. A misstep by the Presbyterian Church "would render it," as he intoned, "a Babel."[63]

Despite such worries, in practice nearly all of these remarkable ceremonies played out in the bounds of the Irish communities that dotted the middle colonies. Here, whatever their positions on disputed points of theology, neighboring Irish Presbyterians could pour together in proud phalanxes. The occasions cleared a path for the best-known revivalists of the mid-Atlantic Great Awakening—figures like Whitefield and Tennent, who rode up and down the eastern corridor of rural settlement, often drawing on communities that were "generally settled with People from *Ireland*." These awakeners became the happy beneficiaries of a powerful shared experience that Irish people had been massing together out of every cranny in the countryside to have.[64]

THE LONG SILENCES that could mark eighteenth-century Quaker meetings might suggest that here, at least, there were no revivals. But even if a revival's central feature were only a great deal of loud, seemingly artless preaching intended to stir a response in listeners, Quaker life before the Seven Years' War was in fact full of revival.

By any standard, the religious life of eastern Friends was robustly evangelical. It teemed with preachers—specially licensed as so-called public Friends, or ministers—who were famous for the chastening power and sincerity of their oratory. Like the reformer John Churchman, these Quaker ministers traveled from meeting to meeting and modeled themselves on the roaring original of George Fox, Quakerism's seventeenth-century founder, reliably addressing great groups of eager auditors. In this period of itinerating orators and weekly meetings for worship that could draw audiences in the high hundreds and sometimes the thousands, there is every reason to think it was unbroken silence, not the sound of impassioned preaching, that was exceptional. The New Jersey mystic John Woolman, for one, noted down in his journal as extraordinary the occasions on his travels when he felt a lack of divine direction at a meeting and so did not preach. The British Friend Samuel Fothergill, whose sermons were attended and even scribbled down in shorthand by Englishmen from all religious traditions, made one of the most celebrated American revival tours of the Quaker eighteenth century, winging down "fair Sylvania's Coast," like an angel of light who blazed and cried out before excited throngs of Quaker believers "With such a moving Grace [and] seraphic Fire," according to one listener,

> As glads the Just & listening Crowds admire . . .
> Bid[ding] conscious Tears from Hearts of Iron gush
> The Villian tremble & the Atheist blush . . . .

But even when it took more phlegmatic forms than a Fothergill sermon, the shape of what happened to mid-Atlantic Quakers in these
years, and especially their sharpened sense of purity and mission—which
has justly been called the Quaker reformation—clearly amounted to
another early American revitalization movement. In its course, Quakers
may have fallen more fully under the sway of nativistic reformers than any
other group, European or Indian.[65]

America's Quaker population was remaking itself into one of the most
morally creative communities in the world. Some of its inventiveness was
shown in Philadelphia Yearly Meeting's sudden acceptance, in 1755—after
rumblings from a few disregarded agitators—of the reformer Woolman's
injunction not to buy or sell other people. In one sign of the close relation in Quaker reform between moral cleansing and a self-advertising
singularity, many Friends expanded the ban on slaveholding to take in
sweeping dietary restrictions—like eating sugar, since it was a slave-
grown crop—and even things as faintly related to slavery as sleeping
between indigo-dyed sheets. Their founding once the war began of the
Friendly Association for Regaining and Preserving Peace with the Indians by Pacific Measures was, if possible, an even more widely unpopular
effort at promoting interracial justice—in this case, by reaching out to the
Delawares who had started to storm Pennsylvania's borders. In the 1750s
and 1760s Quakers imposed on themselves, too, a stricter stand against
war-related taxes and fighting, and began, with the founding of hospitals,
a long train of philanthropies.[66]

The Quakers' vivid new sense of themselves as a crusading people,
shedding corruption to return to a radical past, was not a simple withdrawal from the world. In this first age of mass immigration, the rigor
and novelty of the Quakers' self-transformations came from their fears of
being smeared away or swallowed up by newer arrivals—of losing their
hold, not only on the province's political life and with it on their security
as dissenters, but on their specialness as a people.

So they adjusted their orthodoxies, leaving great gashes in the membership records of Quaker meetings. From the 1740s on, Quakers disowned one another at quickening rates for drunkenness and selling
liquor, for Sabbath breaking, for war-related acts, for sexual looseness,

·and even for deviations from Quaker dress and speech. Like the German language and clothing that some Lutheran observers feared their own youth would abandon, the Quaker norms of plain dress—with unornamented cloth, uncuffed coats, and broad-brimmed hats—and plain speech—in which everyone was addressed as "thee"—could work as constantly flashed badges of membership. These were some of the first things people noticed about one another, and their presence or absence could inspire real ill will: as with the young Ulster servant who lived in the household of a Quaker preacher at Lancaster long enough, it was reported, that "her Dress—Speech—&ca has set her Relations much against her."[67]

But Friends began to be punished and disowned the most harshly for having sex outside of marriage and, more surprisingly, for simply entering into marriage itself in the wrong way. In the early 1710s, perhaps one in eleven marriages had been judged irregular; but by the early 1740s, one in two was—and the rate kept rising, two and a half times as fast as that for all other offenses. Newlyweds could be disciplined if they had a child already on the way or—most significantly—if one of them was not a Quaker.[68] And by midcentury the specter of mixed marriages, making what the preacher Elizabeth Wilkinson called a "motled Generation," held an unhappy fascination for mid-Atlantic Friends. To fight it, Philadelphia Yearly Meeting overturned the long-standing assumption that children with only one Quaker parent could be birthright Friends; and during the thirty years before the start of the Seven Years' War, the prosecution of members for marrying out shot up fifteenfold. Partly because so many people who were about to have children were tossed out, Quakerism's population growth—amazingly, with the population around them doubling every twenty years—simply stopped.[69]

Starting in the 1730s, a book by a Friend named Moses West—the *Treatise concerning Marriage* (originally written in London about twenty-five years before)—was reprinted in Philadelphia. West's tract proved the "UNLAWFULNESS of *Mixt-Marriages*" by Quakers through simple-minded chosen-people thinking. Since modern Quakers were the same as the Israel of old, marriages to gentiles were still forbidden. With much invocation of the Canaanites' tempting daughters, and the forced divorces of those wobbly Jews who had raised half-breed children, West's suddenly popular tract stressed that as the "Peculiar People of God," Quakers simply "*must live alone,* and not be *mixed,*" instead seeking ways to "Shun [non-Quakers], as much as may be." James Reynell, a merchant, felt typical worries over his younger sister. It was vital, as he wrote in 1739, that she "throws her Self not away" with a non-Quaker, for "Mix'd Marriages are the Destruction of Families." When she nonetheless got engaged to a gentile, Reynell cut her off from all contact. "[I] Cant help Looking on her as Lost to me," he wrote bitterly to a cousin.

> The man himself has Written me a Pretty long Letter, . . . [saying] tht their being of Different Perswasions ought to be no Objection . . . . I have not Given him any Answer. . . . Please to Acquaint 'em both not to have any Expectation . . . o[f] any favours of any Kind from me . . . ; But if they be Already Marryed, its to no purpose, to say anything to em.[70]

As their home colony became the focus of all European overseas movement, the Quakers' renewal was shaped by a desire to fence around the familiar community of Friends. Part of Quakerism's reinvention was pressed forward by specific wartime crises. But with its focus on marrying in and shrinking away from other groups; its talk of restoration; its innovations clothed as returns to primitive Quakerism; and its endless invocations of the lost legacy of "our worthy Ancestors," the renovation of Pennsylvania Quakerism was a blatant case of nativistic revival, too.[71]

The reformers' urge for purity could take amusingly literal forms. Despite his friends' worries over "an affected singularity," in the 1760s John Woolman took to going around in a big white hat (since it was undyed and so less luxurious, albeit in the showiest way possible, than a dark one) and, in time, an entire suit of undyed, ice-cream-colored clothing. Reformed Quakers' defensive drive for specialness lent a kind of poignancy to protestations like that of the antislavery activist Anthony Benezet, in 1781, that "[a]s a people we are called to dwell alone . . . to be as a Kingdom of Priests, an Holy Nation, a peculiar people to shew forth the praise of him that called us." For from about 1730 on, dwelling alone was probably the one thing mid-Atlantic Quakers were most painfully aware they could never do again.[72]

RELIGIOUSLY EXPRESSED quests for distinctiveness could be found everywhere in the mid-Atlantic of the Great Awakening. Indian nativists tried to give up European clothes; Quaker dress grew more idiosyncratic. Lutherans petitioned for German-speaking ministers, fearing they would not otherwise be able "to live and die faithful to their mother tongue." An emphasis on marriage within the fold, the unearthing of peculiar cere-monies—even, as a token of Lutheranness, a dogged emphasis on music and the singing of "beautiful, edifying, evangelical hymns"—all of these things were startled into sharper life. And until the eve of the Seven Years' War, the divisions between Europeans showed every sign of grow-ing steadily more serious.[73]

This posed obvious problems for public life, problems that became a source of active worry each time there was a security scare. Such a period came in 1747 and 1748, when (because of Britain's role in the War of the Austrian Succession) Philadelphians faced the frightening prospect of French marauders "cruiz[ing] at our Capes," or piratical Spanish crews of "the very Dregs of Mankind" pillaging houses on the lower Delaware. The best way out of this dilemma would simply be to include more provincial Europeans within the group of people you cared about, and hence could count on being cared for by.[74]

Franklin was one of the first to see this. In November 1747, he pub-lished a pamphlet—*Plain Truth*—to popularize his project of starting an association of volunteer military companies. Franklin's pamphlet, printed in both English and German, fluently used Old Testament examples and the language of chosen peoples to try to overcome the mid-Atlantic's par-alyzing divisions (concluding roundly, *"May the* GOD *of* WISDOM, STRENGTH *and* POWER, *the Lord of the Armies of Israel . . . unite the Hearts and Counsels of all of us, of whatever* SECT *or* NATION, *in one . . . generous Publick Spirit"*). Not for the last time in his career, Franklin set out to imagine entirely new alliances between groups: a "UNION" of his home province's different peoples, like that between the "separate Filaments of

Flax"—as any Irish linen-weaver would immediately understand—when they were spun together into one thread.

To call up such a coalition against the threat from the sea, Franklin understood that he had to appeal to the whole grudging and distrustful spectrum of national groups. And so his appeal climaxed in a long and elaborate series of sops to the separate self-esteem first of the region's Englishmen (known for their *"Zeal"* and *"undaunted Spirit"*), then of its Irishmen ("those *noble Warriors!*"), and finally of its *"brave* and *steady* GERMANS." Franklin was trying to paste together an interethnic public using little more than charm and shared fear.[75]

His idea was adopted with delight by a few units of volunteers in Philadelphia (whose martial mottoes and insignia Franklin contentedly composed, together with soldiers' manuals of his own printing). These "Associators" were in turn taken up by Gilbert Tennent, the onetime Presbyterian wunderkind, now settled in the pulpit of Philadelphia's Second Presbyterian Church, who soon started delivering and printing special sermons for them. At a first hearing, the most remarkable thing about Tennent's productions was the raw exuberance with which they proclaimed that *"The LORD is a Man of WAR"* and imagined Jesus as a general, freeing Tennent to shout out in His voice, *"I will render vengeance to mine Enemies . . . . I will make mine ARROWS DRUNK with BLOOD!"*[76]

But beneath the sound of this thunder, something surprising happened. Tennent had always preached about the community of true believers—especially Presbyterian true believers—and their demanding group relationship with God. Like the Israelites of old, they had to try to stay in covenant bonds with Him, even while alone in Canaan amid apostates and strangers, alternately besieged and seduced by strange customs and gods. Every other major group in the province also referred to this vision—which drew on the parts of the Bible, like the books of Joshua, Judges, and Nehemiah, that were most concerned with wall building, national purity, and the importance of hanging on grimly to God-given ways. When provincials spouted such language at one another, its message was not that they were all in anything together.[77]

But biblical parallels controlled all debates about public action. (If we habitually measure new events against Munich or Pearl Harbor, colonists argued as readily from the curse of Meroz and the sack of the Temple.)

So what Tennent now tried to do, a little awkwardly, was to stretch out this language of a covenanted people to cover almost everyone who lived in the province, sound Calvinists or not.

Even if the language he had to use kept getting in the way, this impulse was in keeping with Franklin's efforts at drawing everyone together into one interdenominational public. The idea was that contiguity might at last become a ground for community—that the group on which the greatest stress was placed should switch from being the band of true believers to something like *the people who live around me*, since in an invasion neither God nor the enemy could be counted on to make finer distinctions. Tennent, and other writers supporting him, started talking about all Europeans' public dealings as a "*Nation* or People" with God, and calling themselves seekers of "the PUBLICK SAFETY." This new rhetoric was mobilized just as individual people were, by the specter of a coming war.[78]

But this motley collection of colonists could not be bundled so easily into a province-wide "PUBLICK" or "*Nation*"—not even by publicly relabeling the president of Pennsylvania's council "KING JEHOSAPHAT," as Tennent did, or demanding that everyone fast and pray together. Especially resistant were the Quaker pacifists who wrote pamphlets to question Tennent's biblical analogies (and to skeptically describe the drilling Associators' "cut[ting] their Capors with crooked Sticks," instead of real guns). They had no intention of being hectored into an interdenominational union in support of a mobilization for war, with its most visible advocate an Irish Presbyterian preacher.[79]

Tennent saw himself as making painful, praiseworthy efforts to be inclusive in his prowar publicity—as nobly holding back from singling out any group for detestation (however richly it deserved it) in pursuit of the "generous *Plan*" of association. If despite all this the Quakers would not wholeheartedly back the "common *Safety* of all the *Societies* in the *Colony*," the reason was not far to seek. Basically, they were bigots. Their lack of interest in arming the people, or joining in military measures themselves, was a small revelation of something larger: their "great *Uncharitableness* in . . . confining Persons of . . . *true Christianity*, to the narrow Pale of the *Quaker Society*" and in talking as if God's blessings flowed "to those, and to no others." This was wrong. So wrong that, briefly and improbably, it suited Tennent to sound like one of those unnervingly ecumenical Moravians whose influence he and other Presbyterians had spilled so much ink against. For "whatever our [Quakers] may imagine to the contrary," Tennent noted, "*Christ's Sheep* are not cooped up in one *Fold*, but scattered in many."[80]

The threat of war had suddenly made politics matter—even in Pennsylvania, in many ways still an almost imaginary state, with no taxes, no military establishment or legal militia, very little public spending, a scant smattering of officials outside Philadelphia, and, in many years, no laws passed at all. But as Tennent's angry protests showed, the urge during wartime to assemble a new public by appealing to as wide a variety of people as possible—and to make one's opponents seem to scorn them— could carry printed discourse in new directions. Despite a few attempts in pamphlets to conjure up visions of Philadelphia under attack—sacked, burned, empty, smoking—no invaders sailed up the Delaware in 1748. News of the peace at Aix-la-Chapelle arrived by late summer, and the arguments over what to do in a war were suspended.

It would take a real war, and not only the passing threat of one, to transform the relations between colonial groups. But what had been suggested was the power a war might have, if one ever really came, both to excite groups of provincial people into shared action and to shove aside anyone in public life who seemed not to believe in, or not to want to protect, those new communities.[81]

WITH THE PASSAGE of a few more years, and the stunning Indian attacks that opened the Seven Years' War, those possibilities became real. The decade that followed would overflow with war. In the 1750s, a long-simmering contest heated up between Britain and France for influence over the Ohio country—a region, fantastically rich in arable land and fur-bearing game, that lay at the intersection of French Canada's southward course down the Mississippi, and of the British provinces' undefined western boundaries. Watching while Delawares, Shawnees, and Mingos moved into the Ohio lands—where they sought relief from both European squatters and Iroquois claims of control—and as a mass of British traders trailed after them, France in 1753 panicked and built a chain of new forts to try to seal its control over the region. Clashes between French and Virginian expeditions in this militarized borderland led the next year to formal war. Most Ohio Indians cast their lot with the French, especially after the summer of 1755, when Canadian and western Indian forces devastated a large, vaunted expedition against the newly constructed Fort Duquesne by British troops under Maj. Gen. Edward Braddock.

After Braddock's defeat, the autumn of 1755 saw a shattering, apparently unstoppable series of Indian assaults on the frontiers. For several years, the countryside was a scene of chaos and rout, with colonial forces hardly managing even to hinder the raids. Finally, in 1757, diplomatic overtures to the Ohio country's Delawares—begun with the help of Quaker reformers and Delawares in the east—set a peace process in motion between the western Indians and the British, and in 1758 a durable truce was agreed at Easton, Pennsylvania. Soon after that, with the British capture of Fort Duquesne (now an exploded wreck, soon to be rebuilt as Fort Pitt), and, after a decisive assault on Quebec in 1759, of French Canada itself, the tide of the war turned. Then it started running so strongly in favor of the British that their problem became how to manage success.

They made a hash of it. With the eclipse of French power and the British takeover of Canada, ill-timed economies and humiliations—Gen. Sir Jeffery Amherst, the commander in chief at war's end, felt that truckling to Indian allies was now beneath the empire's dignity—estranged the region's Indians and helped to spark Pontiac's War. This second full-scale Indian war got under way in 1763, only months after the final signing of a peace between the European powers, with a series of simultaneous Indian risings against frontier forts. Another miserable season of Indian blitzes followed in the countryside. Not until well into 1764, as negotiation, regular army expeditions into the west, and France's clear lack of interest in rising to the insurgents' aid all did their work, were most of the embers of war put out.

But once this train of wars had been set going—to be followed, in 1775–83, by the confused and viciously inconclusive fighting of a drawn-out civil war, the American Revolution—the middle Atlantic would never be the same.[82]

* * *

> And behold in my Dream I thought I was going towards Phi[l]adelpia
> when I arrived . . . the sun was seting, and behold I was at the Gable end
> of the State House, and there was the appearance of a Man in bright
> Cloathing with wings at his Shoulders, who beckoned to me . . . [saying]
> come I will shew the[e] the calamity that is Comeing upon this citty of
> Philadelphia . . . .

This is the way the nightmare of one Quaker from the countryside
started—it would end with his waking to "cries Screeches & Lamentations . . . in mine Ears so pearsing that the Sound thereof . . . cannot easily be forgotten"—in the tense and miserable year of 1757, at the
low-water mark of the Seven Years' War. The nightmare angel guided
the dreamer up a ladder to the city's darkening rooftops ("I said O how
Shall we walk on such Difficult Places, he said stick by me and there
Will be no Danger") and told him to look back down. In the streets
beneath them

> I Saw a multitude of Black Carts or waggons one after the Other with
> four black horses in each, And two men in Mourning with black caps on
> their heads & lighted Torches in their hands . . . and their Loading was
> dead Bodies . . . heaped up of different Sexes . . . I saw all their Actions
> & positions by the Torches which the mourners had in their hands . . . .

On being faced with this vision, of catastrophic death—probably from
some sort of plague—striking Philadelphia, the dreamer's thoughts took
an interesting detour. It seemed important to see in which different
churchyards all of these "promiscuously" jumbled dead were being
deposited. Just who were they? So

> we walked up the street upon the houses till he brought me to a Bury-
> ing place which I took to be the Ground belonging to . . . Christ's
> Church, and looking Down I saw great pits dug like the foundations of
> houses, And saw many of those Waggons unloaded [of their dead]
> which was by the mourners or Drivers with Pitchforks . . . .

Here Christ Church's trademark spire made it clear that these were piles of *Anglican* corpses. And a classificatory dream tour of the dead ensued, with the angel showing him the other burial places, where it became clear "what sort they belonged to." Then, in the last moments before waking, the Quaker dreamer asked to see the sight to which everything before, apparently, had been leading—the capping horror:

> [I] Said Pray Shew me Freinds suffering likewise and how it doth go with them, [on this] he shewed me another place of Interment . . . [where] I looked and saw graves (not pits) and some put in likewise Promiscuously . . . now he said I have shewed thee all.[83]

This partitioned dreamscape suggested how much power the revitalization of religious communities would have to shape Europeans' views of the terror and violence that convulsed the middle colonies at midcentury. In this collection of suspicious, insecurely chosen peoples, nearly everyone would at first understand the descent into Indian war that lay ahead not as a misfortune but as a betrayal.

Chapter 2

FEARING
INDIANS

FOR SEVERAL NIGHTS DURING THE COLD CHRISTMAS HOLIDAYS of 1756, "a Sett of young Gentlemen" at the College of Philadelphia put on a play. Their charismatic young provost, Rev. William Smith, had written almost two hundred new lines for insertion into one of the period's pivotal works. *Alfred, A Tragedy*, by David Mallett, had first been staged in London in the 1740s, amid growing military tension between Britain and the Continent's Catholic powers. The drama celebrated King Alfred's triumph over savage marauders—the Danes—nine hundred years before. By awakening his subjects' love of their country, the story went, Alfred had expelled the invaders from English soil.[1]

The play's lesson that reawakened patriotism could turn adversity into triumph was widely popular, and one of the songs from the play had become a true cultural phenomenon:

> Rule, Britannia! Britannia, rule the waves!
> Britons never, never, never shall be slaves!

In gathering half a dozen of his best-spoken students to practice this play in an empty hall of the college and passing out to them handwritten copies of his verse additions, Provost Smith was not simply having fun. He was carefully writing himself and his teenaged actors into a highly charged national literary property at a time of military disaster. For, as

Smith himself explained, his choice of *Alfred* was "owing to the great similarity of circumstances in the distress of England under the Danish invasion and that of the Colonies at this time under the ravages and incursions of the Indians."[2]

Speaking through the mouths of undergraduates who were, in many cases, the sons of Pennsylvania's leading officeholders, he wanted to proclaim where the colony's salvation lay. Patriotism, public spirit, martial vigor, a love of Protestantism: these were the values, Smith wrote, that the play's lines—"Lines so truly British, so compleatly good and virtuous"—would instill. Pointed, patriotic bluster was everywhere in the play, since nationalism was one of the things that the production was about. (It should have been: the audience included Lt. Gen. John Campbell, fourth earl of Loudoun, the commander in chief of all crown forces in North America.)[3]

But the play captured the interest of its "crouded and discerning Audiences" of Philadelphians during a long winter season of terrible defeats, when the middle Atlantic countryside was regularly being laid waste by raids from the north and west. The winter of 1756–57 was, in fact, one of the lowest points in modern British military history. Understanding this opens a new dimension in one's reading of the play, which was not, on the whole, a bragging or even a really confident production. The backdrop for all its action was a country overrun, a people defeated, an enemy cruel and nearly irresistible. In the world of *Alfred*, Englishmen were slaughtered and enslaved, the enemy torched whole hillsides covered with desperately needed crops, and almost everyone but Alfred had already fled in terror from the Danes.

A different feeling from triumph was also part of this provincial theatrical's appeal, one invoked in Mallett's simple prologue for the play. It invited audiences to think themselves into a time and place where *"Danish fury, with wide-wasting hand, / Had spread pale fear . . . o'er the land."* The experience of Indian war, in this first taste of it during the Seven Years' War and again in the Revolution, was the experience of almost unlimited fear.

To make sense of the spectacle of the mid-Atlantic colonies at war, one has to be able to imagine this fear, and the desperation that comes with continual defeat. For most of the time when they were faced with Indian war, people in the countryside—instead of feeling indignant, enraged, or defiant—were simply terrified.

The fear that they felt had a character and intensity their British cousins could not really have understood. English-speakers in the home island were certainly afraid during wartime, especially of an invasion from France, which most British naval planning—as well as the raising of a nationwide militia—was devoted to forestalling. Once the French landed, this fear went, they would set out with extirpatory fervor to spread Catholicism, burning Bibles and torturing people with the Inquisition's dreadful instruments.[4]

The American colonies went to war with Canada after 1689 as often as the mother country fought France, and they shared in all these fears. As one gentleman farmer wrote desperately to Pennsylvania's provincial secretary during 1756, "Must we in Very Deed become a province of France? . . . If so, . . . farewell Religion . . . must we have Persecution? Images Crucifixes &ca. &ca. Alas! Alas!" A propaganda pamphlet printed in 1754 pretended to translate a Canadian officer's exultant report ("Fire and Gibbet will be their Portion"!) on how, once war broke loose, the British colonies would be naked before a Franco-Indian Catholic invasion, thanks to tireless Jesuit work at "influencing and inlisting the Natives."[5]

But as this last detail suggests, the colonists' fear of their neighbors in New France was always much sharpened by another worry: that the Canadians would "overwhelm 'em," as one essayist in 1744 darkly noted, "with many thousand barbarous *Indians.*" This second fear of Indians was the colonists' alone. And it was powerful and pervasive enough to determine much of what the middle colonies' residents did diplomatically, militarily, and politically from the start of the Seven Years' War until the end of the Revolution.[6]

THE VIOLENCE that provincial Americans found themselves first dreading and then experiencing was, in the most literal sense, terroristic. It had been carefully planned and carried out by the Indians with whom they were at war to induce the greatest fright possible. While retracing the tracks of a group of Indians who had burned houses in New York's

Mohawk Valley during 1780, a company of provincial militia found themselves faced with a frightening and disheartening series of vignettes,
staged at intervals for the first mile of the trail. The group's commander
wrote down carefully these "scenes which I beheld." All around them was
a background of "nothing but houses in flames and people murdered,"
with slaughtered cattle littering the ground. As he and his men walked
along in pursuit, he wrote, first "we beheld . . . a man shot and speared";
then "a little girl, about 6 years old, lying in the crotch of a tree, most cruelly mangled and scalped"; and then, "a little further on . . . a boy, about
9 years old, killed and scalped." Producing tableaux of devastation—like
the scalped and cut-up little body left propped in a tree—was not incidental to such attacks, but one of their basic motives. The "scenes" left
behind were hardly ever the martial versions of crime scenes—showing,
in unplanned, sequential traces, how the violence had unwound. Instead,
they often reflected strangely careful postmortem operations. In the
Seven Years' War most of the corpses that search parties found, for
instance, had not only been stripped but actually dragged, whenever
feasible, to the center of the road. That way, they would be the first things
any traveler saw, and the fear stirred by the sight of them would make all
the connecting roads feel dangerous.[7]

Because these Indian forms of war depended on the multiplication of
panic, they allowed for an extraordinarily economical ratio of attackers.
As Timothy Horsfield, a Northampton County, Pennsylvania, justice of
the peace, lamented late in 1755, amid his first-ever Indian attacks, "40 or
50 of these Banditi or Robbers . . . are able in their Skulking Manner to
disturb the Peace of a whole Province & to baffle the Attempts of 1000ds
. . . sent against them—." It was not really possible to come up with a
plausible scheme of defense against such small-scale strikes, as Franklin
saw more clearly than most. Writing an English correspondent in 1757 to
debunk the idea that a different militia law would cure things, he
observed that "[o]ne might as justly charge to your Want of a good Militia law in England, the Highway Robberies and Housebreaking which
sometimes fill your Newspapers." With much of the war falling into an
awkward gap between conventional engagements and individual killings,
Franklin wrote, even

if every Man in the Country was a Veteran Soldier, our sparse Manner
of Settling on so extended a Frontier, would still subject us to . . . the
Depredations of such an Enemy as the Indians are, who . . . lurk about
for Opportunities of attacking single Houses, and small weak Neighborhoods. . . . We have now near 1500 Men on our Frontier, and yet People
are sometimes scalp'd between Fort and Fort, and very near the Forts
themselves . . . For . . . the Land must be till'd and Business follow'd;
every House and Plantation cannot be guarded . . . .[8]

After a first wave of attacks by French-allied Indians hit the countryside in October 1755, other Pennsylvanians tried to piece together what
had happened. So far as anyone could tell, a few large groups from the
Ohio country—totaling sixty to a hundred men—had arrived at safe
points that were beyond the province's farthest settlements and divided
there into smaller groups. These groups then dropped successively down
the ridges into different settled valleys to reconnoiter, with each spy
"lay[ing] about a House some days & nights, watching like a wolf" to see
"the situation of the Houses, the number of people at Each House, the
places the People most frequent, & to observe at each House where there
is most men, or women." The individual farmsteads they chose as targets
were at last attacked in parallel by still smaller groups, each only big
enough to kill or capture the number of people it was likely to meet.[9]

These violent raids by little Indian parties haunted contemporaries'
imaginations. Usually they were pictured as home invasions that came in
the middle of the night or at daybreak. But whenever the season allowed,
the brunt of the attacks actually fell on people who were outside doing field
work in full daylight. The work of the harvest could not well be avoided,
but reaping crops during wartime left one nightmarishly exposed. One
foggy morning in 1778, the son of a well-known border soldier, Capt.
Samuel Brady, helped to bring in the harvest at Loyalsock, Pennsylvania,
on the northern Susquehanna. Despite Brady's determination not to be
taken by surprise (the other reapers had leaned their guns against a tree, but
"young Mr. Brady . . . . thought this wrong, & put his . . . some little distance
from the rest"), when Indian attackers swept across the field he was shot,
speared, tomahawked, and scalped before he could even reach his rifle.[10]

These farm-by-farm attacks were followed by the capture of as many people and animals—especially younger people, horses, and cattle—as could safely be taken, the showy slaughtering of the rest, and the firing of crops and farm buildings—"Houses, Barns, Stackyards, . . . every thing that will burn." Then, as the larger war band's members withdrew, a sequence of reunions would follow at points further and further west, until the original group was reassembled.[11]

In 1756, William Fleming, a young Pennsylvanian, was captured by an attack party of only two men: the Delaware war leader Captain Jacobs and another Delaware named Jim. The narrative he published gave an unrivaled account of life in one of the little groups that made up these larger expeditions. Freelancing behind enemy lines, the two Delawares showed how bold, and how frightening, such tiny war parties could be. At one point Jim single-handedly stormed the house of Fleming's neighbor, a farmer named Hicks who had "a numerous Family of able young Men." Jim's only protection in making this attack was Fleming, whom he propelled along before him by the shoulder, "thinking they would not shoot at me, and if they did, I should screne him." Captain Jacobs told Fleming that he and Jim were part of a larger, fifty-man expedition of which he was in overall command, and asked Fleming to help them target the most vulnerable households around him. From the first moment the two Indians stopped him on the road, Fleming had literally been too terrified at the sight of them to speak, so much so that "my Enemies, savage as they were . . . endeavoured to encourage me, by clapping me several times on the Shoulder." (When Fleming later led them to his wife, she, for her part, "upon seeing them, had like to have fallen into fits.")

Although they had tried to moderate Fleming's panic during his capture, the Indians went on to instill still more docility and fear in their benumbed captive by subjecting him to a staged killing. Having taken one of the Hicks boys prisoner, they sat Fleming down and bound him backwards to a tree, with special "Leather Muffs" over his hands to keep him from freeing himself. Then they bludgeoned the Hicks boy to the ground with a tomahawk, split open his head—pausing at this point, in "Sport[,] . . . to imitate his expiring Agonies"—and scalped him. They advanced on Fleming, "all over besmared with [Hicks's] Blood," to let him know that only by "good Behaviour" could he avoid the same death. "It is impossible," as Fleming observed, "to describe my Horror on seeing this:"

> Death attended with its most frightful Terrors stared me in the Face, and I even wished I had been so happy as to have been [the] first out of Pain, and not lived to see what I undoubtedly thought next Moment would be my own Fate thus barbarously acted in that of my Companion.

Most Indian attack groups meant to "act" in this way for the country people they were attacking what it would feel like to be tortured and killed. Manufacturing the sort of paralyzed terror felt by Fleming was one of the attackers' ends. However recklessly they fought, the outnumbered war parties could not hope to kill everyone in the countryside, and horror became as much a shield for their campaigns as Fleming's body had been for Jim.[12]

UNLIKE EARLY AMERICANS from other places, most people in the middle colonies experienced Indian war for the first time only in 1755—in Pennsylvania, after a full seventy-five years of peace. As Zaccheus Collins of Lynn, Massachusetts, wrote in 1756 to a Philadelphian friend, "I am Concerned for your afflictions you met with by the Incursions the Indians &c Make on your frontiers it being a new thing to you—allthough we have had the Same among us Ever since my memory—." And so, especially in the 1750s and 1760s, when newspaper accounts describing this "new thing" were pieced together from the memories of survivors, they were so filled with rich, hallucinatory detail that they could themselves become mildly traumatic to read. They usually included the exact time and geography of attacks, what people were doing—sleeping, eating, milking, picking cherries or chestnuts—when the blows fell, and the ways specific people had fought and died. Collectively the image they provided was of a disorientingly close-up and domestic kind of fighting. The Indians' filtering off of forces, ending in synchronized assaults on individual households whose members could "know nothing of the matter untill they [we]re thus labrynth'd," terrified and unnerved country people. They felt, with reason, that a horrible death could come at almost any time and from any direction.[13]

Even three full decades before the mid-Atlantic country people had any real attacks to fear—when new immigrants had just begun moving into parts of the countryside where they came into regular contact with Indians—the bare prospect of Indian war was able to convulse whole settlements in recurrent panics. In the summer of 1727, some northern New Jerseyans were put "in a Fright, [that] made them remove to *New York & Long Island*" by the arrival in their neighborhood of a conclave of Munsees. (It turned out the Indians had come to celebrate the election of their new "Indian King.") Tired of being repeatedly "Alarmed by a Nois of Indians," in April 1728 another group of frightened settlers in northern Philadelphia County petitioned the governor to manage Indian affairs in such a way as would result in their being "freed from These alarms . . . To prevent as well our fears as Danger."[14]

The same spring, groundless fears of Indians bore some people in the newly settled interior far enough to actually kill. A few dozen miles above Philadelphia, on the upper reaches of Manatawny Creek, lay an iron-working corridor. Iron smelting depended on charcoal that had to be made, slowly and smokily, from the timber on great forest preserves, so the iron plantations in this neighborhood—with thirty-foot blast chimneys and open ore quarries—were a sign not of its industrialization but of its lying at the fringe of settlement.[15] Here, amid little populations of slaves and indentured servants who tended flaring furnaces, the power of mid-Atlantic colonists' fear of Indians became clear. One morning in May 1728, Gov. Patrick Gordon heard from the ironworks of an armed encounter with strange Indians and rode out from Philadelphia to investigate. He "found the Country under very great Terror and Surprize." Several families of Germans (among them a man who, though rumored to be dead, was only hurt a bit "in the Belly") had barricaded themselves in a mill. Then Gordon learned something more alarming, and truer, than the rumors of attack. Four English and Welsh men on Cacoosing Creek, perhaps fifteen miles away, had just killed three Delawares.

Here is how John and Walter Winter, the brothers who were eventually hanged for these deaths, explained what had happened. They had made a stronghold of Walter's house and patrolled about to gather in neighbors, because of repeated false alarms of Indian depredations in the preceding weeks. These alarms amounted to a remarkable collective delusion fueled by fear. The Winters heard second- and third-hand news of Indian assaults from German acquaintances at Tulpehocken and the Manatawny works. John Winter met one man who claimed to have talked to a man who "told him, that the *Indians* had kill'd his Wife and eight Children, and they then all lay dead at his house; and that all *Tulpyhocken* was cut off . . . and that he saw Fires." On the morning of the deaths, another "Dutchman" had told Walter Winter that "the Indians . . . killed sundry Dutchmen." None of these reports was true.[16]

Arriving at a neighbor's who had sent to them for help, the Winters saw Indians near his woodpile and started shooting. One Indian man, who had been holding a bow, was badly wounded by Walter Winter's fire and died after stumbling off into a thicket. So did an Indian woman, called old Hannah, whom John Winter knew but did not recognize in the course of this panicky encounter until he had already shot at her. He bashed another woman down with the butt (or cock) of his rifle before the Winters' neighbor swung his ax at her "and sunk a Place in her Scull that I could have laid my Fist in it." They took two Indian girls prisoner. Then, the next morning, plainly starting to feel doubtful about what had happened, they dragged the older women's bodies into a leaf-filled hole.[17]

What came out most clearly in the Winter brothers' confessions on the gallows in Chester was how unmixed their contrition was for what had been—as Walter Winter told the spectators in "the last [words] that I shall speak and you will hear from me"—a horrible accident. He and the "Neighbour *Indians*" he had killed, he thought, were alike victims of the "strong Fear" that had fallen on the upper settlements.

> When I went from home, I had no Ill-will towards the *Indians*, nor did I Design to kill any, if they were peaceable, and made no Assaults upon us . . . . I declare, as God is my Judge, we had a strong Report among us, that there were Wars between the *English* and *Indians*, and that was the only Means that brought me to commit the wicked Murder upon that innocent *Indian*. . . . I did it with no other Intent, than to defend my self, and save our Lives.

Standing beside him on the scaffold, John Winter chimed in that they had "thought all along they were Enemy *Indians*, and that we kill'd them in Defence of our selves, our Neighbours and County," adding, "I am sorry for the *Indians* Deaths, that then were so barbarously put to Death by us, which if we had known at that Time, we should not have been guilty of their Blood." As they understood and explained their own acts, the Winters had been urged on not by any malice toward all Indians but by hearing rumors that they were at war and in danger.[18]

In recognition of this, within days Governor Gordon issued a proclamation urging all Pennsylvania's residents, "the *Europeans* of whatsoever Nations they be," not to frighten one another into forming panicky bands that might provoke neighboring Indians. And "by all Means," he wrote, they should "avoid th[e] unbecoming Practice of expressing or shewing their weak unhandsome Fears" about Indians' movements. The judge of the quarter sessions when the Winters were tried likewise strove to root out the countryside's circuits of fear. "You, with all others the Inhabitants, must have observ'd the Emotion and unreasonable Panick, which lately possess'd great Numbers of the People," he sharply told the grand jury, "some of which may have arisen from Ignorance and Fear":

> This is noted to you, That as you are dispers'd in several Parts of the County, you may, as Occasion offers, in all Conversations, endeavour to quiet the Minds of the People, and perswade them, for the future, not to hearken to, much less assist in spreading, Lyes and ridiculous Tales. . . .
> —We intreat you therefor to excite all the People to use [the Indians] well, and give no Offence . . . [by] expressing either a ridiculous Bravery on the one Hand, or foolish Fears on the other . . . .

But despite officialdom's best efforts, "foolish Fears" would outrun reality in the countryside until, in the 1750s, they were fulfilled.[19]

DURING CONFLICT with Indians, country people commonly found themselves holed up for long stretches in forts or fortified houses, waiting. The speed and selectivity of the attacks meant there was usually much to fear but no one to fight. Soldiers at least could drill, but for them, too, being besieged by an opponent they hardly saw, and by their own apprehensions, was hard to stand.

This was especially true of the units confined in forts. Fort duty was infinitely less popular than guarding the country people or "ranging" the landscape, looking for traces of Indian parties, with all the free motion and sense of initiative it offered. But forts had a reputation as jailhouses— partly because they left men under such direct discipline, and more because they could make everyone in them feel not so much sheltered as surrounded, hemmed in by whatever might be massing around. People in refugee towns could feel uneasy; but those in forts were often terrified.[20]

Scouting parties sent out to clear the forts' perimeters found unnerving signs of having been watched from close at hand—spears stuck in trees, indentations in the grass, marks in riverside mud that showed someone had been "under t[he bank by] Night spying," sometimes even "Beds among the Leaves where small parties of indians have lain." But easily the worst traces were the scalped bodies of straggling soldiers, like James Pattin's in 1756 outside Fort Augusta, near the Indian town site of Shamokin at the forks of the Susquehanna. Pattin, having "happened, to go [to] a Spring about a Mile from the Fort without Arms, (contrary to the Orders given out)," Capt. Joseph Shippen recorded, was "shot by an Indian . . . thro' the Body & scalped & his Scull split open in several places."[21]

Finding these broken bodies could devastate morale. At Fort Hyndshaw in 1757, the frequency with which Capt. Johannes Vannetten and his men took "scouts" outside plummeted after they discovered one of their number "Scalpd. and interely Stript and Shmefully Cut that his Bowels was Spred on the Ground." According to Vannetten's diary, the average rate at which they ventured out fell from once every two days—once every day, most often—in December, even in deepening snows, to only one scout every four or five days in May. In time Vannetten's men were so spooked that in June "the Fort [was] Allarmd by hering many Guns fird. . . . and Some . . . Said they See the Indians and Several was Killd," he recorded. "I . . . found it to be men unwittingly Shooting at fowl in the River."[22]

At Fort Pitt in the frightened summer of 1763, no one was even allowed to pass outside the fortress walls—there being such "evident

Danger of being Scaulped"—without orders. Its nerves on edge, the garrison tried to observe an air-lock-like discipline against inrushing Indians. The gates were never unbarred without the colonel's command. Orders that Maj. William Trent copied down in his journal described how a sequence of sally ports and barriers were to be opened and quickly shut up again early each morning—though only "if the Weather is clear (if not after the Fogg is gon)"—with parties put out to cautiously "reconoiter the Banks all round" the fort before herding the cows outside to graze. Trent watched from the walls as fires flared up and columns of smoke rose over the landscape, with Indians, who seemed to him to be seething everywhere around, burning houses closer and closer to the fort. And he listened tensely when, every few days, Indian voices were heard giving "the Death Hollow which we know must be some of their People who have . . . murdered some of the Countrey People."[23]

The "Death Hollow," or halloo, suggests how unnerving the very sounds of a countryside at war could be. One resident of Carlisle, Pennsylvania, wrote at the height of Pontiac's War of how "you often hear the Indians howling, in their frightful way, between the mountains." The noises in the hills came from returning warriors who shrieked out a "scalp yell" for each one of their victims, making sounds one interested listener described as combining "*glory* and *fear*, so as to express at once the feelings of the shouting warriors, and those with which they have inspired their enemies." The elements of the cry were

> the sounds *aw* and *oh*, successively uttered, the last more accented, and sounded higher than the first . . . and drawn out . . . as long . . . as the breath will hold, and . . . raised about an octave higher . . . . These yells or whoops are dreadful indeed, and well calculated to strike with terror, those whom long habit has not accustomed to them. It is difficult to describe the impression which the *scalp-yell*, particularly, makes on a person who hears it for the first time.

It hardly came as a relief when there were sights to accompany such sounds. Sometimes the Fort Pitt garrison caught unnerving glimpses of its enemies, fleetingly "show[ing] themselves . . . at the upper end of the Garden," or closing in—visible from the fort walls as noiseless figures in the middle distance—toward unknowing work parties, until cannon were fired at them. The treeless spaces around forts could become stages for violence that drew the eyes of whole garrisons. "Yesterday morning," an officer in the Pennsylvania interior reported in 1778, "the barbarians scalped a man in sight of the garrison at Munsey"; a second would have fallen if the troops had not rushed out to interrupt the spectacle.[24]

Not all forts were stocked with soldiers. Ordinary country people often tried to boost their spirits by "forting up," or building and rebuilding strongpoints and stockades for themselves. They plainly preferred to flock to real forts, but in their absence they would try to make their own from mill buildings and modified taverns (like the ferryman John Harris's inn on the Susquehanna), cutting gun slits, heaping up munitions, blocking windows, and gathering in neighbors. They might use blockhouses built for the deerskin trade, or even churches, like Rev. John Steel's Presbyterian meetinghouse near Conococheague. But usually, like the Winter brothers, they used private houses. These may have been the most frightened forts of all.[25]

Explicit evidence for what it was like to be forted up in a house and dreading Indian attack comes from a journal kept by Benjamin Mortimer, a Moravian missionary on the Muskingum River during the War of 1812. Mortimer found that, far from calming the country people, "[m]oving thus together . . . has the distressing effect when conducted as it was here, of encreasing the fears of the people very much:"

> for no guards were appointed about these so called forts; therefore the inhabitants were not more secure . . . & could not think themselves so; and the opportunity was taken, especially on the part of the females, to tell each other the most frightful stories which they had ever heard, concerning the cruelties of the Indians in war, and thence to form strong representations of what great evils *might* befal themselves. The state of things about us was . . . truly awful to those who were under the complete influence of their fears.[26]

Being inside insecure homemade forts could genuinely be much worse than being outside them, since they worked like honeypots for attackers. The largest clumps of country people to be killed or captured simultaneously—as related in newspaper accounts, and reports about European captives—were generally people who forted up together. At a single house on the south branch of the Potomac in the spring of 1757, for instance, one Jacob Seiver "& his Wife & . . . Youngest Child were killed with 14 others at the same time, besides which 21 more were carried away Captives his house being a small fort to which the People had retired."[27]

But however bad it was, being inside a fort with many other people plainly felt better than being outside it and alone. Writing from near Fort Pitt in 1769, the trader John Campbell described the mood of the countryside in a war scare. After a party of (British-allied) Senecas traveling north from war against the Cherokees had killed some livestock and robbed a house to supplement what they saw as an inadequate supply of food from the fort's commander, "the Country People [were thrown] into such a Pannick that they moved off scarcly any Remain[ing]." And when the running people were "Asked the Reason" for their flight, Campbell reported, they "could give none only that all their Neighbours were going and they would not stay alone."

This formless dread of sudden violence was not felt only by Europeans. With the country people struck by fear of the neighboring Indians' intentions, Campbell thought that those Indians had started to panic, too. And though there had been no irreversible act of violence yet, he thought, "Such is the temper of both sides each being afraid of the other that it is too precarious to judge whether it may or maynot happen." In late 1755, after Ohio Valley Indians started attacking the mid-Atlantic provinces in earnest, most Delawares in eastern Pennsylvania and northern New Jersey were so reluctant to go to war that they hung back from fighting for more than two months. "[W]e don't know what to say or do," they wrote to Pennsylvania's governor, "but to be still, and now we hear the Hatchets are a flying about our Ears, which puts us in Fears."[28]

It was a month before they heard any reply from Philadelphia. And in that month, the eastern Delawares' knowledge gap about colonial intentions was filled in with frightening news and speculation—not only of war but of captivity, massacre, and decapitation. They heard persistently that the English "intended to Come to Wayoming & bind the Indians & Carry them to Philadelphia, & if any resisted they would cut his Head of." They heard from a Tuscarora man, with convincing specificity, that

"37 [Indians] were confined by the English & Carried as prisoners ... [to] hang them all." They heard falsely that the Moravian Indians at Bethlehem had been enslaved; and European runaways told them they thought "all those Indians Residing in the English Governmt had been killed by the White People." Unsurprisingly, many became afraid that they were disastrously hemmed in by "the white People who would kill any of thm without making a Difference between Indian & Indian—." And so, for the most part out of fear of what European colonists were about to do, in December 1755 the eastern Delawares did go to war, launching devastating attacks—which they imagined as preemptive—on neighboring settlements.

THE ESSENTIAL FACT about Indian-European warfare in the middle colonies was that the Europeans almost always did very badly. Though the American Revolution brought about a glorified, misleading view of frontier fighters and riflemen, during the eighteenth century country people practically never managed to mount even faintly convincing defenses against Indian attacks. Despite covering the countryside with scouting parties, they thwarted few raids and captured or killed fewer raiders. Over the long term, war-induced shortages of Indian goods and diplomatic efforts could bring some slackening of the attacks. But in the medium term, Indian assaults threw rural areas into irretrievable chaos. Interior communities could try petitioning for more and better soldiers, ammunition, and weapons, or plan pillaging expeditions against Indian towns. But for years at a time, in both the Seven Years' War and the Revolution, many found that none of these things could really slow the stream of deaths. The only thing that worked was leaving.[29]

Local men of note were desperate to puncture what they saw as the myth of Indian military superiority, and the psychological edge that went with it. This was difficult, though, since the Ohio Valley Indians' high military reputation was well deserved. European victories were meager. Late in Pontiac's War, when a regular-army force under Col. Henry Bouquet managed not to lose a bloody, large-scale engagement with Indians at Bushy Run, near Fort Pitt, a letter in one newspaper revealingly exclaimed, "Thank God! ... We hope the province of Pennsylvania will enjoy [the Bouquet expedition's] splendid results, and that the people will be convinced by it the Indians are just as far from being invulnerable as any other men, if they are attacked by an equal number, especially of British soldiers."[30]

But people were seldom convinced enough of this to feel safe, perhaps because most of the responses they saw to Indian attacks were so half-hearted and obviously ineffectual. To be sure, after an attack there were usually men willing to march out and look for the enemy in armed groups. But although such post-attack "pursuits" gave the frightened recipients of Indian news somewhere to go and something satisfyingly concrete to do, there was no discernible military reason to keep sending them off. As contemporaries often regretted, pursuits like the one orga-nized by Rev. John Steel and Sheriff John Potter of Cumberland County, Pennsylvania, in November 1755 that "went in Quest of the Indians, with all the Expedition Immaginable, but to no Success," practically never found anyone to fight. Often they did not much want to. The 100 to 160 men on Steel and Potter's march, for instance, came up and viewed two burning houses. Then, when they "pu[t] it to Votes" whether they should "pursue up the Valley all Night" to find the Indians responsible, they overwhelmingly declined. Only Sheriff Potter's disgust at the cowardice of the party, he claimed later, kept him from continuing on himself with a few sterner men. But as Potter put it, "I will not guard a man that will not fight when called in so eminent manner, for there was not six of these men that would consent to go in pursuit."[31]

Foot-dragging in pursuit was probably more common than such flat refusals. In 1778, a fifteen-man Northumberland County, Pennsylvania, ranging party under a Colonel Hosterman heard "firing and yells" under a mile away. From the sounds, they somehow felt able to guess that about the same number of Indians were attacking a farm there as they had men in their own party, which would make for a difficult fight when they got there. Then, farther off, they heard "a noise resembling a stroke on a Hol-low Tree several Times repeated." This, they decided improbably, was a secret Indian signal, reporting to the raiders how many of Hosterman's militiamen there were. Already unsettled, Hosterman and his band pressed on toward the sound; but they did not press quickly. It took them more than forty-five minutes to cover the three-quarters of a mile to the farm, in the course of which they heard "two death Hollos & one that they Took to be a prisoner Holloo." By the time they got to the farm, all they could find there was burning buildings and footprints, which they did not try to follow. At one mile per hour ("our People," Hosterman explained, "had a very ugly swamp [or thicket] to cross through which took them near a Quarter of an hour"), their rate of travel was not impressive—at least not for a unit of riflemen who found themselves within hailing distance of attacking Indians whom they were meant to engage wherever they could. Their march may have had some of the quality of a nightmare, in which one's feet will hardly lift and move. The same year another American colonel, who had ranged the west branch of the Susquehanna and seen "[t]he Barbarians . . . frequently appear[ing] in open ground," confessed that nevertheless he and his men "are not certain we killed a single Indian." In all honesty, he explained, the trouble was that when he had seen the Indians they "do fairly out run the most of white men."[32]

Even given what was probably the most powerful possible reason for fighting—the knowledge that members of their own families were being attacked and killed—many country people simply could not bring themselves to face an Indian. In his 1756 captivity narrative, William Fleming wrote of watching while a youth from the neighboring family was taken prisoner. The boy and a brother had just stepped out after dinner from his family's farmhouse—with its "numerous Family of able young Men" inside—when one of the Delawares simply jumped out and hauled him behind a tree. And despite his "scream[ing] in a most piteous Manner for help," his brother made no attempt to help, "fle[eing] back to the House with the utmost Precipitation," Fleming reported, "whence not one would venture out." Stories of this sort seldom made it into newspapers, where the actions of people being attacked more often took on an unreal quality of indignant heroism.[33]

Fear triumphed strikingly over family at Northampton County, Pennsylvania, in 1778, as four men, two of whom had with them their wives and eight young children, traveled with a wagon to Lycoming. Despite being warned that shots had been heard ahead, Peter Smith—the father of six of the children—"said that firing wou'd not stop them." As they proceeded, this little party's members heard two gunshots and suddenly saw three Indians rushing toward them. "[T]his occasion'd our men to flee as fast as they cou'd," the area's militia colonel evenly explained, "all but Campbell [one of the unmarried men], who was seen fighting at close Quarters with his Rifle . . . before they were out of sight of the wagon they saw the Indians attackting the women & Children with their Tomahawks . . . ." The next day, the three men came back to the scene of the fight for the corpses, which included the stabbed and scalped bodies of Smith's own wife; of Campbell, who had not fled; and of "a Little girl kill'd & scalped, [and] a boy the same" (two of their other six children had fled, while the remaining four were evidently made captive). They were perhaps surprised to find the wife of the other married man in the party, who—though scalped and brained—turned out not yet to be dead. "[S]he was sitting up . . . but Lean'd on her husband when he came to her, And Expir'd Immediately, she . . . cou'd not speak."34

The experience of finding family members who had been killed by Indians sometimes worked on rural Europeans' minds in durable ways. But for Peter Smith and his friends, at least, even seeing their wives and children cut down by attacking Indians was not enough to make them turn around or fight. They were simply too frightened.

PART OF WHAT so frightened rural Europeans about Indian war was how little its battles felt to them like proper violence. In two fascinating newspaper essays printed late in the Revolution, a New York grammarian named Lindley Murray tried—in his own characteristically systematic, bloodless fashion—to anatomize Indian war's outrageousness. "Every body must have observed," Murray felt sure,

> how frequently the newspapers have been filled with complaints of our enemies, as acting savagely and barbarously—as being guilty of unnatural cruelty—as carrying on a felonious and piratical war—as acting contrary to the rules of war. I have, however, taken notice, that among all these dissertations little or nothing has been said to shew why they have acted barbarously . . . .

Murray's answer was simple: *all acts of cruelty which have no tendency to weaken the resisting force, are contrary to reason and religion, and therefore to the law of nature and nations."* Murray could not see how Indian attacks were meant to make a military difference. (Indeed, almost no one in eighteenth-century America or England seems to have realized that Indian war was designed by its practitioners to be precisely as terrifying as they found it.) After all, the Indians were "neither formidable for their number nor their strength, but [only] for making inroads upon the dwellings of their enemies and putting to death women and children, with circumstances of horrid cruelty." And this, he thought with a fine lack of personal experience, must only make their victims burn to fight the harder. Hence the counterproductiveness of the Indians' terroristic wars, from which their illegitimacy followed.[35]

In many ways, this analysis was disengaged from how people were actually assembling their thoughts about Indian war. But Murray's ideas, not on the uselessness of Indian attacks, but on the laws of war, did get at part of the truth about why Indian warfare seemed so horrible. In account after account from the eighteenth-century mid-Atlantic, Indian attacks were called massacres and, above all, murders. "Murder," in fact, came close to being the stock term for any Indian raid. Hence an officer in New York's Mohawk Valley who wanted to sum up the fusillade of assaults there in the summer of 1782 could use forensic rather than military language, writing simply, "Murder is become so common that it is hardly taken account of." If one word came to mind when Europeans viewed the corpses of Indians' victims, "murder" was it.[36]

To understand why acts of war should have been discussed as crimes, it helps to turn to the most influential early modern writings on the laws of war. Some of the works of theorists like Francisco de Vitoria, Hugo Grotius, and especially the Swiss writer Emerich de Vattel were in every decent colonial library, and discourses on Grotius and Vattel could be found in the pages of American newspapers. In all but a few of their most scholastic provisions, the laws of war they laid out set limits to military conduct whose rightness was intuitively accepted among European peoples, as a kind of cultural background noise.[37]

The central idea conveyed by saying someone has been murdered, and also that people have been massacred, is—besides the act's wickedness—simply the helplessness of the people killed. An incapacity or unreadiness for resistance is what makes the scenes of their death seem, to amplify the etymological echoes of animal butchery underlying the old French word *macecre*, like an abattoir. This led straight to the most basic prohibition in the laws of war: it was forbidden to kill people who could not fight, which meant, above all, children and women. In *The Law of Nations*, probably the century's most consulted work on war, Vattel stressed that the point was not that women and children were somehow not at war. In fact, "being members of the nation, they are to be reckoned among enemies"— "but this does not import that it is lawful to use them as men who carry arms, or are able to carry them . . . [for] these are enemies who make no resistance, and consequently give us no right . . . to take away their lives."[38]

But all contemporary accounts of Indian attacks noted that they had fallen on exactly those people—children, women, farm folk obliviously going about their housework and harvesting, sleeping people "surprised and murdered in their Beds"—who could make no resistance. And this aspect of the attacks plainly had a special power to shock. Taken together, such accounts made a strong, simple pattern, whose outlines would remain clear and easy to recognize in later American culture, even when overlaid with endless local details: a vision of figures with their weapons raised, stooping over others who lay prone, or looked away unaware, or kneeled and pleaded.[39]

A great many things were not condemned by the laws of war. Unless actual torture was involved, the specific manner of taking an enemy's life, however cruel, was of little concern. Nor was the destruction of crops or property shocking. But what nearly every European observer did worry about was a choice of enemies that included dependent noncombatants and, with striking persistence, the treatment of enemies not before but after their deaths.[40]

Rather surprisingly, the right of at least eventual burial was a basic assumption of the laws of war. As the great Spanish theorist Vitoria had observed, it had been considered a clear right under natural law, even for the corpses of executed criminals, since at least the time of the Israelites: and since "piety is a natural thing, even for the dead . . . [i]t is unlawful to abuse their corpses." Unlike those people today who sign up happily for posthumous donations and dissections, early Americans were very far from indifferent about what happened to their bodies after death. When blended with Indians' supposed propensity for mutilating their dead or dying opponents, this dread of posthumous abuse (especially of decaying visibly, or becoming food for animals) accounted for an enormous part of the fear that provincial Americans felt when considering Indian attacks. Their evident fascination with the burning up after death of Indians' victims in flaming barns or houses probably sprang, too, from the idea of the dead's being disposed of in horribly unconventional ways.[41]

Body-burying expeditions had a central place in newspaper reporting—a place that makes sense when we understand the special power the damaged or unburied dead had to shock and depress colonists. The parties of men who trudged off to find victims and "Bur[y the]m in a Christian Manner" became vessels for terror. In late October 1755, after William Parsons heard reports of an attack near Easton and went out "to assist in burying the Dead," he wrote two letters unburdening himself of the horror of the trip. His little party, doubling in numbers as it went, heard of another attack nearer by and decided "to go . . . to these dead Bodies" first, which they soon found "lying dead just in the Road" with "all the Skin of their Heads . . . scalpt off." As darkness fell, the members of the party worried that "their Bodies might be torn to pieces" before morning. So they borrowed a grubbing hoe and shovel from the nearest farm and dug the deepest grave they could in the stony ground, putting them "both in one Grave . . . as we found them with all their Cloaths on."

More remarkable than the bare facts of what Parsons's party did, he said, was the way the scalped, unburied bodies made him feel.

> my dear Friend I have given you as clear an Account as I am able to do in the Confusion & Distress of Mind that I am under. But how shall I find Words to describe the Confusion & Distress of the poor unhappy Sufferers? And if I had words My Heart would burst at the Discription . . . . I have not lived long in the World and yet I have lived too long. . . . I have lived to see an Enimy . . . ravaging my Country and murdering it's Inhabitants Oh! that the Almighty would be pleased to soften the Hearts of the Legislators and incline them with Pity towards the distressed miserable People of this Province. But in writing thus and in unbosoming my self to you I am perhaps reviving in your Breast the aflicting Reflections which fill and overflow your own Heart.[42]

To a surprising degree, mid-Atlantic Europeans would experience Indian war as being about the communication of strong emotions—always starting with fear and ending for some, like Parsons, with a wish to be backed by the full power of the state. The shock they felt at Indian violence was so intense because of the ways it swerved away from what seemed normal to them, even for a world at war.

IN THE early fall of 1755, before Pennsylvania had been attacked, a pacifist printer in Germantown named Christoph Saur was already roundly condemning the tendency of "many of the common people [to be] indignant about the Indians," and their saying—in both the "Irish and German ways of speaking"—that "the dogs should all be shot, they are traitors and rogues." But Saur was writing before the "common people" could actually have had any direct experience of attack. When they saw for themselves what an Indian war was like, many country people's response would be not impatient anger but a terrified solicitude for the well-being of Indians who lived around them. For everyone soon came to believe that any attacks on well-disposed Indians who lived within striking distance of a settlement would inspire retaliatory attacks against the responsible neighborhood by revenge-seeking survivors, or by other Indians acting in solidarity.[43]

From his estate at Islip, Long Island, Lindley Murray, the revolutionary-era grammarian, had taken it on faith that Indian war must breed ferocity in Europeans—being "so far from weakening the force of the people against whom it is practised," as he mused, "that it tends to inspire them with a revenge and fury not to be resisted." But the fear of Indian attack often induced instead a cowed, nearly paralytic dread of doing anything that might antagonize watching, hostile Indians and so draw them closer. Many people in the countryside wanted, more than anything, to simply go unnoticed by their enemies. When a neighborhood felt this way, its strongest denunciations would be not of local Indians but of anyone who harassed or hurt them and so seemed to endanger the lives of their neighbors.[44]

Here is an example. In 1763, a Indian named Zacharias, his wife, Zipporah, their child, and another native woman were killed and robbed by militia volunteers in the countryside near Bethlehem—and near two Moravian mission towns where hundreds of Indians lived. Many rural residents directed their wrath straight at the soldiers responsible for the Indians' deaths. The people in surrounding towns were convinced that Zacharias's relatives would try to take revenge, or tell other Indians to do so. This conviction was the source not only of terror but of vast bitterness. "[T]he Neighbours been very Despleass upon This actions," the local justice of the peace, Henry Geiger, wrote indignantly to the justice in Bethlehem,

> for killing the Indian in their Neighbourhout . . . they Say the Capitain is not able to pay Their Damage What They muss Sofere and the peaple wuld make a Pedition To the Governour . . . The Neighbours Says That They believe the officer have killd the Indians for to have Their Goods and Not for To Destroy the Enemies . . . So They Do Ther Duety . . . the meschifs being Done When the afficer and Soldier being in Liqour Then They have Courage to Do meschife and killing the Indian Woman and boy for to hurt the Poor Abitans upon the frontiers Sir . . . .

To be sure, the worst part for sputtering neighbors like Geiger was probably not that Zacharias and his family had been killed, but that they had been killed "in their Neighbourhout." Still, since their response was to try to gather evidence against the killers, the functional difference between their attitude and one of real concern for the Indians' fate was slight.[45]

In 1766, Sir William Johnson, the British crown's superintendent of northern Indian affairs, received a letter from concerned residents of Ulster County, New York, written in the same vein as Geiger's. The country people wanted to inform him of the recent killing of an Indian "by a vile vagrant fellow" in their neighborhood (which, they said, was "[s]uppo[sed to be for] the sake of what the Indian had"): they implored him to see the wretch responsible "apprehended & punished" so as to avert the Indian retaliation that otherwise surely lay in store. The neighbors hoped that quick, unambiguous action could help to "Reconcile the Indians to us, and be as Brothers."[46]

Far across the Alleghenies the same year, in Cumberland County, Pennsylvania, neighbors of one Samuel Jacobs became convinced that he had killed a traveling Mohawk who was found dead in the neighborhood.

As these neighbors gathered to "view & Bury" the corpse, whose face had been blown off by a shot from behind, their response, instead of silent approval or a cover-up, was to subject Jacobs to the judicial ordeal of bier right—a ceremony, already archaic in the eighteenth century, in which suspected murderers were made to touch their supposed victims' bodies to see if the mysterious electricity of sin brought blood starting from the wounds. This spectacular ritual was thought to offer solid proof of guilt— the guilt, specifically, of murder, instead of any lesser crime. "[I]f a Murderer touched the dead Body," as one of Jacobs's neighbors pointedly noted while they stood there together, "the . . . Carcass tho' lifeless would Bleed." So everyone filed willingly past and "touched [it] alternately," but when Jacobs's turn came, he blanched and had to be forced to make the test. The body did not bleed. But when two of his neighbors, eager to find the evidence of his guilt, nonetheless went out sleuthing the next day and found the Indian's rifle—hidden under a log where Jacobs had been seen—they came running back to "apprehend & carry him before a Justice," only to find that he was already gone, never to be seen in his home again.[47]

Jacobs's neighbors felt a remarkable concern to ensure that the odium of Indian-killing—which they saw in this case, at least, as unpalliated murder—would under no circumstances fall on their shoulders. The power of the fear of attack was shown still more powerfully by what happened after Zacharias's death near Bethlehem in 1763. Residents of the neighborhood were certain they would have to pay a terrible price. When an Indian attack ripped apart nearby houses and a tavern the next month, they interpreted it as direct retribution. In a collective spasm of guilty fantasy, it was said that strange Indians had been seen arriving at the Moravian mission communities just before the attack; that people inside the tavern had heard their attackers outside screaming "you have killed my Brother Zacharias"; and that a militia man who died there had said on his deathbed that he recognized them as being from the Moravian missions, whose residents included some of Zacharias's relations, among them a brother named Renatus.

What the Indians outside had in fact been saying, according to an eyewitness, was "Come out you cowardly Dogs, come out you cowardly Sons of Bitches, what Way of fighting is this? come out & fight fair"; and in response even to leading questions about their identity the dying militia man had apparently said only, "Oh, God! No, I don't know." But the rumors were enough to lead county officials to imprison Renatus and try him for murder, although he proved to have a cast-iron alibi for the period of the attack, with corroboration by multiple German witnesses. The remarkable trial that followed was meant to be a clear statement of how Europeans saw Indian raids—not as acts of war but as acts of murder and revenge. Its course would be controlled by the dread of attack.[48]

It was hard to find jurors for Renatus's trial. In arguing unsuccessfully for a change of venue from Easton, at the forks of the Delaware, his counsel, a German attorney and activist named Lewis Weiss, asserted that Northampton County was a place some of whose residents,

being . . . most severely injured by an Indian Enemy are now full of Resentment against that Nation in general, and not having . . . met with any Enemy Object seem inclined to turn their Revenge upon any other Object whatsoever that hath a Drop of Indian Blood . . . .

And this, Weiss believed, would leave any jury in the county to face

this dreadfull Alternative *Either* to expose themselves to be Martyrs, have their Farms & Effects set afire &c for the Sake of an Indian that is withall of one common Root with the Murderers and Enemies of that Country, *Or* else to condemn an innocent Man.—

It is important to notice that Weiss was not saying any jurors would be so biased against Renatus, simply as an Indian, that they would try to see him hanged regardless of his innocence. He was saying that they might be too frightened of being attacked by any group of country people who disagreed with an acquittal of Renatus not to convict him. If one gives up the idea of a rural populace universally inflamed against all Indians—as to make sense of the evidence one must—Weiss's model makes perfect sense. In this barely controlled countryside, the threat of violence by even a small group could readily create conditions within which much larger populations had to operate, and it is easy to see how Renatus's potential jurors would have been affected at least as much by their fears as by any anti-Indian feelings. They faced two neatly opposed evils: an attack either by any Europeans who were angered by an acquittal, or by any Indians made angry by an unfair hanging.[49]

The result of this dilemma, as a newspaper account noted, was that when Renatus was "brought before the bench, and called to account for . . . murder," somehow "there were not enough jurymen there, so the trial was put off until the following day and the sheriff ordered to bring twenty more." An eleven-hour marathon of listening to evidence ensued once a jury had been settled, with subpoenaed testimony by a former Indian captive and minor celebrity, Sarah Wilkins (who said that she had never seen Renatus in the war parties where she was held). If the notes for his closing statement are any guide, Weiss spent much time telling "Stor[ies]" to the jury about soldiers' anti-Indian atrocities, and turned against Renatus's accusers their own observation of "the Impossibility to know an Indian when painted"—for if that were so, how could any of them testify with confidence that they had seen him?[50]

At nine o'clock at night, the twelve jurymen retired together, to start considering the evidence without break until nine o'clock the following morning. They must have tried to weigh in their debates not only the evidence, which was one-sidedly exculpatory, but the hazards to them and their community of a verdict on either side.

And in the end, despite living amid a countryside devastated by Indian attack and having the chance to punish an Indian for supposedly being one of their attackers, the jurors proved more afraid of Indian than of European retaliation for the wrong verdict. The country people acquitted Renatus, albeit not without thinking long and hard about it. His acquittal did not do him much personal good. Most of his family died while he was in jail, and he was detained long after the trial, supposedly to protect him and the country people from each other. But the acquittal illustrated that sometimes, at least, the fear of Indians was intense enough to drown out even antagonism toward them, which may be the best testimony to its power.[51]

THE RESPONSE of the countryside to Indian war, then, was controlled almost wholly by fear, a fear observers could literally see overrunning the landscape in the people it set in motion. Anticipatory fear could be so great, as Benjamin Mortimer, the Moravian missionary on the Muskingum, reported in August 1812, when rumors arrived of a disaster for the American army, that

> it could hardly have been greater with many, had the enemy actually been at their doors, and had they seen scalping knives in the hands of the Indian warriors. From mere anxiety and dread, all labor appeared to cease now throughout the country.[52]

And the *grande peur* Mortimer described was descending on a relatively flat part of the Ohio Valley, where one could have seen threats coming for miles in any direction. By contrast, the strange topography of the countryside farther east, where Ohio Valley Indians concentrated their attacks during the Seven Years' War and Revolution, was infinitely more conducive to panic. The approaches to nearly every important part of the border were dominated by mountain ridges. Modern contour maps of Pennsylvania look exactly as if someone has crumpled them up in the middle, making an improbable density of abrupt, parallel folds running diagonally from southwest to northeast. Settlement along the border was settlement in valleys, particularly those running between the long, sharp spines of the Blue Hills and the Tuscaroras.[53]

So backcountry people thought and talked about settlement in terms of specific, named valleys. Many of the first Indian attacks struck just such outlying hollows. The so-called Great Cove in western Pennsylvania, so recently settled by squatters, was a typical attack site early in the Seven Years' War. As the provincial secretary Richard Peters observed, it had its name "from its being enclosed in the Form of a Bason by the furthermost Range of the *Kittochtinny Hills* and the *Tuscoraro Hills*." These isolated bowls of settlement—or chutes, wherever a river valley transected the narrow rows of ridges (as was the case all up and down the Suquehanna)—must have made border inhabitants uneasily aware that they could not spy threats closing on them from any distance.[54]

Often—as at the township of Hanover, Pennsylvania, where some of the so-called Paxton rioters would be recruited in 1763—farms spread across the landscape until they ran directly into the sharply rising side of a ridge and could go no farther. The sides and tops of such partition walls, still too steep for cultivation, show bright green even now from an airplane. Here, pressed up against the shoulder of a mountain, a farm's residents must constantly have felt commanded by their landscape. Often farms so placed could not be seen from settlements in other valleys. When the residents of one neighborhood were lucky enough to see their attackers in advance, immediately before Delaware raiders struck farms on the western branch of Conococheague Creek, their settlement's semi-alpine situation against the Blue Hills meant that as they fled they gained an unusually clear and eerie vista on the devastation below. "[L]ooking back from an high Hill, they Beheld their Houses on Fire," as residents of Carlisle, Pennsylvania, heard the next day, and "heard several Guns fired, and the last Scrieks of their dying Neighbours."[55]

When raids caused the death or capture of everyone in a valley settlement, the discovery of its fate could easily be delayed for days. This could make the transmission of attack news—so important to the experience of Indian warfare—still more unsettling. The very first assault on Pennsylvania in the Seven Years' War, a raid at Penn's Creek on October 16, 1755, was not discovered until the evening of October 17, when the only resident who had been away happened to return and was greeted by two bodies. Widespread awareness of her news, and the arrival of burial parties, took several days more. The ghastly discoveries of the expeditions sent to probe such lost settlements' silent wreckage would always fascinate the press.[56]

But much of what made the wartime attacks so frightening was, of course, their total unpredictability, and sometimes Indian raiding parties seem to have played off the expectation that lonely mountain hamlets would be especially open to disaster by popping up, instead, in the centers of thickly settled plains. The payoff in terms of terror could be immense. One attack during Pontiac's War fell on a schoolhouse "right in the middle of the inhabited country." A man walking by the school could see no sign of anything wrong—except, he suddenly realized, that he heard no noises from inside it: no chanted lesson, no schoolmaster's drone. Opening the door, he came across a "blood-bath": "the schoolmaster scalped, with his Bible under his arm . . . [and] one of the scholars still living . . . who told him there had been four Indians there, whom no one had seen till they were inside the house." Eight more students lay dead around him. And "it is feared," the newspaper account of this attack concluded, "that the Indians' striking so far within the occupied part of the country will induce the inhabitants to move away from their places."[57]

SINCE MOVING away was the universal response to both attack and the fear of it, an extraordinary proportion of the letters or newspaper accounts written in wartime included their authors' impressions of the reverse migrations unfolding around them—of how many people were going, and how far. These descriptions were so incessant that it can be hard not to start skipping over them as one reads, but for contemporaries this was clearly the most noteworthy thing about an Indian attack: everybody left.

At its simplest the response was a two-part series of flights, first of men with letters, then of crowds with much of what they owned. Each time a new raid hit, reports of it ran down post roads and rivers from valley to valley. These inflated mixtures of fact and rumor—what the Quaker trader James Kenny called "Indian news"—were borne along to wash in unnerving installments on the residents of such rural entrepôts as Harris's Ferry, Carlisle, Lancaster, Reading, and Bethlehem, Pennsylvania, and Albany and Fishkill, New York. From Lancaster in 1755, Joseph Shippen Jr. described the typical response:

> Inclosed I send you a Copy of Letters which this minute came to Town by Express from Jno: Harris. The Acco:ts they contain have alarmed the People more, than any we have had heretofore. We have got a Man to go Express immediately with the Originals to the Governor.

On the arrival of frightening letters, local notables usually sent out alarm riders to rebroadcast the news to surrounding farm settlements ("the greatest part if not the whole," as John Harris, the ferryman and innkeeper, described one that he had pieced together, "certainly truth"), then had them recopied and carried on by express riders to other county towns and, nearly always within twenty-four hours, to Philadelphia.[58]

Because the network for sensing and reacting to Indian attacks relied so much on the writing of quick, accurate letters at these literary switching-stations, duplicating and retransmitting news for carriage from place to place, one of the most immediate needs in coordinating a military response was, rather surprisingly, clerks. Without enough copyists the Indian-news network started to break down, as a command post of J.P.'s at Reading in late fall 1755 made clear. "We have scarce any Strength left to write," they wrote the governor. With new letters surging in, "We are incessantly employed and without Clerks— . . . we cannot write our Selves any Thing of considerable Length, we must therefore depend upon it that we shall be credited without sending Copies." Express riders were also needed to gallop about, carrying these accounts, and their own vulnerability to attack added further uncertainty to the system. No news was not necessarily good news. With "Indians . . . frequently skulking about the Roads & watching to gain Intelligence," information could be commandeered by the enemy—as happened with one dispatch rider found lying in the highway in 1756, "shott & scalped his Scull split open & one of the Provincial Tomhawks sticking in his private parts."[59]

The hinterland stations where war letters were collected and transmitted were often the same places from which newspapers and the post had been distributed in peacetime. When Indian attacks started, the information flow through these conduits reversed, and those who had once read the news now started to write it. John Harris coordinated most newspaper subscriptions and deliveries for the countryside around Harris's Ferry. In wartime he, for one, proved entirely aware that any of the "More Particular Accot:[s] of the Transactions of the Savages" that he was able to collate and forward east would in many cases "I Expect . . . be Printed in the Next weeks Papers." The most impressive petitions about attacks— like an angry remonstrance passed on in 1756 (with "as many Names to it as he can get") from Rev. John Elder at Paxton, via Col. John Armstrong at Carlisle, then the Shippens at Lancaster, to the Pennsylvania assembly—were likewise the ones coordinated and assembled at these rural nodes. Being weirs for Indian-related letters and news gave frontier notables like Harris considerable power to affect the impressions that were formed by people farther east.[60]

Hearing and reading dispatches about attacks made the country people in wide areas move, adding word of mouth to the system, as the "poor distressed people, in their flight, . . . communicate[d] the pannick to others." But rural Europeans did not flee chaotically into the bush. Instead they rewound the skein of settlement, changing the roads that had been cut out toward them from county towns—and which in time of peace had carried them goods, travelers, and the post—into raceways to flood each larger settlement as they passed in panic to the east and south. "[T]hose who live on this side near the Mountain," as one J.P. at the Blue Hills summed up the trajectory of refugeeism, "are removing their Effects to Tulpehocken. Those at Tulpehocken are removing to Reading, and many at Reading are moving nigher to Philada., and some of them it is said quite to Philada."

What these people were doing amounted to the sudden unsettling of the countryside. Recurring over and over in reports of refugeeism was the shocked observation that some familiar place, improbably far to the east, had now become "the frontier." "I am this Moment arrived at Mr. Harrises Ferry," Matthew Smith wrote to the vice president of Pennsylvania's revolutionary Council of State in 1778, "& Just now Behold the Greatest Scenes of Distress I ever saw . . . the Blue Mountains is now the frontier, & I am afraid Lancaster county shortly will follow." As "[t]he Panic and Spirit of Flight" spread and one county after another "broke loose," putting the process of colonization into reverse, a province could visibly contract and, at some of its edges, start blinking out.[61]

The clouds of fearful refugeeism that encircled any Indian attacks were astoundingly extensive, both in time—usually most people were driven into hiding in the towns for at least six to eight weeks in their wake, with significant numbers staying three months or more—and in space. In midsummer 1755, with the stunning annihilation of Maj. Gen. Edward Braddock's expeditionary force to western Pennsylvania, the outer radius of flight had been a full 150 miles (with many settlers along the Susquehanna left in a "dreadfull way" by the news, believing an imaginary Indian armada would sweep downriver "in a great body to destroy all . . . , alarm'd at the sligh[t]est noise in the night expecting every hour to see the canoes coming down upon them"). After this the radius of fear seems never to have been less than 50 miles, and any attack within 25 or 30 miles reliably triggered an avalanche-like, all but universal movement away. Most rural people's experiences of Indian war were of talking and reading about it, fleeing it, and dreading it, rather than of coming under direct attack. But they were hardly less powerful for that.[62]

With the "Roads . . . continually full of Travellers" and people everywhere "Crowded together in . . . town[s]" (or "gathering into little Forts"), one's first impression at most points along the refugees' routes would have been of a strange abundance of people, almost as with some sort of market day. But these were uncoordinated crushes, with travelers, "most of them barefoot," who had heaped up and brought with them a huge variety of personal things, herding their livestock as they went. The first sight Benjamin Franklin saw on approaching Bethlehem in 1756 was the "Waggons . . . [of] many People moving off with their Effects" (such a column in 1755 included many "Women walking along with their young Children on their Backs"). In westernmost Pennsylvania at the outbreak of Dunmore's War in 1774, Arthur St. Clair—who thought "[n]othing c[a]n be more suprising than the dread the People are under . . . without even the appearance of an Enemy"—found as he traveled that he "did not meet less than a hundred Families, and I think two Thousand head of cattle in twenty miles riding."[63]

More people and animals were physically in motion during these runaways than at any time in the recent past, filling the streets of county towns and milling around "in Droves" to find shelter. "[T]he Neighbouring Inhabts are flocking into this Town," an observer wrote from York in the fall of 1755, "Defenceless as it is." In 1763, there were similar accounts from Carlisle of "Streets filled with People," and of rough refugee camps lining the nearby Susquehanna, with "the Woods . . . filled with poor Families, and their Cattle, who make Fires, and live like the Savages." In 1778, one could again see the strange sight of "the banks of the Susquehanna, from Middletown up to the blue Mountain, . . . intirely cled with the Inhabitants . . . as well as many in the River, in Boats, Canoes, & Rafts, &c." But many people could not get far enough out of the countryside and into the centers of towns, where they tried to burrow into a reassuring density of other people. (This impulse is familiar to animal behaviorists, who study it under the rubric of the selfish herd.) One refugee in Carlisle, saying he was "drove off by the Indians," walked all the way into the literal heart of the town, where he put up and started to live in "a small Hut on the Common."[64]

Though this was usually one of the emptiest landscapes anywhere in the European-populated world, things could seem oppressively crowded. People were rammed in wherever they could fit. Arriving at Bethlehem, Franklin found it "fill'd with Refugees, the Workmen's Shops, and even the Cellars being crouded with Women and Children." At Carlisle in 1763, it was said that "every Stable and Hovel" was "crowded with miserable Refugees . . . [in] Beggary and Despair"; in Bethlehem, the town's multistory Sun Tavern was "so crowded with poor People, who had fled thither from their Places . . . that [there was] scarce . . . a Corner to lodge in, & the Yard was full."

BUT THE MOST obvious way in which these were gatherings of a kind not usually seen was that almost everyone in them was frightened. The country people were nearly always unable to find or effectively fight their attackers, whether real or imagined, and the overpowering fear they felt in response left their houses empty, their crops rotting in the fields, and the roads crowded with animals and people, as nearly everyone in broad swathes of the countryside drove, ran, rafted, or paddled toward safety and away from their unseen enemies.

If most of the country people did not literally move into forts, their presence turned even the county towns—both physically and psychologically—into armed camps with terrified, bristling perimeters, along which, it was understood, "Our Savage Neighbours continue[d] to lurk . . . every now & then Murdering & Carying off" a few unwary people. Even in flight, a feeling of safety would be hard to find.[65]

Chapter 3

WOUNDS CRYING FOR VENGEANCE

IN ALBANY COUNTY, NEW YORK, ONE MORNING IN 1781, A MAN named James Yates came running across the fields to the farmhouse of his mother and father. When they greeted him, Yates's parents saw that he was completely naked and—almost certainly—covered in blood. Yates, who neighbors would later say "had nothing remarkable in his character," told them he had just killed everyone at his house. When his parents walked with Yates the half mile back to his house, they saw "[h]is wife, and infant across her breast, . . . lying dead on the road." Their other three grandchildren were inside, and they were dead as well, "their heads . . . all bruised and battered to pieces" by blows with an ax or club. And as they walked into the farmyard they saw still more signs of the terrible surprise attack Yates had mounted against his own household. The dog, two horses, and a cow were also dead; "in the body of [another] of the cows, which was not quite dead, an axe was found sticking." Looking now at the smashed heads and hacked-up corpses of his children and his wife, whom he must have started to kill while they were all still asleep, Yates had one thing to communicate. "[H]e said they were not his wife and children," observers reported, "but that the woman was an Indian squaw."

Yates may have shown no signs of illness before, but he was clearly crazy now. Little can be said with safety about the mental world of a killer who is likely to have been urged on by schizophrenia. Still, though Yates said his wife was an Indian, and probably believed she was one while he killed her, most things about his rampage—the placement of the bodies, the slaughter of domestic animals, the smashed-in heads, his naked-ness—suggest that he surrendered to an impulse to act out what it would be like to be an attacking Indian himself. Living in the Hudson Valley countryside during one of the worst seasons of Indian attacks in a gener-ation, Yates ran naked and bloodied from room to room to re-create, in his own household, a tableau it would have been hard to tell from those at any of the farms around him where British-allied Indians had struck. Whether by seeing his wife and family as Indians whom he had to kill, or by seeing himself as an Indian who had to kill them, Yates had acted out and made real the one thing he must have dreaded most in that frightened autumn of the Revolution: a sudden assault on his family.[1]

After the 1750s, many people besides Yates learned under the stress of war to associate with Indian attack a surprisingly narrow set of violent images. Preoccupied for long stretches by Indian war, mid-Atlantic colonists often felt compelled to reproduce, or even re-create, its scenes in many mediums. Because some country people thought that to see Indian attacks would be to understand their terror, they tried hard to spread the images of war to people in the towns toward which they fled during crises—among them the provinces' printers and most powerful men. Their ways of doing this showed what they most feared about Indian assaults, and the simple, insistent lessons they thought they should hold for people who heard about them. In time, the images of Indian attack helped Europeans in the middle Atlantic to draw their first lasting pictures of themselves. The rhetoric that spread from printed accounts of Indian war to envelop so much other discourse seldom worked straightforwardly as anti-Indian incitement. Nor did it provide an intel-ligible account of what happened militarily in the countryside. It usually had different purposes: to vilify other Europeans—the French at first, and the Quakers—and to assert the existence of a suffering, victimized community.

This style of war made possible a magnetic rhetoric of suffering, one fixed on the sight of attacks and not their causes. It was a good rhetoric to argue with. Anyone who tried to deny its force could be charged with indifference to the pain of the people. And the voices who cared most loudly about warding off Indian attack gained authority from their protectiveness of the people—whose needs, and even feelings, publicists and politicians started to voice for them. Once public debates centered on their sufferings, ordinary country people who had been dismissed in the cities as worse than Indians were reshaped into grander figures, defined by their hardships more than their religion, their nationality, or any of their own troublesome actions. And, increasingly, they made useful symbols for the "country" as a whole.[2]

As THEY TRIED to bring the Seven Years' War to a definite end in the middle colonies, representatives of the Iroquois, the Delawares, and other mid-Atlantic and Ohio Valley Indians met with provincial officials at large diplomatic conferences every few years—sometimes every few months. These "treaties" could be chaotic occasions, where feasting and drinking led, as a Quaker boy wrote disappointedly of the Indians at Lancaster in 1762, to participants' being "abundance Drunk." Loosely controlled crowds of Europeans from the countryside often turned out at treaties, which could open with "multitude[s] . . . crowded so close upon the Indians that they could hardly get air." Some called out insults at the Indians and railed against anyone willing to treat them as negotiating partners. At its worst, moving through an excited treaty-town crowd might have felt for native delegations something like the way it felt for European captives to run the gantlet on arriving in Indian towns.[3]

Listening to such country people's shouts and looking at the sights they wanted officials to see offers the keys to a mental world filled with vivid anti-Indian imagery, much of which had political (and even artistic) uses far beyond the crises that produced it. Whenever they talked about Indian warfare in terms more detailed than murder, provincial observers understood it as a novel species of attack on bodies and families.

Just before a treaty in 1757, an Indian attack hit Swatara township, in northeastern Lancaster County. Its residents, with "distracted Minds," resolved to appear "in a Body Arm'd" at Lancaster, where the treaty was under way. They were persuaded instead to stay at home, though,

and send four of the Dead Bodies to plead their Cause. These being brought in the morning the Indians were to answer the Governors

Speech and the people Passions thereby exceedingly raised occasioned a Commotion which had a dangerous Aspect many of the people Complaining . . . . [T]heir Clamours . . . were very loud . . . against all that were for making Peace with the Indians were very Insolent and extravagant in their Expressions and conduct and scarcely refrain'd from open Violence—. . . .

These four corpses being carted around on a field were not simply incitements but emblems of what the Indians had done. They were, in fact, the crudest possible statements of the experience of Indian warfare, and as such also arguments of a kind. The corpses were sent—after the country people had finished sending "one Messenger after another [who] came down to Lancaster and gave dismal Accots. of their Situation &c Magnifying the Danger, and calling loudly for Assistance"—to force officials to see just how the people were suffering, and to plead for a detachment of soldiers. The physical rhetoric of this body display succeeded sensationally at provoking a response, where those spoken words and sentences had not.[4]

There were many ways of startling people outside the countryside into sympathetic understanding. One letter to Pennsylvania's governor from the interior tried to make the horrors there tangible simply by enclosing "a tameyhawk which was found Sticking in the brest of one Davd McClelan." More common were the panicked petitions that poured into the city from people like the thirty residents of Lower Smithfield, Pennsylvania, who reported in 1763 that, "from divers reports . . . that the savages Is commiting their cruel barbarities, we have the greatest Reason in life to expect [attacks here] . . . [from] Barbarous savage Indians who delights [in] the shedding of innocent blood." This genre—the anti-Indian petition, infused by a feeling of being cornered with no way to safety—was direct and effective, with officials continually citing its examples.[5]

The standard rhetoric of anti-Indianism also sprang from breathless letters written by the magistrates and notables of interior townships. These letters made the basis of brief reports in the colonies' newspapers, both in English and in German (translated, for the most part, from the English papers). As they moved past these on-the-scene accounts up a

ladder of incrementally increasing ambitiousness and art, provincial readers came across fuller newspaper narratives of Indian raids; polemical
ephemera, like the snowstorm of pamphlets let loose by Pennsylvania's
midcentury political crises; and the sermons of clergymen—like the great
George Whitefield, who often preached "extremely pathetick[ly] with
regard, to the Disturbances . . . on the Frontiers"; or Samuel Davies, a
revivalist and, briefly, president of Princeton; or William Smith, the
incendiary first provost of the College of Philadelphia. From there it was
a short step to the period's most self-conscious literary efforts, like the
fascinatingly overblown poetry of Davies, or of Smith's protégés Francis
Hopkinson and Thomas Godfrey Jr., and to the blood-soaked dramas of
one George Cockings.

All attempts at calling up the terrors of Indian war—whether belles
lettres or misspelled petitions—shared a great deal of self-conscious
straining after effect. Accounts of attack were also nearly always accusations of neglect or partial guilt against some other Europeans. And as it
became clear how extraordinarily hard such accusations were to answer,
they multiplied.[6]

But before each of these repackagings of war came, simply enough, the
bodies. All contemporaries found it remarkable and moving to see before
them the marks that Indian weapons had left on another person. And so
corpse displays, making an emotional point that at once became political,
popped up surprisingly often. Incredible as it seems, at the start of the
Seven Years' War there may even have been a minor vogue for the display
of scalped bodies. Some displays took place not in the far countryside—
though no doubt the bodies' slow, jolting cart rides east stirred excitement
in all the roadside towns they passed—but on the streets of Philadelphia.
Shortly before Christmas in 1755, for instance, the *Pennsylvania Journal*
reported, "two Men and a Boy, who had been killed and scalp'd by the
Indians, were brought to Town in a Waggon, to shew the Inhabitants the
Barbarities that are committed on our fellow Subjects." The next day,
John Reynell, the crusty Quaker merchant, confirmed that there was
great "Confusion" in the capital over the Indians' "destroying our Back
Inhabitants, three that were Murderd were brought to Town Yesterday."[7]

Probably the largest and most politically important body display,
barely three weeks before, actually came to a climax on the steps of

Philadelphia's State House. On November 25, four to seven hundred Berks County Germans marched into the capital to demand the passage of a militia law. Rolling up first to the governor's house and then to the assembly building, they too relied on the eloquence of their neighbors' corpses. As William Smith described the demonstration's second scene, in a very partisan account, "The SCALPING continues! Yesterday the *Dutch* brought down for upwards of 60 Miles, in a Waggon, the Bodies of some of their Countrymen who had been just scalped by the *Indians*, and threw them at the *Stadt-House* Door, cursing the *Quakers* Principles, and bidding the Committee of Assembly behold the Fruits of their Obstinacy."[8]

People hauled these victims around to direct attention to their cut-up limbs and, especially, their missing scalps. Every kind of writing placed immense weight on scalping, which, together with "murder," in fact became a metonym for Indian war. "Every hour," as a letter writer from Fort Pitt summed up his situation during the terrible summer of 1763, "we hear of scalping." Its importance was suggested by the account of a party in Frederick County, Maryland, who took comfort in having stopped a scalping during Pontiac's War: the man they "saved" was shot down and operated on elaborately by an Indian who "cut [him] . . . in the Back, and divided his Ribs from the Back Bone," a correspondent reported: "but we prevented his being scalped."[9]

Scalping was, in fact, such a powerful sign of the horrors of Indian war, and fights with Indians usually went so badly, that when it was inverted— by Europeans scalping Indians who came into their power—it could release an absolute exhilaration. At Reading, Pennsylvania, in 1756, a seventy-five-man expedition found itself face to face with a much smaller group of Indians. The Pennsylvanians "were so terrified" that, rather than attack, they ran headlong into a nearby house, which they then defended by shooting from its windows. When the firing died down, two young men ran outside to scalp two fallen Indians. Then everyone ran pell-mell out of the house and back to Reading, where this undignified encounter was turned into a triumph, a letter writer noted, by the party's having "brought us the two Scalps" to show off, with dramatic effects on morale. "They say the People are so elated with this Success that 150 Men . . . are gone over the Mountain to attack the Indians, and to scalp the others if not removed, tho' they are undoubtedly dead."[10]

It might have been better to show this spirit in the face of actual attacks, but that was rare. For some people, the release to be gained by carrying out on Indians' bodies all of the acts they feared that Indians would do to them was too intense to resist, even when it came too late for battle. The feeling that some Europeans who killed Indians had, while mirroring in their own acts the stripping, mutilation, burning, and especially the scalping they most associated with Indian attacks, was often straightforwardly described as satisfaction or happiness. In the first winter of the Revolution, one American soldier who had seen his dead comrades' bodies dug up by Indians and scalped and "mangled . . . in the most shocking manner" wrote home of being lucky enough to have what he called "the pleasure"—in another inversion like the one that so excited the people of Reading—"to see two of them scalped as a retaliation for their barbarity."[11]

Scalping, then, was the most important of several wounds that made up the standard set of injuries associated with Indian attack, all of which were so strongly patterned as to become compact declarations about the nature of Indian warfare, and—when presented to officials who were supposedly failing in their duties of protection—arguments as well.[12]

Corpses "just reeking after the hands of the[ir] savage slaughterers" were the power source for discussions of Indian war. But for the simple reason that there were not enough mutilated corpses in the middle colonies to go around, most people met them not in person but on the page. Physical rhetoric made way, necessarily, for less corporeal, but no less body-obsessed, ways of writing. Though it might seem to be something that lay outside eloquence, attempts were going to be made, over and over, to cram into words the experience of seeing someone who had been mutilated by Indians—most often by authors who had not themselves undergone it, but only wanted to imagine what it would be like.[13]

SIGHTS THAT had filled rural people with helpless fear could be discussed with confident outrage once they were reduced to newsprint. As much as anything, it was "frequent melancholy Accounts of the barbarous Murthers committed by the Indians" found in the newspapers, as one

Quaker assessment found, that "filled the minds of People in general with a Spirit of Indignation and Resentment against them."[14]

At first, Indian war's transition into print could be clunky. The drawing up in rural counties of "List[s] of all the People which was Killed Since the War begon," as Capt. Jacob Orndt headed one such effort in 1757, was a standard military activity, and the most rudimentary newspaper reports on Indian war simply reprinted these uninflected but strangely powerful lists. Collecting and converting so many discrete lives into a thin column of *"Persons killed the last Week, that are come to Hand,"* made them the most literal possible translation of the impulse behind the body displays. Since these were not obituaries but only processions of names—and sometimes nothing more than identifiers like "three little Boys"—what was twisting down the page was not so much a list of people as a list of bodies. Displaying victims in this way made them not individual stories but exhibits in a grim parade, whose point was simply to bring the dead before the public.[15]

The fuller newspaper reports of body-burying expeditions carried readers' imaginations closer in, inviting them to recapture the shock that country people had felt when discovering the dead. A few quick details would be supplied on how a party had approached a massacre site before the narrative pace dropped to a crawl for a riveting slow pan across a landscape scattered with corpses, usually "scalp'd, all stript naked and laid a-cross the Road."[16]

The body-burying parties' gory reports traced what Europeans feared most about the idea of being in an Indian's power. Besides scalping, there were careful descriptions of bashed-in skulls and cut-out tongues, of sharp objects stuck into eyes and genitals, and of long, deep spinal wounds, as if from chining livestock. The continual requoting of such passages cemented an idea of Indian violence as peculiarly vicious, able to be told at a glance by its injuries. As Charles Read, the chief justice of New Jersey, observed,

Weak Minds are apt to be in an extraordinary Manner inflamed, and get into violent Ferments, on reading an Article in the Gazette of a few Persons being destroyed by *Indians*; and yet these very Persons will with little or no Emotion, run over an Article of a Battle between two Armies, where Thousands fell on a Side. They get heated by the Mode of War, though it is of little Consequence whether the Scalp or Finger of a dead Corpse is taken off as a Token of Victory, or how many Wounds it has.

When the body of a Delaware man turned up near Easton in 1757 with "several Great Wounds . . . on the Side of his Head, one in his Throat, and another on each of his Hands," his inquest's members were able to announce with confidence that "they believed no white Man had killed him."[17]

The newspapers also held dispatches in a strain less devoted to showing damaged bodies: this was the rhetoric of family violation. Starting with the assumption that enemy Indians were especially drawn to kill "helpless Wives, and poor defenceless Babes," this strand guaranteed that countless newspaper stories would zoom in on the sight of women, like "Jacob Allmong's Wife" at Bethlehem in 1763, "with a Child, lying dead in the Road, and scalped." Because of this special interest in domestic death—in the killing of women and children within families—one report actually scattered the contents of a bedchamber across readers' field of vision, just as they had lain strewn across a clearing: "a Bed Tick" at the door foretold "a Child lying dead and scalped" within. Another report edged away from straight narration onto the terrain of the novel, with heartrending dialogue between a husband and wife. Georg Caspar Heiss was in a neighbor's house, when he "heard his Wife cry out in the Garden, *Casper, Casper, come and help me, the Indians are here and will kill me and the Children.*" He rushed to the rescue, but managed only to be made frantic by "hearing his Wife cry out mournfully, *Casper, Casper, farewell I shall never see you more!*"[18]

The newspaper press had frozen in place the basic images of a rhetoric that was tightly trained on the cruelties likeliest to hold European readers rapt with horror. One strain of the rhetoric simply displayed abuses to the human body before and after death, especially scalping, as well as incineration, nonburial, and dismemberment. Facing readers again and again with bodies, "cruelly mangled and massacred, . . . [and] very nautious for want of interment," this mutilatory rhetoric worked to teach them how such corpses should be interpreted: usually as demands for protection and revenge, or accusations of the people's neglect by the powerful. For they were "haggled . . . all over with wounds, which look," as one writer asserted, "like so many wounds, crying for vengeance against their murderers, and yelling at the negligence and insensibility of the administration." The other main strand of writing worked to stir a sense of the piteousness of violated families, with its catalog of "mourning Widows, bewailing their Husbands . . . tender Parents, lamenting the Fruit of their own Bodies . . . [and] Relations and Acquaintances, pouring out Sorrow."[19]

All these descriptions were meant as visual prods to strong feeling— providing "some fresh Object," as a 1763 dispatch put it, "to awaken the Compassion, alarm the Fears, or kindle . . . Resentment and Vengeance." Coming across the press's weeping parents and cut-up bodies—"the very Thoughts of which," as the ferryman John Harris wrote encouragingly from the countryside, "ought to excite Us for Satisfaction"—readers were meant to take away a set of feelings now tied to them. Feelings, as the newspapers taught, that would naturally take the shape of reckless grief and "vengeance" (in the sense not only of retribution but of its associated anger). The panic such sights aroused in life was missing in these reports. "To-day a British Vengeance begins to rise in the Breasts of our Men," as one account ran in 1763. "One of them that fell . . . as he was just expiring, said . . . Here, take my Gun, and kill the first Indian you see, and all shall be well.———"[20]

To accuse other people of not having sufficiently "soften[ed] . . . Hearts" (as one body burier put it) for the sufferings of rural families was to question their fitness to take part in the mid-Atlantic provinces' emotional communities, and soon in their political ones, too. The shrill tone of triumph with which party pamphleteers would soon accuse one another of wanting feelings suggests how much authority the right mix of sorrow and anger, and its anchors in Indian-injured bodies and families, had taken on. "For Heavens sake, let not the Blood of our Brethren, any longer Cry for Vengeance," as one effort at anti-Indian—and anti-Quaker—incitement exclaimed. "Let us rise and prove, we feel."[21]

In 1755, Capt. Joseph Shippen of the Pennsylvania regiment—a young man who would grow up over the next few years of Indian warfare, and the son, nephew, brother-in-law, or cousin of the province's most power-ful men—sat down to trace the precise impressions that he felt stirred in his own mind and heart by hearing about frontier calamities. (Until the pace of Shippen's military career quickened, hostile Indians remained as imaginary for him as for any newspaper-reading Philadelphian.) "To me," Shippen wrote his old schoolmaster,

> such tragical Scenes are sometimes truly pleasing. Not That I can rejoice in other's Afflictions, far be from me so cursed a Disposition.—But when I view either really or imaginarily any of the human Race on the Precipice of imminent Danger, or actually suffering the keenest Strokes of Cruelty, my Heart melts within me with Pity & Compassion for the unhappy Object, whom I have no Power to relieve. Yet as the softer pas-sions of the Breast inflame the Soul with a Disposition, to do its utmost Efforts for its Relief, I enjoy in that Respect a secret pleasure . . . .[22]

To make sense of this response to Indian war, we have to venture a lit-tle way into aesthetics—in particular, the aesthetics of the sublime. The pre-Romantic literature of sensibility, which rose during the eighteenth century to dominate poetry, drama, and especially the new genre of the novel, was the first body of writing in English to systematically exploit the aesthetic value of emotions. At the heart of this shift was a fascina-tion with the very experience of having intense feelings, and above all with sublime sensation: the feeling of being awed, struck with wonder—or horror—at something outside oneself.[23]

Huge amounts of writing and thinking about Indians after midcentury were shaped by the pathetic sublime, a mode of writing engineered to overwhelm the reader with emotion at the sight of suffering. The strain of rhetoric that provincial writers slowly perfected to describe Indian affairs—by percolation from sources as diverse as the urgent letters in newspapers, nights at the theater to see new plays, and expeditions to relieve besieged forts—was consistent enough, taken in bulk, to warrant its own subspecies name: the anti-Indian sublime.[24]

The anti-Indian sublime's thematic hallmarks were its habit of always describing society, so far as it was the setting for the "melancholly Scene[s] . . . acted" in Indian warfare, as a set of little families; an emphasis on the ripping apart of these families, as husbands, wives, fathers, mothers, sons, and daughters were made spouseless, parentless, and childless; and an obsession with the helplessness before attack of mothers and infants, especially when twinned in pregnant women. There was, too, what would in religious poetry be called a "composition of place" of incredible, gory vividness, with authors thrusting wounds and blood before readers' eyes; a close focus on unburied bodies, left sprawled at random for decay and wild animals to work on; and an insistence about making the audience look at such distinctively "Indian" injuries as scalpings and knocked-in heads, often using direct commands ("See!").[25] The stylistic tics of the anti-Indian sublime were its direct or apostrophic requests for readers' sympathetic sorrow and anger, with writers taking frequent narrative time-outs for expostulation and venting; and its grammar of brokenness and interjection, as words, shot through with exclamations (especially "O!"s) and long dashes like ripples over water, were made to visibly reflect their writers' agitation at the things they described.[26]

Joseph Shippen's "secret pleasure" in picturing frontier attacks was conventional, since both main strains of anti-Indian writing—the physical and familial—exactly fitted current theories of the pathetic sublime. Edmund Burke, in his widely admired *Philosophical Enquiry into the Origin of Our Ideas of the Sublime and Beautiful* (1757), was the first critic to put the observation that terror and horror were, in most ways, the sublime emotions par excellence—if sublime sensation was what dilated the soul, roused the senses, and worked on the emotions, inducing a rapt, stunned unself-consciousness—at the heart of a fully worked-out system of aesthetics. "Whatever . . . operates in a manner analogous to terror, is a source of the *sublime*," Burke suggested. Since "terror is a passion which always produces delight when it does not press too close," the sight of physical pain and suffering was the wellspring of the strongest emotions we could possibly feel: and accordingly, he concluded, "there is no spectacle we so eagerly pursue as that of some uncommon and grievous calamity."[27]

The familial strain of anti-Indian writing played more on pathos, turning farmhouses into little theaters of love and pain. A stress on women and children was doubly determined: the laws of feeling within the pathetic sublime and the European laws of war both guaranteed it.

"Now we are shocked," as a front-page piece in the *Pennsylvania Journal* rather enthusiastically observed, "with the frightful images . . . of Infants slain at the Mother's Breast . . . [and] Families butchered in their Beds." Though many Indian strikes were genuinely directed at individual households and the families within them, they were so often described in part because of colonists' compulsion to understand events using the pathetic sublime. Over and over, children and parents died within inches of each other. In the postscript to a 1755 letter, for instance, Conrad Weiser simply "c[ould] not forbear to acquaint" Pennsylvania's governor with a vignette being talked of near Tulpehocken: a woman "with her Babe in her Arms," he reported, had been poleaxed while she "gave it Suck," on which "she fell upon her Face with her Babe under her, and the Indian trod on her Neck and tore off the Scalp."[28]

Unborn children being cut from wombs were almost as common—as with the story of the hidden frontier husband who Col. John Reid reported had watched Indian raiders "rip up his Wife, who was with Child . . . . Barbarous, Inhuman Monsters." Writers were drawn to this motif of "mothers ripp'd," which made an unmatchably tight cluster of associations with vulnerability, pain—not least the pain of birth—and especially the family. The mother-to-be, neatly tying off parenthood's loop of dependence and love, was the pathetic sublime's logical endpoint. For nine months, a single body could contain a whole family, so one atrocity could show bodies and families torn apart at a stroke.[29]

As a way of talking about war, the anti-Indian sublime excelled at sweeping away contexts. Long chains of cause and effect had led to the scenes that provincial writers kept describing. But with one sight—a mutilated corpse—forever swimming into view, the back stories faded. The high emotion of this kind of writing was, on its own terms, unanswerable: it could not only convince readers but do so in a way that made argument seem tasteless. William Smith, the college provost and an eager political writer, could paint the Friendly Association's efforts to learn the causes of Delaware belligerence as simply ridiculous, like quizzing a man who has just rushed over for buckets to douse his burning house ("Was [the fire] by Design of any malicious Person? . . . Did he receive any Affront?").30

Once it was understood and unbottled, the anti-Indian sublime proved a volatile essence. Since it was little more than a set of verbal strategies and ready-made images—working at one full remove from the wordless rhetoric of the body displays, and worlds away from the roiling fear with which real victims were discovered—it could be used to argue almost anything. The rhetoric was a toolkit, first assembled to unleash overpowering sympathy, that many writers could not resist turning to the triggering of their readers' political reflexes.

Since the anti-Indian sublime was at bottom only a grammar—not a logic, with necessary conclusions—it would have been easy to uncouple from its standard targets, which were Indians and, at midcentury, Quaker politicians and the French. Benjamin Franklin proved this in one of his best efforts at propaganda, *A Narrative of the Late Massacres . . . of a Number of Indians* (1764), written after the anti-Indian Paxton riots of winter 1763. Franklin's pamphlet was an expert, strictly conventional specimen of the anti-Indian sublime—so full of incoherent sorrow at seeing the scalped and "butchered half-burnt Bodies of . . . murdered Parents, and other Relations," that it might have served as a textbook. The one difference was that Franklin was describing Conestoga families, not European ones, who had been ambushed by "CHRISTIAN WHITE SAVAGES." Franklin's pamphlet made something of a sensation, but this was only a shock of reversal: it depended on the existence of a well-established formula to upend.31

During certain spells, the anti-Indian school of writing soaked through all mid-Atlantic writing, coloring the thoughts—sometimes, indeed, supplying them—of anyone who could read or listen to others do so. In the 1750s, even the famously peaceful naturalist John Bartram was to be found lapsing in a few letters into the unmistakable phrases of the anti-Indian sublime, echoing its every convention with a fidelity so naïve it was eerie. His own father was probably killed by Tuscaroras during Bartram's early childhood in Carolina, but as an adult plant fancier he usually worked with Indians closely. His limpid reproduction of the anti-Indian sublime suggested how standardized, and unreal, Indian war's image set had become.

In one paragraph of a 1756 letter to England, Bartram described the winter weather with a spare, scientific tone. In another, he described Indian warfare in a vomit of prefabricated phrases, drawn from the letters published in the provincial press—which had, as he wrote a friend the summer before, "astonis[hed] & moved" "both town & countrey . . . as the leaves on the trees with A wind & the sea with A storm at the relation of such . . . tragical sceen[s]." As Bartram moved into an area that he himself had experienced only through anti-Indian reporting and literature, his tone at once became desperately agitated, just as if a switch had been thrown:

> by what we can understand by the reports of our back inhabitants . . . if th[e Indians] come to A house where the most of the family is women & children thay break into it kills them all plunders the house & burns it with the dead in it . . . O Pensilvania . . . —all ages sex & stations hath no mercy extended to them the young man . . . perhaps with hasty steps & heart filled with raptures of love is going to visit his intended spouse is unexpectedly pierced by A silent ball shot by distant secreted enemy . . . his vigorous sinews is relaxed his body rouled in blood & exposed to the fouls of the air: our tender Infants hath thair brains dashed out our wives big with child hath thair bellies ript open those killed within thair houses is mostly burnt with them . . . if thay flie into the woods or hideth in the hedges the murderers soon finds them & plunges their hatchets either into thair brest or skull where thay are exposed to the enclemency of the weather day & night their once sweet cheeks & lips now stained with dust & blood & thair bosom filled with clotted gore— until by chance they are found by our Companyes who comitts them to a private grave without winding sheet or Coffin or surrounding weeping relations.

A corner of Bartram's mind had been very strongly impressed by every major anti-Indian formula, as the choice of topics and high-flown words (complete with "O"s and "clotted gore") suggest. The holographic ease with which many early Americans could now imagine the sufferings of what Bartram called not only "our wives" and "our . . . Infants" but "our back inhabitants"—often in more or less the same words, and the same order—came from their being constantly inundated with anti-Indian rhetoric, in high culture as well as low.³²

MANY AUTHORS with artistic leanings found the anti-Indian sublime too seductive to even try to resist. The most ambitious written productions circulating in the middle colonies soon teemed with its themes and tactics. Even looking only at verse and drama, it is easy to uncover a rapturous vein of literary Indian hating. In 1761, Francis Hopkinson, a young gentleman-composer—and recent graduate of the College of Philadelphia—traveled to Easton to take minutes at an Indian treaty. This inspired him to write "The Treaty," a remarkable rural ode that turned, partway, into an evocation of an Indian raid. It had all the ingredients of the natural sublime, from lonely moons to glittering rivers; but Hopkinson quickly dressed them in a more striking sublimity of pathos and horror, built up from descriptions of the Delawares' warfare.

Because Hopkinson was fascinated as much by the intimacy and vulnerability of family ties as by gory word pictures, his reverie opened with a forest cottage, its inhabitants soundly sleeping. Then, suddenly, "At dead of night a savage yell was heard; / . . . And death in horror's darkest robe appear'd." For Hopkinson's strongest fascination was with family ties that Indians rent apart. This was a sight that the energy of his verse suggested he found thrillingly awful, as Hopkinson's tone swung from rapture over the lovely Lehigh River to transporting horror—"My swelling heart," as he interjected, "beats quick within my breast"—at the specter of a couple cut down, children beaten into captivity, the torture of prisoners, and an orphaned farm daughter who had to watch her lover's "life bubbling from [a] recent wound!"³³

Another poet whose main interest undeniably was in gory word pictures was Rev. Samuel Davies. Around the time that he became president of Princeton, Davies wrote some breathtaking meditations on rural atrocities. He launched one effort by ushering readers to the frontiers at the outbreak of war, where

> . . . Horror rang'd, and her dire ensigns bore,
> Raw scalps her trophies, stiff with clotted gore;

The heart and bowels smoaking on the ground,
Still warm with life, and mangled corpses round.

He then picked up momentum through a long, hit-parade compilation of all the most mutilatory anti-Indian images. Families, asleep in their innocence, were cut to ribbons by Indians who would slurp blood out of "fresh wound[s]" after "tar[ing]" "[f]rom the raw skull the hairy scalp." The victims

. . . start, and struggle, but in vain the strife,
To save their own, a child's, or parent's life,
Or dearer, still, a tender bleeding wife.
Now mingling blood with blood, confus'd they die,
And blended in promiscuous carnage lie.
Brains, hearts and bowels, swim in streams of gore,
Besmear the walls, and mingle on the floor.

The jet of blood-soaked images continued through discussions of battle-field butchering and scalping of the wounded; the infliction of post-mortem mutilations; and the sight of bodies lying "toss'd in heaps . . . naked, unburied" till their bones were bleached by the sun. The moral that Davies found amid all these "mangled limbs" was grimly program-matic. For the bodies could speak: "Behold them with their latest gasp of breath," he instructed readers, "Implore their country to revenge their death."[34]

A five-act tragedy by George Cockings called *The Conquest of Canada* was put on in Philadelphia by the American Company of Comedians over three nights in February 1773, in an "unusually rich" production that featured actual artillery, soldiers, and jolly boats. Enthusiastically rehash-ing Britain's conquests by land and sea in the Seven Years' War, much of Cockings's writing made up a loving catalog of the military sublime, with thundering guns and blood-drenched battlefields (a favorite rhyme was "roar" with "gore"). He wrote closely related central scenes into both the *Conquest* and its prequel, *War*, that tried to show how inspiring scalping was, and what an electrifying sense of purpose it should give to all Britons.[35]

Landing at Quebec in *War*, General Wolfe was already exasperatedly

> Conscious of British blood, by murder spilt!
> Of treaties broke! and sportive scalping guilt!
> Of mothers ripp'd, and helpless infants cries![36]

The British campaign against French Canada went on in triumph, to end in a picture of wounded, fallen soldiers on the field of battle, still hacking away resolutely to keep Indians from "mangling, and scalping" their helpless comrades. ("O can! can I bear the cruciating thought!" one cried in a splendid transport, "And in idea see my gallant friend . . . / [with the] tomax sink[ing] into his head; / His body mangled; and his scalp torn off'"?)

Cockings's source for the image of mutilation-maddened soldiers showed how the body-centered conventions of anti-Indian writing had unfolded and spread from local zones of conflict to English-speaking culture as a whole, taking on new applications and growing steadily more unreal as they served in succession to plead, to argue, to denounce, to inspire, and at length simply to excite. His source, Cockings explained, was the "letters from America in the news."[37]

Then there was Capt. Paul Jackson of the Pennsylvania regiment, an ex–classics tutor at the College of Philadelphia, whose verses surveyed pastures where "the grim savage devastation spread, / And drench'd in gore his execrable hand"; and his pupil Lieut. Thomas Godfrey Jr., who wrote an archetypal poem on the "deep distress that overwhelmed our Frontier Settlements, when every field was stained with . . . blood . . . by the merciless hands of unfeeling Savages." Godfrey drew his readers with him on patrol to "shew [them] fatal field[s], all drench'd in gore," and urge them to "let . . . the briny torrents flow" before farmhouses whose inhabitants had all been killed:

> The lonely prospect strikes a secret dread,
> While round the ravag'd Cott we silent tread,
> Whose Owner fell beneath the savage hand . . . .

But the outlines of the anti-Indian sublime's uses in high culture should be clear.[38]

* * *

WHAT DIFFERENCE did it make that mid-Atlantic colonists spent so much time using dead bodies, both paper and real, to show one another the effects of Indian war? Part of the answer can best be grasped by making a detour across the sea, and backward in time—to Paris, to consider the funeral customs of the French monarchy in the age of religious wars. The French kings (like English ones) were thought of as having two bodies. One was personal and mortal, like our own, but the other was political, impersonal, and deathless, with a continuous existence apart from the life of any one king. And in accord with this idea, the sixteenth-century French set about hammering together ever more detailed effigies of their dead kings to represent the second body—the constitutional body, to which, in a sense, they all belonged, and which would flourish even after a king's death. Sometimes they did extraordinary things with these funeral images, which "w[ere] treated as the live king in his Dignity": dressed them up sumptuously; had them sit in state; gave them public, multiple-course meals with finger bowls; carried them about in processions from place to place. The impulse behind this form of display, however entertainingly bizarre, was straightforward: the figure on display was needed as a visible embodiment of the body politic.39

The corpses that were carted through the streets and fields of the wartime middle colonies, and shown off over and over again in print, were every bit as much an image of the community, and of its current state, as the European funeral effigies had been. In this case, the community whose condition could be seen in the paraded figures was not flourishing but hacked up and disfigured, bleeding and poorly clothed—a downtrodden, pitiable people, visibly in want of help. Dismemberment and mutilation were the worst fates a state, or a symbolic body politic, could suffer. In pre-revolutionary American rhetoric, being cut into pieces became a vital pun—a visual point of concentration that intertwined and doubled private and public emotions. The metaphor was easy to grasp. In his 1757 manuscript essay urging attacks on Indian villages, Col. James Burd of Pennsylvania gave a careful tactical account of the Delawares' methods in making their "strokes" against exposed families and settlements exactly in order, he said, to reveal how "we of the

Province of Pennsylvania [have] been Embarrassed & had our Limbs lop't off." Since the seventeenth century the Iroquois, too, in the cautious dispersal of their captives between regions, had imagined themselves literally dismembering a body politic. "They used the term, WE-HAIT-WAT-SHA, in relation to these captives," as one early student attests; "[t]his term means a body cut into parts and scattered around. In this manner, they figuratively . . . sunk and destroyed their nationality, and built up their own."[40]

Unexpectedly enough, death and dismemberment—in the shape of Indian-mangled bodies—were coming to provide mid-Atlantic Europeans with a preferred image of themselves. More broadly, in an enormous range of writings, at midcentury and again in the Revolution, they talked over and over again of their "bleeding country." This was an image so inescapable that even an arch-pacifist like Israel Pemberton Jr., the figurehead of the Friendly Association, had to recognize and use it, at one point protesting awkwardly to New York's governor of "[t]he real concern which I feel day and night for my bleeding Country." In 1757, the Pennsylvania assembly charged a Chester County justice of the peace with seditious libel after he petitioned too bitterly for a militia law. His much publicized defense, in part, was that seeing "the savage Knife of the Enemy hourly plunged into the Breasts of the miserable Frontier Inhabitants" had made him feel "too deeply affected with the Sufferings of [his] bleeding Fellow Subjects, to be silent."[41]

This phrase called up the obvious picture of a community bent and bloodied by attack, but because "bleeding" also had a broader meaning— "[f]ull of anguish from . . . deep pity, or compassion"—it emerged as the region's master image during times of attack. Linking physical injury to an overmastering sympathy for the suffering that it caused among the country people, the image of the bleeding country came with a strenuous agenda. *Let the country's suffering affect your feelings,* it said, *and then do whatever you can to save it, to defend it and bloody its attackers back.*[42]

During this period, the most potent symbol of the "country" in the middle colonies was a body warped and burdened by Indian attack. At its angriest, this was an unanswerable rhetoric, but at its simplest—in drawings—it probably did not occur to many people to try to answer it at all. Two engravings designed by Philadelphians suggest the political power

3.1: Blood streams from the dead man's and woman's chest injuries, whose head markings may be meant for scalping wounds; the woman's eyes have been gouged out, and a child's body is at center. *Detail of [James Claypoole Jr.], "The German bleeds & bears the Furs / Of Quaker Lords & Savage Curs . . ." (Philadelphia, 1764). Courtesy of the Library Company of Philadelphia.*

3.2: "The Colonies Reduced." Franklin first had this hugely popular image printed for distribution on small cards to members of Parliament during debates over repeal of the Stamp Act (*London, late 1765 or early 1766; reproduced from frontispiece to Dec. 1768* Political Register and Impartial Review of New Books). *Courtesy of the Lewis Walpole Library, Yale University.*

and flexibility of the rhetoric of mutilation. In figure 3.1, a detail from a 1764 cartoon attacking Pennsylvania's so-called Quaker party for coddling enemy Indians, the lower body of a captive with an Indian master on his back can be seen stumbling through a clearing filled with corpses: the dead lie quietly pouring out blood at his feet and under bushes. The second image (figure 3.2), which Franklin himself designed the next year against the Stamp Act—quickly recycling the rhetoric of injured bodies, as he tried to keep ahead of political changes in the colonies—is a cartoon allegory of the colonies "Reduced" by parliamentary oppression, with Pennsylvania and New York lying lopped off beside British America's bleeding, dying trunk. It was one of the most widely reproduced images of the pre-revolutionary decade.[43]

The point of midcentury body displays was to advertise how horribly the bodies being shown off had been abused, and that their mutilation had come at the hands of Indians and Indians' supposed abettors. The slippery passions they aroused were easy to redirect toward political issues. When the dead were carried into the public arena, being seen by so many people pulled them out of the realm of private grief and fear, abstracting corpses into public statements. In the cities, they came to act as demands: for laws favoring the governor's authority, for instance; for the continuance of war against the western Indians; or, several times, for a new government. The dead were given lines to speak, and they proved hard to answer.

In a variety of mediums, some colonists struggled to conjure up a community that could be seen as uniform in its suffering and resentment—a community first embodied in dead Europeans from the countryside—and then to speak for it against all its supposed abusers. The most powerful of the rhetorical forms and strategies they arrived at outlived the opening shocks of war, tumbling through the political life of the provinces and the new nation in an ungovernable cascade. Literary anti-Indianism was an electrifying set of images, purpose-built for the interpretation of suffering in terms of injury by outside attackers. By the time of the Revolution, it was ready to be applied to the British and their allies. The sense of indignant vulnerability that many Americans felt—what could literally be called their violent self-pity—would be one of the new nation's most characteristic and long-lasting cultural products.

Chapter 4

THE SEVEN YEARS'
WAR AND THE
WHITE PEOPLE

WHEN WAR CAME IN THE FALL OF 1755, THE SMOKE FROM
fields and farmhouses burning over the horizon sometimes hung in the
air for days at a time, making a bitter, persistent fog—like a smudge of
fear that you could see and smell. If farming families in the outer valleys
of European settlement besides this saw the rolling column of white-gray
smoke that showed a haymow was on fire, or heard a thin crackle of
closely spaced gunshots—coming "as Quick after each other as one could
count"—they had one overpowering impulse: to run. If they could hear
other, closer sounds, like their own doors slamming or the bellering of
frightened cows—let alone the "hoot[ing] and cr[ying]" of attackers—
flight would do little good, and they might try to hide.[1]

But for most country people the signs of Indian war parties were
fainter and farther off. If what they had to go on was not the evidence of
their senses, but excited "Indian news," and if they had not yet made up
their minds to flee, dozens or hundreds of men might decide to troop
about with guns instead. Lacking guns, some marched with axes. Such
swarms of would-be volunteers were likeliest to form on the plains near
country towns that did not themselves come under attack. The crowds'
members seldom had clear objectives in mind, and they often milled, a bit
alarmingly, around—like the hundred men from Heidelberg, Pennsylva-

nia, who arrived, ten evenings after the first attack in the province, at the mountain pass bounding their farming plain. They tromped up to the ridgeline, from which outlook "those that had ammunition, spent most of it in shooting up into the Air, and then returned back again, firing all the way, to the great Terror of all the Inhabitants."[2]

Often these marching groups took shape around important local men, like justices of the peace. Their members sought direction from these notables, or tried to learn the latest news of attacks, or asked them to send away for guns, ammunition, and soldiers, or—most often—complained to them of their defenselessness. And when their complaints turned bitter, as they generally did, a surprising side of these gatherings became clear. With hardly any prodding, they could turn into attempts at finding local people to hold accountable for the crowds' unhappiness.

A FEAR OF undeclared enemies and betrayers nearly always swept the places where people felt themselves under threat of attack. Indian warfare's close-up killings could change the way the world looked. Its special power to unnerve and stun disordered people's faith that they understood how things around them worked, as each part of a landscape once taken for granted—the landscape of home—was scanned for hidden threats. At the start of the Seven Years' War, people in this frame of mind readily fastened their blame not only on the idea of Indians but on other Europeans, showing special anger toward local officeholders and people tied to government. A danger that was more impersonal or easily seen—a column of French marines, say, trooping down the Lancaster road—might not have produced such self-fracturing suspicion. But when Indian violence came, it was so close at hand that it felt as if its causes must be, too.[3]

Conrad Weiser, an Indian agent and justice of the peace on the plain of Tulpehocken, Pennsylvania, learned about all these things in mid-November 1755, when a crowd whose size he put at four or five hundred men gathered in the road near his house, where he had been meeting with Iroquois representatives. Weiser and some other leading men of the neighborhood went out nervously to address the assemblage, reading aloud a "sheem" they had drafted to have the people scout and guard against Indians for two shillings a day.

But the men, some of whom may have already abandoned their farms, took a dim view of this offer. Weiser said they preferred the declaration of a scalp bounty. (Within a few days he was promising that the province would someday pay them one.) And as the men's dissatisfaction gathered, it turned into loud mistrust of the government in general and of Weiser, a magistrate and conspicuous Indian go-between, in particular. "They begune," Weiser wrote,

> Some to Curse the Goverr. Some the Assembly. Called me a traitor of the Country who held with the Indians and must have Known this Murder before hand I sat in the house by a low window some of My friend Came to pull me away from it telling me some of the people threatned to shoot me . . . The Crie was The land is betrayed & Sold. The Comon people, from Lancaster County, were the worst . . . I was in danger of being Shot to death . . . .

But at this tense moment, to Weiser's relief, a smoke plume was sighted and an express came galloping up to announce (mistakenly) that there had been an attack near the mountains—on which "The People ran and those that had Horses rode of" pell-mell.[4]

As this seriocomic scene suggests, there was something woven closely into the fear of attack that made it attractive, in the face of it, to single out what the Tulpehocken crowd called "traitor[s] of the Country." This compulsion to condemn was a peculiarity of Indian war that did not go unexploited for long, since one of the most striking things about these suspicions of betrayal was how political their underpinning logic was. Whether the governor, or assembly, or local agents like Weiser were to blame, such outbursts assumed that someone in power must have done the people wrong.

It proved irresistible to translate such experiences into the stuff of written partisan debate. As ideas about public safety and the public good that had last been aired in the crisis of 1748 were revisited—with steadily less innocence—many writers would try not to weave all Europeans together but to master the power of division instead, by decrying traitors in print. For as painful experience goes to show, the discovery and denunciation of enemies can often lend authority to those who do the denouncing.

* * *

THE WARTIME EXPERIENCES of the middle colonies' few Catholics and Moravians, as well as of their many Quakers, suggest how easy publicists would find it to help the population in seeing some groups as suspiciously involved with Indians, and from there as somehow colluding in the attacks that had started to buffet Pennsylvania and northern New Jersey.

Catholics came under pressure from angry antipapists at the war's start. A dread of Catholic-Indian conspiracy had long pervaded colonial society, and nearly two centuries of panics over Catholic plots against British governments had trained English-speakers to *chercher les catholiques* in times of trouble. The black-robed Moravian missionaries— working among Indians out of sight of other Europeans, with unfamiliar religious ideas—were also harassed, sometimes while being accused of secret Catholicism.5

But real Catholics had the worst treatment. A visitor to Philadelphia noted that news of Braddock's disastrous defeat in the west was received by "The Mob here . . . [becoming] very unruly, assembling in great numbers, with an intention of demolishing the Mass House belonging to the Roman Catholics." A worried observer at Goshenhoppen, Pennsylvania, triggered another panic by reporting on a "parsell of Indians . . . laying . . . about three miles from the Roman preasts Chappell . . . [who] were well armed with swords and guns and were Stout fellowes." The country people's concern over Indians "lurking" near the chapel, and their desire to "disarm or otherwise . . . disable the Papists from doing any Injury to other People who are not of their vile Principles," were strengthened by these Catholics' having supposedly seemed glad after Braddock's destruction. In 1760, "ill-minded persons" in Lancaster burned St. Mary's Catholic chapel to the ground.6

Well-known Quakers in the countryside also became targets for the suspicion set in motion by Indian alarms. As a class, Quakers had come to be associated not only with government and with pacifism in the face of danger, but with persistent attempts at seeing Indians' side of things. And so for some rural people the Quakers simply had to be to blame, somehow: it would explain everything.

Edward Biddle traced the dream logic of one emergency meeting in a letter he posted from Reading in the first season of raids, amid "horror and Confusion," with "The Drum . . . beating to Arms, and Bells ringing & all the people under Arms." This rural borough was never attacked. But "Oh my Country! my bleeding Country!" Biddle scribbled.

> Within these two hours we have had different tho' too [c]ertain Accts. all corroborrating each other, and this moment is an Express arrived . . . .
> This night we expect an attack, truly alarming is our situation. The people exclaim against the Quakers, & some are scarce restrained from burning the Houses of those few who are in This Town.7

The singularity at the heart of Indian war was that when faced with attack, Europeans would fall out among themselves further, looking inward at a supposedly Indian-tainted elite for traces of guilt instead of outward at more obvious enemies. Many executive-appointed authorities were happy to encourage the forging of an intuitive link between violence in the countryside and Quakers in the assembly (in part to deflect it from themselves). At the end of October 1755, for instance, the magistrate James Read claimed to be on the verge of leading down a frustrated crowd to quarter themselves on "our *Friends* in Philada., who think themselves vastly Safer than they are."8

The attacks made possible a politics of opposition to everything and anyone who could be suspected—credibly or not—of threatening the people. Indian war's powerful and readily politicized mistrusts soon started nourishing a one-sided contest by the Quaker assembly's opponents to win the authority that would come with being the colony's font of patriotism, martial spirit, public-spirited activity, truly Protestant opposition to popery's myriad agents, and—not least—hostility to the people's enemies, both Indian and internecine.

THE MAIN VEHICLE for popular suspicion of the Quakers was supplied by their own reformers, in the shape of the Friendly Association for Regaining and Preserving Peace with the Indians by Pacific Measures, an exclusively Quaker charity set up in the first springtime of the war.

Despite its being among the most enlightened, open-minded groups founded in provincial America, the Friendly Association lent itself perfectly to the vilification of Quakers and Indians.

It was led by stringently evangelical activists: people like John Woolman, the antislavery writer Anthony Benezet, and the fantastically rich former merchant Israel Pemberton Jr., its guiding spirit and public face. They hoped to return Indian-European relations to the course of "upright dealing and Hospitable Treatment" that had marked William Penn's time, when Quakers ran provincial Indian policy. This they would do by watchdogging the diplomatic dealings of the latter-day Penns (who had gone Anglican), by making cash payments to poor, sick, orphaned, or distressed Indians who visited Philadelphia, and by giving generous presents to the native delegations at provincial treaties, in the form of the clothing, iron goods, powder, and adornments that were the day-to-day stuff of forest diplomacy.[9]

But what could be wrong with any of this, even for the most unfriendly observer? Part of the answer lay in a contrast between the Friendly Association and other associations that were founded in midcentury Philadelphia. From the 1740s on, ethnically and denominationally based charitable clubs had sprung up, the products of quickened immigration and rising national-group consciousness. The Scottish founders of the St. Andrew's Society at Philadelphia (set up in 1749) had been inspired by their "meeting frequently with our Country people here in distress"; their German equivalents in the Deutsche Gesellschaft zu Philadelphia (1765) similarly sought the "help and support of the poor strangers of the German nation in Pennsylvania." The Hibernian Club (by 1759), the Corporation for the Relief of Presbyterian Ministers, Their Widows and Children (before 1760), and its Anglican opposite number (1768) were to be joined before the Revolution by the Society of the Friendly Sons of St. Patrick, as well as the Society of the Sons of St. George Established at Philadelphia for the Advice and Assistance of Englishmen in Distress. Most of these societies had less formal precursors, and they came to meet four times a year, with dues and fines—for such failings as forgetting to wear their special neck medals—that were applied to charitable giving and to blowouts held every St. Andrew's, St. Patrick's, St. Michael's, or St. George's Day.[10]

With the war, refugees surged into the city—a dislocation Rev. Heinrich Melchior Mühlenberg, for one, could watch in begging visits by the "poor Lutheran brethren . . . driven naked from their homes" who came "ask[ing] for old clothes, etc."—and the societies' focus turned toward charity for the victims of Indian attack. In the 1760s, for instance, the St. Andrew's Society (having expanded its working definition of Scots to include Ulster Presbyterians) regularly disbursed relief to refugees from Cumberland County who showed up in Philadelphia.[11]

Like the other societies, the Friendly Association was a charitable club devoted to easing the misfortunes of war, with members drawn from a single national or religious group. Entirely unlike them, though, it spent its funds not on European refugees but on Indians. It is hard to overstate how much this made some Europeans resent the association, and the Quakers behind it, at a time when it was already true that "many ignorant as well as ill minded people are enreached towards friends, ascribing to them all mischief done by the Indians without any sound reason."[12]

As an attempt to retrieve a lost tradition—a tradition of Indian-Quaker diplomacy—the Friendly Association was like many other, more plainly religious stirrings that filled this age of immigration and revival. It was meant to be as conspicuous as possible, to other Europeans as well as Indians—the better to stand as a shining example of how intercultural relations could be conducted, and of who might best conduct them. Like its sister New-Jersey Association for Helping the Indians, it was meant, in short, "to exhibit . . . a standing Memento of Justice and kindness."[13]

The themes of sectarian rebirth and righteous self-assertion underlay one of the association's first gatherings, a banquet that Israel Pemberton held in Philadelphia for the Friendly Association's founders and representatives of the Iroquois confederacy. Pemberton's house was a long, two-story structure, first built for a governor, whose imposing touches included a garden "in the old stile of Uniformity, with Walks & Allies nodding to their Brothers, & . . . Evergreens carefully clipped into Pyrammids & Conical forms." In the course of the "Occasional Conversation . . . after Dinner," Pemberton made some studied remarks. We still have what seem to be the notes he cupped in his hand while talking. Pemberton probably stood up from his place as if he were in a Quaker meeting for business, glancing down to recall the right words while he spoke to the weighty Friends and Indians sitting politely along the length of his dining-room table, amid the littered plates and glasses of their meal.[14]

Though Quakers had founded Pennsylvania and made many treaties of friendship with its native inhabitants, Pemberton said, it would be understandable if the Indians should have grown confused about Friends' importance, or begun to wonder whether they had disappeared. For in late years the Quakers had more and more "lain hid and almost buried, by the great Numbers of other People who are come hither many of whom are Men of different Principles from Us." But from having been entombed in this rubble of other peoples, Pemberton said, "all true Quakers" were now more determined than ever to

> Arise, and shew Ourselves to You . . . and as a proof of our Sincerity we give you this Belt (a large white Belt) which . . . as it is made of many Peices which were small and of little weight of Strength before they were Knitt together But is now Strong and firm, So We when Collected and United together shall appear . . . .

The reply by Scarouady, an Oneida half-king in the Ohio lands, played on Pemberton's images of reemergence, agreeing that he "thought the People of that Profession had been all dead or buried in the Bushes or in the Ashes"—because, since William Penn's time, "there has . . . come . . . another sort of People different from the first Settlers, And we lost him"—before expressing his joy "that you rise again from the Dead."[15]

Pemberton had an air of being richer and more superb than Pennsylvania's actual governors, and a special knack for maddening the members of their faction. He embodied a danger they often decried: that the province's diplomatic powers would slip into the hands of the Friendly Association's "extreamly wicked" members. And it was true that both Indians and Europeans sometimes addressed Pemberton as "Governor Pemberton"; as "your honor"; or even—in keeping with the idea Scarouady had advanced in his dinner speech of a reincarnated William Penn—as "Onas," a ceremonial name, punning on an Iroquois word for pen ("feather"), that had been reserved since the founder's day for Pennsylvania's governors.[16]

Before long, Quakers and their rivals all believed firmly in an unpopular Quaker-Indian special relationship. This impression owed much to some Quakers' determined efforts at proving themselves open to Indian influences, especially in the realm of the spirit.

THE SIGNS of Friends' special interest in Indians were proud and obvious. Working at Fort Pitt before Pontiac's War, whenever he could the Quaker trader James Kenny noted down in his journal amiable conversations that he had about the "Good Spirit Above" with Indians who stopped in, as well as Indians' telling him that "Friends were . . . yᵉ best People," being "kinder and better humour'd [to them] than any others," and his own belief that there were "frequently better & honester Men amongst them [the Indians] than Most English People" professing Christianity. It was simple to disarm even hardened characters among the Indians, Kenny told Pemberton, since as a Quaker "the Principle I act from, makes . . . my Love toward them . . . not in deed feigned but Sincere." Indeed, he confessed, he was so happy to serve them in every little way—fetching drinks, serving special cuts of meat—that "I have had the Satisfaction to hear [a European associate] Say . . . I was fonder to wait of the Indians than of him."¹⁷

For his part, by 1763 John Woolman was sharing with Indians in ecstatic meetings for worship, after paying a remarkable visit to a village near the New York border. Pluckily traveling "over mountains, swamps, and barren desarts" just as news of Pontiac's War started to trouble the countryside, Woolman finally reached Wyalusing—a mainly Munsee town, where he was a little let down to find a Moravian missionary already visiting. In worship services with the Indians, Woolman had such a sensation of spiritual communion—he called it "feeling the current of love run strong"—that he asked the English-speaking Wyalusingites to "omit interpreting" what he said and simply let his unintelligible flow of words wash over the rest.

Because Woolman believed that many Delawares he met were already communing with the divine light inside them, and that the "almighty Being . . . hath an equal regard to all mankind," he could seek a kind of spiritual tutelage from Indians. It is hard to imagine a member of another denomination writing about this trip quite in Woolman's tone: after his first, overwhelming experience of worship, he wrote simply, "in mine own eyes I appeared inferior to many amongst the Indians."[18]

Woolman had been drawn northward by Papunhang, an extraordinary man who came to embody the idea of a kinship between Friends and natives. Papunhang was an elderly Munsee prophet who had renounced violence and collected a following in the early 1750s—"a sort of religious People," whose members called him "Minister"—to found the settlement at Wyalusing. His spiritual experiments bore him steadily closer to evangelical Christianity, and by 1761 Pennsylvania's governor was mistakenly praising Papunhang as "a good Christian." Two years later, he would in fact ask for baptism (from the Moravians), but in the early 1760s his religious position was still floating about pretty freely, in a way that seems to have made Quaker reformers like Woolman wonder: What if Papunhang became a Quaker, too?[19]

There were grounds for hope. Papunhang and thirty acolytes paid a high-profile visit to Philadelphia in July 1760, "want[ing] to see the Friends" and talk about religion. As their delighted hosts recorded, they regularly attended meetings for worship in the Quakers' Greater Meetinghouse—a building at the heart of the city, catercorner from the covered market in High Street—where they would have sat on the facing bench amid a quiet collection of broad-hatted elders. Plying the prophet with questions and taking down his table talk, the Friends "made a great deal of him" (as a jealous Moravian noted), "ke[eping] him to themselves." Papunhang seemed tantalizingly close to joining the Quakers ("I have heard a Voice say to my Heart, that the Quakers are right," he announced), but in the end nothing solid came of his visit.[20]

But the spiritual crush it confirmed opened the way to more joint worship—especially at the treaty of Easton in August 1761, which in some Quaker accounts seemed more back-and-forth Quaker-Indian prayer fest than diplomatic event. The Wyalusingites stuck to their usual routine of worship, meeting around low fires under a collection of awnings at dawn and dusk. Now, however, Quakers sat beside them, marveling at how "Solid" and orderly the Indians were, and listening while Papunhang spoke in Delaware out of the silence, holding up his hands so they could see him gesture in the air. The Wyalusingites repaid the favor with early-morning "religious Conversation . . . on divers weighty Subjects." At the end of one long session, the spiritually wrung-out participants took their leave of each other, sighing and crying, "all much broken, & . . . [saying] it was such a time as they had never known before."²¹

The Friendly Association's members were pinning some of their hopes for peace on Indians' and Europeans' being melted down together before God. This vision reached its climax in the hot Sunday meetings that the Quakers held at Easton under a huge tent of their own, with hundreds of treaty-goers attending—Quakers, Wyalusing Munsees, assorted Nanti-cokes, Conoys, and Delawares, Pennsylvania's governor and council, local Germans (who were noisy, and fidgeted), and the merely curious. Here, on an outdoor stage, the ideal of Quaker-Indian brotherhood was acted out for all.

Side-by-side worship with Indians caused a sensation in the Quaker and German sectarian communities. Mennonites and Schwenkfelders wrote to Philadelphia, asking for details about these religious Indians. (Not least "whereabout . . . they live, if a Place on Lewis Evans Map of the middle Settlements could be indicated," one potential contributor to the Friendly Association wrote, "that would gratify my Curiosity.") But Quaker reformers hoped Papunhang's story would hold a moral even for less sympathetic Europeans. They saw him as an exemplar of the innate piety of "Indians" generally. His people—wise, gentle, artless, abstemious, full of "wonderful . . . Zeal & goodness to the English"—were ready for spiritual instruction, opposed to violence, and eager to redeem captives and pacify other natives. And if the Quakers and Papunhang could fuse their very spirits, "caus[ing] our Hearts," in his words, "to be tender to love one another and to look upon all Mankind as . . . one Family," what was to stop colonial and Indian negotiators from settling a peace?²²

In 1761, members of the Friendly Association were worried that the old man had died. Israel Pemberton sent a speech to Wyalusing to ask after him, noting that "if He is Dead we have no doubt He is gone to everlast-ing rest, & will recive the reward of willdoing." This confidence that Papunhang was lodged in heaven—and that their contemporaries' "prej-udice, custom &c." notwithstanding, in the eyes of God spiritually

minded Indians and Christians were the same—put the Quaker reformers proudly at odds with many other Europeans.[23]

THE INDIAN CONFERENCES of the 1750s and 1760s were never
unruffled affairs. Consumed by mutual loathing, the people attending
from both the proprietary faction and the Friendly Association saw the
treaties' decisive struggles as being those they had with each other. Quakers like Israel Pemberton found executive scheming everywhere they
looked. At a time when public eating was still a numinous thing, even the
dishing out of food could touch off struggles. During a celebratory lunch-
eon at Easton in 1756, resentment flared when Pemberton got no trout to
eat—while the Penns' secretary got two. (Since he was "more dispos'd to
promote [peace] than to indulge in Feasting," Pemberton said, he had
"attended solely to prevent any exception being taken"—but still.) As
Pemberton wrote bitterly in the association's minutes, with the secretary
conveniently

> not having provided . . . Tables for near so many as were asked, it caused
> some Confusions . . . but tho' he disappointed others of a Dinner he did
> not himself, taking Care privately, to secure one out of the first & best
> Dishes of fine Trout and after he had eat it appeared very much con-
> cerned about some for whom he saw there was not Room and with much
> Complaisance . . . dine[d] with them at a Table he ordered . . . pretend-
> ing to have been so engaged as not to have got his own Dinner . . . .

For their part the proprietors feared these Quakers would transform
negotiations that could otherwise be brisk, businesslike, and—why
not?—a bit unequal into public ordeals, full of humiliating new demands,
by "tamper[ing] with" the Indians. Many of the Penns' men felt the proprietors were in reality bargaining only with their own Quaker subjects,
hidden under an Indian shell, so they were maddened any time they
thought they had proof that—as the trout-eating provincial secretary
rushed upstairs at Easton and yanked a Quaker's door to yell—"you are
putting things in the Indian Heads.—"[24]

Besides suspecting that Quaker puppeteers were "guid[ing the Indians'] every Motion," some proprietary men had an ominous sense that the Friends and Indians might be blurring their very personalities together. At the Easton treaty of 1757, two proprietary youths—the sons of the provincial secretary and the Anglican rector of Christ Church—were told to look out for Quaker mischief. The young watchers came to suspect that the whole conference was underlaid by a set of secret arrangements, meant to be undetectable by anyone not an Indian or a Quaker—or pretending to be one. For more and more they

> perceived a very remarkable Distinction made by ye Indians between Q^{rs} ... & others ... when we us'd to meet Indians any where in ye Streets, or in our Evening Walks after Business, they woud generally accost us wth this Question in their broken English—Are you a Quaker, a Quaker—and if we answer'd No, they wou'd frown & look very stern & illnatur'd ... But if we answer'd in ye Affirmative, (as we did some times to try them) ... they woud smile & carress us, & call us Bro^{rs}, & say we were good Men—Quaker good Men ....

The Quakers and Indians had held meeting after meeting ("at least 20 times"), never letting a word of what they said escape. Their cooperation seemed to come not so much from friendship as from a sort of unnatural intimacy, an amphibious inter-identification that approached outright identity. For on one of their walks, as the boys advised the public in a sworn report, they had met an Indian dressed very plainly, wearing "a broad flat Hat, like a Q^r." This inspired a remarkable question—as the two warily reversed the inquiry so often made of them—and a more remarkable answer. "[W]e askt him if he was a Q^r, & he smiling, answered Yes, Yes, I a Quaker now—but when I go away I—Indian again—or to y^t effect."[25]

If unmasking such hybrid nightmares was the great concern of the Quakers' opponents, then when the treaty rumpuses—already so much like satires brought to life—were put into print, they would have a chance to let the public look under the mask as well. The anti-Indian sublime's explosive little kit of politicized images had made it easy to "display" mutilated bodies on the page. Anti-Quaker polemics after Pontiac's War would take the experiences of these treaties—seeing Quakers help Indian speakers to rehearse their arguments, or watching them bestow bales of goods on Indian delegations—and make of them a short, shrill indictment. Did Indian attack naturally feed a search for hidden betrayers? Here they were. In acts the Friends saw as open and unbigoted, their political opponents could claim to see only collusion with killers, crying out to heaven. The Friendly Association's members tried earnestly to use "Published Papers for the opening of the Eyes of the Public Relating to Our Indian Affairs"; but in an increasingly hostile world of print, their image was not their own to control.[26]

The retreat of many Quakers from government was a push-me-pull-you process. On the one hand, Quakers were chased out by their opponents' harsh mastery of the rhetorical signs the war supplied (like the bleeding bodies of country people, and Indian-Quaker intimacy). On the other, Quaker reformers actually welcomed other Friends' exclusion from office, since they felt that to stand, conspicuous and unpopular, outside the turbulent currents of the wartime colonies would be to keep one's virtue safe. The Friendly Association was meant to embody their urge for singularity and withdrawal—it was a private body, in which only Quakers could hold office. But since the publicists who wrote on behalf of executive power proved so adept at warping even this charity's works into expressions of distaste for other Europeans, if not downright treasonableness, in the end the Friendly Association, too, seemed too much part of the hurly-burly of public life to be healthy for Friends' spiritual lives, and it was given up.[27]

Each time Friends wriggled against the snare of guilt by association in which their rivals had caught them, it only cut them more deeply, since all their efforts to bring about peace could be presented as acts of treachery.

As Pennsylvanians underwent the last shocks of Pontiac's War in 1764, one poem in a cheap eight-page pamphlet made the idea of a special spiritual closeness between Quakers and Indians—the very idea the reformers had been so careful to promote—into the basis for a bitter attack. "[Y]ou can hear an Indian bellow," the angry doggerelist wrote,

And praise him for a pious Fellow,
Though what he means you cannot tell,
Nor if he talks of Heaven or Hell.

The kindly figure of Papunhang became a sign of Quaker hypocrisy, along with all the Friendly Association's charitable projects, from the provision of treaty gifts to the support of sick or elderly Indians in Philadelphia. So understanding toward Indians, so scornfully dismissive of other Europeans' lives! "Go on good Christians," the poet urged,

. . . . never spare
To give your Indians Clothes to wear;
Send 'em good Beef, and Pork, and Bread,
Guns, Powder, Flints and store of Lead,
To Shoot your Neighbours through the Head; . . .
Encourage ev'ry friendly Savage,
To murder, burn, destroy and ravage . . . .

The image of an Indian-Quaker affinity was easily twisted into a stinging self-indictment—one a single couplet could sum up:

In many things change but the Name,
Quakers and Indians are the same;—. . . .[28]

This simple observation was one that Papunhang and Woolman would both have been glad to embrace. But in a culture at war, and in the hands of publicists who were as eager to clip Quakers out of the polity as they were to denounce Indians, the image turned poisonous.

WITH SNIPING and backbiting at every turn, can it be that a decade of war against Indians did nothing to draw together the different kinds of Europeans who faced it? Not quite: for despite the country people's tirades against suspicious officials, and the attacks against Catholics, Moravians, and Quakers, the war did also bring about mass rural meetings and crushes of refugees.

The raids in 1755 and 1763 that started what contemporaries came to call the "first" and "second" Indian wars pushed thousands of country people down roads and rivers and into county towns. These frightened pulses of motion poured together more—and more varied—Europeans than had ever been the case before. There were no precedents for coming together in the countryside in this way, and sometimes the experience inspired at least fleeting feelings of unity. The only large, cooperative gatherings many country people could have known were the biannual markets held in a few boroughs. The fair at Lancaster was well enough known as a time when rustics came together to earn a mocking description in one Philadelphia almanac:

> Hogs there eat hogs—Pigs cry come eat me;
> There's wine, if you it drink, will heat ye:
> The rustic clown and greasy frow do prance
> To th' doodlesaack, the hipsisaw [bumpkinish German jigs]
>   they dance . . . .

But since Lancaster's was the one regular fair in New Jersey, Delaware, or Pennsylvania that was not held along the dense eastern edge of colonization, in a town perched on the Delaware River, even the fair-day feeling of cutting loose together was one that few people in the interior had had for themselves.[29]

The sudden flurries of refugeeism and mustering that followed Indian attacks—with English, Welsh, German-speaking, and Irish people from different townships and churches, from both county towns and the countryside, tumbling together in efforts to make themselves safer—must have struck their participants as new and strange. They were embodiments of the less exclusive communities that publicists had first tried to call up in the 1740s, amid the French and Spanish invasion scare. The people in these defensive groups had simply been driven together, so they could not be choosy about who else was in them. Most such clusters were short-lived—after a few weeks of quiet, many people whose farmsteads were not laid waste would trickle back, since leaving for good meant pauperism—but the gatherings' novelty and high emotion made them matter nonetheless.

Emergency meetings were often called by alarming letters circulated "as quick as possible"—like one dispatched in 1763, requisitioning a farmer's house so that

> the whole of the inhabitants of Upper Smithd: Township might Meet together . . . to the Advantage of the whole in General, especially if these, like Troublsome Times should continue . . . Warn the whole, of the People above you . . . for the more the better. . . . N:B. take care & keep a good look out there is Enemy Indians on Our Cost [i.e., boundary], & where they will fal first We cannot tell.

In emergencies, inclusiveness felt like safety. As three magistrates wrote in 1755 to "all other well wishers of this Province" in Northampton County, with everyone in the countryside equally at risk, they should all pool their strength simply "as Friends and Neighbours who are also exposed to the same Dangers as you are."[30]

Panicky catchall gatherings resulted, with authorities trying vainly to organize "confused Multitude[s] destitute of Arms & Ammunition & without Discipline."[31] The most urgent need (as Franklin observed) was usually just to "quiet the Inhabitants, who seem terrified out of their Senses," by making them feel that proper steps were being taken. Since otherwise the whole countryside would be left a wasteland, managing the people's fears—what one J.P. called "spirit[ing] up the People all I can"— became a valued political skill. At the start of the war, the unreliable Susquehanna ferry-owner John Harris was known for "discourag[ing] the Folks . . . [and] buzzing them in the Ears of their great Danger." (He seems to have actually set off a rural panic with mistaken warnings of an invasion by fifteen hundred Indians and Canadian troops.) But by 1763, after years of helping to run meetings at his inn in Paxton township, Harris had learned to tamp the people's anxieties down instead of fueling them. Though he was still "not the Man in all respects that I could wish him," as the grandee Edward Shippen Sr. wrote to the council from his home base in Shippensburg, "yet I cant think he ought . . . to be disregarded . . . —I am sure he has a great deal of Merit in Spiriting the People up to Stay at Pextan."[32]

The people at emergency meetings did what they could to cement their group resolve. Some swore to "live and die together"—as at the first mass meeting of adult men in the valley of Tulpehocken, where "All unanimously agreed to die together and engage the Enemy . . . till others of our Brethren should Come up and do the Same." Such promises helped the country people to imagine themselves as linked together against outside threats in a league of "well-wishers of the people." Sometimes they joined in prayers or heard ministerial "Exhortation[s]." The Tulpehocken men were addressed by a local Lutheran named Kurtz, who was known to have a thunderous voice, a "hot-headed and dictatorial" manner, and a crowd-pleasing habit of preaching "partly extempore."33

Such rallying may have helped a little to create new sensations of trust. This was true especially in the first months of excitement, when large groups of men stood ready to march about at any word of danger. In October 1755, disorganized forces formed at staging points in Berks and Lancaster counties and trooped toward the Susquehanna. (They were expecting to counter John Harris's imaginary army of Indians and Canadian soldiers.) What set them moving seems to have been not unmixed altruism so much as a wish to head off attackers before they could get to their own home townships. When a force under Weiser arrived at Paxton to find no enemy, with most of the local men gone upriver, it streamed back east at once, "as we did not come up to serve as Guards to Paxton people."34

But sometimes crowds did move about just to offer one another help. At Carlisle, Pennsylvania, in November 1755 there were "large companys here dayly from York Co:ty"—which was to say from the other side of a daunting Appalachian ridge—"assureing us that they are Reddy to come to our assistance at the shortest warning, [and] people from Chester Co:ty and Lancaster County daily up at Harris's Assureing them the same." Large groups gathered the same month in Northampton County and across the border in New Jersey, so that one had only to "sen[d] Letters out to Alarm the Country," as the J.P. Timothy Horsfield found, "& People came from all Quarters." When Horsfield wrote about a rumor "of a Body of Indians being like to fall in upon the White People &c," by nightfall he was hosting several wet companies of "the People in Easton & the Jerseys [who] were alarmd & got together to march for the Defence of the Back Settlements" to him through a storm. Hundreds of men from northern New Jersey were ready to come across, "as willing as tho' they were going to help a Neighbour at any piece of Work" (though, an observer at Elizabeth wrote, "we understand . . . the back Parts of Northampton is settled with the Church of England and Presbyterian Members, otherwise People would not go with so much good Will"). By December, the Moravian bishop at Bethlehem was urgently asking Horsfield "to write some Letters both to the Jersey People, and to our good Irish Neighbours"—with whom Bethlehem's Moravians had had virtually continuous friction for years—and ask them to march over to stop "the Enemy from going on so boldly, yea I may say so devilishly."[35]

It seemed possible at first that some of this marching and pledging might break down the walls between denominations and townships. Weiser's October march to the west, for instance, seemed to work like a rolling social snowball, packing on new members as it went. When he heard at Heidelberg that the "paxton people . . . had been murd'd," Weiser "Immediatly sent my Servants to alarm the neighbourhood"; then, riding to the Heidelbergers' muster, he found a hundred "Tulpehockin-people" already gathered who at once "unanimously agreed to join Heidleberg people." As this coalition marched through the diverse upper Lancaster County townships, Weiser could watch "our Company encreasing all along": even some nonviolent Anabaptist "long Beards" pitched in, including "a Menonist who declared he would live and die with his neighbours; he had a good gun with him." Weiser wanted to believe (and to help the readers of his reprinted letters believe) that in the face of French and Indian danger, everyone in the countryside would choose to live and die together, sweeping away previous distrusts.[36]

But even at these fancied last stands there were signs of trouble. People who had never had occasion to talk to each other, or perhaps to speak in public at all, finally did in emergency meetings—but sometimes it only made their differences plainer. Mobilizing militia and paramilitary groups could lead to endless squabbling over who should be in charge, where defenses should be concentrated, and how Europeans from different national backgrounds would work together. In Lancaster, Edward Shippen reported, "Our People"—both German- and English-speaking—came together for an open strategy session, "to consult upon some Measures for the Defence of themselves & others." But the bilingual meeting broke up without agreeing on anything, requiring a second, segregated round of talks. "This Morning the Dutch have got a Meeting among themselves," as Shippen noted; "we shall know the Result of their Conference very soon."[37]

During these times of trouble, officials wanted to play what Conrad Weiser thought of as "the part as fathers of the people." But as human material for the unified, resolute reaction forces and mutual-support leagues that they had in mind, mid-Atlantic colonists proved messy and hard to shape. Emergency mobilizations moved too fast, and owed too much to shifting currents of fear, to be guided for long by a few leaders' wishes. When these "Convention[s] of . . . undisciplined People" did manage to act or feel united, it was because of their shared terror at a seemingly imminent threat. But like most oppositional identities, this one shrank rapidly back into irrelevance once the stimulus of fear was taken away. Whatever sensations of unity the country people had generally evaporated with the crowds that felt them.[38]

BUT IN THE REALM of rhetoric matters were different. Here it was far easier to find agreement, since printed accounts of what happened in the countryside could simply pass over the untidiness of actual mobilization. In arguments about what political lessons the crisis held, and in many misleading invocations of settlers' unanimity, an assumption took hold, at least on paper: that whiteness was a useful rubric—more so than Lutheranness, for instance, or Presbyterianness. What gained a purchase was the premise that being one of "the white people" said something about how one thought and acted about Indian war, and toward Indians.

Whether publicists wrote of "the white people" or simply "the people," images of a single, suffering peoplehood that encompassed nearly all the mid-Atlantic's European groups—except Quakers—came to flourish in the press. If all the people had truly been of one mind, public figures who could voice their needs and demands would have been oracles worth heeding; but even the pretense of doing so proved powerful. Like the bleeding country, "the white people" became a building block for public discourse, and the first outlines were sketched of a coalition that would help to push all pacifists out of the middle provinces' governments, and most Indians from their territory, by century's end.

It is hard to appreciate this without grasping the relative novelty of the language of whiteness. "White" as a human descriptor had been hit upon long before, in other milieus of confrontation with non-Europeans. But in the heterogeneous middle colonies, where color-based coalitions had not struck anyone as especially self-evident before, the word "white" was lastingly shaded, and given an enormous boost in power, by its use in Indian wars—from the recurring need they set up to contrast the Europeans of the middle colonies, en masse, with the Indians they had started warring against and worrying about.

By the time the war started, Indian nativists were already apt to identify Indians and Europeans as separate orders of creation. In keeping with their precocity at seeing all Europeans as a uniform color group, there are signs that (at least outside New York City) the very name for "the white people" first gained currency in mid-Atlantic writing—rising to favor over rival words, like "English"—as a faintly exotic-sounding translation of Indians' and Indian-hands' standard usage. The phrase expressed a broad contrast between the interests of a diverse body of non-Indians and those of Indians themselves—a contrast whose importance Indians had felt more sharply, and rather earlier, than Europeans. Naturally enough, part of its wartime rise was owing to Indians' reported speech—as when Pennsylvanians learned in 1756 that disaffected eastern Delawares had flatly said their war aim was to "murder all the white People"; or that the Ohio Delawares had tried to tempt the neutral Iroquois by telling them "it was best . . . to take up the Hatchet against the White People, without distinction, for all their Skin was of one Colour and the Indians of a Nother."39

Even in the wake of the war, Europeans did not treat the phrase as self-explanatory in all contexts. In the 1768 journal of his evangelization tour through Pennsylvania's back counties, the minister Charles Beatty felt obliged to define it, helpfully appending to the phrase "white men" in his transcription of an Indian conversation "(for so they distinguished the *English*)"; and glossing what another Indian had said about "the white people, (which is a general name they call other nations by, that are white).'' As this suggests, "white people" had an initial flavor of strangeness for many English-speakers; and perhaps of seeing the people it described from an interestingly awkward, outside point of view. With Indian war, as the phrase grew more fashionable, that angle of vision haltingly started to become more Europeans' own.[40]

THESE WORDS are resonant and deceptively familiar. They sound so much like staking a claim to racial superiority that it is hard to understand how they could have been bent, so often, to the job of debasing and insulting not Indians but other Europeans. For talk of "the white people" was more often political than racial—just as anti-Indian animus was often applied most eagerly to other Europeans. This is not quite the puzzle it seems, since most of Europeans' thinking about Indians was still preracial, and surprisingly unconcerned with innate color. Allegiance, environment, and class explained so much of human difference that many believed they could see the European poor darkening before their eyes.

When Indians' own opinions about human difference were asked, they were often unforgivingly exclusive. Their practice with captives, by contrast, was never so concerned with unerasable boundaries, since the capture of even teenaged Europeans was often followed by their successfully adopting their captors' language, clothes, religious ideas, deportment, and even appearance.[41]

Europeans' views about human separateness are often assumed to have been as essentialist as any Indian's, but in fact they were not so tidy. For religious reasons, Europeans were explicitly and very widely committed to the unity of mankind, or what one American observer called "the doctrine of one race." What was more, though they thought it a slow and unlikely process for an Indian to pass over into being a "white" person, they did not see it as impossible: and they were at least as ready as Indian captors to accept that Indian-raised "white people" could become fully Indian in a matter of years.[42]

In 1787, the vice president of Princeton, Samuel Stanhope Smith, addressed the American Philosophical Society in Philadelphia on differences in human appearance. He turned with relish partway through to the case of George Morgan White Eyes, a young Indian enrolled at his college since 1779, whom Smith had been watching. He could see that the young man was becoming more "Anglo-American." His mouth was still bigger than the other boys', his cheekbones higher, his face a bit darker— "[b]ut," Smith assured the audience, all "these differences are sensibly diminishing." He had already "los[t] that vacancy of eye" seen in other Indians, and from living amid Princeton's softening influences, White Eyes's skin, too, Smith was ready to pronounce, "is much lighter than the complexion of the native savage."

Another tale of assimilation came from Pennsylvania's borderland in 1763, as Pontiac's War began. A refugee paddling away from Redstone Creek by night reported a narrow escape from "a White Man named Hicks and an Indian" in a bark canoe. "Hicks told him that an Indian War was broke out," the refugee said, "and that he would kill the white People wherever he found them." This was almost certainly Gershom Hicks, who appeared again at Fort Pitt a year later claiming to have just escaped from captivity. He acted suspiciously, and under harsh questioning confessed he was spying on the fort for the Delawares, then described his own recent "Murder[s] and Scalp[ings]" with an eight-man war party. Hicks's reportedly undiscriminating rage against "the white People" may seem surprising in someone who was himself born a European. But he plainly no longer considered himself to be part of "the white People," of whom he meant to kill as many as he could.[43]

Mid-Atlantic Europeans had been slower than Indians—by a couple of decades—to commonly see themselves as a coherent group, and they were as slow to see a basic, unbridgeable chasm between Indians and "white people." Like Hicks, in fact, they may have learned to do so partly at Indians' hands. From the 1740s on, Indian religious movements had forwarded precisely the view of human origins—a belief in polygeny, or separate creations of the differently shaped and colored races—that would underlie the most extreme opinions of mid-Victorian racialists. But until nearly the century's end, Europeans were hobbled by Christian thought from seeing human varieties as so different that they might have had separate origins (much less separate creators or afterlives).[44]

The book of Genesis, squarely at the start of the Bible, dictated that speculations about human origins could never be casual: their implications for scripture's authenticity were too direct. Any polygenist "opinion," as the jurist Henry Home, Lord Kames, grudgingly noted, "we are not permitted to adopt; being taught a different lesson by revelation." And despite Renaissance speculation that Indians might represent a kind of human unknown to Genesis, by the middle of the eighteenth century the most striking thing was not what a challenge Indians posed for Europeans' biblicist worldview but how easily—and persistently—they were folded into it.[45]

English-speakers shared a comfortable consensus. As the early *Encyclopædia Britannica* (and its innumerable plagiarists) stressed, there were certainly not "sufficient grounds for determining [the Indians] . . . to be a race of men specifically distinct from all others"; and above all, authorities agreed, "mere colour is by no means the characteristic of a certain species of mankind." It was widely observed that the Inuit were "a white people, without anything peculiar . . . to distinguish them from the rest of mankind"; and the existence of "white Americans" in Panama—whose color Oliver Goldsmith thought "exactly like that of an European"—was reported repeatedly through the end of the century. It seemed clear to the thoughtful that if Indians went "several generations" without painting their skin, and took "the same precautions to brighten their color that an European does, it is very probable that they would . . . come to . . . dispute the prize of beauty" with them. One would have to be ill-informed or doctrinaire to use skin color as an index of something essential.

The commonest analogy in such discussions was with the way social class controlled the appearances of Europeans themselves. If poverty was a small-scale version of savagery, Indian traits could be traced to the Indians' seedy lives in the woods.[46]

IN HIS ORATION on human difference (and a hugely influential book he based on it), Samuel Stanhope Smith, for one, endlessly compared the poor and savage, showing how hardship, fatigue, exposure to the sun, and "poverty and nastiness" would darken anyone. Smith, who was nothing if not consistent, noted that living in the American climate was shifting the appearances not only of Indians but of Europeans. Each new generation of Americans was straighter haired and more sallow (à la Indians) than the last: since this happened a little faster east than west of the Delaware,

New Jerseyans were "somewhat darker in their colour" than Pennsylvanians. The most persuasive case for Smith was that of Europeans who took on Indians' color and other "habits of the body." Despite the transmutation of George Morgan White Eyes, this was mostly a one-way process, since "a dark colour can be [more easily] impressed, than effaced." And the changes went furthest among captives, whose physical "resemblance . . . [to] the native savages" could become "so strong, as at first to strike every observer with astonishment."[47]

Contemporaries were riveted by the idea of Europeans who "attempered" with Indians. If captivity was an experiment in the intersections between European and Indian life—could one become the other?—the answer seemed to be yes. Many captives gave up even a memory of their European pasts. Observers were full of wonder at how much of a person could be erased, as Rev. Heinrich Melchior Mühlenberg showed in retelling the Blondel-and-Lionheart-like story of one German girl's recovery. After her release at a treaty, she and other unclaimed captives were taken from town to town in what became a kind of rural roadshow. When she arrived at Carlisle, being now in her late teens, "grown big, strong, and formed like an Indian, and . . . sp[ea]k[ing] the savage tongue," she was only identified when, by luck, her mother tested the group's knowledge of particular hymns. On this her Indianized daughter (who after nine years was otherwise unable to speak German, though she still understood it) "sprang forward from the rest" and managed to sing "Jesum lieb' ich ewiglich," her girlhood favorite, to general weeping and recognition.[48]

Not only looks and language but nearly everything could be altered. Other captives, like "Elizabeth Tell," whose very name was in doubt, were advertised as trying helplessly to remember who they were or where they had lived. By 1760, such cases of released captives who wandered around without speech, money, or European identities, never "recollect[ing] their Surnames, nor from what Place they were taken," had even proven appealing enough to spin off a little class of impersonators. Most of the impostors who feigned ex-captives' amnesia and cultural dislocation were runaway servants, for whom it was useful to be able to take charity without—supposedly—having enough command of English, German, or their own memories to answer meddling questions.[49]

The idea behind such stories was that basic human traits could wash freely in and out of anyone's constitution. People's own actions and environments could alter them even at the deepest levels—which was one way of saying that no levels of difference lay especially deep. A person with "short, and thin, and frittered" hair (like most slaves) and one with enviable locks, for instance, differed only in whether they had grown up poor or living outdoors. Vice President Smith confirmed this by taking an indigent girl—"frittered" in hair and body—into his household and watching narrowly while she shifted, slowly converging with Smith's own children, until, by the age of fourteen, the scientist in him was gleeful to find that his servant's hair was now "long and flowing, and she is not badly made in her person," either.⁵⁰

This environmentally driven vision set outer boundaries to intolerance—even in the harshest essay about Indians' nature and descent to see print in the mid-eighteenth-century middle colonies, a 1758 letter in Philadelphia's *American Magazine*. It carried the question of "from *what Race* these savages are descended" exactly as far back in time as orthodoxy could allow (without recourse to creations before Adam). The Indians laying waste to Pennsylvania must, the essayist allowed, be "descendants of murdering *Cain*," having survived the Flood from their place of exile in the Land of Nod, or America. As part of "the race of cursed *Cain*"— who was probably the first scalper—they were "still skulking wandering murderers, retaining their original thirst of blood." Even "[t]he colour of their skin and hair, with the peculiar *Cast of their eyes*, . . . may be impressions of the MA[RK] imposed on *Cain*; [as may be] their *Sight* being so quick and discerning." In short, as he concluded, "From their hellish cruelty *good Lord* deliver all people"!

But even the Cainite coin had another side, and this essay was balanced at once by another heartfelt prayer, this time for their conversion (which "May *God* of his infinite mercies . . . be pleased speedily to effect"). For such differences were all in the family: "as *Cain* was within the first promise *of the blessed seed* . . . and his posterity are included in . . . the blessings and benefits procured by *Christ Jesus,* we have grounds to hope that god . . . will mollify their obdurate hearts." Precisely because they and Europeans shared one blood, instead of writing the Delawares off, "[i]n this grand work it is our duty," he announced, "to exert our most

... vigorous cooperating endeavours ... that they seeing our good christian works may ... glorify our father," too. Inescapably undergirding most thinking about human differences—and, skeptics would see as the century waned, supported by it in turn—was the vision of Genesis, of a humanity made by one God, sharing one destiny.[51]

THERE WERE two main ways of thinking about what kind of people were likeliest to drift across the gap between Indians and Europeans. The first stressed social position. After the 1720s, with the arrival of Irish and German voyagers, observers had noted nervously how ready the unruly people streaming into the countryside seemed to be to slump toward savagery. Their un-English cultural backgrounds made them alien, and for want of landownership or wealth, many frontier people were unlikely to make proper farmers. Vice President Smith's perceptions about how poverty reshaped and recolored bodies along Indian lines—among not only captives but anyone who sought opportunity by "removing ... to the western countries"—were in tune with this way of thinking.[52] When many in a group of long-term captives who were turned over to Col. Henry Bouquet in the Ohio country seemed mad with grief at the prospect of coming "home" to the settlements and tried to run away again, it was assumed they must "have been of the lowest rank, ... bred up in ignorance and distressing penury." Being like Indians was a specialty of the lower sort.[53]

But a rising way of talking about Indians and "white people" had less to do with class than with individual actions. Here personal loyalties did most to determine what kind of human you became: choices you made, instead of choices already made for you. Not only environmentally caused "habits of the body" but people's allegiances, too—as with Gershom Hicks's loyalty to the Delawares—were at the heart of what we now imagine as racial sorting.

In accounts of Indian-European differences during the 1750s and 1760s, whether bitterly polemic or filled with wonder, these two explanations slowly peeled apart and started to oppose each other. What made "white people" and loyal subjects now was not where they lived, or whether they hunted for a living, or worked outdoors, or drank too much, or kept clean or went hungry or owned their own farms. It was whether they had suffered alongside other Europeans at Indians' hands. "The white people" was not a straightforwardly racial group, and that was why it began to matter politically, at least a little: because you could leave it, or be drummed out of it.

Since the best proof of loyalty to the "white people" was to have been abused by Indians, arguments over Indian war imbued those who had undergone attacks with great authority. Shortly after Gershom Hicks's interrogation at Fort Pitt another Indian-dressed settler, James Bell, turned up with his own tale of escape. Referred to simply as "the Indian Spy," Bell posed the same puzzle Hicks had. In the end, his identity as an enemy of Indians was settled to the garrison's satisfaction not by anything he could tell them but by what they found out about his family's sufferings. A letter from the J.P. in Bell's home township laid out matter-of-factly the reasons for belief in him:

> His father was killed at the Same time [he was taken prisoner] & one of his unkels & his Cusen a while Before . . . His Brothers & Cusens Has Been Several Times out with me I[n] Pershute of the Indians & are well Known to be Loyal Subjects . . . .

So Bell could come home, and try to become again what he said he had always wanted to be: an ordinary European person.⁵⁴

"THE WHITE PEOPLE" were Indians' paired opposites, and what they had in common was an aggrieved sense of victimization. Shared suffering dictated that when mid-Atlantic Europeans showed the corpses of war dead, they would parade with the bodies of their own and not their enemies. "The white people" could also have been called something like *the suffering European inhabitants of the colonies*—or, as the title of one of 1764's most important pamphlets would in fact make it, *"the distressed and bleeding Frontier Inhabitants Of the Province"* of Pennsylvania.⁵⁵

This would be the basis for the middle colonies' first mass political nation. Like most working nations, the community glimpsed during these decades was not really a logical structure. Though it was jerked into motion by something that could be called "white people's nationalism," the patriotic new politics of the war pointedly shoved many Europeans—including Quakers—out of the charmed circle. Exclusion was essential. What lent passion to the testing of loyalties, and to the cinching up of new coalitions, was the idea that some people within the provincial surround were in sympathy or secret collusion with outside attackers. This stress on submerged sympathies—on the betrayal of the white people's common interest before a looming Indian front—gave public life much of its drama and power in the popular mind.

This perspective turned the world topsy-turvy. By its reckoning, some of the most prominent people in the provinces had crossed over into the Indians' territory of treacherousness, while some of the most obscure stood revealed as downtrodden but praiseworthy subjects. In the hands of polemicists, a new cast of characters would emerge: the humble, much put-upon people of the countryside, including its squatters—"the poor People," who had until now been so easy to dismiss as thoughtless, shiftless, and stupidly provocative; as too much like Indians to get along with them; or as being beaten by a rod they had perversely made for themselves (since Indian attacks were "their own fault" for pressing onto unbought lands).[56]

A sensational series of anti-Indian and anti-Quaker riots was to break like a storm in the winter of 1763–64. Their aftermath drove home a new and far more flattering view of dwellers in the back counties. These events showed how few just claims some country people—and nearly all their urban defenders, who imagined a furious populace, knitted together with indignation—had started to think that Indians or their supposed European sympathizers could make on the scorned and suffering white people. The reasons for the violence lay deep in the nature of intercultural relations in the countryside, a countryside that had come alive with fear.

Chapter 5

ATTACKING
INDIANS

On a lovely August day in 1889, the people of Milford, Pennsylvania—a small town perched on a bluff of the Delaware—woke to a cannon blast. Its boom "swept like thunder through the valleys," and it marked the opening of a festival: what posters plastered across the town proclaimed to be "an Historic Occasion!" That afternoon, after patriotic singing, oratory, and marching, while a brass band and the cannon's "frequent roar exhilarated the surging crowd," a stubby zinc monument was unveiled to the memory of a colonist named Tom Quick. The inscriptions girdling its base made it clear that Quick—"THE AVENGER OF THE DELAWARE"—had been a man with a burning mission. "MADDENED BY THE DEATH OF HIS FATHER AT THE HANDS OF THE SAVAGES" in the Seven Years' War, "TOM QUICK NEVER ABATED HIS HOSTILITY TO THEM TILL THE DAY OF HIS DEATH, A PERIOD OF OVER FORTY YEARS." Milford's obelisk celebrated his role as a founder of the township—and as a famous "INDIAN SLAYER." Quick was the ultimate Indian-hater.

Since the late eighteenth century, a brisk local current of storytelling had been in place, with old men ready to elaborate, when prodded, on Quick's lifelong project of killing. In most accounts, he killed ninety-nine before dying of smallpox, when, to his posthumous satisfaction, Indians dug up his infected corpse and started an epidemic. "Like the Wandering Jew," Victorian readers learned, Quick was ever roving—and ever killing. Travelers on the railroad that wound down the Delaware gorge could even read about him in their official guides while they looked out at the picturesque places where he might have hidden.[1]

Even at this monument's unveiling, some scorned the Avenger, while others were happy to fête him. But what few considered was that this grim celebrity's career might be almost wholly invented. Though Quick was probably not a lifelong serial murderer (he verifiably killed one man), the stories of Indian-killing that he plainly told rang true for his contemporaries, who were convinced that people who saw their family members die in Indian attacks formed wild, unstoppable urges to kill. In 1758, Gov. Francis Bernard urged all Indian envoys coming into New Jersey to do so below the forks of the Delaware, "because," he felt, "the People above who have lost their Friends and Relations are so inflamed, as to render it unsafe . . . to enter this Colony above Trenton."[2]

In 1755, Tom Quick's father had unwisely gone back to the family mill in the Minisinks, a little north of the forks of the Delaware, to do some milling for his neighbors a few weeks after an Indian attack. He and some soldiers were found "scalped, stripped naked, and most cruelly cut in many Places." After his father's death, Tom Quick turned up in the contemporary record only once. In fall 1761, a magistrate was writing down news "heard amongst the people" over the Blue Mountains. There were rumors that war with the Delawares would soon resume, or already had, with one family twice being warned by Indians "to be gone from their place," as well as cattle killed, Indian dogs set on European sheep—and a barn inadvertently set alight by a quarreling Delaware couple, with the plume of smoke, as always, setting off a panic. In the Minisinks, many residents were too frightened to go to their farms, with "the people on Pensylvania Side . . . much more in fear then the People in the Jarsey's, . . . [being] Under Strong Apprehention the Indians will fall upon them." Much of their dread was over "the Death of the Indian [named] Maudlin, Killd on the Jarsey Side by one Quick (as the Messenger heard)." For the Quicks' farm was on the Pennsylvania side, in Upper Smithfield, and that was where retaliation could be expected to fall.[3]

In the least embellished account of Maudlin's death—after which "a hundred Persons or upwards . . . d[id]nt care to return" to their homes in Smithfield—he and Quick were at a tavern together, almost certainly drinking and talking threateningly to each other. When they left, Quick shot Maudlin in the back, ransacked his body, and hid it in the pit ripped out by the roots of a fallen tree.

In following Maudlin from a tavern, sniping at him, rummaging through his pockets, and hiding his body, Quick acted less like the popular idea of someone with a grief-maddened thirst for vengeance than a garden-variety felony murderer. Nor did Maudlin act as one might expect. He was described in the earliest oral tradition as taunting Quick with having been in the party that killed his father, and "mimick[ing] the grimaces of the dying man" to him. But these unlikely sounding details closely match other accounts of drunken interwar socializing between natives and Europeans, while what made Quick most like other Europeans who actually killed an Indian was his surreptitious opportunism.[4]

It was Governor Bernard's sense that most intercultural violence came from obsessive Indian-haters, men left with no peace by their family members' deaths. Like Bernard, we may still instinctively expect to find behind anti-Indian violence a special class of people, pricked on to acts of boundless malice by their belief in Indian savagery and inferiority. The idea of this animus—described by one Pennsylvania governor as the anti-Indian "Ardour of the People," a drive lying deeper than reason—grew stronger and clearer in political rhetoric and literature, together with an image of the passionate Indian-haters who felt it, from the eighteenth century through the nineteenth, when they reached their most elaborate flowering.

But to understand how Indian-European brawling and killing really came about, the least glamorous elements of Quick's milieu—the bullying talk and visits, the raw panic in rural neighborhoods at the prospect of attack, the everyday episodes of drinking and conviviality, the blusterous stories about earlier acts of violence, the potshots and furtive pillaging—all turn out to be far more useful than the impression of a countryside filled with vendettists. Before the 1780s, killing Indians was usually an opportunistic business with little connection to the discourses that sprang up to dignify and decry it. Most other anti-Indian activity unfolded in accord with a fascinating shared grammar of face-to-face intimidation, as Europeans and Indians worked to instill fears and counterfears in one another.[5]

* * *

THE MIXED-UP COMPLEXITY of interests behind most anti-Indian acts was shown surprisingly well in one of the eighteenth century's strangest and least appreciated works: *Ponteach, or The Savages of America* (1766), a play by the self-promoting Indian fighter Maj. Robert Rogers. Rogers saw himself as an unmatched professional among Indian-hands, and his scorn for other Europeans' capacity to contend with Indians made his effort a usefully skeptical, unprettified source. Though the play included much stunning stage violence, its harsh picture of the killing and robbery of two Indians was of most interest. This scene, wooden as it was, distilled something true from Rogers's own experience.

Two European hunters named Orsbourn and Honnyman wandered into view. Luckless in the hunt, grumbling over a scarcity of deer and unfair Indian competition, they started to complain about Indians in general and to wish it were legal to "hunt" them. Here the two men, trading speeches, laid out overlapping reasons for the murders the audience would see them commit as soon as two Indians appeared in the wings. Indians were not Christians; and their actions in the recent fighting meant they "deserve[d] no Mercy" after it. Above all, both said, because they had lost relations in the war they had a sudden, overmastering response (which the audience would have seen as ironically "savage") to seeing or even thinking about Indians. "Cursed revengeful, cruel, faithless Devils!" Honnyman observed:

> They kill'd my Father and my eldest Brother.
> Since which I hate their very Looks and Name.
>
> *Orsbourn.*
> And I, since they betray'd and kill'd my Uncle; . . .
> . . . . 'twould ease my Heart
> To cleave their painted Heads, and spill their Blood.

Orsbourn loudly spoke of "eat[ing] an Indian's Heart with Pleasure," while Honnyman agreed: "I'd join you, and soop his savage Brains for Sauce; / I lose all Patience when I think of them." And when two unfortunate Indians appeared, the Europeans (who had just been vowing to "pop . . . down . . . the first [Indians] we meet well fraught with Furs") hid themselves; shot them dead; seized their fur packs; hid them in the bushes; took their rifles and hatchets; and scalped them.[6]

But throughout all of this Rogers could not help undercutting Orsbourn and Honnyman's high-flown account of their feelings, by letting his audience see that they had another motive besides past trauma—namely greed—for what they did. For as the killers chucklingly observed over the corpses, their victims' furs were a fantastic windfall. In minutes they had made a full autumn's take their own. The hunters' frustrated itch for profit was shown as leading them to seize not only the "lawful Prize" of the Indians' rifles but their scalps as well, almost as an afterthought. (As Honnyman offhandedly noted, if there was another war, "their Scalps will sell for ready Cash, / Two Hundred Crowns at least, and that's worth saving.")[7]

These many, thorough forms of theft ended by making the scene seem more felony homicide than crime passionnel. Indeed, since Orsbourn and Honnyman discussed mugging Indians if they came across too many to kill (in which case they would "ease the Rascals of their Packs" at gunpoint), these characters' basic aim was not Indian-killing, but Indian-robbing. And yet, because hovering over everything they did was the audience's awareness, and their own, that they had seen relations killed by Indians, it was impossible to tell a simple story about what they did. Whatever predisposition toward anti-Indian violence their pasts had given them coincided perfectly with their material interest.

In this, Rogers told an accurate story, since the motives for anti-Indian violence so seldom came singly. More than any other one thing, fear underlay Europeans' reactions to Indian attack. Hate had a place in motivating violence, too, especially in the shape of an urge for retaliation among some of the people whose family members died at Indian hands. But often even in these cases it would take the prospect of profit to tip animus into killing.[8]

ONE WHOLESALE EXCEPTION to everything I have just said came in the form of soldiers during wartime, whose attacks and threats against neutral Indians were the commonest, if least surprising, sort of anti-

Indian violence. Their main reason for lashing out at allied and neutral Indians was interpretive fatigue. Garrisons spent more time dreading attack than undergoing it, and before the Revolution large numbers of Indians were often found close to forts, trading furs, negotiating, and supplying venison. In winter 1758, Capt. Joseph Shippen kept a tally of the Delawares living at Fort Augusta. In mid-January 1758, he made their number 33; ten days later, 43; and by mid-February, a full 62. As all this counting shows, although it was common to have Indians around, soldiers never stopped noticing their presence.

And operating in a sea of uncertainly aligned natives produced in many men, including Shippen, a draining state of constant wariness. Shippen became convinced that one of the Delawares at his fort was really a spy when he "disswaded" some young Indians from going out to strike at the French (their agreements with Pennsylvania did not require active warfare). Shippen's unprovable "Suspicion that [the man] intended to decoy . . . our Soldiers over the River, in order to get their Scalps" led him to have scouting parties sneak about outside the fort in elaborate, vain attempts to catch him consorting with French-allied Indians.9

But some soldiers who felt the same uneasiness showed less caution. Many plainly felt that it took an endless effort to tell which Indians were heartily on their side and which were not, a "problem" made more frustrating by their almost never seeing those Indians who attacked them. ("[In] all Likelihood," as one officer observed after a summer in the woods, "we may be upon the same [errand ti]ll the last trumpet sound wt out finding One Indian.") Some decided to end their suspense by seeing it as impossible to draw distinctions between Indians.10

With so many allied and neutral Indians about, this was not a commonsensical choice but an expression of soldiers' unhappiness at their uncertainty-filled intermixture with Indians. Often it led to attacks on those natives whose help they needed most, as with the Forty-fourth Regiment's treatment of "The Indian Jerry" near Schenectady, who "was killed last Night, and his Head found this morning Stuck upon a Pole in the Camp. . . . some say it was done by Officers, some by Soldiers"; or the case of the Indian man at Fort Pitt who, in the wake of a scalping nearby, "being charged with the fact by one of the Soldiers was without more ado run through with a Bayonet!"11

Soldiers' outbursts centered on the idea of enemies masquerading, with maddening success, as friends. Near Bethlehem in 1758, the provincial Capt. Samuel Neilson cursed Teedyuscung—the eastern Delaware leader then helping Pennsylvania to negotiate with the Ohio Indians— and "declared that if he met Teedyuscung or any of his People . . . let them come on what Occasion or with what Pretence soever, he would kill them without asking Questions." Neilson also talked as if he would march his men against the Wyoming Valley, where Teedyuscung's people had just been promised a little homeland, with houses built for them by European carpenters at the province's cost, and said "he wished that the Indians had scalped but not killed all those who went up [to a recent Easton treaty] that thereby they and others might be convinced we had no friends among the Indians."

Neilson's rodomontade (which did not really lead to any killing) was one in a series of demonstrations against the presence of neutral Indians that soldiers acted out during the midcentury wars. In the simplest protests, soldiers shouted—like the sergeant who was jailed when, after looking over two Conestogas being escorted on provincial business, he suddenly screamed that "they had Fought against Capt. Jamison's Party Last Winter, for he knew them by their Tassells and if he should meet them in the woods . . . would shoot them as soon as any Enemy Whatever taking his Gun into his hand at the same time." (This, it was reported, predictably "so intemidated them that they did not think it safe to Pursue their Journey and said they would return home.")[12] Other protests were more sustained, like Cpl. Christian Weyrick's extraordinary crack-up at Fort Allen in 1756. When Weyrick wanted to "drive [Teedyuscung and two Indian women] out of the Fort" but was stopped by an officer, he went on a screaming rampage. He attacked the lieutenant and other onlookers and "took a Gun and drove about . . . like a Beast and not like a Man," brandishing swords and muskets, pitching fireplace stones through windows, and "behav[ing] so violently that [the Indians] were forced to leave" for a lean-to "a Good Distance of the fort." In the wake of this, the commanding officer wrote, "I am Resolved to let no more of them into [it]."[13]

The provincial and regular armies produced not only such protests but many of the worst atrocities against nonhostile Indians—as well as the most scorching anti-Indian talk, in some cases nearly genocidal, to be committed to paper. During the Seven Years' War, it became an official policy to kill Indian prisoners, whom in time many officers simply called "those Vermine." As the colonel of the Royal American Regiment ordered at Loyalhanna, Pennsylvania, in 1758, if while on patrol the Royal Americans found an enemy party, "they must attack without counting and aim at a Prisoner if there is white People"; "But for Indians Let them all be knoked on the head." It has become well known that the garrison at Fort Pitt presented blankets and a handkerchief from their smallpox hospital to some Delaware envoys, as a captain wrote, "out of our Regard to them . . . . I hope it will have the desired effect." By the summer of 1763, army officers speculated freely about using not only smallpox but hunting dogs "to tear them to pieces," as well as "Every other Method that can serve to Extirpate this Execrable Race" of Indians. At a minimum, as Gen. Sir Jeffery Amherst directed Bouquet with unnecessary strictness, "I Wish to Hear of *no Prisoners.*"14

When Bouquet marched an unopposed expedition toward the Ohio towns in 1764, Col. John Reid wrote from Fort Pitt to voice what he saw as the sense of the army. It was maddening that Bouquet's march might end uneventfully, with a peace. "Should these Brutes, who distinguish themselves by the Names of Wolf, Fox &ca. (beasts of prey)," Reid shrilly asked, "be still indulged with the liberty of calling Britains their Brothers?"

> [O]ught they not on the contrary to be . . . taught to know the deference due to a People who have it in their Power to reduce them to the most abject State of Slavery, or to raze them from the face of the Earth.

The better to punish them, Reid had a proposition: let him undermine any chance of an end to the fighting with an atrocity.

> [M]ight we not, before we have intelligence of a Peace being concluded with them, send a Party from this Garison to their nearest Town . . . and cutt them off? Ensign Hutchins who knows the Country thinks it very practicable, and that it might be done with safety, there being only about Twenty Wariors, and not nearer than Twenty Miles to any other

Town. This might have another Effect, that of preventing the ratification of a Peace, from it's nature, odius to almost every man under Your
Command.[15]

Such punitive, even animalizing talk among soldiers anticipated a way
of discussing Indians that first became truly widespread after the Revolution. Before the 1780s, there were vanishingly few records of Indians'
being compared to animals in civilian life. As critics of African slavery
sensed, it was when Europeans talked as if they thought another kind of
people to be more animal than human—as Reid was starting to do—that
their actions became most vicious and, in modern terms, most racist.[16]

So such regular-army attitudes were noteworthy, though given the
nasty rhetorics that early armies spun off for most of their enemies—
whatever their color or nation—it might have been more surprising if no
soldiers thought or talked like Reid. (The French were long the subjects
of an English-speaking military discourse that came very close, in its
stress on cruelty and perfidiousness, to the discourse on Indians: in fact,
"take the Indians with all their faults," as Capt. James Stevenson of the
Sixtieth Regiment noted in 1770, "& I give them infinitely the preference
to the Rascally Race of French.") Reid's comments suggested the power
of woodlands war, and its frustrations—not the least of which, at the
close of Pontiac's War, was the elusiveness of conclusive-seeming victories—to darken armies' views of the Indians they were trying to fight. In
peace, or toward Indians they could not believably see as veiled enemies,
most soldiers' anti-Indianism was more muted.[17]

THE SECOND, LESS important exception—another group of people
who sometimes really did want to kill any Indians they could—was the
relations of the dead. This category swelled up unwarrantably in contemporaries' minds, but though there were never many revenge killers about,
they did exist.[18]

One true story of passionate, openly attempted revenge can be pieced
together because of the rare Ulster surname (Mitcheltree) of the family
at its heart. In February 1756, a soldier at Patterson's Fort, a stockaded
house near the Susquehanna, ended a litany of people killed in a recent

Delaware raid with a special bulletin: "Just now a Man came to the Fort and informs us of the Death of Hugh Micheltrees Wife." The next week, a nearby missionary reported that "Hugh Micheltree . . . [was now himself] dead & scalp'd, with many Children." And in March another surviving male "Metcheltree, [was] taken . . . within sight of Patterson's fort"; this Mitcheltree was close enough that he frantically "call'd to the Garrison, told them the Indians were but six in number, and desired to be rescued, but [as] none went, he was carry'd off."

And so it was, a dozen years later, that the Delaware headman Killbuck, "homwards Bound" through the Susquehanna towns from a treaty at Fort Stanwix, New York, suddenly found himself being "pursued a consederable distance By Jno: Mitcheltree who with a Gunn presented," as Killbuck complained, "attempted to shoot me." Mitcheltree flatly declared to the local J.P. his intention of "putting [Killbuck] to Death, whenever it shall be in his Power"—a resolve that certainly owed much to the killing or capture by Indians of so many members of his family in this neighborhood thirteen years before.

After Mitcheltree's sincere effort at assassination—which had, provincial officials felt, "so dangerous a Tendency to involve the whole Contry in an Indian War, that they think it is absolutely incumbent . . . to take strict Notice of such alarming Villainy"—he had to put up a £400 bond guaranteeing indefinite good behavior. In any event, "my life was preserved," Killbuck believed, only "by the Help of God & . . . means of my speed in run:g."[19]

THERE WERE never many Mitcheltrees about. The bulk of anti-Indian acts arose less from vendetta-like ferocity than from fear, and they unfolded in almost scripted ways. Ordinary people in the countryside were often described as berating Indians, and apparently coming within an ace of trying to kill them—just before being found out, or dissuaded, or held back. In March 1756, an Indian man walking alone near the Admiral Warren, a noted highwayside tavern and inn only twenty miles from Philadelphia, reported having "very narrowly escaped with his Life from a Number of Men who assembled together on the Road . . . and were with Difficulty restrained." But despite the volume of such homicidal harassment, over time it practically never led to deaths, or even bloodshed.[20]

When they had a chance, "the lower Class of People" would sometimes "take advantage of the Indians" at treaties by crowding around to "curse, swear and rail at them & endeavour to incense them against us, within their hearing which appears to be very offensive to them." In a 1756 conference at Easton, Israel Pemberton vividly described how "divers of the Jersey People behaved with great Imprudence . . . appearing Outrageous" after a dinner, presumably by shouting and threatening from a little distance away, "now they think they could without Danger to themselves."

That same evening, the Delawares who had come to the treaty with Teedyuscung started trickling worriedly away. And indeed for several nights, from the loud "Imprudence of the People there was so much Cause to apprehend Mischief" that the governor had the Indians' lodgings and the river boats guarded "to prevent People coming from the Jerseys, as they . . . threatned." When a peddler tried to interest the soldiers in taking his "Knives, and to join . . . in cutting the Throats of the Indians, himself engaging to destroy the King"—Teedyuscung—he was thrown into the borough jail.

But all of this had a predictable effect. It made the authorities unhappy about asking Indian delegations to Easton again. The town was geographically too convenient to give up, but the next year Governor Denny was worriedly trying to shunt toward Bethlehem any Indians who might wait around Easton before the opening of a new conference: "They know," he wrote, "the Disposition of the Jersey People towards them." But most Indians would need no urging to avoid places where they had been threatened, since that was the whole point of the threatening.[21]

Before the war, some strangers who needed to nose around the countryside had thought it "absolutely necessary to bring 3 or 4 Indians along" to avoid "being Stopt by the Irish with guns." But with war underway, things were inverted: many Indians, including crucial allies, now felt that for their own protection they had to travel with Europeans.[22]

In February 1756, the Iroquois representative John Shickellamy had to "declar[e] positively" that even with a guard for a trip to Philadelphia, he and his wife "would not go thro' Tulpyhoccon, being apprehensive that the Dutch would fall upon them, and either kill them or do them a Mischief." He had already fled Harris's Ferry because "the Irish People . . . threatned to kill him." He had had enough of being terrorized by "the fearful ignorant people," who "Sometimes told [him] to his face, that they had a good mind to Scalp him," and in the end he did not dare go out for fear. As the half-king Scarouady summed things up, "At present your People . . . think every Indian is against them; they blame us all without Distinction, because they see nobody appear for them; the common People to a Man entertain this notion, and insult us wherever we go."[23]

The cases of threatening were not all near-misses at murder. They were meant not to provide fair warning of imminent attacks but to bully and posture. Intimidation offers real pleasures, so some people surely found it "very Agreable and Cherefull . . . [to be able to tell a] Storrie of bulleing y Indians." But the central aim of "ill Language . . . from the meaner Sort of our People" was venting, and transferring fear, amid the precarious setting of rural war: like some of the railing that they "had a good mind to Scalp him," directed at John Shickellamy. The obvious goal was to get the Indians who were being threatened to go away, taking with them Europeans' ache of fear.[24]

The self-discovering plots against travelers; the peddler at Easton, undoing his glinting knives; the cries of bravos that (as some shouted when a Conoy couple and a Mahican left Lancaster) "these Indians deserved to have their brains dashed out; and they Should not Scruple to . . . if they Should meet them on the Road": such bullying expressed a deep desire—one potentially but not immediately violent—to get the Indians who were its audience out.[25]

Most diatribes played out in the amphitheater of the highway, down which many men and women who took part in roadside anti-Indianism plainly meant to propel Indians until they were "quite clear of the Inhabitants." Instilling a counterfear in Indians before as many other people as possible felt good to these "fearful ignorant people," and it nearly always worked. Neutral Indians and messengers moved away or traveled in fear, sometimes hidden in the backs of quick-moving wagons.[26]

Threats moved closer to action when groups of men paid loud visits to Indians they wanted gone. (Although, just as most killers did not shoot Indians in the middle of the highway, really lethal visits seem to have been unheralded.) In 1756, after such a group terrified Iroquois delegates at Harris's Ferry—who "made off privately"—Pennsylvania stopped holding conferences there and relocated Indians in the neighborhood to what seemed the safety of Conestoga Manor, a little reservation in settled farmland thirty miles farther to the south, and "deeper within the Inhabitants."[27]

SOMETIMES THREATENING VISITS by armed men went on for so long and at such a high pitch without violence that it seems fair to say they became a wartime institution. Europeans already thought of Indians as experts at producing fear through menacing visits. Often Indians' stopovers at farmhouses led to complaints from frightened or unwilling hosts, who resented more than the expense (which could be considerable). The visitors they complained of most were ones who said frightening things about war: like the Indian man being entertained at a farm in Sussex County, New Jersey, who "threaten'd the owner of the house to burn it, & assured him that an Indian War would soon break out."[28]

Europeans had a theory of what such "insolent" visits meant. Indians "before they come to actual Hostilities" would telegraph their wish for war by "behav[ing] surly and saucily," one Pennsylvanian warned in 1755. They

> come into [colonists'] Houses and insult the Families and . . . peremptorily demand victuals or any thing they have a mind for and . . . perhaps draw their Knives or present their Guns at you to terrify you . . . telling the land is theirs & you shall remove away with all kind of brutish Menacings . . . .[29]

Europeans' menacings needed less interpretation, perhaps because their own visits were nearly always made in groups. After soldiers killed a traveling Indian family in the Blue Hills in 1763, the nearby Moravian mission town of Wechquetank underwent a gale of European visits. With their neighbors frightened that the deaths would bring about a revenge raid, it seemed a good idea to several companies of volunteers from over the hills to show up every few days and try to browbeat Wechquetank's residents into going away. They came "mean[ing] to fight with our Indians," as the missionary, Bernhard Adam Grube, recorded, "since [they] suspected that our Indians already knew" about the killing, and so would not feel the crisis was over until all the Indians had left.

For weeks throughout September and early October 1763, a collective slaughter seemed to Grube always about to break out. One Irish militia company's threats were typical: they "were very exasperated against our Indians," Grube wrote after a visit, threatening to shoot anyone they found walking in the woods, "and said . . . if even one man was to be killed on this side of the Lehigh the whole Irish Settlement would . . . fall upon us and kill us." On September 22, another company came and flatly "told the Indians that they should leave the town, or they should be killed in one weeks time." But this deadline came and went.³⁰

The most terrifying visits came after an Indian attack finally did occur (in part, as feared, as retaliation). One group promised "they would fall upon us in the Night & kill us all," and the same night still more came "with the intention of killing our Indians, they were very enraged and charged our Indians with committing the murder in the settlement." But somehow the missionary and his wife were able to put them off, remonstrating "that this was impossible . . . . I really had to fight for my poor people or else the Irish would certainly have revenged themselves on these poor innocent people. At last they were a little appeased when I gave them something to eat from my little supply."³¹

Certain he had just staved off an atrocity, Grube at once oversaw the town's evacuation, loading all his congregants into wagons to start on a miserable quest for safety that would carry them to a dysentery-ridden royal barracks four blocks from downtown Philadelphia. They were gone from Wechquetank, and they would not be back.

During the War of 1812, a similar series of visits was made to the mission settlement of Goshen, Ohio. (Goshen was one of several Moravian towns on the Muskingum River that helped to make the eastern Ohio country the site of a fascinating, if flatter, rerun of many rural activities and problems that had taken shape in the mid-Atlantic during previous decades—sometimes even with the same people.) The Goshen missionary, Rev. Benjamin Mortimer, recorded month after month of threatening visits. There were many tense times: once a single gunshot at dusk was enough to send three hundred nearby Americans "fle[eing] during the night." Militia musters, and routed American soldiers passing down the road before the mission, were a continual source of trouble. Some of the soldiers (who "came along as beggars") "spoke loudly," Mortimer said, "that they would kill every Indian here, and take their horses to ride home on." People in the neighboring forty-house hamlet of New Philadelphia, Mortimer reported, had "said plainly, that every Indian here must be killed"; others made "a threat very seriously repeated, that a number of persons . . . were privately deliberating about coming to burn our town." Naturally Goshen's residents were "not a little terrified," and some spoke of evacuating.[32]

Mortimer knew that the townspeople's threatening might echo and grow until it either tipped into action or so frightened his charges, and his family (Mortimer's wife was "several times" actually sick with fear), that they had to leave. Determined to defeat the "endeavor to frighten us away," the missionary some days spent "most of his time on the street, conversing with & endeavoring to pacify these people as to our Indians." He made it known that he had hired spies to monitor the talk at "vendues, taverns, and other places of public resort," so as to make the neighbors "more cautious . . . in their expressions." These spies—as well as local officials to whom Mortimer continually sent messages—rode over to Goshen any time an armed visit seemed likely to prove frightening. The result, as he proudly noted at the end of one intimidating string of "conversation" and threats, was that "A general surprize appeared to be excited" in New Philadelphia "that we did not, out of fright, leave the country.—"[33]

But Mortimer was an exceptionally observant man, and he soon hit on a way to stop the visits and threats altogether—by adeptly reversing their source, which was the New Philadelphians' nearly craven fear of Indian attack. Everyone could feel the townspeople's fear: it made a steady, humming presence, like an electromagnetic field almost strong enough to strum. Even some of the townspeople themselves found it irresistible to play with. One night when a band of neighbors left Goshen, they started firing their muskets into the air, so as to "frighten," they said, the tensely listening "women in New Philadelphia, and make them think that murderous work was going forward." (This entertainment succeeded in driving one of the town's families into hiding in the woods until dawn.)[34]

But beside such crude improvisations, Mortimer proved a virtuoso of fear. In mid-September, there were Indian attacks very near by, and Mortimer reached the point at which Grube had been on the night of Wechquetank's evacuation, almost half a century before. Threats against the mission Indians were peaking, and it seemed they would have to leave their houses behind, perhaps to be looted. Mortimer had started getting ready for exile when he had an idea. Since he doubted plans for their murder had really been made, he decided to try a new approach. He would do some threatening of his own, carefully writing out a devastating advertisement for general circulation to the county's citizens. As it appeared on handbills and in newspapers, its "effect," Mortimer proudly noted, "every where answered our utmost wishes. . . . Truly a fear from God accompanied it."35

If the Goshenites were driven away by their neighbors' threatening treatment—let alone if those neighbors moved in to sack the mission—what, Mortimer's advertisement wondered, would the British-allied Indians attacking Ohio think? Would they stay away? Or would they fall with special, vengeful fury on New Philadelphia and "beg[i]n to commit murders in that neighborhood," which had so far been peaceful? "[I]t is feared by many," as Mortimer politely wrote, that "you . . . [will] be in great danger of suffering from other Indians," and what a pity that would be. An evacuation could be the start of the story, not its end: whether or not the Europeans liked it, they and the Indians were each other's hostages.36

And within one week of this gambit, the tide, Mortimer saw with delight, had turned perceptibly, with nearly everyone "by this time well disposed towards us." The threats and visits stopped. The one group visit that Mortimer really feared that fall—it included soldiers with dead relations, and he had heard nothing about it in advance—was slowed and turned back, in part, by a local man's "sharply" saying to its members that they should not "com[e] so far to interfere . . . in Goshen, when *every sensible man in this neighborhood* . . . accounted [the mission's Indians] the very best safety that the country had."37

Moravian Indians always made resistant targets for intimidation, with their large numbers, oversight by other Europeans, and celebration of suffering—even martyrdom—over flight. The reaction of one congregant to the endless menacing he faced at Wechquetank in fall 1763 seems to have been an ideal: Grube proudly reported his saying that "if it should happen that white people want to kill us, I will not defend myself at all." And by the end of this period, Moravian villages would be still more willing to ride out European threatening, having painfully learned to navigate the torrents of anti-Indian visiting that military defeat and the specter of attack could unleash. The trick was to make neighbors more afraid of having them go than stay.[38]

Behind many rural threats against Indians lay a wish to instill fear in Indian neighbors—imagined as a kind of counterfear, one equal and opposed to the boundless terrors that nearby Europeans felt. The idea was to drain the threat from a local surround by frightening Indians into moving away, as Europeans so unstoppably did whenever they heard news of war. If this terrorizing failed, it was simply because, as at Goshen, the currents of fear had been rerouted to arrive at a different result.

OFTEN INDIAN and European men narrated flatly for one another the violent things they had done in previous wars or expected to do in ones to come. Simple talking, often mixed with drinking, was one of the commonest forms of intercultural threatening. So it was that around Goshen an Indian named Kaschates "used . . . to relate to the white people very circumstantially, what murders he had committed among them during the last Indian war, & what excessive cruelties he either has—or pretends to have been—guilty of"; while another "spen[t] much of his time in going from place to place to hear & tell news. . . . occasionally t[e]l[ling] . . . the white people what acts of cruelty he had committed among them during the last Indian war (. . . altogether probably his own fabrications)." In the 1760s, the Indian Joshua James boasted unnervingly to a Lancaster County listener "that he never killed a white Man in his Life; but *six Dutchmen* that he killed in the *Minisinks.*" Europeans, too, could be found ominously "glorying in their former bloody exploits" before Indians.[39]

If the level of excitement around such war stories rose, narration could turn to confrontation. When bluster became most pointed, certain lines cropped up regularly, as if scripted. After prefatory "whooping, Yelling, and Swearing," someone might go on to make you feel that he really, truly meant to kill you by "sw[ea]r[ing] Blodily that he would Shoot [you] through the Heart"; or by declaring that after whipping you with an ax handle he would "cut [you] to Pieces, and make a Breakfast of [your] Heart."⁴⁰ It is striking how seldom Europeans seem to have moved on in the same gestural breath from such posturing to deadly violence, instead letting fly with even more vivid promises of what was just about to happen. But Europeans may have been more used than Indians to talking trash without result. One Lake Superior trader, killed by his Chippewa drinking partner, evidently was. In the middle of a quarrel, the trader petulantly hung his head in the distinctive posture used by Indians waiting for a death blow, and "dar[ed the other man] to kill him, which the Indn."—to his everlasting surprise—"readily complied with."⁴¹

Liquor was the lubricant for threatening talk. Both Europeans and Indians enjoyed the fear they could stir in other people while intoxicated and seemingly capable of anything—"taking pleasure," as an early Jesuit observed, "in seeing themselves dreaded." There were rules and norms even of stupefaction, and many Indians saw complete drunkenness as a hugely desirable state to be striven after. It offered not only an opening for nearly consequence-free violence—it was axiomatic that the liquor, not its drinker, bore the blame—but a license to let out resentments. In 1762, an Indian man "came here Drunk early in the Morning," the lieutenant in charge of Fort Augusta reported, to dress him down for not buying a certain deerskin, "and was very abusive, Offering several times to Strike me, . . . Boasting at the same time of what he had done during the War & Could yet do." While drunk it may have been more or less "Usual" for Indians to tell you, as Sir William Johnson described for English correspondents in a 1767 survey, *that [you] are Cowards, that they will put [you] to death, that they are the Lords of the Ground they live upon &ca.* That *"&ca."* suggested how much inebriated death threats seemed to him an Indian-European institution, about which soldiers and traders would need to be knowledgeable.⁴²

Liquor was often flowing, too, when Europeans told Indians frightening stories or actually attacked them. European killers might have drunk with their own victims, since inebriation could be not only a disinhibiting mechanism in anti-Indian violence but a tactic. Worried officials' belief that "if the Indians are suffered to . . . get Drunk, they will be in danger of their Lives" was grounded in experience. Many of the Indians who died at European hands were assassinated while drunk, or even sleeping in a stupor. "On all occasions, when the object is to murder Indians," the Moravian missionary-historian John Heckewelder wrote bitterly, "strong liquor is the main article required; for when you have them dead drunk, you may do to them as you please."43

THE MOST PERILOUS TALK came when Europeans accused Indians of having taken part in killing other Europeans. Such speech did not need to sound dramatic, for it drew a clear frame—the frame of retaliation— around anything that followed. The importance of tracking all these conversational gradations was shown by an encounter in 1756 between three Delawares and Johannes Vannetten, a captain in Pennsylvania's provincial forces, halfway up and halfway down a hillside. Vannetten and his men had gone into the countryside to guard harvesters. Calling to one another as they fanned into a field, they were surprised to be "Hollowed" at from the shoulder of the mountain, by an Indian asking for Vannetten.44

"Come you to us," the voice said, and when Vannetten climbed a little up the mountain, then stopped, a conversational standoff followed, with each man trying to slow things down and decipher the other's intentions. Vannetten wrote their words out later, so the verbal minuet (in which neither man spoke his first language) can be written as a script:

DELAWARE MAN. "[Are you] alone"?
VANNETTEN. "Yes" (*"ma[king] a sign for Sergeant Cole and the Company To Stay Back"*). "Come to [me]."
DELAWARE MAN (*perhaps shaking his head*). "Come you more up the mountain."

Vannetten wanted to talk all of the Indians down into the farmhouse: there he could decide whether they were friends. The Delaware wanted to coax Vannetten uphill for the same reason. A balance of invitation and threat underlay all their words. Seeing only two other Delawares, Vannetten edged higher.

"[T]hey me[e]t and Sh[a]k[e] Hands Together."
VANNETTEN. "[W]hat [do you] wan[t]"?
DELAWARE MAN. "[T]o Know if [you a]re Busy to work in [you]r Harvest and How it [goes] on."
VANNETTEN. Why not "go down with [me] to the House"?

He could see for himself.

DELAWARE MAN. "No, for the Indians . . . Have done so much mischief Here Last Winter that [I am] afraid to Come down."

Here Vannetten bumped up the conversational pressure. Instead of the reassurance he had just been asked for, he laid out a blandly self-serving formula:

VANNETTEN. "[I]f you are a friend you Need Not Be afraid, for you shall Not Be Hurt."
DELAWARE MAN. "[I] w[ill] not Come In." (*Looking for safer conversational ground.*) "[I] w[ill] Return th[is] Day again to Wigwamonck."

The eastern Delawares living at Wyoming were about to conclude a peace with the province. But Vannetten had now decided that the other man was not really friendly (and probably not from Wyoming, either). His hospitality and its accompanying undercurrents of threat grew more pointed.

VANNETTEN. "[Will you] drink a Dram with [me]"?

This, a standard offer to any Indian over whom a European wanted some advantage, here made the other do something with his hands besides gripping his gun.[45]

DELAWARE MAN. "Yes."
VANNETTEN ("*sen[ding down the hill] for the Bottel and dr[i]nk[ing] to Him,*" *then passing it up to him*). "[F]rom whence [do you] C[o]me"?

This redundant question showed that Vannetten "knew" that the other was misleading him.

DELAWARE MAN. "[F]rom Wywamonck."
VANNETTEN (*with an alarming shift in tone*). "[You] Ly[e]."

After this flat insult, the conversation accelerated toward dangerous ground. Now, Vannetten said, the Delaware admitted he was from Tioga—a town whose people would launch raids for a longer time than those from Wyoming. Vannetten made it clear that he thought Tioga an unfriendly place:

VANNETTEN. "[H]ow many [European] Prisoners [are] there"?
DELAWARE MAN (*trying to establish that Tioga's hostile days are over*).
  "[F]our ha[ve] been there, But [are] gone."

Having none of this, Vannetten bluntly repeated that the Delaware would continue to be safe if he let Vannetten ratchet up control over him.

VANNETTEN. "Call the other two Indians to Come to [you] if you are friends and you shall Not Be Hurt."

So the Indian man did call to his companions, and a "young Indian Came, But the other would Not."

At this point (with his own five men having edged up behind him), Vannetten introduced the single topic that planted everyone present past a line of no return: he "talked to Him about the four that was murdered the week before on Minisinks Road." Everyone who heard him understood at once that with direct talk of Indians killing Europeans they were in the middle of a new conversation, one that would not end well. There was a sudden flurry: "[W]hen [I] talked to him about that," Vannetten observed, "He was for going away and Kept himself well guarded with His gun While He was surrounded" by Vannetten's men.

Vannetten walked the "young Indian" farther uphill and asked him to call the third Delaware in. The young man "s^d He would," Vannetten wrote, but then sensibly ran, with Vannetten shooting after him. He thought "By His Cauling"—the quality of his screaming—"That only the Swan shot Hit Him." But downhill nine more reports sounded. "[T]he other hearing the gun, forst himself through the Company and Run of," Vannetten's men reported when he jogged back, on which they had all fired. Whether that was true, or the soldiers had taken Vannetten's firing as a signal to shoot, the result was the same. They scalped the corpse, retroactively making the whole conversation—from halloos to captivity— into an act of war.[46]

This hillside exchange showed how some subjects—especially the past deaths of other Europeans—could mark out an epoch in Indian-European conversation, tipping dialogues into showdowns. The most dangerous thing a European could tell an Indian was that he thought he was a murderer.

THERE WERE faster ways than words to make a threat. Like the two Delawares who writhed before the captive William Fleming in 1756, miming the death agonies of his neighbor, or the Lancaster County men, marching toward Philadelphia in 1764, who acted out the motions of scalping on frightened passersby, many Indians and Europeans relied on gestures to intimidate. Guns were the best props, amplifying one's every move. If someone being bullied did not respond to rural men's "shak[ing] a stick" or fist at him, with a gun at hand they could work their way through a whole catalog of menace: pointing and "present[ing their] Piece[s]"; holding their "thumbs upon the locks of their Guns"; audibly "cock[ing] their Guns at his Breast"; "mak[ing] a push . . . with a Gun" barrel. Even when face-offs turned physical, guns were often wrestled with and "catched hold off" rather than fired.[47]

But one mimed action was especially well attested: that of sighting a rifle from a distance, again usually without firing. There are few things so uncomfortable as having one's movements followed by the bobbing tip of a gun, and sighting—in a pinch, even with sticks—seems to have been a universally used gesture. When David Jones, a pugnacious New Jersey Baptist, plowed into the Ohio Indian towns in 1773 to look for converts, he met with countless menacing receptions. At one town, when three masked shamans bustled over to frighten him off, one "stooped down by a tree and took sight as if he designed to shoot at me," Jones wrote; "but I could see that he had only a pole in his hand."[48]

Militiamen who drilled under Virginia's aegis in the contested lands near Pittsburgh on the eve of Dunmore's War, in 1774, were similarly complained of by frightened back inhabitants for sighting their weapons over the river at "friendly Indians, in their Hutts on the Indian Shore," and sometimes taking potshots as they left their musters. Though none of these salvos caused an injury, their message could not have been plainer. The same summer, the Delaware leader White Eyes formally asked "that you will not suffer your Foolish young People to Lie on the Road to watch and frighten our People by pointing their Guns at them when the[y] Come to trade with you, for some of our People had been so scared," he said, that they had put their villages on a footing for war.[49]

One killing that was first discussed as a straightforward case of an Indian's being murdered, as Sir William Johnson put it, "Meerly because he was an Indian," seems in fact pretty plainly to have been a case of such menacing gone, almost inadvertently, too far. Since one of the most determined advocates of intercultural harmony throughout the mid-eighteenth century had been the translator and go-between Conrad Weiser, it came as a horrible shock when in 1769 Weiser's own nephew, a teenager named Peter Reed, shot the son of Seneca George, an Iroquois half-king among the Nanticokes and Conoys at Chenango, just over the New York line.

Toward nightfall, Reed and some companions were in a fishing canoe on the Susquehanna, while Seneca George's son was "in an open Bark Cabbin with some other Indians on the bank of the River." As the canoe drifted past, with the forms of the Europeans inside lighted up strangely by the fire for fishing that they had burning in its prow, Reed, "in the Stern present[ed] his Gun towards the [Cabin] and fire[d]," blasting Seneca George's son right through the torso with what would have been an impossibly skillful shot—from a moving canoe, from a distance, in partial darkness—if it had been meant to be more than a terrifying pot-shot. The Indians on the bank recognized this, for instead of scattering they shouted indignantly to the canoeists that "they had killed one of them, upon which" the Europeans paddled away in a panic. Reed was captured the same evening, and imprisoned to await a settlement of "whether the Affair was accidental or designed."

Perhaps because it fell somewhere between, in the realm of threat and half intention, Reed was later "discharged by Proclamation," after the provincial and imperial Indian establishments had been put on alert and a full condolence conference held for Seneca George.[50]

ANTI-INDIAN VIOLENCE that did not overflow from attempts at inspiring fear could play out with hardly any posturing at all. Less common, and less visible, than bluster or fear, but far more often deadly, was opportunistic greed.

In spring 1766, an Oneida man was robbed and murdered after venturing down from the northeastern Susquehanna to trade a pack of furs on the New Jersey side of the Minisinks. The locals could not say what his name had been; he "neither understood English, nor was acquainted with any of the Inhabitants." But his two-week-old corpse was uncovered after their worry over his disappearance led to the mounting of a search. They were "greatly alarmed" and "in the greatest Anx[iety that] . . . Indians will fall on them in a Hostile ma[nner]" as a result of what they found: the Oneida's body was crammed into a grave (so hurriedly scraped that his back and legs were broken to fit it) near the cabin of Robert Seamor, a recent deserter and "base Vagabond Fellow" with "no Property." At Seamor's they found "a Rifle and some Beaver skins . . . as plunder" from the victim, and he and the Oneida had been seen leaving a public house together around the time he disappeared.[51]

After Seamor was put into Sussex County's crude log jail, then sprung the same night by huzzahing men with clubs who "threatned Destruction" to anyone who interfered (which, as Gov. William Franklin observed, "deterred" the constables "from doing there duty"), he was nonetheless recaptured by law officers from the next county over, put on trial in his frontier neighborhood, convicted, and put to death after confessing on the gallows. Despite being the new county's first execution, the hanging "did not" excite "a Murmur among the People" of upper Sussex, at least some of whom had already taken up a subscription to "make . . .

a present of something handsome" to the widow and two brothers of the dead Oneida man when they turned up a few months before the trial, riding home again with forty-four dollars and the victim's rifle.[52]

Nightmarishly full evidence of robbery and murder was to be found in the actions during 1763 of two short-term companies of provincial soldiers. These men, paid to range in the shadow of the Blue Mountains, were led by two German brothers, Nicholas and Jacob Wetterholt. A majority were German-speakers, but many came from Craig's (or "the Irish") Settlement, a place where the Moravian bishop at Bethlehem thought traveling Indians "in greater Dangers of being Hurt . . . than any where Else in all the Province."[53]

The "prodigeous Hilly" sector that the Wetterholts' men patrolled, tilting into the Lehigh, had long been a backwater of the war, and they were idle much of the time. Nicholas Kern, Nicholas Wetterholt's ensign, kept a tavern in a house abutting the steep-sided mountain gap carved by the river, and locals presciently feared that "the Soldiers will . . . lay there drinking & playing mischief, and guard only that house," with "a Constant Frolick . . . much like the Indian Mode."[54]

The companies also squatted just upriver at the abandoned Fort Allen, a shabby, long-walled structure, shuttered and stripped of its cannon, around which the undergrowth must have been reasserting itself. The men, whose discipline was also in disrepair, enjoyed the power of soldiering: a corporal "ravished two women, while . . . upon a scout"; others carried on illegal private trade with Indians from the upper Susquehanna who stopped on their way to Bethlehem.[55]

The worst was Lieut. Jonathan Dodge, a tall and brutal New Englander who frankly despised the Germans around him. Anything could set him off. Ranting, "I will have my will. . . . I will have my will," this frightening young man had berated and beaten a wide selection of people, from Ensign Kern's wife at the tavern (for not serving him "to his mind"), to a private whose arm he smashed into a broken hash with his gun butt. He pillaged food from neighboring farms, and he made a specialty of attacking Indians under ambiguous circumstances.[56]

Dodge had started by confiscating packs of deerskins from Indians traveling to Bethlehem. One party of four men whom he robbed—luring them into the tavern for a drink, then suddenly seizing their rifles and furs, sending them fleeing in fear from his threats and a volley of gun-fire—netted Dodge at least half a month's pay, or about two-thirds what his men would earn over the whole of their enlistments.

Dodge was violently touchy about this incident, and he wrote an implausible account of it for his colonel that changed the men he had mugged into unintelligible, heavily painted, housebreaking "Rogs." As Dodge explained, they "Behaved very strang . . . I thought I would Do for the Best as you told me not to hurt aney of oure frinds But to my faith I could not think thay Was frinds." Dodge's story was a transparent fraud, but no one could really contradict its kernel, which was just that he "could not think thay Was frinds." Such stories of how Indians had acted like enemies before coming under attack—improbable and overelaborate, but for all that watertight—appealed to Dodge (as to other men like him), since he used another barely a month later.57

In September, a Delaware named Mahalas traveled with a friend through the Wetterholts' territory. Each had a bundle of trade goods from Bethlehem. Some of Mahalas's goods were pilfered at a tavern in the Irish settlement, and when they got to Fort Allen, Mahalas's companion, "uneasy to go," unwisely headed across the Lehigh without him. Maha-las decided to spend the night at the fort.58

Meanwhile, Dodge asked whether he and the Carolina-born Cpl. Jacob Warner—perhaps, like him, an outsider of a kind—could go and look for a lost gun. They returned that evening with a rifle. But when Mahalas traveled onward the following day, he began to feel suspicious. Retracing his footsteps to a point about two miles from the fort, he spot-ted in the path a little piece of leather from his traveling companion's bundle, together with "other Marks, whereby they concluded, that he there had been murdered & . . . the Traces of something draggd along the Ground" as far as the river, into which it had then been flung. Nothing more was found of Mahalas's friend or his goods.59

Mahalas raced back to Bethlehem to notify Timothy Horsfield, the J.P. and militia colonel, whom Dodge and Warner were soon telling about an unheralded act of heroism. They had not liked to mention it at the time, but on the night that they found the gun they had also had a battle with no fewer than three enemy Indians. They saw them, "painted Black" and "look[ing] like devils"—according to Dodge, by "esp[ying them] upon a Mountain"; according to Warner, by "hear[ing] a Noise of Something in the Bushes"—and pluckily charged forward, Dodge said, "halloo[ing]" defiance, when the warriors "sprung behind trees, and made several attempts to fire, but I was too quick." Their story was not yet quite straight, and Warner's version preserved more of how Mahalas's friend really died: after he and Dodge yelled, "Jumped out o[n] the road," and fired, "Werner first Scalped, the Dead Indian the Indians had not fired one gun." The dead man probably sensed little more than a sudden rush from the bushes, if they did not snipe at him from under cover.[60]

This time Dodge had something else besides an Indian's valuable rifle and hunting profits to sell. He wrote a letter—it must have repeated their exciting tale of an adrenaline-filled firefight—that Warner carried "to a Certain Gentleman in Philada.," together with the two-week-old scalp. This secondhand urban Indian-hater gave Warner eight dollars (this was a month's salary or more to a corporal) and "Wished him good Luck."

The simple, stealthy tactic of "following," or trailing after Indians who had left a known location—a tavern, a fort, a village—to waylay them on their route, was the method used by most actual killers. It made sense wherever private space and pretexts were otherwise hard to come by (it was used among Indians, too). Though little craft was really needed, an excuse would nearly always be made for going after someone who had left—like looking for strayed horses or, in Dodge and Warner's case, a gun. This calculating meanness of methods and motives was typical of most cases in which Europeans actually killed Indians, rather than threatening to. Dodge's surreptitious following—with his eager snapping up of deerskins and salable new goods—was hard to tell from robbery. The Philadelphian who acted as Dodge and Warner's benefactor offered an even plainer financial motive, making their victim's body part of the plunder.[61]

These killers and victims had had no strong connections to the neighborhood: Dodge loathed it. But when the tactics of profitable murder came to a disastrous consummation that fall, the killers were a cross section of the Wetterholts' youngest men, and their Indian victims had dozens of relatives living nearby in Bethlehem's satellite village of Nain.

On a Saturday at the end of the summer, Zacharias, a lapsed Moravian convert who had been visiting near Bethlehem, started back toward the

Great Island in the Susquehanna with his wife Zipporah, their young son, and another woman. (These were the unlucky people whose deaths led to the murder trial described in chapter 2.) By Sunday afternoon, they had gotten near Kern's tavern. Zacharias wanted to go into the house to "buy Sum Good[s] . . . but Whas in fear To be kilt," according to Niklasz Oblinger, a neighboring farmer whom he "beg[ged] To Go With him." After buying fabrics in the tavern—blankets, some linen, blue stroud-cloth leggings—Zacharias and the women sat drinking with the soldiers until Oblinger "perswade[d] him to Go af." The women and child rode off on one horse, and Zacharias got ready to follow on another. But he could not find his gun. "[M]ebee your Wife has the Reyfell," Oblinger suggested—so Zacharias rode off into the slanting light, with a saddle pack full of goods and no gun.

They were followed and overtaken in a field. According to Moses Beer, a private who later confessed to shooting Zacharias, Jacob Wetter-holt asked him and Samuel Custard "if They would Go afther," and, Beer reported, "They answer yes." When he saw the soldiers, Zacharias "Wuld Defend him Selves With his knif," but it was no use. The family's horses and corpses were stripped of everything of value, the horses sent off—to be found straying in the woods a month later—and the bodies pitched into the river.[62]

And then Custard, Beer and his brother Enoch, Ensign Kern, and four other men, all of whom played some part in the murders or the disposal of the dead, retired to the second-floor room at Kern's tavern to stage a nearly Calvary-like scene of division. They held a pari-mutuel auction among themselves over the family's possessions, with one man acting as "Cryer at the Vendue." Each bid for the different goods that the group had retrieved—including not only the leggings and cloth Zacharias had just bought, but the rifle he could not find, his powder horn and spare gunlock, his two-quart kettle, his "half worn Sadle." With these distributed, they split the resulting pool of cash—held by the cryer as the "bank"—until everyone was even, with the men who had gotten more, or more valuable, goods taking less money "in the Settlement or Dividend." In the end, each made about thirty-five shillings, or three weeks' ranging salary.

This ceremony seemed familiar to the men who later described it. Soldiers were used to disposing of things taken from dead enemies, and even from each other. (When one militiaman died at Fort Pitt, an observer disgustedly noted that he "was no sooner dead than Robb'd by some of his Fellows, they stripp'd the Corpse of all the Cloaths . . . [and] also stole his Gun—.") But with their techniques of following, pillaging, and group sharing, these men of the Wetterholts' were working as a murder gang.[63]

So it could be dangerous for Indians to travel about with valuable goods. Smaller gangs than the Wetterholts' might form on the fly when they saw what Indians had, as "two Scotch-Irish strollers" did in 1766—one, James Annin, a man in his fifties, the other, James McKinsey, a halt, beardless teenager who claimed to be the batman of a Scots officer killed at Pittsburgh. They had met in Philadelphia, and were walking very slowly along the highway toward New York on a summer midday when they came to Moorestown, a crossroads at the heart of southern New Jersey's drowsy countryside. Here they begged their lunches, and noticed Hannah and Catherine, two Indian women "who had long resided in the Neighbourhood," probably at the Indian reserve of Brotherton.

Hannah and Catherine were carrying their shopping—some fancy fabrics they had just bought in town. McKinsey was heard to "g[i]ve them abusive Language," and the women went away to sit in a roadside wood-lot. One was visibly pregnant. The two men, according to their separate confessions, decided to follow and "ravish them, if they should refuse their Offers." The encounter ended with Annin knocking both women down, and McKinsey giving one a coup de grace with a hatchet. Within an hour the men sold the cloth goods two miles down the road and split up. When Hannah's and Catherine's bodies were found, the two were at once suspected, arrested—though McKinsey had fled to Philadelphia, he was recognized from a neighbor's horrified description in the newspapers—jailed, tried, and convicted.[64]

The aftereffects of these fairly straightforward felony murders were now almost at an end: the men were to be hanged together within the month. But on the scaffold Annin continued flatly denying that he had killed anyone. And even if he or McKinsey had, he said appealingly to the crowd—which included delegates from Brotherton—he "thought it a Duty to extirpate the Heathen." Perhaps this was an Indian-hater's defiant declaration of core principles. More likely it was an effort, a few moments before death, at finding any kind of palliating context for his crimes. After an instant more, he and McKinsey were dangling in the air before the crowd, with nothing left to say.[65]

IT WAS A COMMONPLACE among officials like Sir William Johnson and Gov. John Penn that instead of making up a passive, worried audience for Indians' killers, most country people would actively back them. Writing dismissively to Penn about the uselessness of chasing a killer who had crossed the Mason-Dixon line, the governor of Virginia put it baldly. "I have found by experience," he wrote, one governor to another, that "it is impossible to bring anybody to Justice for the Murder of an Indian, who takes shelter among our back Inhabitants. It is among those People, looked on as a meritorious action, and they are sure of being Protected."[66]

In the middle colonies, the strongest support for this impression came when crowds sprang the killers of Indians from jail. Easily the most notorious case—one that came to the attention of George III (who "lament[ed]," as his colonial secretary reported, "an Event so big with Mischief"), as well as sending hundreds fleeing over the Susquehanna in midwinter with their livestock and heaped-up possessions, and costing officials months of panicked diplomacy, not to mention £2,500 in Indian presents—was that of two shabby, dark-haired Germans, each able to get by in English "but indifferently," who lived in upper Cumberland County, Pennsylvania: Friedrich Stump and his indentured servant, John Ironcutter (or Eisengräber).[67]

In January 1768, Stump was visited at his house near the forks of the Susquehanna by four men and two women. They were part of a mixed group of Indians from the Great Island, living that winter at a cabin fifteen miles up the creek, and they had just stopped in at the house of William Blyth, the area's leading illicit vendor of liquor to Indians. Some might well have been drunk or a bit threatening. Stump did not like having them there, because at some point after one or more of the men was asleep he killed them all, scalped at least one of them, "dragged them down to a Creek near his House, made a Hole in the Ice and threw them in." When one of these corpses was discovered the next month, having bobbed seventy-five miles downriver under the ice, it was found to have been stove in at the front of the skull by Stump's tomahawk (having been "struck, as appeared . . . two or three times with the Pole End"). The next morning, Stump went with Ironcutter up the creek to the remaining woman, two girls, and infant. After murdering them in turn, with Iron-cutter's help, Stump "set Fire to the Cabins and burnt them" for good measure, so that only "some remains of the Limbs" were left.[68]

The next day, Blyth confronted Stump. "[B]eing apprehensive that [the six adults] intended to do him some Mischief" when they came to his house "in Drink, and disorderly," and would not leave, Stump claimed that in his fright he had had to kill them—and then killed the rest "to prevent them carrying Intelligence" of the other deaths back to the Great Island. But after checking on Stump's story—and finding charred corpses at the cabins—the horrified Blyth carried the intelligence out of the creek himself, riding off to see the governor in Philadelphia.[69]

On his way Blyth paused to tell rural J.P.'s of Stump's murders. They brought word to Carlisle, Cumberland's county town, where, with the quarterly court sessions starting, many lawyers and magistrates were ready to discuss the news. They decided to send a posse after Stump. But several valleys to the north, William Patterson, a young ex-militia captain, had already gathered nineteen neighbors and captured Stump and Ironcutter himself. Patterson's party bound them so tightly that the boy's hands were later "much swelled with the tying," dispatched a messenger to the Great Island to break the bad news, and deposited their prisoners at Carlisle jail on a blustery Saturday night, a few hours after the first letter arrived from Philadelphia to call for Stump's capture.[70]

The governor's letter ordered that Stump be sent to Philadelphia for examination—a legally delicate long-range cross-jurisdictional transfer, to be carried out by sheriff-to-sheriff relay teams, carefully releasing and accepting the prisoners on the borders of four counties in turn. Because it also stated, a little ambiguously, that once in Philadelphia he would be "dealt with . . . according to Law," things started to unravel.[71]

Did that mean he would be put on trial there? Some in Carlisle noted the flat illegality of trying Stump for his life before a jury in a different county, and on Monday, after hearing out a delegation upset by this "Indignity intended to their County"—and deciding that the river's roughness made it hard to cross securely with the prisoners—Carlisle's senior J.P., Col. John Armstrong, kept Stump and Ironcutter in jail and wrote for more instructions. The area's other J.P.'s gathered in Carlisle to make a show of legal resolve.[72]

But the situation was ripening. Stump told whomever would listen that "he expected his Trial in the County where the Fact was committed," and soon some men rode up to town to announce that they would stop his removal. But on being told the prisoners were not "cruelly treated" and would be tried in Carlisle, they said they were satisfied, "fired their Muskets" as punctuation, and went off without nearing the jail. After this the authorities relaxed—until Friday morning, when Armstrong at his breakfast table watched unbelievingly while another crowd rode in and surrounded the jail.

Bellowing that "they were acting a bad Part . . . a Part that must subject them and their Country to Misery," Armstrong ran out with the sheriff, other magistrates, assorted townspeople, and a Presbyterian minister for a showdown on the jail's front stairs. Some of the rescuers shoved Armstrong roughly down the steps. After shoving back, and gathering himself for a speech ("Gentlemen, . . . it is in your Power to kill me, but I will die on the Spot before you shall rescue the Prisoners"), Armstrong was surprised when Stump and Ironcutter appeared, already free though only minutes had elapsed, and he and the other officials were "jostled or borne away into the street" at the points of guns and cutlasses, while the prisoners were carried off by their surging, cheering rescuers (together with a useful blacksmith "with a Pistol held to his Breast").[73]

Did the rescue amount to an affirmation of the folk that it was a good act to abruptly, almost psychopathically murder ten Indians? The hundreds of people who fled their farms probably did not feel this way. The gathered magistrates thought that what the affair meant depended on its ending, and on the "prevailing . . . Sentiments of the People." If it was "the hearty Inclinations of the Body of the County to see public Justice administered," there should have been signs of this. And, as it happens, there were.[74]

Many of the people at court week talked about Stump's overblown "Story touching the Conduct of the *Indians* at [his] House"—"which I take," Armstrong said, "to be false"—with perfect seriousness, "draw[ing] upon him the Compassion of many who would otherwise have regarded him with Abhorrence—." (The second day's murders were less discussed.) The story's core idea of forced hospitality for menacing guests resonated with country people who later spoke to Armstrong, complaining that they "must be threatened and insulted by Indians . . . before they dare say it is War."[75]

Above all, though, there was fear that a special act would be passed to try Stump and Ironcutter in Philadelphia. This was unwelcome not only to those who thought of them with sympathy, but to everyone in Carlisle who believed in the common law's clear rules about trial by a jury of neighbors in the vicinity of the crime. (Governor Penn later pronounced himself "astonished at the impertinent insolence of those who have taken upon them to Suggest or even to suppose" that he would ever "do so illegal an Act" as move a trial.) That local jury trials—before "Neighbours of the Fact, [and] of the Party"—made things easier on defendants was the entire point of the precept, which was thought to be specified by Magna Carta, widely celebrated as part of British liberty's bedrock, and spelled out in the manuals for magistrates on which Armstrong and his peers relied. Nor was this some idiosyncratic quibble: fury at the prospect that local juries might be overridden by fiat of a faraway legislature was a strong current in the crisis between troops and Boston crowds that began the same fall.[76]

In short, Armstrong observed—though he "greatly complained" of the argument—"an Alarm [wa]s raised in the Minds of many, touching their Privileges" if Stump were removed: it would be, as some of the lawyers in town warned warmly, "yielding up a most valuable privilege." When the rescuers became convinced that soldiers were going to sneak Stump away in the night—in a "generally prevailing mistake," which "spread almost beyond credibility, like an electrical shock, over all the county"—the crowd took him into its custody. Otherwise, as Armstrong said, this "they say they would by no means have done."[77]

And so, bizarrely, discussions about Stump's return started even before his rescue was over. While the rescuers were streaming out, two clergymen trotted after them, "persuading them to bring back the Prisoner," and got ready agreement from "About one Half of the Company" if they were promised he would not be taken to Philadelphia. A message from those holding Stump—for two weeks he and Ironcutter were reportedly "ke[pt] . . . confined" by "These Madmen" somewhere in Shearman's Valley while negotiations unfolded—similarly asked for assurances of nonremoval. Twice posses of law officers, clergymen, and concerned citizens rode over the mountains for large outdoor meetings, at which they denounced the rescue, read aloud more recent promises from Philadelphia about Stump's trial venue, and labored toward a settlement.[78]

Many of those they talked to seemed "convinced of their Error"; and "all declared their willingness to return the prisoner" and "promised to use their best endeavours"—committing, at one point, to deliver the men to town on February 5. But this deadline passed with no sign of them. Stump, having been "unluckily permitted" to go and visit his father over the river, had evidently kept on heading east. He and Ironcutter were never recaptured.[79]

Stump's rescue was unremarkable, although the things he had done to be imprisoned were extraordinary. For it is hard to overstate how common unpunished crowd actions were in the back counties after the Seven Years' War. Beyond the longest-settled parts of the mid-Atlantic plain, the law's coercive resources were strikingly weak, even very close to forts. From 1765 through 1766 and again in 1769, for instance, there were running conflicts in the west between soldiers, magistrates, and the so-called Black Boys (who sooted their faces for anonymity), including firefights, floggings, horse killings, arson, robbery, mail interception, whippings, gaggings, hostage taking, the capture of soldiers as "the King's prisoner[s]," and endless rescues. Hundreds of country people "appear[ed] daily in Arms, and seem[ed] to be in an actual State of Rebellion" (roaring "shoot the Bougar"! when they saw a fort's commander). There were full-fledged assaults, lacking only artillery, against garrisons. Fort Bedford was for an interval actually captured, and at a siege of Fort Loudoun, which lasted two days and nights—with dozens of the rioters' fires flaring in the surrounding darkness—hundreds of rounds were fired. There was at least one actual death and, repeatedly, the pillaging of pack trains bearing goods and army supplies from fort to fort over the steep, twisting spine of the Alleghenies. At times, much of westernmost Pennsylvania was made a no-go area for any outside forces of the law.[80]

This fighting started in an effort to halt trading into Indian country, trading that was about to be carried out sooner after the end of Pontiac's War than the law allowed. But quickly everyone "got entirely out of the channel of the civil law"—as a central figure in the excitement, James Smith, later reflected—and did "many unjustifiable things." This, he said without irony, "convinced me more than ever I had been before, of the absolute necessity of the civil law, in order to govern mankind." Smith's insistence that the rioters genuinely did embody "Civil Authority," so that they were only trying (most of the time, anyway) to honor the common law, was at the heart of these events.

For Smith, the constitutional course of action was something to be negotiated, when necessary, between officials and public-spirited men with guns. Until he was dismissed from the magistracy, Smith's brother-in-law, the J.P. William Smith, issued legalistic passes to travelers whose behavior he judged such "as becomes loyal Subjects"—by contrast, he said, "no Military Officer's pass would do"—and when James Smith was imprisoned for a shooting during the second wave of riots, he called off hundreds of milling rescuers from the Carlisle jail, "declaring his Desire to have a Trial by the Laws of his Country, [and] begging them to return Home."[81]

With a perverse legal legitimacy mattering so much to even the Black Boys—who offered vehement arguments from acts of Parliament—the Stump affair likewise delimits the difficulty of simply dismissing eighteenth-century constitutionalism as a self-serving pretense. The language of popular constitutionalism that made Stump's rescue possible was at the core of a roughly consistent ideological system, one with far more power than the state itself to shape events in the back counties. Stump had many more sympathizers once it seemed he would be "unconstitutionally" tried than he had had after his murders.[82]

BEYOND THE SEABOARD and its increasingly shrill political struggles, Europeans actually murdered or threatened Indians for a blend of reasons, none of which had much to do with an anti-Indian culture that gripped the whole mid-Atlantic population or made its members, en masse, into potential killers. Though some people in the countryside really did hate all Indians and want to see them dead, for most people, and for very long stretches of time, prudence dictated that their actions while living amid Indian attacks would be controlled by fear. Since fear and respect are allied feelings, sometimes the results could be surprisingly favorable to Indians.

But in the city, meanwhile, most people—among them armchair hard-liners like James Hamilton, who served as Pennsylvania's on-again, off-again governor for about ten years during the generation of the Seven Years' War—could indulge whenever they liked in a comfortable anti-Indian indignation. The vicarious anti-Indian culture that such city dwellers shaped from their fantasies—with its sharp partisan and literary uses—became pivotal to the human relations of the whole region.[83]

Chapter 6

A SPIRIT OF ENTERPRISE

IN SPRING 1756, GOV. ROBERT HUNTER MORRIS STOOD ON the steps of the Philadelphia courthouse while a proclamation of war was read before "a large Concourse of People." The proclamation announced huge bounties for any subjects willing to "pursu[e], tak[e], kil[l], and destro[y] the . . . Delaware Indians" in volunteer scalping parties. The adherents of such bounties—like Governor Morris, and country people who clamored for them after defeats—believed unshakably in their power as wartime cure-alls. After only a couple of months of Indian war, Morris's councilor James Hamilton already felt sure that "large" bounties were "the only way to clear our Frontiers of . . . Savages, & . . . infinitely cheapest in the end."

The troubles with bounties were obvious. They rewarded freelancing over steady soldiering; they symbolized a ruthlessness bordering on barbarization; and because body parts could not say whose they had been, they were blatantly indiscriminate, no matter how carefully they excepted allies or young children. But these problems were exactly why scalp bounties attracted their backers. In place of duty pinned down in forts (with it sometimes really seeming as if "the Indians . . . Glor[ied] in doing mischeif near them"), they offered displaced farmers the prospect of scouting about independently—like Indian attack groups—and making sudden fortunes. Their showy pitilessness suggested resolve, and the taking of the offensive: the first things stripped away by the flights and defeats of

Indian war. And with the depressing lack of spirit that followed most attacks, it seemed clear the country people would need some such "encouragement" to stay on their farms.[1]

The hopes of a turnaround that were held by the scalp bounties' boosters, as well as their detractors' fears—that bounties would cause the murders of many nonhostile Indians—were both misplaced. The surprising thing was that, though everyone talked about scalp bounties, practically no one could claim them: only eight were awarded to private subjects in Pennsylvania during the whole colonial period. But if the idea of scalp-bounty windfalls was an illusion, it was an illusion with some power to shape events.[2]

Because of the flurry and notice that preceded Morris's courthouse ceremony, four men over the border in Somerset County, New Jersey, burst at midnight the day before into a darkened hut with cutlasses, a gun, and an ax they hoped would serve for scalping. They had formed a criminal "Combination" to kill the family who lived there—George, his wife, Cate, their eleven-year-old daughter, and their one-year-old twins—"to take their Scalps, and to carry them to Philadelphia, where they were to swear that they were Enemy Indians, and that they had killed them in . . . Pennsylvania, with Intention to get the Reward." This would have brought them a small fortune (650 Spanish dollars in coin), but in the event it was a panicky, botched encounter. George crashed through the back of the hut to safety, and—after losing their gun to Cate but managing to "cut her Head all to Pieces" in the dark, and laying about at her unseen children—the conspirators, too, fled into the night, being correctly "afraid the Neighbourhood would be raised upon them by the Indian Man." But Cate died, and her killing showed that if a whole population was given a strong financial incentive to seek Indians' deaths, at least a few people would act on it.[3]

Almost always, though, scalp bounties' effect was less direct. They brought about neither epidemics of murder nor great victories, but they did create a different—and, it was hoped, more menacing—context for intercultural relations. They helped rural Europeans to feel they might, after all, be a people to be reckoned with. Above all, they awoke a "Spirit of enterprize"—a euphemism for greed, written about during wartime as being mingled with a noble ardor for revenge and "service to king and country." This "Spirit" invested many anti-Indian efforts more pedestrian than scalping—but almost as profitable—with the spontaneity and glamour of merciless war.

In the resulting excitements, it became simpler to relocate Indian groups. Amid talk of scalp-hunting, officials could let their hands be willingly forced—by what Governor Morris, after issuing his bounty in 1756, insisted were the "Demands of the enraged People"—into actions that advanced the segregation of European and Indian populations.[4]

ANTICIPATORY FEARS of Pontiac's War convulsed the Susquehanna-side settlements in summer 1763, though there were no attacks east of the river. As news of military disasters trickled in through June and July, John Elder, a Presbyterian parson in Paxton township (and, as a "Gentleman of . . . Prudence & Influence on the Spot," an honorary militia colonel) found that his neighborhood had no appetite for fighting Indians. Despite almost a decade of experience, "the frontier Inhabitants are . . . quite sunk & dispirited," he wrote embarrassedly to the governor (who could only confess "surprize to find the people so very inattentive to their own safety"). As Elder flatly reported, "it's to be feared that on any attack . . . all seem inclinable to seek Safety rather in flight, than in Opposing the Savage Foe": people could hardly be brought to enlist. At one point, he tried to see whether men could be recruited from around the urban borough of Lancaster and sent upriver to guard Paxton.[5]

What changed the neighborhood's mood was a declaration of scalp bounties. It had started with bullying. On July 7, three Conoys and Nanticokes appeared in Paxton at Samuel Hunter's roadside tavern and mill, where the Susquehanna narrowed and cascaded, with frightening news. Pontiac's attacks were a sweeping success: hardly a western fort was left intact, and many Iroquois had joined the war; so that now, they announced—or gloated—a united native force was gathering "to march in a large Body," nine hundred strong, and obliterate Fort Augusta, at the forks of the Susquehanna—an irritant to the valley's Indians since its construction—before wheeling down toward Paxton and all the riverside towns, dealing destruction as they came.[6]

Samuel Murray and three other men answered these fantasies by "t[h]reatning the Indians, to Sculp them, and telling them" a lie: "that they have fifty Dollars reward from the Governor, for Every one theyle take." But the next day the men were still at Hunter's, and—as an officer in the nearby stockade worriedly wrote—Murray's friends now acted as if they "Were goeing to S[h]uite [them] Down": if someone had not intervened, he thought, they really would have. The Indians were now "as mad as Ever the Devill can make them," and the officer feared what they would say back in Indian country.7

He need not have worried. The next day, six men led by Murray trailed the three Indians a dozen miles back up the river road, then shot and scalped them. Murray rode off with the scalps to see Gov. James Hamilton in Philadelphia, where he swore that the Indians had been shot while stealing and asked for a reward, trying to make his own threats about bounties come true.

Hamilton knew his answer would be pivotal. As a letter that he gave Murray to carry home observed, he was "disposed to give the fullest Encouragement to persons who . . . Exert themselves in the Defence of the Frontiers," so he asked two local J.P.'s to quiz Murray and make sure that that was what had happened. Hamilton was too eager to kindle the country people's flickering flame of courage into brilliant, unconquerable life to see in Murray nothing more than a bully and assassin. The J.P.'s gave the report he hoped for, and he issued a careful-sounding but more or less open-ended reward for the scalps. "[I]t is not certain," Hamilton decided,

> that those Indians had any intention of murdering the inhabitants at that time, yet as they were taken in an Act of Felony, but more particularly that We might not Damp the Spirit of enterprize against the Savages in the beginning of the War, We have come to a Resolution to allow . . . Ten Pounds for Each Scalp . . . .

The response was immediate. One of Murray's examiners, Edward Shippen of Lancaster, had long been arguing that a scalp bounty was the only way of "quelling the Indians." Shippen thought the terrified people needed "Spiriting . . . up" from "some Stirring Leading man"—someone like himself, but with several thousand pounds of public money to pay out. Now he rejoiced that the governor had "judged the matter So right."

He was soon reporting happily on plans for a large-scale harvesting of scalps. "Mr John Read says that as soon as he returns for Pextan," Shippen wrote his son Joseph (who was now the provincial secretary),

> a Number of about 40 or 50 Scalpers will immediately join Mr. Murray & himself & set off Post haste, for the big Island beyond . . . Fort Augusta. . . . —I would fain have the £30 for the Indians Scalps sent by the next Post if you can possibly manage to get it paid you—.

Not forty or fifty "Scalpers," but three times as many, poured up toward the Great Island, a landmark in the Susquehanna's west branch on which a mostly Munsee town was settled. One resident was the eastern Delaware headman Nutimus, Pennsylvania's steady friend for decades. But semi-informed observers felt certain that this island, and other Indian towns along the Susquehanna, must be "Receptacle[s] & retreat[s] to all the scalping Parties that have infested our Northern Frontier." Their innocuous-acting residents should be chased away, and their fields and houses ruined, to stop warriors from using them as refuges or listening posts. Of Wyalusing, another upriver town (this one filled with pacifists under Papunhang, the elderly Munsee visionary), Elder observed, "it's Evident that till that Branch . . . is cleared of the Savages, the Frontier Settlemts. will be in no Safety.—"[8]

THE LARGE, UNSTEALTHY GROUPS that flooded north in August were wrecking and plundering expeditions. The towns these paramilitaries meant to "clear" were not warriors' camps, and most Great Islanders had already left for the hunt, so there was little risk of fighting. As the exasperated colonel of the Royal American Regiment wrote witheringly to John Harris, "After all the noise and Bustle of your young Men on the Frontiers . . . . Call[ing] very loudly . . . for a Reward for Scalps, . . . I don't hear that any of them Stirrs to obtain it." But simply imagining themselves as resolute "Scalpers" proved enough to convert the unwilling soldiers of midsummer into eager, marching crowds. With the booty from any village they sacked, they could come out not displaced and impoverished but richer, and perhaps more respected, than before.

There was a gap between this dream of steely frontiersmen countering Indians in "the *Indian* Manner of fighting"—"picked Men, who could shoot with great Exactness," as one approving petition put it, who were careless of hardship and well versed in the woods—and such efforts' bumbling reality. When the Great Island expedition of August got a little above Fort Augusta—where the garrison tried vainly "to persuade us not to go over, as the Monsey Indians were friendly"—its members found Indian traces as darkness fell: a lately used fire. After consulting in panic, they turned around to return to the fort.9

The expedition was already over, but despite so dreading an attack, they now walked into one. Four men died in the confused firing (and were quickly secreted in the creek to prevent scalping), but they couldn't really say whether any Indians were dead, thinking it "not . . . prudent to follow and Scalp them, for fear of . . . the Indians falling in with our wounded Men." So the expedition fell apart into little bands that squirreled homeward in the dark, arguing about which direction was south and blundering into one another. Even their attempt at preemptive retreat had ended in a rout.

In the morning, having traveled the wrong way all night, fifteen or sixteen men from one splinter group found themselves on the Bethlehem path, where they suddenly saw three breakfasting Indians with new goods from a trading trip. "[D]ont shoot brothers, dont shoot," the Indians cried as the excited group approached. So they took the three prisoner. When the Indians said that there were no war parties on the Great Island, one of the volunteers flatly told them they were lying, and talked pointedly about the fight they had just had "with some of their people" on Munsee Creek Hill. Then, most ominously, he recounted the recent European deaths in Cumberland County, until the Indians "began to tremble."

The Europeans muttered while they walked on. The man who had called the Indians liars did not want to turn them over to be released at Fort Augusta. "[W]hy," said the group's most experienced member, "would you kill them yourself, for you can get no person here to help you." But six men were in fact willing to shoot at the Indians while they walked ahead of them. And so, after waiting for them to get about a hundred feet in front—perhaps making things feel more like a repetition of that morning's first contact—they did, then scalped and pillaged the bodies and went on.

But not all here was as it seemed. When one man lagged behind to take a new pair of leggings from one of the three corpses, he watched in shock as another of the Indians—who had been managing to play dead, despite what must have been excruciating pain—jumped up suddenly and ran downhill, "the skin of his face, the scalp being off, [flapping] down over his eyes so that he could not see." The volunteers were not especially good even at murder. But in time they found the rest of the expedition again, and all marched home in seeming triumph and "high Spirits," with the scalps and rifles, leggings and brand-new Indian goods. People at home could not have guessed that three of the expedition's four scalps came from passersby who were nowhere near the Great Island—and one, at that, still a living man.[10]

Local officials like Elder and Shippen gave an exultant reception to the "Pextan and Shippensburg brave Boys, who lately defeated . . . about 50 naked, black painted Serpents" (a reference to the conceit that one of the Indians was the war leader called the Snake). John Harris sent grandiose letters to the Philadelphia newspapers about their dauntlessness, "notwithstanding [the Indians] had the first Fire." It was a moral duty to encourage such gutsy "Young Adventurers"—who, "i[f] properly treated, are . . . willing to try their Skill again." With enough bounty money, Shippen could unleash a fearsome rural war machine, fueled by the people's rising spirit. "I wish a Reward of £50—P Scalp were offered," he wrote hopefully,

> . . . but it may be one half of the money would do; however I hope that £100—will be immediately sent up for the 4 Scalps now brought In. The Young fellows are in high Spirits and resolve as soon as possible to take another Trip—Five hundred Pounds will go farther in the above way than ten times as much in the Common way. . . .—let a hundd. pounds be sent up for ye voluntiers 4 Scalps which I expect will come to me first . . .—If the Volunteers hear that the Scalps are to be paid for, they would . . . go out a little way to meet the Indians, who will most certainly come down very soon . . . .

As summer turned to fall, more enormous pillaging expeditions rolled upriver. They left without asking the government's permission, but were

always described as full of confidence that they would meet with mone-
tary encouragement.

This time the Great Island attracted an unpaid four-hundred-man
army from Cumberland County under Col. John Armstrong, which
broke apart in disagreement when it reached the island (already empty of
people and livestock). While a third of the volunteers went farther
upriver, the rest headed to Fort Augusta (into which at long last they
staggered, "half starved [and] without any Success," to plead for rations).
Armstrong's other men found a town with five or six Indians still in it,
who fled, and some leftover livestock. They promptly held an auction
over "the little Plunder they got" and divvied it up.

Inept and fractious as they were, these wrecking expeditions promised
plunder, and provincial enlistees around Paxton all started straining to be
excused and go with the volunteers. By the time one group of militia
turned private came back from pillaging Wyoming, according to a gleeful John Harris, the governor had agreed to grant £25 per scalp to the
Munsee Hill volunteers, and seemed likely to allow the same amount to
anyone else. No more scalps were taken by the autumn's many "active
lively" "Scalpers," but the dream remained a draw, as a sort of lottery and
for the way it dignified looting. On the whole, Hamilton's offers
amounted to "Some Encouragement for the Troops & Volunteers to
Exert themselves," Harris contentedly noted, "as Soon as the Weather
will Permit."[11]

ON HEARING of the Munsee Hill march, Governor Hamilton had
grumbled that the volunteers were "most unaccountable, headstrong People, and have no Authority from me for what they are doing." Giving
them too much credit for finding Indian victims, or even the island itself,
he thought they would in their "unbridled and undistinguishing rage"
probably "butcher" allies like old Nutimus. In quieter times, he said, he
would never have overlooked their proceedings.

But the times were not quiet, and the people's feelings seemed to
Hamilton to have been stirred. Then, too, the reports of a martial spirit's
at last "animat[ing]" the countryside—a "public Spirit, that reflects Honour on our Country"—were exactly the kind of news the governor longed

to see in print. He would not for the world do anything to "give the least check to the noble ardour that seems to Prevail among the People in your parts," as he now wrote deferentially to John Elder. He sensed the politically attractive chance to act as an open-handed father of the people, and started reporting knowingly to the assembly about the "noble Ardour among our Frontier People," which should be "cherished and improved."

After so much humiliation, lassitude, and panic, Hamilton was delighted to interpret the volunteers' passion for sacking as an itch to engage the enemy. Relieved high officials, puffing up the country people's actions, started to regard them all as seized by "rage"—a word whose military connotations were mostly positive. (It was a poetic commonplace to speak of soldiers' feeling a "generous," or gallant and high-minded, "rage," a "glorious rage," or simply "British rage.") Officials grew immune to anything that challenged this view, since as political discourse it seemed so right. This, they knew, was how war should make them react: not "tamely" or in cringing flight, but with a towering, righteous wrath that swept their enemies away.

After invoking a people so ardent, so unruly and inspired, the governor was inclined to be open-minded about any mishaps, in the way of innocent deaths, that resulted from their overflow of "Spirit." The rhetoric of a populace all irresistibly afire for revenge was politically convenient, since it came appealingly close to excusing everything else that was wrong with the whole disjointed war effort, drowning out what might otherwise seem a series of blameworthy fiascos. It also let Hamilton vie with the assembly over who was a fiercer backer of the people. The main point about the volunteer expeditions, surely, must be that by means of them "such . . . Terror is . . . thrown into the Minds of the Savages," as one newspaper letter put it, that the Susquehanna's native residents would not choose to "tarry on this Side of the Allegheny; and we may hope under God, for some more Quiet." Beside this great good—the shifting of fear, and populations—less fortunate facts should be overlooked.

Indeed, Hamilton wrote, "it will not be long possible to restrain the Ardour of the People for revenging the horrid Cruelties [of the Indian raids] . . . on all of that Colour whether Friends or foes, whenever they come across them.—It is indeed enough to wear out the Patience of a Saint.—" In a boisterous sea of high-spirited countrymen, Hamilton could simply dismiss it as unrealistic to ask whether war parties really sheltered at the Great Island. His assurances of safety to even the province's most useful Indian friends grew perfunctory: for "what Protection can I give them?" as he sighed to the Moravian Indians' agent in Philadelphia. To Papunhang and his people, Hamilton offered still colder comfort. If anything nasty happened after the volunteers finished ruining fields at Wyoming, the Wyalusingites must blame not him, and not the volunteers, either, but the Indians who had first struck Cumberland County: for "People who have been so much hurt," as Hamilton intoned, "cannot be restrained from taking Revenge." His candid advice was that they evacuate promptly.[12]

And so by the time that Bethlehem's magistrate tried to tell Hamilton about the vanishing Delaware Zacharias and his family—who were murdered and enthusiastically pillaged by some of the Wetterholts' men—the governor had a dismissive pigeonhole ready for what he was hearing. Instead of really condemning unprovoked anti-Indian violence, he saw it as inevitable. There was just no stopping the rage of the people; and in fact "I can not desire of hearing any thing further upon that Subject," he wrote testily, "at a time, When One hears of nothing but the most Savage Cruelties & Butcheries committed by [the Delawares] . . . —I know nothing of their being Killed, but, in case it was so, I doubt not but they deserved it."

When Hamilton made this observation there had been no Indian attacks in Northampton County for at least three years, though there would shortly be another. War parties soon started to pass down against Pennsylvania from the northeast Susquehanna. When Newoleka, the headman of a town between, tried to intercede—much as Papunhang, below him at Wyalusing, had stopped one raiding party before the first peace, by "A-Colecting a Large quantity of wampom with good Speeches to stop them"—the attackers imprisoned Newoleka's men and "threatened . . . to lay my head on the Logs & cut off my head for taking the White people's part." There was no compromise left in them. And what made them "so strong" against the settlers? "[A]fter those four Indians [Zacharias and his family] were killed at Fort Allen," Newoleka reported, "I could not stop them by any means at all. I thought they would kill me, and my people, many a time, for offering to stop them."

Things that looked from Philadelphia like a few regrettable details in a turbulent panorama of war could be seen, in Indian country, to be more like the whole of the picture. Despite this, the retaliatory attack against Northampton County that followed Zacharias's death would soon be cited by Hamilton and other would-be experts as exactly the kind of thing that made it impossible for Indians to reasonably hope to go wandering about the countryside—like Zacharias—in safety. Most of the neighborhood was up in arms, not against Zacharias's family, but against its murderers. But this made no difference to Hamilton's theory of how the countryside worked during wartime. So far as he could see, local Indians simply had to leave or be attacked; and if they were attacked, he did "not desire of hearing any thing further upon that Subject."[13]

THE SADNESS of events was twofold. Neutral Indians suffered, and so did their European neighbors. High officials' determination to find something—anything—grand and deadly in the response to Indian war led them to treat a few killers, like Murray, as a fair sample of the frightened mass of country people. Though their intermittent decisions to pay for murder could not really set off waves of killing, they did encourage wrecking and looting expeditions, which could be imagined as spirited strikes. (Their failure to successfully engage Indians in battle—in 1763, even once—was brushed aside.)

The rapturous press treatment of these events, based on letters sent east by news brokers like John Harris and Edward Shippen, helped to build up a politically useful perception that the countryside was full of ardent anti-Indianists. If the people were all thirsting for Indian blood, real murderers (like the men who shot their prisoners below Munsee Creek) could be seen in an indulgent, misleading frame—an inflated context that, during wartime, floated free from the moorings of fact.

But coddling vicious opportunists like Lieut. Jonathan Dodge did nothing for most of the countryside's residents, as some desperate petitions showed that they perfectly well knew. Nor was it much military help simply to push some Indian settlements farther away from the back counties, as the "scalping" expeditions did. Still, the idea of segregation had a real charm for the official mind. To people like Hamilton, having Europeans and Indians near one another simply felt like trouble; and it seemed to make sense that if Indian villages were abandoned, European farms were less likely to be.

But this piecemeal ethnic cleansing was unreliable even as a buoy for the country people's spirits. The fear of Indian attacks had fascinatingly elaborate effects—among them, at least sometimes, a desire to keep Indian neighbors around at any cost. "[A]s long as You stay here, we will not move," two farmers settled over the mountains in Northampton County came to pleadingly tell the Indians at Wechquetank in September 1763, "but if You leave Your Town then we can stay no longer, and all the people behind the blew mountains will come in Confusion." When Wechquetank was evacuated, a refugee crisis unfolded, just as they had predicted.

As a rule, misguided official encouragement of a few genuinely homicidal people in the countryside—and the new borders of moral understanding and human neighborhood that that encouragement brought—could be horribly damaging to the people who actually had to live there.[14]

THIS WAS TRUEST for those Indians who scrambled to stay out of the pillagers' way. The Conoys and Nanticokes and the Munsees, Mahicans, and other Delaware-speakers who had found a contracting refuge among the branches of the Susquehanna were pushed west and north. Several looted town sites were not resettled. When the Wyalusingites came back after the war, many started another village—Friedenshütten, or the Tents of Peace—under Moravian tutelage in a new location. Cross-border towns in New York like Chenango and Oquaga, more tightly within the Iroquois orbit, now held most of the Nanticokes and Conoys with whom Pennsylvanians came in contact. And for their part, Delawares were being called to the Muskingum Valley, two hundred miles to the west, by the visionary chief Netawatwees, who hoped to establish a new confederacy there.

But even after 1772, when Papunhang's people decided to sell out and move west, Indians still lived seasonally in eastern Pennsylvania, and year-round in New Jersey. As one fledgling minister traveled through the

6.1: An Indian delegation is proudly shown the sights of Philadelphia by the state assembly speaker—Heinrich Melchior Mühlenberg's son, Frederick—in about 1793. *Detail of William Birch, "New Lutheran Church, in Fourth Street Philadelphia" (1799), in* The City of Philadelphia . . . (*Philadelphia, 1800), pl. 21. Courtesy of the Library Company of Philadelphia.*

so-called new purchase lands around Fort Augusta in summer 1775—imagining the tender feelings with which "the wandering Natives" must have left the land behind—he was a little shocked to be faced so often with real Indians. Many trees along the road that he nervously followed were "cut . . . in strange Figures," and everywhere he found fire pits and bark huts: in one place, the stripped hind quarters of a buck, still warm, hanging "over the very Road." Then, in a settler's house, "two Indian Boys bolted in (they never knock or speak at the Door)" and cooked some venison, sitting among the ashes and "bit[ing] it off in great Mouthfuls." Surrounded by flies, dogs, dead fish, ashes, and patches of jelled blood, with "Naked Indians & Children" running in and out, the young man found himself happy to pretend to be busy at his writing when six Indian men entered and stood silently before his host. "I am," he wrote, "in Fear—." When a Scottish tourist visited Philadelphia the same spring, he was diverted to see several

Conoy, Nanticoke, and Tuscarora families from the Susquehanna's head-waters who had just traveled down to request supplies. They were shoot-ing arrows at a halfpenny on a post in the State House yard, which they could often hit "with such force as was very surprising."

But increasingly such visitors—like the group shown in figure 6.1 as they looked while being guided through Philadelphia's brick elevations in the mid-1790s—would be just as much tourists as the Scotsman himself. A perceptibly increased segregation was one of the legacies of the 1760s. And in part this was because of what happened during the winter after all of the expeditions to the Great Island: an expedition, unexpectedly, to Philadelphia itself.[15]

BY EARLY 1764, Sally Wilkins, a teenaged girl from a tiny settlement on the far side of the Kittatinny ridge, had spent several years living as a captive on the upper reaches of the Susquehanna. She lived in Tioga, a mostly Munsee and Seneca town. One midwinter night Tioga's residents started to wail, and the town erupted with horrible sounds. "[T]hey were extremely enraged," the girl reported, with "the Squaws screaming all Night, and tearing their Hair, and the Warriors promising them Revenge." They also "began to be very cross to the Prisoners," treating Wilkins and the other Europeans worse than before. This was the night news arrived in Tioga of a series of murders far to the south, in the farm-lands around Lancaster and in the county town itself.[16]

The story of that winter can be told as one of an unlikely assortment of groups, all emerging from the interior to close in on Philadelphia. First to arrive in the city, in November 1763, were nearly two hundred Delaware-speaking men, women, and children, who rode in carts and walked from Moravian settlements outside Bethlehem, especially Nain and Wechquetank—the mission town from which they and their minis-ter, Bernhard Adam Grube, had at last been bullied into moving by threatening visits. Then, a few months later, the Indians were followed to Philadelphia by hundreds of other people: European men with guns and horses this time, many of them volunteers like those who went against the Great Island, others possibly along for a lark. They meant to achieve the last word in threatening visits.

All of these people were drawn to Philadelphia because it was the colony's capital, the seat and symbol of all government. Here at the heart of executive authority and military power—with a sizable new barracks just four blocks north of Market Street—it seemed the Moravians could safely sit out the rest of the war. But for the European "rioters" who followed them there in February 1764, the city offered the attraction not only of these Indian refugees themselves, but of being able to throw defiance directly in government's face—and not least in the face of Philadelphia's concentration of Quakers, whom they imagined holding the government captive. Because it was the focus of all provincial politics, printing, and public contention, for everyone Philadelphia seemed the region's most visible point—like a city-sized stage set, where their actions would loom with added meaning. So the countryside came to the city, in an encounter that unsettled both places.

ROOM WAS MADE in Philadelphia for the Wechquetank Indians at the insistence of the assembly, which wanted to move them for fear less of what might befall them than of what they might do. The provincial Indian commissioners claimed that the Moravian converts secretly traded powder and rifles with belligerent Indians, or sneaked out to help in attacks. They had to be disarmed and excised from the countryside—granting them a public stipend to live on, in lieu of their crops—so that "their Behaviour may be more closely observed." Each military setback was the clue to some devious betrayal—aid or information given to enemies, as the trustees of the Presbyterian Ministers' Fund darkly noted, by "the Indians among us." By this official logic, they had to go.[17]

Many people over the mountains did not feel this way, of course. Within days of their evacuation, the members of a Lutheran congregation in nearby Lower Smithfield were unhappily petitioning Governor Hamilton to send the converts right back to the neighborhood, so as to have their help in tracking and "Detecting Evil Indians"—at which, the Lutherans noted, the Wechquetankers were much "more capable . . . than White People as We, are"—or, failing the Indians' return, to "Appoint such other Assistance, as in your Wisdom shall seem . . . Effectual." But even if some of the Europeans closest at hand felt safer with the Moravians about, the "Scurrilous Reports Propagated . . . by those who Did not rightly know the Vallue & Benefit of having them for Neighbors" during wartime seemed, for now, to drown out such worried voices in the ears of officials.[18]

So the Moravians were riding down to the city for their own internment, even if it was an internment they were ready to welcome. The Indians and ministers were ferried to two large buildings amid the meadows of Province Island, a publicly owned tract four or five miles from the city center that was farmed for hay. It was not where the Moravians were meant to stay, but at their intended destination—the new barracks in the Northern Liberties, which was filled with royal troops and some of the refugees who were packing the city—they had been rebuffed in a way that made Northampton County seem cosmopolitan.[19]

Soldiers turned out to stop them from entering the barracks, clambering aboard and "dr[iving] the first three wagons out again." Philadelphia's sheriff tried to decide what to do, and they all waited in the street while the ragged people whom Grube referred to, in his Anglicized German, as the "Mop," gathered. "The concourse of people was very great, and from 10 to 3 in the afternoon we were much abused," Grube wrote. "We had to listen to all revilements, mockery, and scorn"—so that without God's help he thought the crowd would have "destroyed" them. Then they all rolled back to the Schuylkill again, a thoroughly alarming experience: "thousands of people accompanied us, the boys [in the streets] set up a great cry, and our good and loving Indians," Grube later noted—not without some typological satisfaction—"were like sheep among the wolves."[20]

But nothing happened, and once the Moravians were on Province Island—where they were soon joined by Papunhang and some other Wyalusingites—they settled down to the most ordinary routine they could manage: worship and woodchopping, morning boat rides for the women to work as dairy maids, and "going to the city and shopping" in little groups, so as to avoid more unwelcome attention. But it soon became part of the routine, too, to receive curious visits from boatloads of "people from the city . . . [who] came to see our Indians," as well as from the island's hay farmers, most of whom came by "in a very friendly way" (though two did break in among the hundreds of worshiping Moravians and "ma[k]e an interruption" on their second night).[21]

It soon became clear that the novel spectacle of the Indians gathering for sermons in German, and especially the sound of their singing—than which "[n]othing charmed the people more"—were proving irresistible to onlookers, "young people in particular," who flocked to watch them on the island and wherever they went. ("[I]f we had a bigger assembly place," Grube wrote speculatively after they were back at the barracks, "we could have some hundreds of listeners every day.") Shiploads of unsophisticated new immigrants from Germany trooped through Philadelphia's streets "to see the Indians," only to be heard afterward grumbling that they were nothing more than gypsies. And without other work a trade in handicrafts developed, with customers streaming in for moccasins, carved spoons, and baskets: "many boys from the city" commissioned bows and arrows from Indians the same age. On the whole, even in this tumultuous, overstuffed city—where much of residents' knowledge of Indians came from printed accounts of wartime atrocities—gaping crowds were more often a problem than angry ones. Grube thought that even soldiers, usually the greatest bullies, had come to "get a different idea of our Indians" from watching their frequent and melodious prayers.[22]

BUT THE SAME WINTER, sixty miles to the west, another, less worried collection of Indians—surrounded by European neighbors they had known for decades—came to a different fate. What happened to them was carefully written down years later in a cheap notebook by a woman named Rhoda Barber. She had grown up in Hempfield, a few miles outside Lancaster and just beside a riverside "manor," retained by the Penns, on which a few Indians lived; about twenty-two in all by the early 1760s. These were the Conestogas, the remains of a larger group who had first settled there some seventy years before. The Conestogas had since been repeatedly assured of the government's protection in public treaty ceremonies.[23]

"One of the first things in my recollection," Barber wrote as an old woman, "is hearing an account of the masacre of the poor conestogo indians." She had not been born until three years later, she said, but "the great interest which every one who I heard speak of it took in it seem'd to fix it in my memory at a very early age." The Conestogas were "great beggars," who also went hunting and bartered brooms, baskets, and other handi-crafts around Lancaster and its adjacent ironworks, a business that often left them on the road, "spen[ding] the night by the kitchen fire of the farms round about." As the Conestogas reminded Governor Penn when he took office, the provincial government had "always" "allow[ed them] . . . some Provisions," with their supplies being overseen by two trustees who lived nearby. With Pontiac's War, those neighbors seem to have increased the grain dole and "advis'd [them] to keep in their town."24

One Wednesday in the middle of the month—it was a "Stormy day, & a deep Snow upon the Ground"—Barber's father had entertained guests from some distance away. Sometime that morning at the family's farm-house

> five or six men came in, they had guns which the[y] left outside, . . . their coats [were] cover'd with snow and sleet, I dont think my father was per-sonaly aquainted with any of them tho he knew from what part of the county the[y] came, he made up the fire . . . while they warm'd them-selves the[y] enquir'd why the indians were suffer'd to live peaceably here, my father told them they were quite inoffensive living on their own land and injuring no one . . . the[y] went away without telling what they had been about, in the mean time my two brothers . . . had been out looking at the strangers horses (as such boys are wont to do) . . . after they were gone my brothers said they had tomahawks tyed to their sad-dles and they were bloody, that they also had Christies gun (Christie was a little indian boy about the age of my brothers . . .), while they wondered what it could mean a messenger came . . . giving information of the dreadfull deed, my father and some others went down . . . the dead bodies lay among the rubbish of their burnt cabbins like half consum'd logs . . . .

Eight Conestoga residents had been at home. Two of those managed to run away before the snow-covered men—who were part of a bigger group, more than fifty riders in most accounts—came among their cabins, killed everyone they found, scalped and mutilated their bodies, and burned the Indians' few houses down. As everyone recognized at once, whether with interest or disgust, except for the lack of captives this sudden, indiscriminate irruption was a stereotyped, detail-by-detail reenactment of how Indian attacks on rural farmhouses had unfolded during the war.

The dead were all conspicuously, heartbreakingly nonbelligerent, living isolated in a thickly European neighborhood. (The massacre site was that safer place, "deeper within the Inhabitants," to which other Indians near Harris's Ferry had been moved in 1756.) But that was not what most enraged official observers. As Edward Shippen, the Lancaster grandee, indignantly wrote, "Every body must have known [they] were under the Protection of . . . and Supported by the Province." The killings were not only individual atrocities, but acts of "riotous behaviour . . . flying in the Face of the Government."

From Lancaster the coroner, Matthias Slough, rode out at once through the day's "great Snow," still falling fast, to "hold an Inquest over, & bury the Corpses." The jurymen returned the obvious verdict of homicide, and one of John Penn's first acts as governor was to proclaim a reward for the murderers. The remaining Conestogas, many of whom had been in Lancaster, were quickly found and shut up in the borough's new brick workhouse, an annex of the jail. As with the Moravian Indians' shift to Philadelphia, the Indians were confined partly to ensure their safety, but partly out of official fear of them: in this case, the fear that, "harmless as they might have been before," the survivors might launch on a retaliatory murder spree. As Shippen mused to his son in Philadelphia, without the thick and hampering snowfall on the day of the first deaths, perhaps "they would immediately have Sought revenge: and as their Custom is on such occasions killed . . . some of their next Neighbours, and then made off."[25]

Within days, threats began spreading about what might happen to the Conestogas locked up in the Lancaster workhouse. On the night of December 20, a few hours after the full moon rose over "Streets . . . full of Snow & ice, and the weather excessive cold," the town's jailer was told by two worried German-speaking men that they had just seen and heard "a parcel of the Rioters" collected at a tavern up the Donegal road, where it sounded from their talk as if dozens were going to rendezvous for a descent on Lancaster to "pul[l] down the Goal" and kill the Conestogas at midnight. The magistrates held a council that night, deciding to order the borough constables to ride "out as Spies" to confirm this report in the taverns around town. But when the spies returned at one o'clock in the morning, "almost perished with the Cold," they had found everything quiet. And though it was the first of several nights that the "Goaler . . . Armed himself & sent off his Childn.," nothing happened that night, or any other.

Instead it was under the midday sun, two days after Christmas, that fifty or sixty men rode through the borough's central square "with . . . Muskets, Tomahawks, & Scalping knives" at their saddles and tied up their horses in the innyard of Matthias Slough, the coroner who had examined the six half-burned bodies at Conestoga Manor only ten days before. The men all jogged down King Street to the workhouse. And there, in a brutal reverse jail break that took only "eleven or twelve Minutes," they did stave in its door—with a knot of people including the sheriff and Slough, who had sprinted after them down the street, trying to "prevail with them to stop their hands"—and did kill all its occupants as they tried to hide or bolt past them into the prison yard, scalping and hacking at some of the corpses: three adult couples and eight children. Squire Shippen heard the shots and screams and got there in time to see the killers running back uphill from "the bloody Place" to their horses at Slough's. Then, presumably, he watched them "[go] off hopping & hallowing having rode round the Courthouse in an inglorious triumph discharging their pieces &c."[26]

Even before this second attack, a group had paid a threatening visit to Wright's Ferry across the Susquehanna, where they taunted James Wright—a lapsed Quaker J.P. who had helped to administer the Conestogas' flour allowance—with news that "they would soon raise a large Number of Men and go & put all the Indians to Death at the Province Island." In the wake of the workhouse killings, the volume of these threats picked up, and their geographic scope widened. "[T]hey say their Name is Legion," David Henderson reported from Lancaster on the afternoon of the killings, "& they are Many & will stand by one another."27

Secondhand accounts of "frequent meetings . . . the people have had in diverse parts of the Frontier Counties . . . [for] an Expedition" to Philadelphia, and of "riotous people . . . Collecting, Daily increasing, & Coming down in parties by different routs" now started to stir unease in the capital. One man was warned anonymously that many residents of Paxton, Hanover, and Lebanon—the rural townships that ran from the Susquehanna along the south flank of the Blue Mountain, like three beads on a string—were forming volunteer companies to march to Philadelphia, "with a Design to Kill the Indians that Harbour there." They hoped to number two hundred in all, with "Many Farmers near the Mountin," the informant wrote, offering forage and "contribut[ing] largely to Defray the Expences of Such as are . . . not of Ability to procure Horses."

As had been true before, the talking, drinking, and planning centered on backroads taverns. "[W]e are told," James Wright's sister Susanna recorded two weeks later, "they are still roving about in companys, and that in all their Revels, they Breath vengeance against Is[rael] Pemberton, Jos[eph] Fox"—a Quaker assemblyman and Indian commissioner, who, as barracks master, personally administered the Moravian Indians' dole of meat, fish, flour, and firewood—"and my Brother, By name, as well as against many others who they do not name."28

THE VIOLENCE in Lancaster was more horrible because it was so impersonal: it is likely that none of the victims or killers knew each other more than glancingly. At the same time the lives of the dead were cut off, their personal histories were taken over by their killers and contorted to serve as part of someone else's story. For instead of being crimes of passion, these killings were meant to make a point, and they did.

Most obviously, they carried a message of intimidation to other Indians, whose impulse to simply evacuate the countryside on hearing such news would be overpowering. But beyond raw intimidation, and beyond their being much the closest thing any of the country people had yet managed to a reenactment and mirroring of the household raids that so transfixed them, these killings were meant to convey a message about what government policy should be.

It is striking how much the official reaction to the murders was controlled by concern that, as David Henderson wrote, "If these Outrages are passed Over . . . all Civil Govt. is at an end." The killings seemed to put the government at risk, both as attempts to see that "Government [itself] became in some measure intimidated" and as crimes that spectacularly discredited its competence. Official talk quickly centered on a need for "Government . . . to support itself"—which was to say on questions of "Power" and "Obedience," of "Force" and "Insolence," and who would now be master, exerting true "control [over] the Conduct of the Administration" in Pennsylvania: the "tumultuous Insurgents" or the authorities themselves. With the people apparently spinning out of control, they would again be discussed—for a while at least—as savages.[29]

However callous it was, metropolitan observers' overriding worry about a loss of face by the government was neither surprising nor misplaced. The rioters themselves seem to have discussed the murders as a deliberate assault on officialdom. To the killers and people who made excuses for them, the Conestogas' being under government patronage was itself a provocation. In an echo of popular unhappiness over the Friendly Association's gifts to Indians, what they said they found most maddening was the idea of government officials' going out of their way to "Harbour" and, above all, spend public money to give Indians food and supplies. With "extremely burdensome" numbers of uprooted country people visibly crowding the cities, raising the poor rates and overflowing Philadelphia's almshouse and churches, the assembly had just turned aside various petitions from rural areas for reimbursement of their locally raised and paid guards, and for tax exemptions to recoup the damage of Indian attacks.[30]

In this setting, the psycho-financial grievance of Indians' being cared for by the government at public expense became central to the riots. The specter of high or unequal tax burdens and financial machinations by the powerful had huge power to anger eighteenth-century Americans, and probably at least part of the Conestogas' doom was sealed by their attractiveness as targets for a protest over public spending. Europeans on both sides of the controversy were certainly convinced of this. In the country-side "& Even ye City it self," the Philadelphian Samuel Foulke wrote as he tried to make sense of the disturbance, a strong "prejudice . . . pos-sessed ye Minds of a great many . . . against . . . ye maintaining them at ye publick Expence." As John Elder had reported from Paxton at the end of January, the idea of "Savages [being] maintained at the expense of the province" was so disliked, and

> the minds of the Inhabitants are so exasperated against [here Elder first wrote and then scribbled out "the Quakers"] a particular set of men, deeply concernd in the Governmt. for . . . the heavy burden, by their means, laid on the province, in maintaining an expensive Trade, & hold-ing Treaties from time to time with Indians, without any prospect of advantage to the province, how beneficial soever it may be to individu-als . . . [that there was] at first . . . nothing intended by some, but to ease the province of part of its burden . . . .

Besides being acts of anti-Indian terror, the attacks had been demon-stration killings, meant in part to show how much "the people" resented government support of Indian refugees. Protect and spend money on *us*, they said.[31]

NEWS OF the second attack stirred responses everywhere. At Tioga, Sally Wilkins's captors set up their nightlong funeral wail. In Philadel-phia, the Moravian Indians at once prepared to evacuate Province Island. False alarms of approaching "Irish rebels" kept them on tenterhooks—first scrambling to move farther offshore into the Delaware, then consid-ering a rapid passage to Nantucket (explained to them as "a certain island where none but Quakers live"), then petitioning the assembly for an evac-uation to England. The assembly declined this but did form a commit-tee, headed by Franklin and Fox, to draft in a matter of hours an entirely new law on trials for murder "by and between white Men or Women and *Indians*." Instead of giving pause to potential rioters, the bill's specifying that all trials of Indians' killers should be conducted close to the capital—

in the southeasternmost "home counties" of Philadelphia, Chester, and Bucks—only proved an additional grievance, and it never cleared committee.[32]

But it did strike the government as feasible to move the Moravians a few dozen miles above Wyalusing to the headwaters of the Susquehanna—by a long, indirect route designed to skirt Pennsylvania itself, passing through New Jersey, up the Hudson, and through Sir William Johnson's sphere of influence in the Mohawk country. And so the converts and missionaries packed their possessions, boarded wagons again, and trundled off on what became a circular odyssey through New Jersey, trying to get to New York Harbor and the Hudson. As one would expect, the crown troops sent to escort them—many of whom had just "come from Pittsburgh and been in the last battle with the Indians"—were one of the Indians' greatest problems on this voyage. At first, the soldiers acted "quite wild . . . plaguing our young women folk in particular," and pointedly talking about their sufferings when Pontiac's War began.[33]

The Philadelphia mob seemed less alarming to the Moravians now, though once again a crowd followed them through the streets ("the press of people was very strong, so that we could hardly push through"). New Jersey seemed still better—though its governor, William Franklin (Benjamin Franklin's illegitimate son), asked Penn to make sure the Indians did not settle down for too long there, observing that Jersey people "will be as averse to them as those of your Province, if they find they are like to be put to any Expence on their Account.—" Everywhere they went, the group's members drew gawkers who were eager to hear their sermons and watch the Indians pray, often "ha[ving] to let themselves be inspected pretty much." In Princeton, an especially "pleasant spot," they drew "a great press of young people who . . . conducted themselves entirely discreetly," including one undergraduate who could chat in Mahican. A few times they faced angry words; and in one innyard a "wicked person with a stick" came up to a missionary's wife and two Indian women, who were sitting unattended in a stage coach, "and poked Elizabeth in the side, so that she fell into a faint."[34]

But as abuse none of this compared to the words of New York's elderly governor, Cadwallader Colden, when he learned that the Moravians were to settle in his province. Colden, though crotchety, was far from a hater of all Indians, having once written an admiring history of the Iroquois; but so far as he was concerned, the Susquehanna-side Delawares were merely "Rogues and Thieves, Runaways from the other Nations, and for that Reason not to be trusted." Writing to deny them permission to board a Staten Island ferry, he spat that "The Minds of the People" in New York were too "generally irritated" against the Delawares to brook their entry. As, plainly, was his own.[35]

The Moravians had just been hastily expelled from Pennsylvania—so that, seen as a threatening visit, the country people's rumored march had nearly succeeded before it started. But now, with Colden's resistance, the Moravians had no choice after three weeks on the road but to turn their wagons around and roll back to Philadelphia. There they were put up in the barracks, this time with no protest from the soldiers.

With the Moravians' return, increasingly grand rumors of an assault on the capital again started spreading. A Philadelphia merchant traveling home was told at the Hat Tavern, a few miles outside Lancaster, that men were gathering in the surrounding townships "to kill the [Moravian] Indians," so that "in ten days fifteen hundred Men would come down . . . [with] Five thousand . . . ready to join them." In the capital, the governor and assembly pored in rising panic over such reports, promulgated the riot act—with Penn reading it personally, amid "driving, cold rain," on the State House steps before three thousand citizens—and called for volunteer companies in the city. Perhaps in recognition of the pressures being brought to bear on them, in a tax bill the assemblymen prepared that week they carefully allowed a two-year tax holiday for any frontier residents who had been "driven from their Settlements, and lost their Effects by the late *Indian* Ravages."[36]

As the reports from the countryside came to a crescendo in February 1764, much of the usual life of Philadelphia stopped. Assemblymen fled the city, leaving the assembly without a quorum. Where there had been snowdrifts and sleighing in the streets, now the weather wavered between intervals of "Exceeding Cold" and a pitiless rain that kept people inside. The rain sent channels of water slipping down the centers of paved streets, slowly turning the unpaved ones to cold mud. It pricked out intricate structures of slush under overhangs; icicles crashed from eaves, snowpacks came suddenly sliding off cedar roofs. It "Blowed hard in the night," and the Schuylkill and Delaware—whose turbid surfaces could be glimpsed between buildings at the ends of many streets—were loud, cold, and swollen, running too quick for fording. At the ferries for miles up river and down, all of the flatboats and passenger dinghies were made fast on the Schuylkill's eastern bank to impede the rioters, and the "large Fires" for waiting passengers at the ferry sheds were left to burn themselves out. Philadelphia shrank into itself.37

A confused and frightening series of nights followed, interrupted by continual false alarms. On February 4, news arrived that the rioters would sweep into the city the next morning, a Sunday, at eleven o'clock, with "a Number . . . surround[ing] Frds meeting houses . . . while the rest were attackg the barracks." The Indians were hustled up to the second story of the barracks, and a breastwork was built before it. John Penn spent the whole of the next "very uneasy" night there himself, amid the Moravians and soldiers, as did about two hundred gentlemen militia; the slightly dopey young governor "visited our Indians at midnight," Grube recorded, "and encouraged them, and was particularly friendly toward the children, of which our Indians were very glad." But the morning came, and the next day passed, without any sign of rioters. Cannon, wheeled into intersections, were test-fired, and the blasts shattered windows. Then, that midnight, "it was given out that the Rebels would be at the Barracks by day Light." Thousands of citizens were turned out into the streets by the shouted "yoho, rouze, get up to Arms, to Arms!" of expresses cantering past, as well as by inaccurate cries of fire, by drum tattoos, and by the watchmen's "Thump, thump, Rap, rap, rap, ket up, ket up" at every door. At two o'clock in the morning, with all the bells of the city clamoring together—"[t]he ringing sounded dreadful in the night"—hundreds of men mustered in the marketplace. "Strong Watches" stayed on guard in the city until dawn, by the light of candles placed in every door and window against the moonless dark. But still no rioters came.38

Once "[t]he alarm bells finally ceased at daylight," the anticlimactic Monday that ensued was a long, bleary round of mustering and milling about, with volunteer companies trooping and galloping and trumpeting their way on "tour[s] in and around the city," sometimes almost shooting or shelling one another point-blank in their excitement. In the course of the day, about two hundred members of Philadelphia Monthly Meeting appeared in public with guns. The armed Quakers made a powerful impression, as Mühlenberg reported, especially on one "whole *troup* of small boys [who] followed a . . . Quaker down the street shouting in amazement, 'Look, look! a Quaker carrying a musket on his shoulder!'"[39]

About two hundred riders and marchers had in fact arrived by mid-morning on Monday at Chestnut Hill, about ten miles northwest of the city, and stopped. There some of the rioters took into custody for a few hours Rev. Paul Daniel Brycelius, a Swedish Lutheran who, like a number of other clergymen, had been riding around trying to intercept them. From Brycelius they learned that the city was in arms and approaching it could cause what he called "a great and horrible blood-bath"—which, he reported once back in Philadelphia, "appeared to give them pause." The men from Lancaster County who talked to Brycelius that morning said they were there not to kill the Moravian Delawares but to do two other things: to take charge of the Indians to forcibly "conduct them out of the province" again, as the crown troops had done the month before ("they were ready," he added, "to put up a bond of ten thousand pounds that this was their intention"); and to present a statement of grievances to the government and "people in . . . Philadelphia [who] lived a pleasant, protected life and had no feelings for the[ir] great need."[40]

At roughly this same time, a rural assemblyman—having already run into the marchers earlier that morning, farther above the city at Whitemarsh—was riding into the capital with a first copy of these complaints. This paper—which ended "G O D Save the King," in a stab at sounding unrebellious—devoted no room at all to what the armed marchers might do once they were in Philadelphia, and surprisingly little to the December killings at Conestoga and Lancaster jail, which it tried to smooth to one side as only extreme expressions—perhaps "not so agreeable as could be desired"—of the march's real wellspring: a "Disquietude" common to "by far, the greatest Part of the good Inhabitants" over

Indians' being publicly "support[ed], in the very Heart of the Province, at so great an Expence." It turned the European ratepayers into "Dupes and Slaves to *Indians*."⁴¹

When news came that this remonstrance was being brought to town, there were mistaken reports that it demanded, as Israel Pemberton's brother James recorded, that "my bror. . . . be given up to them," as "one Object of the [rioters'] Enmity," and Pemberton rode off hastily to New Jersey. But it became clear from Brycelius and other go-betweens that the marchers would stay that day at Germantown, where they were packing into the taverns. After receiving the written complaint and talking with his council, that evening Penn dismissed for the night the volunteers who were swarming in the city.⁴²

THE NEXT DAY, Tuesday, February 7, was a day of negotiations. In the predawn darkness, a leader among the marchers, calling himself Matthew Smith, came alone into Philadelphia and viewed the newly fortified barracks, then went to talk with the governor. Perhaps in response to this visit, later that morning at five o'clock Penn sent a delegation of notables—including Franklin, the mayor, some of his councilors, the assembly speaker, and prominent Anglican, Lutheran, and Presbyterian clergymen—to Germantown, where, together with Col. John Armstrong of Carlisle (whom both sides more or less trusted), they met with Smith at Coleman's tavern, "where the largest band was assembled." It was presumably an edgy conference. When William Logan, a Quaker councilor, rode up to Coleman's, an eruption of angry catcalls—"There is that scoundrel Logan, that Quaker!"—frightened him into galloping away.⁴³

Upstairs, Smith and the marchers' other spokesmen again blandly disclaimed wanting to do more than "take the Indians out of the barracks . . . to conduct them out of the province," and laid out their grievances. One—lifted from the political points that James Hamilton, the recent governor, had been scoring over the assembly—was a lack of financial encouragement for local expeditions or the payment of neighborhood rangers. Another was "the leading Quakers t[a]k[ing] those Bethlehem Indians (among whom were murderers) into the city and treat[ing] them like lords at public expense. . . . [while] nothing at all was done for the suffering frontiersmen." And, disorientingly, another grievance was the opprobrium that the December attacks had aroused against frontier people as a group—with "the[ir], the backwoodsmen['s], [being] insulted by Quakers and other disorderly people who jeered at them, 'See there! There are the murderers of Paxton who have slain the Indians!'"

As this suggests, it seems possible that an urge to answer back—especially in print—after being derided for the killings was a motive for the march, or at any rate for ending it. The last demand confirmed this: the rioters would disband if Smith and another marcher were allowed to stay behind and prepare a further remonstrance, to be printed up in Philadelphia and presented to the assembly. In this task of publicity, incredibly enough, they asked for the expert help of Franklin himself, which they were refused. The marchers were no more innocent of their own representations in the press than they were of the Indians'. Their actions were shaped by those representations, and by a concern for them, to a startling degree—one that showed print's steadily rising power over events.[44]

The Philadelphians accepted this bargain of the rioters' dispersal for a pamphlet, and when they got back to the city Penn dismissed all of the milling volunteer companies for good. But the next day, when "a poor Raged Com[pan]y" of thirty or so marchers taking advantage of the agreement "did goe [into Philadelphia] on Business, (& to See the City)" (where, according to an indignant Quaker, they were "much taken notice of by some"), there was again a massive military response, with a thousand volunteers mustering in thirty minutes, until the presence of the "Shabby Gang" of "ragged Arse . . . Fellows" was explained. The day after that, one of the march's leaders went less conspicuously to the barracks with an Indian commissioner, where he "looked [the Moravians] earnestly in the face," trying to find one he could decry as a known combatant, "but knew none."

And that, in terms of the action that Philadelphia saw, was that. The marchers evaporated from outside Germantown without entering the city. The Moravians stayed on in the barracks for more than a year, long after the crown troops had left. There they dealt with barely manageable influxes of tourists every Sunday at sermon time (on the weekend after the excitement, Grube noted, "the Indians . . . were forced to bar their rooms, so that they had a little rest"). Young converts played the harpsichord for parties of curious gentlemen, and they all died steadily from the waves of smallpox and dysentery that coursed through the barracks.

That spring the Moravians also read aloud with concern many of the pamphlets and broadsides that were printed in Philadelphia, "see[ing] from the writings that appear almost daily, ... many accusations and great enmity toward our Indians," and coming to fear "that thereby the people are stirred up against us more and more." For what the marchers, soldiers, and volunteers left behind them within a few days was an unprecedented storm of printed polemics, nearly all of which rehashed the riots and drew bitter political lessons. It was a kind of paper blizzard, a silent explosion of print—as if, when the cannon in the streets had been touched off, they had shot out not fire and powder but tens of thousands of sheets of paper, all twisting and fluttering down over the city.[45]

Chapter 7

THE QUAKERS
UNMASKED

In 1764, Philadelphia's printers put out twice as many pamphlets as in any year before. "There has not been a Week since you left this [place]," the merchant William Bingham told a correspondent in May (enclosing for him a new effort called *The Plain Dealer*), "but there has been One or more Pamphlets published & sold about the Streets some of them against the Presbyterians & others against the Quakers." By January 1765, the pace at which pamphlets, poems, cartoons, and bad plays were being printed up still had not slackened, and they had only grown bitterer. One crude broadside showed a huge and lowering "Prince of Darkness," with an anti-Quaker writer kneeling before him in fealty—and this irreligious image, the Lutheran pastor Heinrich Mühlenberg wrote in shock, was actually "hawked about the city today and sold by a harlequin on horseback! Oh, the poor young people! . . . God's judgments cannot be far off!"[1]

The paper war that started that winter amplified and reshaped a pre-existing struggle between politicians and publicists who backed Pennsylvania's assembly, and others who backed the wartime powers of its proprietary governors—an exchange that had in fact been rumbling along intermittently for a full decade. Its first salvos were fired at the start of the Seven Years' War by Rev. William Smith, the provost of the College of Philadelphia, whose first efforts at propaganda had laid out a matrix for all the printed fights that followed—fights in which, through the creative logic of debate, the authority of all the countryside's unwashed Europeans would be steadily exalted.

BENJAMIN FRANKLIN had rescued Smith, a promising young Aberdeen-born Episcopalian, from his position as a Long Island tutor, sponsoring him to lead the college in 1753. During the war years, many of Smith's students folded elements of the anti-Indian sublime into their belles lettres. Reading their teacher's writings, it seems clear that Smith himself pioneered most of this rhetoric's most distinctive features, gradually refining anti-Indianism into a literary system amid the scrappy printed arguments that came with war. In his unsigned pamphlets and newspaper pieces—with annual flurries in September, before the elections—Smith had been working to undermine the assembly even before the onset of violence late in 1755. The differences in this self-consciously expert rhetorician's efforts before and after that autumn can illustrate in embryo how the war would change all public discourse in the middle colonies.[2]

In December 1754, Smith wrote a pamphlet on the dangers that Pennsylvania faced from French territorial encroachments. This first prewar effort, printed in London, was meant not for a wide local audience but for a small, specific one across the sea: the parliamentary majority at Westminster, whose help Smith and the Penns' governor, Robert Hunter Morris, were hoping to enlist in making the Quaker-dominated assembly less powerful, or at any rate less Quaker.

The most striking thing about this pamphlet was the frankly bigoted persona in which Smith wrote it. He thought a French land grab in the West was made likelier by Quaker assemblymen's lack of interest in funding preventive military measures; and it was a danger that he doubted the Germans settled there (improbably many of whom he assumed to be Catholic) would do much to resist. "They say it is all one to them," Smith scoffed, "which King gets the Country." Nearly all of Pennsylvania's woes could be laid at the door of the "uncultivated Race of *Germans*," whose "insolent, sullen, and turbulent" ways Smith tirelessly decried. These foreigners' apathy and "extrem[e] ignoran[ce]" left them easy puppets for

Quaker politicians, whose German sectarian allies had long pumped out German-language propaganda against the Penns.

Short of slowly "making *Englishmen*" of the foreigners by English-only education, Smith thought the best solution was to cut out all German participation from the public sphere. This could be done by voiding wills and legal documents in German, outlawing the German press, so that "no News-Papers . . . or any other periodical Paper" could appear except in English, and—most simply—stripping German monolinguals of their right to vote. For why should this "Body of ignorant, proud, stubborn Clowns (who are unacquainted with our Language, our Manners, our Laws, and our Interests)" have any electoral power? It was also urgent to end the tolerance shown to Catholics (and others, like Moravians, "suspected to be a dangerous People . . . much a-kin" to them), since in Smith's view an insane, Quaker-dictated toleration of non-Protestants had left the colony a prey to fifth columnists and invaders. In short, the province's salvation lay in systematically erasing the divisions that came with religious and linguistic diversity.³

Like Smith, most public writers before the war took it for granted that there was a wall between German and English print. Like him, too, they worried less about American opinion than about swaying "the Minds of our Superiors" in Westminster, and assumed that the Quakers erred in their approach to other Europeans—if they did err—by being too tolerant. (Smith's side, by contrast, prided itself on not keeping quiet about the Catholic menace out of any shrinking "Fear of stirring up a Persecution.") Most writers were also alike in assuming that the assembly, as the "popular" part of government, represented the people's will, if anything, too closely; that "the Power of the People," lodged in the assembly, and "the Power of their Governors," lodged in the executive, were in perpetual tension (an assembly writer described the governors' *"Interest"* as *"totally distinct* from that of the *People"*); and that it would not do for people outside the legislative chamber to become too involved in politics.

For no one was "so absurd as to 'design a Democracy.'" Public life could never be guided by "a *fickle*, and *confused Multitude*": *"no such Absurdity* and Inconveniency was ever *allowed* of, as to give the *Persons represented*, a Power to *controul* their *Representatives."* In the technical sense, the people were still a thing quite different from—and more ideal than—those individual people who happened to be living in the countryside at a particular time. The people were a principle made tangible only through the magic of representation. Collections of real individuals out of doors, however numerous or excited, could never embody the people as their representatives could.4

Given this abstracting filter between politics and the living public, Smith's first writings were dense and intramural, with much quotation of parliamentary messages that the assembly and governor had batted between them. Relying on the unfriendly parsing of legislative minutes, this plodding, he-said-they-said style of argument made for tiresome reading—as one assembly writer admitted in a 1759 pamphlet (also printed in England). "It would be endless to wade through all the Minutenesses of so tedious a Contest," he apologized, after dozens of pages;

> and Odds if the Reader did not leave the Writer in the Midst of it. . . .
> Into the Hands of what Number of Readers . . . this Treatise shall fall,
> is out of Calculation . . . . : But whatever the Number may be . . . the
> Majority will by this Time, probably, exclaim, Enough of this Governor!
> or, Enough of this Author!

Still, the assembly's publicists had long been happiest in exactly this mode. Many assemblymen saw themselves as liberty's guardians—devoted every day on the house floor, as one confided in his diary, to the job of "detesting and despising" the Penn family, "that Monster of arbitrary power." So maddened by the monster's legislative maneuvers that they felt driven to reproduce them all, verbatim, on paper, the best rhetorical effects that many assembly writers could manage came simply from salting their pamphlets (as a parodist pointed out) with "the Words 'Liberty, Property, Proprietary private interest and Power, Injustice, Misery, Slavery, Thraldom, Bondage, Captivity . . . [in] double Handfuls."5

Smith's first pamphlet stood out from this background mainly for the harshness with which it "cu[t] and slash[ed]" at Quakers and Germans. Even so it was popular, falling—according to Smith—"as a Clap of Thunder," with nowhere near enough copies anywhere to meet demand.

When a few arrived on a London ship, as Smith smugly noted, "there was a Run after them Night and Day for a Week. Thousands would have been sold here, if they had been sent over." From Lancaster, a young gentleman wrote to thank his Philadelphia schoolmaster for sending him a hand-written précis "of the late Pamphlet that has made so much Noise in Town"—since in the countryside he had no other way of reading Smith's attack. Still, in both style and distribution, the effect of Smith's first effort was self-limited.[6]

BUT AT MIDSUMMER 1755, with the rout of Maj. Gen. Edward Braddock's expedition to western Pennsylvania, the war started to seem terribly real to large numbers of people. As one of Smith's rhetorical pro-tégés, Rev. Thomas Barton, told a hushed congregation in Carlisle, the atmosphere around them now should be seen as charged with dread—with "Calamity . . . roar[ing] at our very Doors":

> Ruin and Desolation . . . with gigantic Strides, approach our once peace-
> ful Habitations! . . . we who inhabit the Frontiers left an unarmed Prey
> to a savage Multitude, who are cruel, and have no Mercy! . . . The News
> of Battle and Murder daily wounding our Ears! . . . our not very remote
> Neighbours . . . wallowing in their Blood, and biting the Ground . . . !
> And we ourselves just on the Brink of sharing the same Fate!

In this new milieu, Smith prepared a second, startlingly different round of anonymous writings. As fears of war overran the province, he had come to understand how one might simply squash the Quaker assembly and its *"democratical* Schemes of Power": not by appealing over its head to Parliament but by appealing beneath it, to the people them-selves, and in particular to the suspicions that Indian attack were stirring in them.[7]

An electoral solution to the problems of Pennsylvania's proprietary faction—which had seen a series of governors brought to heel by assem-blymen who controlled, not just their salaries, but an array of patronage posts at which the executive could only look longingly—seemed within reach. Smith and his circle began to be hopeful in late 1755 that, with war, the patterns of public life might truly be transformed: the executive freed to run provincial affairs "with Secresy, Ease, Expedition, [and] Success," and a new grand coalition of patriots formed to sweep away the old assembly. Smith—and with him Robert Hunter Morris, the governor at the start of the war—had an issue with which the people might be awakened and the Quakers' electoral spell dissolved.

So in his next major pamphlet, in December 1755, Smith looked back on a fall filled with Indian attacks. He now had livelier subjects than Bourbon land claims to take up. For "My Life is at Stake," as Smith announced from the study of his Philadelphia house, "and the Cry of Blood, Death and Desolation hourly pierces my very Heart from the Country round about." The title page of his new book promised readers "an Account of the shocking Inhumanities, committed by . . . the Indians," because it was becoming clear that they made for a kind of reading mid-Atlantic buyers would seek out very eagerly.[8]

This had been established that winter by William and Elizabeth Fleming, a husband and wife who lived through raids at the Great Cove. Having "lost all they had in the world," the Flemings set up house in Philadelphia. There they wrote a gripping double narrative of their "Sufferings and Surprizing Deliverances" at the hands of the Delaware war chief Captain Jacobs and started selling copies from their Second Street lodgings, asking that "all . . . who are curious to read this little pamphlet, will purchase from the authors . . . only, for th[eir] Benefit." Although a description of their own miseries was the only property the Flemings had left, they did well enough this way for their story to see at least three Philadelphia editions in six weeks, as well as two German editions sold as far away as Lancaster. There was an immediate popular audience for wartime horrors. Like Smith's new work, every piece of public argument printed in Philadelphia after 1755 would have to take account—and, if possible, advantage—of this.[9]

Smith made the new polemic easy for his fellow colonists to buy and to like. The pamphlet sold widely, and to sensational effect, at Bradford's bookshop in Philadelphia. Smith aimed it squarely at a local audience, and filled its pages with the long dashes, the shattered families (a scalped mother, who had "her new born Child horribly mangled, and put under Head for a Pillow"), the exclamations, and the horrible vistas ("mangled

Limbs . . . promiscuously strewed upon the Ground . . . !") of the anti-
Indian sublime. But Smith also entirely switched about his approach to
those unreliable Germans who filled the western settlements, and who
had started populating his own atrocity accounts.

He knew that he had to do this, and how to do it, because of newspaper exchanges with his critics, all of whom quoted his nastiest passages
about Germans as proof of the Penns' sinister intentions toward their
own people. Smith's first effort, one such writer observed, "is filled with
personal Scurilities and Reflections against whole Bodies of People, in a
Language purely *Billinsgate.*" This was easy to show: "The *Germans,*" as
he noted, "are called [in it] a Body of insolent, false, turbulent, proud,
ignorant, stubborn Clowns; and the *Quakers,* [and] *Menonists* . . . mentioned in Terms full as respectful."

The accusation of having intolerantly aspersed whole categories of
people sent Smith into such a tailspin of self-justification that he plainly
believed it could ruin his whole project. He had to somehow keep up his
attacks on Quakers as a political class, and on the German role in supporting them, without seeming to vilify those groups as groups. Tolerant
intolerance was tricky to manage. Smith tried apology: he had not meant
to attack all Germans, and if he had, "he is wrong." He tried denial: "He
is so far from *reflecting* on the poor, misled *Germans,* that he pities them."
He tried blaming a few bad apples: "all the Reflections thrown out against
. . . whole Bodies . . . are due only to a few *designing* Persons, who have
made the *Cats-paw* of the Rest." And—simplest of all—he tried going
unapologetically back on the attack. He was not bigoted, but his opponents were: and that was exactly why he had to denounce them.[10]

From a writer who lit endlessly into "Foreigners," and everyone who
pandered to them, in his second pamphlet Smith reemerged a champion
of the oppressed German and Irish country people against *"our haughty
Masters,"* the Quakers. What was the Quakers' worst flaw? Unflinchingly
Smith named it: their intolerance toward other Europeans. For "I see my
poor Fellow-subjects," he wrote, *"bleeding and suffering"* all around—and
suffering from the Quakers' political machinations. While Quaker
assemblymen had been cruelly footling about, "finding means to intro-
duce Quarrels, and spin out the Time," all the while "their Country was
bleeding beneath the Outrages of a savage Enemy." That blood now

drenched the province's ground was the fault of Quakers as much as Indians. For "alas!" he wailed,

> who shall gather up the innocent Blood that has been spilt upon our
> Borders, and in the very Heart of our Country . . . . a Multitude of our
> Quakers . . . are the bloodiest People in our Land; and the Blood of those
> who are murdered thro' their Default, cries to Heaven against them . . . .

"[T]he bloodiest People in our Land"—it was an incredible transference. And these Quaker men of blood could behave so cruelly because they did not care about other Europeans at all. In fact, they scorned the Irish and German people pouring into the countryside as garbage to be swept aside, taking a "secret Satisfaction in seeing their increasing Multitude *thinned* and *beggared.*" To establish this, Smith adduced an apocryphal Quaker in Lancaster, who when told of a new series of Indian attacks had "replied with great Indifference, that *there were only some* Scotch-Irish killed, *who could well enough be spared.*" This naked bigotry was the cue for more transports of indignation:

> This is the common Language of many of these People [the Quak-
> ers]. . . . My very Soul rises at the Thought! And these hard-hearted
> Wretches will find that *God* will require the Blood of *Scotch-Irish* at their
> Hands as soon as the Blood of *Quakers*. . . . Their Consciences are
> mighty tender of shedding the Blood of *Indian* Murderers, but hardened
> and seared as to shedding the Blood . . . of the *Scotch-Irish.*

Always going about, "insinuating that other religious Denominations are not upon an equal Footing with themselves" and fancying they had been "set . . . apart as the CHOSEN OF GOD," Smith's arrogant Quakers might, in fact, be too bigoted to live in an open society like Pennsylvania at all. For "where lies the Difference," Smith asked bravely, between the Quakers and a more obviously subversive group like the Catholics? "Both . . . are *staunch, bigotted,* and *pharisaical* alike. . . . SUCH A RELIGION ought to be rejected, and, if possible, extirpated from the Face of the whole Earth." Smith wrote happily of signs that if they were pushed too far by Indian attack, the country people for whom he now claimed to speak might well try to end Quakers' connivance in their agonies by the "Expedient" of "cutting their Throats." He himself would of course "by no means think of them all alike": but the Quakers' own murderous intolerance was plain to see.

Smith suggested that a fair remedy for the country people's suffering might be to give them new assembly seats—since the back counties, being "settled with People of many other Denominations" and clearly accounting for "so great a Majority" of "the whole People," had been "very sneakingly" slighted by the Quakers. With this simple step taken, "it would be impossible to tie up the Hands of the People." Precisely like Smith's earlier scheme to disfranchise Germans, this proposal to pack the assembly with new members would have short-circuited all the existing structures of politics. The brilliant difference was that, this time, the grounds for doing so sounded transparently democratic, inclusive, and tolerant rather than the reverse.

The attractiveness and seeming urgency of Smith's program came from the terrifying immediacy of the rural war: people were dying out there, after all, as you had only to riffle his pages to see. In grasping how readily—and gainfully—Indian war could be presented as an ethnic issue, Smith had sketched out the direction for most rhetoric over the next decade. Even before the war a few polemics had tried out some of the separate attacks that Smith combined—like the idea that any pacifistic Quaker assemblyman should "be branded with the Name of a Betrayer of his Country, and be hated and despised." But now the language of blood crying for vengeance, and the accusations of Quaker bigotry and pharisaism that it always enfolded, lent all such charges much greater power.[11]

IF IT WAS to change anything other than literature, this language had to affect live voters and officeholders, so Smith's most powerful ally—the governor—soon started to help in remolding public discourse. As his opponents in the assembly knew, Robert Hunter Morris was himself a master rhetorician, one able to gain the fullest advantage both from his dramatic spoken addresses to the assembly and from their reprintings. Morris's excited rhetoric was so eerily like Smith's own—with the governor's *"artful* Messages" invariably packed full of "pathetic Calls, and loud Demands," Indian dangers and damning questions ("Had you really any Tenderness for your bleeding Country," he asked the assembly in August 1755, "would you have acted the Part you have done?")—that its frustrated members charged him with having written all Smith's unsigned work, given their "perfect *Sameness* of Sentiment, and even of Expression."[12]

As one skeptical assemblyman noted, when Indian news reached Philadelphia, Morris seemed personally to "ma[k]e it [his] Business . . . to increase the Terrors of the Times"—calling the assembly's members up to the State House council chamber to stand before him as, "with all the Circumstances of Alarm and Terror his Imagination could furnish," and "a Face, and a Voice, . . . suitable for the Practice . . . to be tried," he declaimed on the dangers all around (though his auditors thought "he seemed more delighted than shocked with the Recital"). Braddock's defeat, especially, Morris apparently "thought . . . would render his Eloquence irresistible," together with whatever other "Matter from the Frontier could give the Governor any new Advantage." All of it made a repetitive catalog of "Stuff" that, by autumn's end, "he had talked over and over, till the Ear was weary": "the Devastations, Cruelties, and Murders committed there, and the Horror they excited in him," with such other "good terrifying Ingredient[s]" as a repeated invocation of the province's supposedly *"naked"* and defenseless state ("almost in the Stile of Invitation") if the assembly did not grant him more money or men.[13]

These performances, all printed up for the newspapers, infuriated many assemblymen, who knew even as they stood listening that they were not Morris's real audience. Like Smith, Morris hoped instead to reshape politics with the weight of the eager reading public outside the State House doors. The assemblymen were already funding war efforts at levels seldom reached in the region. Many probably felt that Pennsylvania's Indian attackers could be dealt with better by negotiation than by force (as proved true of the eastern Delawares); that rural raids could never really be prevented; and perhaps that most of "the Losses [the country people] ha[d] suffered were owing intirely to . . . the[ir] loose scattered Manner" of squatting. But they knew, too, that none of these arguments would please or reassure those people outside the State

House who wanted something definite to do against their attackers, and someone to blame. For "Fear," as one of Morris's listeners glumly moralized, "though most an Enfeebler of any of the Passions, has the strongest Dominion over us; and while we are scarce half of ourselves, it is not to be wondered, that we become the Property of any Body else."¹⁴

Throughout 1755, petitions asking for arms came to Philadelphia from the banks of the Susquehanna and the foothills of the Blue Mountains. But mixed in with these pleas were harsher addresses, from closer by, that blamed instead of asking. One, submitted by a justice of the peace named William Moore, flatly ordered Quaker assemblymen to stop "neglect[ing] the Defence of the Province"; Philadelphia's mayor and 133 co-signers presented another, petulantly making "a positive and immediate *Demand*" that they relieve their "bleeding . . . suffering Fellow-Subjects" by agreeing to every provision of a militia law on which the governor insisted.¹⁵

Both addresses had been written by William Smith—who privately boasted that by means of such "clamorous Things, signed by great Numbers of Hands" the assembly would be *"pelted"* into laws to the governor's liking. The very cool reception the assembly gave the petitions showed that they knew they were contrivances, aimed at "hectoring the Assembly into . . . Measures" they would never otherwise adopt. But if they kept coming in, the assemblymen sensed there might be little they could defensibly do against the "Power of Numbers."¹⁶

When the newspapers printed one especially inflammatory address that Smith had written for Justice Moore, the best reply the maddened assemblymen could manage was to call Smith before their bar—wheeling, with misplaced fury, to seize and fine a listening group of city gentlemen who dared to set up a "loud tumultuous Stamping of Feet, Hissing and Clapping of Hands" at their chamber's opened doors when Smith finished speaking—and to jail him for contempt. Though Smith had lost his anonymity, he had succeeded in shifting public debate—and, at times, in *"pelt[ing]"* the assembly into buckling to the governor.¹⁷

The first years of war had falteringly shaped a culture of public argument that drew its style and conviction from descriptions of Indian attack and allegations of intolerance. The printed arguments made by the war were linking up the German- and English-speaking worlds in novel ways, and recurring more and more often to the sanction of the people—

the people not as an intangible ideal, but as the suffering mass of Irish and German country people: people who, far from being to blame for their own problems, were discussed with rising confidence as the victims of a corrupted politics.

Nearly a decade later, in 1764, the printed debates that followed the Paxton riots brought each one of these changes forward again with startling speed, volume, and ferocity, carrying them, in a little less than a year, close to their fullest possible extension.

FOR A WHILE after the December 1763 killings at Conestoga and Lancaster, everything put into print deplored what the rioters had done. "[A] Piece from [the rioters'] side of the Question appearing," one pamphleteer noted, "was thought impossible." There was agreement that the murders in December had been acts of total cowardice, the kind of thing "no Man of real Courage or Bravery would bear the Thought of doing." The meaning of the crisis still lay in what the Lancaster County killers had done to Indians—not in, say, what Indians (still less Quakers) had done to them. It seemed obvious that the marchers had meant to do more than protest on reaching Philadelphia: they were insurrectionists. The Quakers' taking up arms had been unprecedented but admirably "spirited," full of neighborly good intentions. (One amused cartoon showed volunteers peeking from an upper window in the Friends meetinghouse, calling down happily, "bring the Grogg up Stairs.")[18]

As a matter of course, most writers disparaged the country people behind the killing and marching as "more savage than *Indians* themselves." They were simpleminded creatures with semi-intelligible Ulster brogues, and full-throated ethnic mockery was at first the rule. "Hoot Mon," one was made to ask another in a popular dialogue, while hearing his account of the killings: "Were not you frechtened to facht so mony Indians?"[19]

The idea that the rioters were the true savages was best expressed in Benjamin Franklin's anonymous *Narrative of the Late Massacres*—a stunning achievement that so dominated the first weeks of debate that it became a public issue in its own right, driving the frustrated marchers to demand Franklin's own help in answering it. In the *Narrative*, as we have

already seen, Franklin upended the achievements of the anti-Indian sublime by using all its favorite tactics—down to italicized groans of horror,
and the display of mutilated bodies—only with European murderers
written into the Indian role. (This was easy enough to do, since the
killers' own actions were meant to make the analogy explicit.) Franklin
then tediously traced the ways that "strangers" fared in the power of people from an immense sweep of other eras and places. Heathen Greeks, the
Muslims of Dagestan, popish Spaniards, Indians—all scorned to kill
innocent outsiders. Even "a poor unenlightened *African Negroe*" would
know that *"you must not kill a Man, that has done no Harm, only for being
white."* And then the payoff came: in a fast paragraph of condemnation—
like an anchor chain of contrasts, rattling unstoppably out and dragging
the rioters down with it—Franklin noted that the Conestogas would thus
have been safe among any other people anywhere on earth, no matter
how primitive, except "the CHRISTIAN WHITE SAVAGES of *Peckstang* and
Donegall!—"[20]

He offered in passing an account of the murderers' motivation—one
modern observers usually accept as clearheaded, but which made almost
no impression on contemporaries. The Lancaster County rioters had
been driven to kill, Franklin supposed, by the hate they felt for all people
who shared the Indians' color and physiognomy. The Indians' "only
Crime" was "that they had a reddish brown Skin, and black Hair"—a
phenotypic hatred as senseless, he wrote, as if he were to take it into his
head to start "killing all the freckled red-haired Men, Women, and Children, I could."[21]

But for now contemporaries all but ignored this theory, since another
ready-made explanation for the rioters' acts seemed to them so compelling. This was (in the words of a comic dialogue) that besides being
European savages, they were also certainly "aw *Presbyterians,*" who had
stupidly understood what they did as "fechting the Lord's Battles" against
Old Testament enemies. It became a truism that the killers had seen
themselves as the predestined elect and their victims—real and potential,
Indian or European—as heathens. The idea had no detectable documentary basis, but contemporaries felt strongly that it made sense. The idea
of bigoted, self-sanctified Presbyterians, who thought "all other *Profes-
sions* intermix'd among them, the *Heathens* with whom they have to con-

tend," gained a purchase in explaining the riots where the idea of skin-color prejudice did not. Because bigotry of this kind applied as much to other Europeans as to Indians, public debate soon turned far more on the attractive problem of Europeans' prejudice toward one another than on prejudice against Indians.[22] And this focus on intolerance between Europeans would not have to work against the rioters. William Smith's bigoted Quakers were standing in the wings.[23]

The brilliantly titled *Declaration and Remonstrance of the Distressed and Bleeding Frontier Inhabitants*, which was put out (after a week's drafting) by the marchers' spokesmen, started a revaluation of what the rioters had done. It tried hard to show that all the tumult had been about nothing less than the people's right to be heard by petitioning government—about what recourse an oppressed people could seek. How could anyone condemn this? As a sympathetic poet put it, when Philadelphians rode to Germantown to meet the marchers,

> They came, they saw, they found 'em civil
> With no intent of Harm or Evil
> But humbly to request Redress
> For cruel *Indians* Wickedness.

It developed now, too, that all along the march had been about getting a voice for the people of the backcountry by means of more assembly seats: a demand unthought of in the rioters' initial declaration, but now exhumed from William Smith's pamphlets at the start of the war.[24]

Writers took strongly to the notion of "a bereft and injured People," humbly asking for help, and then fused the marchers with the whole of the rural population. If all were alike "beggar'd, ruined, miserable Fellow Subjects," the rioters were the people and the people were they. And whatever "your city Quakers" might think, the country people were "a great Majority": "nine Tenths of the Inhabitants," or "three Fourths"—or at any rate some very large number, all of them on the marchers' side. The goal was to transmute the Paxton crowd from an "ignorant and enthusiastick *Mob*" into an index of popular opinion, making it harder to resist them as savages from "the barren Mountains of . . . *Slemish.*" Their ethnicity did not matter, and their numbers did.[25]

But after the manufactured petition drives at the start of the war, writers who supported the assembly were used to looking on crowds and petitions as performances, gotten up for political ends by their enemies, rather than the real voice of the people. At first, they reflexively dismissed any discoverable mass opinion in the province as trumped up or irrelevant. The sense of the people, one observed, could never be grasped without "setting aside the common People of the Town"—or, indeed, all "the inconsiderate Part of the People," "not One in Fifty" of whom, another easily maintained, "understands what he reads." As public actors they did not matter.[26]

This rich, unself-conscious vein of antimajoritarian language made it easy to present the marchers' opponents as unfriendly to the people. And that it was completely out of step with the public response to the crisis was proven by the explosion of print. At least as far west as Lancaster, where the covers of many imprints now said they were for sale, even "the Vulgar, [and] People Ignorant of the Matter" were clearly reading, listening to, and buying polemics as they had never come close to doing before. The debates over the riots were truly popular, and they offered a matchless opportunity for hustling, cut-rate entrepreneurs of print—who responded by pirating all of each other's most popular pamphlets, making up fresh combinations of tracts and poems to reissue together, printing humorous double-sided handbills (one side for each side of the question), supplying helpful little collect-them-all lists of riot-related imprints (at one shop, fourteen could be had for a total investment of just four and a half shillings)—with a delight that shone from their pages: "The Demand for this Piece has been so great, that *this Fourth Edition* is call'd for in a few Days!" Suddenly there were topical engravings, too: "real cartoons," in one cartoon scholar's approving assessment, the likes of which had never been cut in America before. Many of these prints—like the one meant to illustrate citizens turning out and "scampering away, Helter Skelter, one tumbling over another," in alarm at the rioters—showed the cobbled square in front of Philadelphia's courthouse steps (figure 7.1). It was a public setting familiar to

7.1: A pastiche of highlights from the Paxton crisis. Watchmen pound on doors, the Friends meetinghouse is filled with volunteers, one unit nearly fires on another, and the governor dismisses the crowd. *Henry Dawkins, "The Paxton Expedition, Inscribed to the Author of the Farce . . . ," illustrating* The Paxton Boys: A Farce *(both Philadelphia, 1764). Courtesy of the Library Company of Philadelphia.*

every marketgoer, and to anyone who climbed those steps to vote in the elections each October. Such crude cartoons started presenting the people to themselves—at first only to amuse, but soon enough with a sharp political edge.[27]

Not wanting to miss all chance of celebrating the people at large by too roundly denigrating the "suffering" rioters described in the *Declaration and Remonstrance,* even the harshest pro-assembly writers gave up saying that the marchers had been bent on bloody treason. Instead they, too, made kindly noises about "sympathizing with them," and the marchers became not bandits but "poor despicable wretches that were made *Dupes* of" by other public figures.[28]

This retreat was called for because the argument about Europeans' mutual intolerance had started swinging strongly around in the rioters' favor, under the influence of a vicious new view of Quakers (in part taken intact from Smith's earlier efforts) that was best laid out in a pamphlet called *The Quaker Unmask'd.* This production by David James Dove, an extraordinary schoolmaster, broad-mindedly proclaimed itself unwilling to "condemn the Lump" of Quakers—but events had already proven them all wickedly intolerant. They had not subscribed to relief funds for frontier people: no, "not . . . a single Farthing." And ocular proof of their intolerance was provided by what Dove made the primal scene of Quaker betrayal.[29]

No one had really seen it before, but Quaker men's mustering in the crisis was nothing to smile at. It was chilling if you thought about it right, because it proved that Quaker pacifism was a selective sham, maintained solely to keep the country people in danger's way. But just let those same rural Europeans come within range, Dove observed grimly, and "Behold . . . the Quaker unmask'd, with his Gun upon his Shoulder, . . . eagerly desiring the Combat, and thirsting for . . . Blood"! Dove imagined one of them confiding, in that mild, Quakerly way,

> Friend . . . It is true, we profess to have an Aversion to War: but . . . we secretly rejoice when we hear of whole Settlements murdered and destroyed. . . . And tho' our Malice at present is openly pointed only at the Presbyterians; yet to be plain with thee, we are as much in our Hearts against all who differ from us in Opinion . . . . thee knows it would be impolitic to discover our Resentment to too many Sects at once . . . .[30]

This reading of what Philadelphia's Quaker men had done was obviously a stretch. But the accusation stuck. Writers on the Quaker side fell into a dazed silence about Quaker arms-bearing, even as their opponents returned endlessly, and with rising glee, to the image of a violent Quaker who stood ready to shoot down, not Indians, but other Europeans. In vivid contrast, as another pamphlet written in Lancaster reminded readers,

> When a Waggon-Load of the scalped and mangled Bodies of their Countrymen were brought to *Philadelphia* and laid at the *State-House Door,* and another Waggon-Load brought into the Town of *Lancaster,* did they rouse to Arms to avenge the Cause . . . ? . . .——O my dear Friends! must I answer—No? The *Dutch* and *Irish* are murder'd without Pity.[31]

So Quakers liked to see the people dead. On February 6, Quakers had strained to attack them in the shape of the marchers, and they schemed to do so every other day as well, by curbing war spending. If you traced their design to endanger other colonists back a little in time, you found that they were to blame for a collection of horrors: for the Indian raids in the countryside, of course; for the Paxton killings and the march on Philadelphia those attacks called up (for "[w]ho is it," one writer shrewdly asked, "has made them Rioters, and then . . . desires they may be *Shot* or *Hang'd* for being so?"); even for the breaking out of the Seven Years' War itself, with all the carnage, "Misery and Ruin [it had] entail'd upon Millions of their Fellow Creatures" over three continents. As one pro-Quaker writer protested, "You might with equal Justice . . . impute . . . the late Death of the Emperor of Muscovy, to them": but the continuance of Indian attacks was nonetheless more and more commonly discussed as something one might ascribe to Quakers.³²

THE SUBJECT OF DEBATE was veering sharply away from anything the rioters had done and moving toward the policies of government: a government somehow embodied solely in Quakers. As this happened, and the Friendly Association came under heavy fire, it started to matter a great deal that the wartime treaty conferences had been carried out with so keen an eye for future publicity.³³

After a conference at Lancaster in 1762, Sir William Johnson, the northern Indian superintendent and a foe of the Friendly Association's "Sinester," "Unjustifiable interfereing," had urged the translator George Croghan to see into print accounts of the Quakers' "Immense . . . profuseness" toward Ohio Delawares at the treaty—as well as Croghan's claim that Israel Pemberton had had sex there with an Indian woman. As Johnson advised him, this story "of the Head of the White Hatts" (like John Woolman, Pemberton was by then a wearer of undyed clothing),

> is verry merry, and I think verry worthy of haveing a place in the Publick prints, sure I am, that many things not half so diverting or Interesting are daily published in Papers and Magazines, and I must say I heartily wish that the Worthy Member had some kind freind, who would make known his . . . pious intentions of propagateing the Species . . . .

No one made anything of the gossip that year, but plainly few images could encapsulate so well the notion of furtive, morally contaminating exchanges between Indians and Quakers. It made the Friendly Association's best-known member a literal Indian-lover.[34]

So as the paper war raged on, Pemberton's supposed encounter at the treaty did become the subject of a propaganda fantasy, *King Wampum* (see figure 7.2), lovingly describing how "a pregnant *Squaw* he spie[d], / Which made his lustful Passions rise; / . . . (For Hungry Dogs love dirty Pudding)." Pemberton "f[ell] to her"—only to get his comeuppance when he found that

> . . . while he did this clever Jobb
> She div'd her Hand into his Fob . . .
> He storms, he raves . . .
> Thee impudent! Thee saucy Huzzy!
> Whilst I rub'd up thy Tuzzy Muzzy
> Thee stol'st my Watch![35]

After *King Wampum* saw print, Pemberton became a negative celebrity of incalculable value to anti-Quaker writers. Everything about him came in for abuse: his hot temper, his panicky flight from Philadelphia, even his son-in-law's manslaughter charge. What would otherwise have been abstract assertions that a starving people had been forced to feed their enemies—with the Indians brought to Philadelphia and "invited from House to House, to riot at Feasts"—could all come into sharp focus around the figure of Pemberton, with his mansion and his taste for "embracing BARBARIANS." "It is said," as one pamphlet put the case, "that ISRAEL, that great Patron and Friend of Indians, hath kept his House and Stable open for these Wretches and their Horses, whilst the beggar'd Frontier-People have been drove from his Door." He valued them not only beneath Indians, but beneath Indians' animals.[36]

A few other Quakers made usable targets, too: like Joseph Fox, the assembly speaker, barracks master, and Indian commissioner; or Abel James, a merchant who served as the Friendly Association's clerk, or effective head. One cartoon showed James doling out tomahawks to a group of Indians, urging them to "Exercise those on the Scotch Irish & Dutch & Ill

7.2: Quaker mischief. *Left:* A view of the *King Wampum* fantasy, with Israel Pemberton "embracing BARBARIANS" at a 1762 treaty conference. *Center:* More of the same. *Right:* Friendly Association clerk Abel James hands out tomahawks for use on non-Quakers. *Detail of [James Claypoole Jr.], "An Indian Squaw King Wampum spies . . ."; two details of "Exercise those on the Scotch Irish & Dutch . . ." (both Philadelphia, 1764). Courtesy of the Library Company of Philadelphia.*

support you while I am Abel" (figure 7.2). But Pemberton was the supreme Quaker villain, as even this picture showed: the lesser merchant pulled his tomahawks from a bulging barrel marked "I P," for Israel Pemberton.

Such assertions gathered power in the prints, suggesting that Quakers' special closeness with Indians was only the other side of an undue distance from other Europeans, whom they despised. If that were so, the marchers had done a public service by cleaving through the distracting jumble of Quaker apologetics for Indians, to show that at heart the Friends' position was really about the neglect and abuse of other Europeans—they had

> . . . expose[d] a Jugler's Box,
> Contriv'd by P[emberto]n and F[o]x

By which, they with a Magic Trick
Could shew white Folks as black's Oldnick
And what's as wonderful agen,
Make *Indian* Villains honest Men.37

This indictment of the Quakers for bending government policy against "white Folks" and in favor of their friends, the Indians, opened another front on which writers who favored the assembly seemed to feel they must stay silent: few publicists wrote in defense of Quakers as a group, or of the Delawares. And no one on the assembly's side even tried to come up with an apology for Pemberton and the Friendly Association. It was a sign of "The Dexterity and Success" of the attacks at "bring[ing] the Society of People called Quakers to publick Shame" that even one of their defenders felt obliged to weakly allow that the Friendly Association's members "have shewn too much lenity towards" Indians. Pemberton, in particular, became everyone's goat, and, surprisingly, much of the legacy in Indian relations that Quaker reformers had spent a decade painstakingly building up was publicly cut loose as indefensible.38

For rather than try to mount a coherent defense, writers on the assembly's side responded by attacking Presbyterians: no longer as a casual matter of course, but with a unity of purpose that showed they now saw Presbyterianism—as their opponents saw Quakerism—at the core of all the colonies' troubles. This was supposedly because so many of the marchers had been Ulster Presbyterians—or, as they would now sometimes be called, *"Ulceration"* "Piss—Brute—tarians"—and in truth because the Quakers' defenders needed a bête noire of their own. By now the lines of attack were clear. "It is I say," one lacerating anti-Presbyterian writer avowed, "a Task no ways agreeable to me, to compare the Conduct of different religious Societies"; and of course no one had any "desire to throw harsh Reflections on the *Religion* of this sect of people"—but all the same the Presbyterian clergy themselves were "determined to defame a whole Society of People," and the public simply had to be warned against their burning, theocratic thirst for dominion over not only the Quakers but every other group.39

Bloated by bigotry and party spirit, "Enemies to every Society but their own," and convinced that Pennsylvania was their Canaan, where they could "use . . . the same Means in extirpating *Quakers,* Indians, or any other . . . Enemies, that the *Israelites* did," the Presbyterians aimed at using the unrest to somehow push through an establishment of their church. Once they had the public in a yoke, "[thei]r Progress to lawless Power, the great Object of [thei]r Wishes" would end in their "reduc[ing] all other Societies, the Church of England not excepted, to [thei]r Will and Pleasure."[40]

Writers on both sides suggested what shape the debate was taking in public opinion by what they would and would not try to defend. Hugh Williamson and Isaac Hunt were the most skilled anti-Quaker and anti-Presbyterian writers, respectively. Hunt wrote endless, fluent pages of anti-Irish and anti-Presbyterian word music, but there were two subjects that, as a rule, he would not touch with a barge pole: the Quakers' Indian relations, and the accounts of frontier horrors so often used by the riots' defenders. Williamson, for his part, doggedly refused to be drawn by Hunt on the merits of Presbyterianism, instead sticking to his best-received theme: the treachery shown by pro-Indian Quakers, with their bigoted hope for other Europeans' destruction. Since each side's favorite subject was the other's vicious intolerance, a spiral coil of antibigotry resulted, one that seemed able, as a practical matter, to go on endlessly tightening. Every tirade only gave the other side fresh evidence, until all the participants in these printed debates were more loudly and explicitly proclaiming their own commitment to respect between European groups than they had ever had any cause to do before.

It became the condition of entry into this hall of mirrors—an obligatory opening gesture—to decry the wickedness of "attempt[ing] to blast the reputation of . . . a Body of People," right before doing so.[41]

So BOTH SIDES cobbled together fantastical enemies, and in a couple of months a compliantly wicked collective Presbyterian and Quaker had each been perfected, whom their creators sometimes scolded in direct address. Panic and depopulation hurt the people, Williamson berated his eternal Quakers (who lurked behind all events, plying the levers of the state), "but you are the persons who gain by it." "[Y]ou have tyranniz'd over the good people on the frontiers"; you "lead them blind-fold . . . bound hand and feet."

But you have a "Thirst after Power, never to be satiated," an anti-Presbyterian pamphleteer would respond, "until all other Societies are reduced to your Domain." And I am at a loss to know why you are even arguing with me: "Is it because you are attached to every Villain . . . who is of the same Denomination of Religion with yourselves?—or because you think it no Offence to take away the Life of a human Creature who is of a different Colour or Persuasion?" The Presbyterian was welcome to choose.[42]

The way out of the stalemate was pointed by Williamson, and by the young Philadelphia engraver James Claypoole Jr., who illustrated Williamson's first pamphlet with the era's most extraordinary print. There had been few attempts to enlist the outrage of German-speakers: at first most of the back-and-forth was not even translated. The Quakers were indicted for stirring up attacks on the Scots-Irish, or on frontier people generally—but not on the tens of thousands of Germans who lived in the countryside and made up what contemporaries all thought to be the region's most cohesive electoral bloc.[43]

It was Williamson, as much as anyone, who changed this. He labored to join "The miserable Dutch and Irish on the frontiers" together as abused peoples, stumbling in tandem under a Quaker yoke. The people were simply being "rid" by the Quakers, "[t]he Scots and Irish . . . rode by main force; and the unhappy Germans"—usually pro-Quaker stalwarts on election day—

> being . . . blindly led . . . and patiently groan[ing] under the burthen, while their wives, their children, and all were perishing by fire and hatchet. But . . . [now, Williamson hoped,] the Hibernian winches beneath his yoke; the German, having lost everything else, begins to pray that you would spare his life:—[And i]n short, the voice of misery and distress is no longer to be stifled . . . .

Williamson's paper Quakers not only exploited the Germans but scorned them for inferior beings, as he made clear in one ferocious pas-

7.3: The Irish and Germans, ridden by Quakers and Indians. *[Claypoole]*,
"The German bleeds & bears the Furs . . . ," illustrating [Hugh Williamson],
The Plain Dealer, or a Few Remarks upon Quaker Politicks . . . Numb. I
(Philadelphia, 1764). Courtesy of the Library Company of Philadelphia.

sage. Williamson was the College of Philadelphia's mathematics profes-
sor, with a mathematician's taste for quantifying daily life. Putting the
sums at issue in the assembly's and governor's rival versions of a military
supply bill (one taxing and one exempting the Penns' estate) at no more
than £110, Williamson impressively computed that without the bill's passage "the Indians would kill about 900; make slaves of about 1100; and,
wound, banish, and reduce to beggary about 13000" over the coming summer. Fifteen thousand country people, then, saved from terrible fates. In
his bitter arithmetic, this "would make each one of them cost us about
seven farthings," or less than two copper pennies: half the price of the little pamphlet his readers held in their hands. "But it may be a question,"
Williamson concluded, his pen atremble over his sums, "with some,
whether the life of a Dutch or Irish man, be worth so much?———"44

Claypoole, the engraver, needed no mathematical pathos to make of
Williamson's piece a stunning, brutally explicit print—a cartoon that
summed up all the directions in which the paper war was driving public
debate (figure 7.3). Claypoole's image illustrated every stock theme of the

anti-Indian sublime. It showed mid-Atlantic colonists to themselves on new terrain—marking out as public ground, where political actors met in civic battle, not only Philadelphia's paved courthouse square but the flaming fields of the countryside. And such colonists: "The German bleeds & bears the Furs," the caption helpfully observed, "Of Quaker Lords & Savage Curs"; just in front of him, "Th' Hibernian . . . kicks to fling his broad brim'd Master." Here were the people being "rid" indeed, a people both German and Irish, the one "bleed[ing]" and staggering behind the other.

Expanding the attack on Quaker intolerance to take in Germans shook Pennsylvania's electoral foundations as even the first outbreak of war had not, with anti-Indian rhetoric whirring tirelessly throughout to add ardor to the charges. A key to success in this campaign would be a newly adroit use of German-language media, one that broke down English and German readers' mutual insulation and broadened the circle of printed debate. As with Israel Pemberton's embodiment of Quaker Indian-loving, the complex issues would be personalized around one man—in this case, Benjamin Franklin himself.

IN A WAY it was Franklin's fault. In the open political warfare that followed the Paxton crisis, he saw the chance to try out a big idea. By arguing that the problem before the public was the regular breaking out of feuds between the governor and assembly—and not their wearisome specifics—perhaps, Franklin thought, he could build support for simply transferring the government of the province out of the Penns' hands into those of the king. Becoming a crown colony would obliterate Pennsylvania's proprietary faction. Though this campaign for royal government was a losing battle from the start—one that nearly took down its authors with it—it carried the debate over the country people's marching and killing into the heart of a transforming election, and pointed the way toward a new kind of politics.

"[W]e are all heartily tired of these Disputes," Franklin observed in starting the discussion, but struggles between lordly proprietors and "Popular Liberty" were in the nature of any proprietary government. No one who lived in Pennsylvania was to blame for its woes: "Religion," as he tried in his characteristic way to assert, "has happily nothing to do with our pres-

ent Differences, tho' great Pains is taken to lug it into the Squabble."
Franklin was trying to cool things off in the best way he knew: by changing the subject. A drive for royalization amounted to blaming the Penn
family—instead of either the Quakers or Presbyterians—for the crisis of
dividedness by which the province's citizens could feel themselves consumed. And by substituting Penns for Quakers as objects of hate, it could
neatly knock away the underpinnings of any campaign to throw out all
the members of the assembly—be they Quakers or "Quakers' Creatures."
If peace could be restored between hundreds of thousands of people by
making scapegoats of a single family, the Penns, Franklin was ready to try.
"We are," he noted, with the hope of somehow flattering all the region's
ethnic groups into each other's arms that had now marked his pamphlets
for more than fifteen years, "chiefly People of *three Countries*." All of
them, together, were being ridden by the Penns:

> *British* Spirits can no longer bear . . . the Chains prepared for them by a
> Fellow Subject. And the *Irish* and *Germans* have felt too severely
> the Oppressions of *hard-hearted Landlords* and *arbitrary Princes*, to wish
> to see, in the Proprietaries of *Pennsylvania*, . . . the one and the
> other united.

But royalization was a tough, doomed sell. It asked the electorate to
swallow too many things on whose disparagement provincial political
culture had always been founded. A standing army presence, a possible
establishment of the Church of England, with a bishop or tithes: these
were just not promising issues. Worst of all, it meant giving up the great
charter granted to Pennsylvanians by William Penn himself in 1701—the
glittering guarantee of privileges that had, in theory, drawn so many
Europeans to the mid-Atlantic countryside in the first place.[45]

The assembly party's means of overcoming this problem was more bold
than clever. It was, for the most part, to try for a sweeping inversion of all
the anti-Indian rhetoric that had come to define the idea of a distressed
frontier—calling it up, and admitting every bit of its force, only to step
aside at the last moment, as if in jujitsu, so that with luck it would smack
the proprietors instead. Hence the assembly now formally accused the
Penns of "extort[ing] Privileges from the People . . . with the Knife of Sav-

ages at their Throat," and in a handbill "distributed gratis by thousands," as Williamson noted scornfully ("least people should too soon forget the proprietors hatred of the frontier counties and the Quakers great love for them, tho' most of us had formerly thought contrariwise on this subject"), Franklin explained that the Penns had savagely waited till "the Frontiers were bleeding in every Quarter . . . [from] the most relentless Barbarities" to break the people to their will. "—Bleed, Bleed on and Die," another assembly piece hopefully imagined the Penns as cackling to their people.[46]

But the assembly's backers had been driven by their opponents into conceding too much rhetorical terrain. The more loudly they bandied their opponents' language back at them, the more they ensured its ascendancy. And throwing out the proprietors—besides the assembly itself, the only unchanging pole of power available to be denounced for betraying the province to Indians—would mean throwing out the universally treasured 1701 charter. This meant that accepting the new language of politics left assembly writers on impossible ground.

Still, they tried. Beyond dressing royalization up with anti-Indian indignation, Franklin and his allies—especially the clumsy assembly speaker, Joseph Galloway—did their best as well to claim the language of democratic majoritarianism. So they circulated a petition in special open-house nights at taverns, as well as more soberly, with "Quakers go[ing] about . . . in pairs to every house" like visiting missionaries. Their petition put the problem baldly: there was "in the Proprietaries a Dislike of the People," which made them unfit for power.[47]

In enlisting the visible, written support of as many ordinary citizens as possible, the assembly's backers were admitting that its decisions, on their own, need not perfectly embody the will of the people. It was bizarre to see Galloway, who had lividly resented Smith's trumped-up petitions during the 1750s, trumping up one of his own. The sight said something basic about how public life had been changed by the war. Now the assembly, too, would seek, if it could get it, the sanction of numbers, working tirelessly to get the literal people out of doors to seem to demand things of it—to publicly "dictate . . . to the Representative Body of the whole People," the assembly itself.[48]

But Smith and his fellow strategists proved hard to outdo in their passion for the people, or for what is now called democratic transparency.

The assembly had that very spring considered petitions asking that all freemen be allowed to watch it (or at least have "the Assembly Doors . . . left open, and . . . [be] permitted to stand without, so as to hear the Debates")—only to turn them down flat. "[T]he good people of this province" could have no notion what was going on among high-flying members in the assembly chamber, Smith wrote accusingly, when they had failed to publish "so much as their *yeas* and *nays*" for a full year. The house must stop its scheming and "openly, and avowedly, . . . lay the whole before their constituents . . . to whom they are accountable." In this way, as October approached, Smith laid about him with the club of democracy wherever he could, finding "very great Affront[s]" in the assembly's every action against "that respectable Tribunal, THE PEOPLE OF PENNSYLVANIA."⁴⁹

Such appeals to the people as "absolute and sole Judges" carried an air of conviction in part because they were made against a larger background: this was what everyone agreed was the politicization of daily life, at every level. The whole tenor of politics out of doors seemed rowdier and more expansive, as if it had come unstoppered. A Chester County writer observed sadly that "Neighbours, who from their Infancy, lived in the greatest Harmony, cannot now spend an agreeable Evening together." The sheet of light verse passed out each Christmas by the *Pennsylvania Gazette*'s delivery boys (prodding customers to give them a tip) agreed: the endless paper war had "Set peaceful Neighbours by the Ears," as "Pamphlets . . . madden'd round the Town." There were evening political lectures in the churches; election handbills, meant to be mulled by voters while they waited to turn in their ballots; and scores of other imprints, with sponsors on each side buying even fairly expensive engravings by the hundred to give away free. In Philadelphia county and city, the fall 1764 elections would for the first time in memory be contested by a full slate or "New Ticket" of anti-royalization candidates, with its members all listed in many newspaper pieces and pamphlets. The crises of the winter had stirred things into angry new life.⁵⁰

GERMANS WERE especially skittish about abandoning the charter, and uncertain of what a change might mean. What if there were no more elections for sheriff—so that a royally appointed one had no need to beg for German votes or politely "call them gentlemen," but could simply "tie prisoners to his horse's tail, and make away with them"? There were grounds for doubt here, to be sure.[51]

The prospect that most upset German readers, though, was that the assembly party's English members—personified by Franklin—might privately scorn and be scheming against them. A remarkable pamphlet (probably paid for by Chief Justice William Allen and overseen by William Smith) first rolled this issue onto the table, where it went off with the force of a grenade for Franklin's hopes. Ten years before, it told German readers, shocking and defamatory pamphlets had been spread against them in England. This referred to Smith's first anonymous piece of 1754: except here, in a wonderfully brazen move, its authorship was foisted on Franklin. After all, Franklin had signed his name to a digest in the *Gentleman's Magazine* in 1755 of his speculative paper, "Observations concerning the Increase of Mankind"—in which, German readers could now be told, he called them all "clod-hoppers" (*Bauerntölpel*) who immigrated in a "herd."[52]

Franklin's sneers, tossed off in the course of a demographic essay—and, above all, in the comfortable belief that they need never come before German readers—had indeed been horribly incautious. Attempts at repair (like pieces lamely claiming that, though Franklin had perhaps once written of "Palatine Boors . . . swarm[ing] into our Settlements," anyone could tell you "the English word *boors* has no wider meaning than farmers") only spread the damage. Hugh Williamson took up this charge about "Palatine Boors" in a new English-language hit piece that soon inspired more German pamphlets. The bigot Franklin, Williamson said, had not only "privately made a Merit of it, That he had effectually put an End to th[e Germans'] growth," but had himself worked actively to deny the Germans assembly seats. And this, at last, gave the charge of frontier underrepresentation devastating force in the German press. Rather than an abstract inequity that one had to draw on a map to see, it was an act of disrespect for Germans as Germans.[53]

When a longtime backer of the assembly party, the Germantown printer Christoph Saur, came out only three days before the election with a stunning sixteen-page attack in German on both royalization and

so im ersten Blat gedruckt, ist recht nach dem eigent-
lichen Sinn und Verstand der Worte und des ganten
Satzes von sechs Männern übersetzt, so beyde Sprachen
verstehen. Um denen Lockvögeln unsere Unparthey-
lichkeit zu zeigen, folget hier der gante Satz in englisch
und teutsch.

And since Detachments of English from Britain sent to America will have their Places at home so soon supplied and increase so largely here, why should the Palatine Boors be suffered to swarm into our Settlements and by Herding together, establish their Language and Manners to the Exclusion of ours.	Und weil die Schaaren von Engländern, welche man von Brittanien nach America abgeschickt hat, in ihrer eigenen Heimath so bald wieder aufgefült werden, nach dem sie hier gelandet sind, sich selbst so zahlreich fortpflanzen: warum ley-den wir, daß die teutschen Baurentölpel in denen Land-schaften die wir angebauet haben, überall so lange her-um streichen, bis sie endlich wie eine Heerde von ihrem eigenen Gezüchte sich zusam-men lagern und ihre eigene Sprache und Sitten unter sich beybehalten, damit die unsren niemahls auf-kommen mögen.

Nun mag es ein jeder nach belieben selbst übersetzen,
so gut er kan, daß weiß ich gewiß, daß niemand einen Ehren
Titel oder eine Lobrede daraus machen wird. Der Leser
kan selbst urtheilen ob diese Lockvögel samt ihren Helf-
fern und Helffers-Helffern, Versetzer oder Verfälscher sind.
    Ich will ein wenig erklären, was das englische Wort
Boor vor eine Bedeutung hat.   Unter denen Eng-
                                            ländern

7.4: Parallel columns of English text and tendentious German translation lay bare the meaning of Franklin's prewar comments about Germans. *Getreue Warnung gegen die Lockvögel . . . (Philadelphia, 1764), p. 10.* Courtesy of the New York Public Library.

Franklin's supposed anti-German bigotry, Franklin was sunk. Over and over, with a bitterness that was palpably not contrived, Saur dragged in Franklin's insult, never writing of "Germans" where he could sarcastically write of "so-called Palatine Boors, . . . [which] swarm so, they multiply like a herd, and stick by their language and their coarseness." The old assembly's members, Saur charged, had worked ceaselessly to keep those "stupid farmers," the Germans, out of their membership. "Then what," he wanted to know, "are we naturalized for?"[54]

Perhaps because German monolinguals knew they lived in a walled garden of print, such pamphlets' pose of ripping away a veil proved sensationally effective. Another pamphlet just as bitter and thorough as Saur's made brutally short work of claims that "Palatine Boors" was not an insult, exposing the meaning of Franklin's pamphlet in parallel columns of German and English text (figure 7.4).

As always, the best way to make charges of ethnic maltreatment stick enough to really inflame public opinion was to translate them into lives horribly lost in Indian war. In 1755, Franklin had organized the delivery of Lancaster County wagons, largely driven by German owners, to supply Braddock's doomed expedition against Fort Duquesne. For years, Franklin had cited this proudly as proof of his civic handiness. But now that he stood exposed as a bigot, the wagon drive's real motive was clear. "Because he loved his countrymen more than the Germans, perhaps he thought, the Germans are good enough for [the wagon service], let them just go along bravely ahead, where the danger is greatest, and when people on the frontiers were miserably murdered by the savages, one did not often have to hear of a certain kind of people [Quakers, or the English]," as one indictment ran. "O! it is only Germans and Irish."[55]

Such harsh charges opened a door—as a despairing pamphlet for the assembly observed—to "changing . . . proven old friends for new ones." The monolithic German vote seemed in danger of pulling apart in favor of a newfangled interethnic appeal. "We appeal to you as Germans," this last-minute pamphlet pleaded, trying to fit the familiar old coalition's pieces together again. "[Y]ou may well be Lutherans, Reformed, or Mennonists, you may be called Dumplers, Herrnhutters, or what you will"— only do not take the risk, whatever you do, of throwing power to Presbyterians, who burned to strip away all the Germans' privileges.

But with the creation of a polemic German media, full of rapid-fire exchanges between writers for and against the old assembly, who jostled to interpret for a broad German-reading audience the arguments that unfolded in the Anglophone press; and with printed calls on Germans to assert themselves in the face of supposed bigotry and abuse, a change had come. At least part of the German-speaking community now seemed ready, come election time, to imagine an alliance with their supposed fellow sufferers, the Irish, next to whom they had first appeared in print as corpses.[56]

* * *

ALL THESE APPEALS to the public had a stunning effect: rates of voting in Pennsylvania exploded. After years with no more than 1,000 or 1,500 total voters in Philadelphia County, in 1764 suddenly 3,874 men pressed up the courthouse steps to hand in ballot papers—as even more printed "squibs, quarters, and half sheets, were thrown among the populace"—in a slow-shuffling upward surge that packed the steps until almost midnight. The assembly's partisans handed out free cartoon sheets on election day, showing a black-gowned Presbyterian minister haranguing the queues before the courthouse ("Saving Grace for a Vote"!). It was an amazingly close contest. Both sides used spies, mounted messengers, and deceptive late-night turnouts—including a "reserve of the aged and lame . . . brought out in chairs and litters" at a crucial moment. But on the morning of the second day, as the polling stretched on toward thirty straight hours, its decisive turn came with the mass entry of perhaps five hundred voters from Germantown, assembled by the new ticket's "horsemen and footmen," who had just been blanketing the suburb.

"Never before in the history of Pennsylvania, they say," Mühlenberg noted, "have so many people assembled for an election." He was right: probably more than 40 percent of eligible voters had taken part. In 1761, the rate had been only a little over 10 percent. In effect, the electorate had abruptly quadrupled, and when the ballots were counted Franklin found that the blasts against him and the Quakers had worked. He was out of the assembly, and eight of ten candidates listed on the opposition ticket for Philadelphia County and City were in. "They carried (would you think it!) above 1000 Dutch from me," Franklin wrote morosely to the assembly's London agent. "This is quite a laughing Matter."

At the end of the year, a parody of the assembly's election-day cartoon was published. It reproduced the first drawing with derisive precision, only with new speech-ballooned dialogue for the milling voters to voice. And in this triumphant account, the whole election was shown as an exercise in German pride. "See how these Palatine *Boors* herd together," a cartoon Franklin was made to lament, as sturdy ranks from Germantown lined up to onlookers' cheers, indignantly asking one another, "Who dares defame The German name"? And above, somewhere in the Jersey Market's air-

7.5: An angel hymns the 1764 Pennsylvania election results as a triumph for German self-assertion. *Detail of "The COUNTER-MEDLY, being a proper ANSWER to all the DUNCES of the MEDLY and their ABETTORS" (Philadelphia, 1764). Courtesy of the Library Company of Philadelphia.*

space, an angel soared, happily chanting through a trumpet the message of the season: "THE *Germans* are Victorious" (figure 7.5). The assembly's opponents had succeeded brilliantly at making its leading members seem to be "jealous of seeing [English-speaking colonists] treat th[e] Germans as fellow citizens on a level with [them]selves."57

The German electorate's breakup helped to install new men—including two actual Germans—in the assembly, and many observers thought they could now see the outlines of a new order. One was Samuel Purviance, a "very Zealous" promoter of Presbyterian unity who started cantering around Pennsylvania in election seasons, forging political alliances and hatching what one of his Quaker counterparts grudgingly called "tolerable Plans, to divide us" by misinformation. To his way of thinking, the future would belong to a league between "our Society" of Irish Presbyterians and the German church people (who were not pacifists, unlike many Mennonites and other "long Beards," and would he hoped no longer vote like them).

In 1764, Col. James Burd wrote to Purviance from Lancaster County about an election-day "push," tracing the shape of the coalition that Purviance wanted to summon up. The Quakers and German sectarians on one side; the Anglicans, Presbyterians, and "all the Lutheran and Calvanists Dutch" on the other, if possible with some "popular Germans" put on the ticket, too—this was what they would try for. As Purviance wrote before the 1765 election, we have appointed a considerable meeting of the Germans, Baptists & Presbyterians to be held next monday at Neshaminy, where some of us [Presbyterians] some Germans & Baptists of [Philadelphia] . . . have appointed to attend in order to attempt a general confederacy of the three Societies in opposition to the ruling party we have sent up emissaries among the Germans which I hope will bring them into this measure . . . .

It turned out to be difficult to hire suitable German agents "for the purpose . . . [of] work[ing] upon their Countrymen"—but in lieu of that Purviance now had handbills to offer. He had dispatched free copies of an electoral piece in favor of the opposition ticket, addressed in German by the printer Christoph Saur to his "Most Worthy Country People," Purviance noted, "which may possibly have some effect." The power of the right kind of print to lift and rattle the political order's lid had been proven.[58]

HAVING LOST his assembly seat, Franklin left for London to help represent the province there. When he boarded ship, his hurt pride was revived a little by a ceremony contrived for his departure, with a salute by ship's guns and an honor guard that rowed him out amid "the Huzza's of the People," while an anthem composed in his honor drifted over the water. But before Franklin said goodbye, he wrote a tantrum of a pamphlet against the New Ticket's backers, taking exception to their claim that he could not embody the people's will in anything—being "so extremely disagreeable to a very great Number . . . of all Denominations and Societies" that he had just been rejected.

He was *not* unpopular, Franklin said, and he had hardly been rejected ("if *not being chosen is to be rejected,*" which struck him as debatable). And, as he cack-handedly observed, he would have won if the New Ticket—which could find safe seats only in "the out Counties, the remotest of the Province"—had not electioneered "among the wretched Rabble" and then, on top of that, perverted his humanitarianism toward the Conestogas and Moravian Indians, simply "to stir up . . . those religious Bigots, who are of all Savages the most brutish."

It was now child's play to eviscerate him. Franklin—who, as one of David Dove's hummable verses reminded the public, "GERMANS was always reviling"—had done it again. Having been spurned by the voters, he responded by "abus[ing] almost the whole body of the people." He scorned the Irish and the Germans equally :

One set of men who opposed him . . . [was] his majesty's faithful subjects the *Presbyterians* . . . this numerous and loyal people are called *"religious* bigots, *of all savages the most brutish."* The industrious GERMANS, to whom this province is so much indebted . . .—they too are called by him *"a wretched rabble, brought to swear themselves intituled to a vote."* Much in the same manner he had treated them on a former occasion; calling them "a set of *boors herding together,"* as if he was speaking of *swine.*

These observations came courtesy of William Smith, to whom it had become clear, in the decade since the war began, that this was no way at all to speak of Germans. "None but a very bad man," as he concluded complacently, "would utter such language . . . against whole bodies of people."[59]

In this new electoral world, one had to be tolerant and popular, and make direct appeals to the people, especially the Germans. Given the intolerant, antidemocratic, bitterly anti-German slant of his own forays into public writing before the war's first frightening autumn, this was an unlikely place for Smith to have arrived. War had made the idea of prejudiced misrule horribly tangible, and by the time he thrashed the Quaker party's giant into an exile overseas, Smith had had to seize every opportunity Indian war provided, and to learn some unexpected electoral lessons. Franklin learned them, too.

THE DEBATES eddying around the Seven Years' War had made it generally accepted that the bulk of the people—especially when they spoke in urgent supermajorities—could instruct their representatives. A distrust of the invisible, magic process of representative deliberation had hatched new demands for transparency and direct dictation. In 1764, for the first time, divisions were recorded in assembly votes, and dissenting members went to the press. Updates were printed on the progress of bills. And, when imagined in terms of ethnic fair dealing, the "equality" of seats between counties became a live issue. It all amounted to a democratic shift in tone for the language of politics.[60]

The debates were energized at each step by ethnic resentment, springing first from the idea of secret betrayals: of Quakers' "partiality" before Indian danger, and their bigoted drive for dominion at any cost. The well of anti-Indian rhetoric was returned to again and again to crystallize dissatisfaction toward the powers that be, who had patently failed in their duty of protection: "For what obligation can there be," as one writer asked, "to a government that refuses protection"?

The authority of the people—a people coarse and disorderly, perhaps, but honest "white folk" all the same—had been exalted. The country people had taken on a new shape, dignified by a suffering one could never sneer at. They were bloodied and killed, in ways everyone could now imagine, and it was their attackers' sneaking abettors, not the country folk themselves, who were to blame for their woes. For after the Paxton crisis, as Franklin saw, it was not "the mad armed Mob" but rather "the Assembly and their Friends" whom most pamphlets would make a habit of "representing . . . as worse than *Indians*."[61]

This compressed, extraordinary period of change had not yet found its fulfillment, which would be an internal revolution against both governing elites—the assembly and the executive faction—in the name of this new people. For now, after the crisis of 1764 was past, its legacy was mostly one of rhetorical change—rhetoric eagerly absorbed on both the proprietary and assembly sides, neither of which had any interest in using the new language to genuinely remake politics.

But an exquisitely articulated set of arguments and tactics had been fashioned for the next time they were needed. It was essential now to appeal to all the people, and to at least profess to love them equally, no matter what their creeds or tongues.

Chapter 8

BARBARISM AND THE AMERICAN REVOLUTION

FREE STATES, attend the song,
Now independent on
     The *British* throne:
To earth's remotest bound
Echoing skies resound
The sweet melodious sound—
     LIBERTY'S our OWN

Virginia's fields unfold,
Where our great fathers bold
     Intrepid stood:
On what embattled plain
The ever glorious train
Pil'd hills of *Indians* slain—
     Pour'd seas of blood.

—*Song to the tune of "God Save the King" (1776)*[1]

*   *   *

FOUR WEEKS after the Declaration of Independence was signed and printed in Philadelphia, John Harris of Harris's Ferry sat down at his desk a hundred miles to the west, in the grand stone house his decades-old monopoly over ferry traffic on the Susquehanna had bought him. He was writing to Owen Biddle, a member of the Committee of Safety in the capital, about the problems and opportunities of fighting a war in the western lands. "[F]rom my love for my bleeding country, my acquaintance with y^r self, knowing y^r situation & Influence, is the Reason I make free to write you this long Incorrect Epistle," he told Biddle.

Although large-scale hostilities between the rebelling Americans and northeastern Indians had not yet broken out, Harris wrote, they would. When that day came, it would be the Indians' doing, so the Americans should ready themselves to mount a punishing offensive expedition. Harris's Ferry had been a gathering place in the Seven Years' War. Here the river's banks had been covered for miles each way with the rough camping sites of refugees, and from here, often stopping in at Harris's inn, expeditions had set off against the Great Island up the Susquehanna and, some said, against the Conestoga Indians down it. "You may depend on it," Harris wrote wisely,

> that the Indians cannot be kept Neuter, no Treaty or Presents can Prevent their being concern'd in the warr . . . . I know the Indians well from my infancy, warr is their delight, & they will be concern'd on some side & Likely both for & ag^t us . . . .

But this, he proposed with a logic that other men would refine in the years of war ahead, did not have to be an entirely bad thing.

> If a general Indian warr shoud Happen, (may God forbid) that an Indian Warr shoud take place, but . . . if there is now no preventing it, Let the Warr be pushed on with the Greatest Vigour into their own Country, (they Begining first) Surely their Territory of the best lands in America is a fine prize for our Warriors to fight for . . . .

With a sense of dread that was more and more often colored by an instinct for opportunity, rebelling Americans now set to the task of sorting out their enemies from their friends. The result of their efforts would be a new place in an old landscape, a country Harris could love and serve. But to reach it would take almost a decade, and another plunge into Indian war. Since few people really wanted this yet, the start of the Revolutionary War in the middle colonies or states was halfhearted and hesitating.[2]

WAR CAME SLOWLY to the mid-Atlantic interior. In this its experience was unusual—different from that of New England, where the first clashes between crown forces and Americans had started in the spring of 1775; different from that of the Chesapeake, where Virginia's exiled royal governor was already raiding and burning coastal strongpoints by December 1775; and different from that of the counties near New York City, which faced a long series of pitched battles after the British invasion of Long Island in summer 1776.

Although the mid-Atlantic countryside was long haunted by fears that an Indian war might be about to start, here—as in the southern backcountry—an uneasy peace was maintained through 1775 and most of 1776. Wholesale expeditions into the interior were held up at first by a diplomatic competition for the allegiance of the Ohio country's Indians between Congress and the crown forces at Detroit. At least for the first eighteen months of the revolutionary crisis, it seemed possible that the Anglo-American war in the middle Atlantic might not have to be an Indian war, too.[3]

In fact, what one could find most often in the press during this period was an overwhelming dread at the prospect of fighting off Indian attacks. This dread was coupled with a doggedly open-minded hopefulness that all the continents' inhabitants—Indian, American, and even French Canadian—might find themselves naturally united against what it was felt they all had reason to see as Britain's long history of oppression. And so, as the war began, mid-Atlantic newspapers described nearly all Indians as steadfastly rebuffing British requests to fight against Americans.

"We can't yet learn," as one correspondent reported in August 1775, "that a single tribe of the Savages on this continent have been persuaded to take up the hatchet against the Colonies, notwithstanding the great pains made use of by the vile emissaries of a *savage* Ministry for that purpose." In 1775, the short-lived *Pennsylvania Magazine*, edited by a recent arrival from England named Thomas Paine, summed up the case for northern Indians' natural neutrality in what, it was widely reported, they saw as an unnatural war. "*Brothers*, Possess your minds in peace, respecting us Indians," Paine reported an Oneida speaker saying. "[W]e cannot intermeddle in this dispute . . . . We are for peace."[4]

Though there was never a widespread and wholehearted adoption of the British cause, there were still pretty clear signs that the allegiances of important Indian groups were shifting. Determined groups of anti-American fighters emerged, working to force other Indians' hands, and with time the vastly superior ability of the British to supply their allies became plain. The Royal Navy's command of the ocean was unchallenged throughout the war, with disastrous consequences for the economy of European Americans, let alone any Indians who tried to depend on them for rifles, clothing, metal goods, or powder. The opportunistic assassinations by country people of some important pro-American figures among the Ohio Delawares did not help matters. And, in time, Americans had to give up the idea that the Revolutionary War would be one most Indians sat out.[5]

So the picture gradually darkened. An assumption of Indian enmity did become part of the mid-Atlantic war effort. Once an association between the British and Indians had really begun to be made, it proved to have incredible propagandistic power—so much so that it could affect political debate even within Britain, and for nearly two years before it had any substance. In America, as John Harris had foreseen, the linkage of British and Indian enemies would pay visible dividends: by war's end, in the "fine prize" of Ohio Valley lands, but for now in the ease with which Indians and their allies could be fought in print, if not in the field.

In early 1776, despite almost a year of fighting by the haphazard armies of the United Colonies, America's estrangement from Britain was uncertain enough that members of the Continental Congress still loyally toasted the king at dinners, albeit with noticeably muted enthusiasm. As a region, the middle colonies were more unreliably rebellious than any other part of America. Matters were especially muddled in Pennsylvania, where most formal governing institutions, including the assembly and the city of Philadelphia, frankly opposed the idea of separation. It would ultimately take a kind of putsch to shove the colony into statehood. But in this uncertain interval there came a minor cultural eruption in Philadelphia of poems, plays, speeches, sermons, parades, and pictures devoted to demonstrating, with delicious clarity, exactly how the process of American alienation from Britain might be effected. All took as their subject the fall of the Continental army's most dashing general—an Irishman, recent emigrant to rural New York, and onetime regular-army captain named Richard Montgomery—in the siege of Quebec the previous winter, during America's first preemptive military strike.

As a general matter, the gravest political mistake George III made in response to the American crisis was to be seen as encouraging his troops to shed American blood. In abandoning his own part of the monarchical contract of protection and allegiance as decisively as he believed his subjects to have abandoned theirs, the king opened himself to the charge of having become an anti-sovereign, an unnatural destroyer instead of a guardian. As the Declaration of Independence would succinctly charge, the king had "abdicated Government here, by declaring us out of his Protection and waging War against us." It seemed the king had not done this halfheartedly, either, but had actually gone out of his way to hire "large Armies of foreign Mercenaries" to more definitively destroy his own subjects. Both Americans and the British opposition made much in their newspapers of an unsuccessful royal attempt to hire Russian troops from the empress Catherine, and knowingly deplored Hessian cruelty even before German troops set foot in America.[6]

Most Britons made their own leap, over the course of the war, from seeing Americans as turbulent fellow subjects to seeing them as foreigners. And according to one careful study of the British press, the thing that at last made Americans alien in British eyes was not simply their violence or evident ingratitude. It was their entering in February 1778 into formal alliance with France, the Catholic archenemy of all English-speaking

Protestants. "Fir[ing their] Indignation at the Thoughts of an Invasion by the Monsieurs of France" from that point on, Britons' perceptions of Americans were rapidly swamped and embittered by their powerful ready-made associations with Frenchness. "Are they not now aliens, and enemies?" a writer in the *London Morning Post* asked of the Americans, within weeks of the alliance's becoming known. "And what hope have we they will be our friends again, who are joined with Frenchmen, and Papists"? By leaguing themselves with a bogeyman that was charged in the English imagination with such fantastic power, the rebels made the war less internecine and less painful to home opinion. It was precisely this process—guilt by alliance—that would help the rebels to publicize how little the British nation deserved to hold the regard of American hearts.7

The most useful antitypes on the American side, of course, proved to be not Hessians or Russians but Indians. But because in the first phase of the war there were so few credible grounds for seeing most Indians as enemies, it took more than a year of fighting for press coverage to really take up the idea of a cruel and unnatural Anglo-Indian connection. In the meantime, the route to introducing Indian atrocities into revolutionary publicity would be indirect. It lay through Canada, and it passed by the body of General Montgomery.8

ON NEW YEAR'S EVE DAY in 1775, Montgomery led his men on a doomed assault through a storm of howling snow and grapeshot toward Quebec's walls, hoping to topple the city and draw Canada into the rebel orbit. The grapeshot fired by the city's defenders killed Montgomery, and the army fled. The Americans left his body behind them, sprawling in the snow, where it would be found by the British, thawed out, and buried with the honors befitting a general. But as the traumatic unraveling of the Canada campaign sank into the popular imagination, these poor facts would be twisted and swollen in a way that confirmed Americans' characteristic preoccupations whenever they confronted defeat. The defense of Quebec was reimagined as an assault on Montgomery's bleeding and broken body, and American publicists began to describe British predilections for mutilatory combat in phrases that had been reserved, as recently as the era of the Seven Years' War, for Indians alone.

In February 1776, the Continental Congress turned to the most studied rhetorician in Philadelphia—Provost William Smith—for a funeral
oration on Montgomery. The ceremony surrounding it started with a
parade of congressmen, Pennsylvania assemblymen, Philadelphia's officials and revolutionary committees, and city militia and Continental soldiers wending somberly through the streets. At intervals throughout the
oration itself, a full choir and a section of violinists took up Smith's words
and illustrated them musically, with songs and "solemn music" specially
composed for the occasion. The production had almost everything, in
fact, except Montgomery's body, since it had been left behind in Quebec.
The text itself was affecting, and Smith wrote in passages where he could
act out being overcome with emotion. ("But whither am I borne? to what
heights have I ascended?") Montgomery, Smith made it plain, was America's *"Proto-Martyr,"* and his "streaming wounds" were the same as his
country's.

But since Montgomery had been killed while launching an unprovoked assault on Canada, to make him a more convincing martyr Smith
had somehow to make attacking seem like defending. So, he announced,
the Canada campaign had not been one of *"hostility and offence."* Though,
of course, the British would try to "misconstrue" it, the attack was
launched only because Americans had learned that the Catholic Canadians, "together with numerous tribes of savages, were instigated and
preparing to deluge our frontiers in blood." And in these circumstances,
he piously exclaimed,

> let God and the word judge whether it was an *act of offence;* or
> rather, whether it was not *mercy* to them, to ourselves, to the whole
> British empire, to use the means in our power for frustrating the bar-
> barous attempt. Indeed there was benevolence in the whole plan of his
> expedition.

Because the British were about to unleash an Indian war, the attack was
an act of prevention, one humanity demanded. In Smith's experienced
hands, simply touching on the horrors of Indian war could transmute
guilt into blamelessness. This was a rhetorical alchemy to which other
publicists of the American cause would have steady recourse.[9]

"[C]ome and view the bloody corpse of our hero!" a similar funeral oration from New Jersey invitingly exclaimed, together with many others. So it was that an early Philadelphia edition of Thomas Paine's *Common Sense* came to be bound together with a dialogue between the dead Montgomery and a congressman, in which the general's indignant ghost pointed out that the British had "called upon Russians—Hanoverians—Hessians—Canadians—Savages—and Negroes to assist them in . . . butchering your wives and children." But by far the most notable account of Montgomery came in a verse drama by an aspiring young man of letters, Hugh Montgomery Brackenridge, whose *Death of General Montgomery* was to be much republished. It was not a good play. Brackenridge's own preface observed that it would have been improved if he had spent more than a few weeks writing it. But considered less as literature than as political writing—as an attempt to work on readers' loyalties by subjecting them to repeated images of British and Indian cruelty—the play was little short of a masterpiece.[10]

It was also a reflection of how the war was causing Brackenridge's rhetoric to shift. Five years before, he and Philip Freneau had together written an extended verse epic, *The Rising Glory of America*, for delivery at their Princeton class's commencement. This prewar poem had had a great deal to say about the nature of the British empire, treating it as being very much a special glory of the kindly British colonists that they, unlike the Spanish, were "Undeluged with seas of Indian blood." Though they treated Indians in passing as fierce enemies, Brackenridge and Freneau singled out Sir William Johnson for special poetic attention as a Briton who had won the Indians' allegiance, along with many souls, simply "by humanity."[11]

The contrast between all of this and Brackenridge's efforts at immortalizing Montgomery in 1776 could hardly have been more striking. The *Death* caused a sensation, and not because it portrayed the relationship between Britons and Indians with approval. Instead, the play's most coherent thematic element was the two peoples' shared lust for American blood. Because there was not very much by way of cruelty—still less Indian cruelty—to work with in the conduct of Canada's defenders, Brackenridge had to inflate some episodes and invent others to make his play hang together.

The first powerful image of the drama, arriving within a few lines, was accordingly provided by a bloody communion ceremony that the British and the Canadian Indians had supposedly celebrated even before the Canada campaign began. In December 1775, at Congress's urging, most American newspapers printed a letter from Gen. Philip Schuyler about how the British had tried to recruit Indian allies the preceding summer. In a conference at Montreal, Schuyler had heard, the son of Sir William Johnson

> delivered to each of the Canadian tribes a war belt and a hatchet, who accepted it. After which they were invited to FEAST ON A BOSTONIAN AND DRINK HIS BLOOD. An ox being roasted for the purpose, and a pipe of wine given to drink, the war song was sung. . . .

The substitution of a juicy roast ox for an actual American body did little to lessen the dismay of Schuyler's American readers. The ceremony's metaphorical cannibalism must have seemed to them frighteningly likely to induce the real thing. Brackenridge managed to work the episode in by showing the figure of Montgomery, wakeful and alone the night before the attack on Quebec, crying out unhappily, "O God!"

> Are we the offspring of that cruel foe,
> Who late, at Montreal, with symbol dire,
> Did call, the Savages, to taste of blood . . .
> Of a Bostonian, made the sacrament?

At this point a footnote from Brackenridge helpfully laid out the conclusion to be drawn. "What indeed could serve," he wondered,

> to give us a more horrible idea, of the diabolical spirit of tyranny, than to have, presented to our view, General Carlton, or his officers, by his direction . . . roasting an ox, and inviting them, under that symbol, to partake of a Bostonian? I know this may be called an Address to the Savages, in their own dialect . . . but certainly it is a style of figurative language, which only the imagination of an arbitrary and cruel Englishman, could in our age have conceived.

8.1: Montgomery's corpse, amid other American dead, with a grieving aide standing over the "mangled remains"; Wolfe's ghost hovers approvingly. *John Norman, frontispiece for Brackenridge,* Death of General Montgomery . . . *(Philadelphia, 1777). Courtesy of the Library Company of Philadelphia.*

The most important parts of what followed could be found summarized in the frontispiece to the first printing of the play, an engaging engraving by John Norman, a Philadelphian (figure 8.1). It showed the ghost of Wolfe rising, like a pale, beneficent mist, over a plain strewn with "mangled remains" of which (in the words of Brackenridge's explanatory key) "[t]he principal figure on the fore-ground is the corpse of Montgomery, with the arm thrown back and stretched at full length." The display of bleeding wounds and mangled bodies—and, in particular, of Montgomery's—was the power source for the play. As quickly as he could manage, Brackenridge swooped with his readers to the general's corpse, lying in reddening snow at the foot of the city walls. Standing above his dead commander, another American military aide let loose with the o-captain-my-captain moment that Brackenridge had selected as the subject for the frontispiece. "O father, father," he cried out to Montgomery, "groaning, fainting, dead!"

> Let me embrace thee to my grief-sick heart,
> And pour my warm soul in thy bleeding veins,
> Wet with the crimson of thy noble blood . . .
> And shew my countrymen each ruddy drop . . . .
> .   .   .   . O bleeding corpse,
> Let me not leave you to the insulting foe,
> Who will .   .   .   .
> .   .   . tear thy body uninhum'd, expos'd
> To the wild Savages, or birds of Heav'n.
> .   .   .   . Sight deplorable!

But, of course, the army did leave Montgomery's cadaver behind in its headlong rush, and the Quebec garrison took it into the city. Except that, in Brackenridge's improved version of events, the British did not bury it with honors. Instead, the next thing the audience saw was the British commander, "CARLETON, from the wall of the Upper Town, exposing the body of MONTGOMERY" at the defeated Americans. Gleefully calling for American prisoners to be tortured and eaten—while anticipating "[t]he deep-struck tomahawk, in the trembling heart; / The curv'd knife, ready to unroof the scull; / And body roasted in slow-scorching fires"—this fictional Carleton tried to discourage the brave Americans below. "Behold the body of your General slain," he taunted: "The great Montgomery bleeds upon the wall."

Except Brackenridge's readers knew, deep in their bones, that American soldiers simply could not find the spectacle of their dead general anything but inspirationally enraging: that was the way things worked. Since the historical Carleton did not do anything remotely like this, the play's reworking of an otherwise unsatisfying campaign represented another instance of Americans' displaying for one another the dead bodies of their own so as to stir themselves up to political change.

But Montgomery had been cut apart by cannon fire, not Indians; and in the play the Canadian Indians stayed offstage, still somewhat uncommitted as rhetorical foes. It was by no means certain yet that the main use of Indians in revolutionary publicity would be as co-villains with the British, even as the flurry of representations around Montgomery did ensure that the British would be linked to Indian-style mutilation and cruelty.[12]

IT WOULD have been easy to argue that British rule had not only saved Americans from the worst depredations they might have suffered at Indians' hands but would continue to be their best safeguard in the future. In 1775, Isaac Hunt, the Philadelphia attorney who had become a one-man pamphlet shop during the Paxton crisis, did exactly this, writing a moderate-minded disquisition on the Anglo-American relationship that made much of the regular army's "sav[ing Americans] from the butchering knife." He also tried to make the specter of other European powers flocking to "hav[e] an opportunity of stirring up the Indian natives to massacre, and butcher" independent Americans into an inducement for staying under Britain and her navy. If Hunt's effort quickly came to seem quaint, it was because it struggled so ineffectually against what became revolutionary America's dominant currents of rhetoric.[13]

In Pennsylvania, still a proprietary government, the most pressing problem for pro-revolutionary writers was to discredit, not the crown itself, but the Penn family. Almost incredibly, their instinct even in this case was to tie the Penns somehow to Indian attack. But since there had been no attacks on the province since Pontiac's War, and even then the proprietary family had come down strongly on the side of militias, it was hard to see how to make the Penns seem pro-Indian. The answer was audacious: simply scoop up all the passionately anti-Indian rhetoric that had been used against Quakers during the 1760s and slather it on the proprietaries instead, trusting the rhetoric to supply its own logic. The Penn family, the Philadelphia Committee of Inspection and Observation suddenly realized in May 1776, had been behind the sufferings of the country people all along. The assembly had to be dissolved and a new, "free" government established, or terrible things might happen. "We have seen, and some of us have felt," the committee wrote in a breathtakingly cynical circular letter, soon reprinted in the *Pennsylvania Evening Post*,

the melancholy effects arising from the opposing interests of the Proprietary and the people—Who can recollect the horrors of the late Indian
war, and not shudder at the idea it brings to his mind. Fire, sword, desolation, and *death in the most infernal forms,* will be presented to our
view—Parents and children weltering in their blood—Infants torn
with savage brutality from their mothers wombs, and made the food of
dogs! ! !——Objects yet more terrible than these will press upon our
reluctant minds . . . .

And now for the crucial maneuver.

Little does it avail to inquire *who was most to blame,* the Proprietary or
the *people then in power*—It is plain, beyond the possibility of doubt, that
the horrid ravages of that dreadful war were long permitted to spread
. . . by means of the unjust claims of haughty and *"absolute Proprietaries."*

Plainly much was at stake—including "Infants [being] . . . made the food
of dogs"—in Pennsylvanians' choice between the old assembly, which still
reported to Gov. John Penn, and the proposed new provincial congress.[14]
As the war actually being fought during the 1770s continued on its
muddled course, and pro-revolutionary publicists gained fresher, more
promising material to work with, they could strain less to achieve the
same effect. Perhaps the most discussed episode in the first half of the war
was a July 1778 assault on the Wyoming Valley. Militia in the valley had
found themselves overwhelmed by a superior force of Loyalists and Indians, sweeping south from Canada and Iroquoia. As their retreat became
a rout, most of the Europeans in the valley broke loose and fled, many as
far as Harris's Ferry. Contemporaries wrote with concern of how the terrified, pitiable crowds of Wyoming people spread panic wherever they
went. Long, loving passages in the press were devoted to recounting the
scalping and burning that the survivors described as accompanying the
"Tory" and Indian advance.

One such account, printed from the tales of refugees who had "run
away from the blood-bath" to Poughkeepsie, explained how, far in
advance of the attack, the Wyoming settlers had imprisoned nine suspected Loyalists, who subsequently fled to live among the Iroquois. Then,

in early July 1778, more than a thousand men, "about 300 of whom were thought to be Indians . . . the rest, Tories, painted like them"—the Loyalists and Indians had converged so much that it was hard to tell them apart—had invaded in force, "kill[ing], scalp[ing], and mangl[ing] in the most inhuman manner," despite the settlers' continual attempts to surrender, before shutting men, women, and children into houses that they set afire, on which "all perished together in the flames."

At least through 1778, the revolutionary press's fascination with Loyalists who tried to cross over to the Indians and conspire with them—inciting and personally directing raids against other Americans, like the Wyoming settlers—still easily exceeded its interest in Indians. That Loyalists were indicted so improbably often for the specific crime of being like Indians might suggest they were soaking up some feelings that had in past wars been directed at Indians. But the revolutionaries' striking stress on betrayal by disloyal Europeans agreed perfectly with the rhetoric of treachery that had started to flourish during the Seven Years' War. And so everyone talked incessantly of Loyalists who tried to intermingle themselves with Indians, "painted and dressed like them," so as to gratify their own need for revenge—Loyalists who were, indeed, "more savage" than the Indians themselves. "[T]hese backward Counties are in real distress," as Col. John Piper informed the Pennsylvania Supreme Executive Council in 1778, "between Indians (and the still more savage) Tories."15

Because Loyalists were full of "the horrid design of joining the Savages in murdering and scalping their neighbours"—the very people beside whom they used to live—a special rhetoric of internecine killing blossomed around them to justify the charge of their being "more savage" than enemy Indians. This idea of Loyalists' hurting people close to them surprisingly often took the literal-minded form of discovering them to be parricides and fratricides. In descriptions of the Wyoming affair, some stories were always given pride of place—like that of "*Thomas Hill* (whose father was killed by the Indians, last Indian war)," but who nonetheless "with his own hands killed his own mother, his father in law, his sisters and their familes"; or of

Partial Terry . . . [who] had several times sent his father word, that he hoped to wash his hands in his heart's blood. Agreeable to such a horrid declaration, the monster, with his own hand murdered his father, mother, brothers and sisters, stripped off their scalps, and cut off his father's head.

The obvious evidentiary problems with such stories (whom in his household did Partial forget to kill?) were no obstacle to their reprinting, nor to their giving pro-revolutionary readers a satisfying feeling of moral distance. Since the American rebels were continually upbraided in the British media as unnatural political parricides against their mother country, it was a relief to see that the real parricides were on the other side.[16]

Anti-Loyalist atrocity literature in the middle states, and especially in New Jersey, also made a sideline of attacking the so-called refugees—Loyalists, including slaves who had run away to join the royal forces, who came back to attack their old neighborhoods in raids that were nearly always described as including Indians, or being carried out in full Indian style. The hanging by Jersey refugees of an American captain, Joshua Huddy, inspired one of the most vehement anti-British newspaper pieces that Thomas Paine wrote in his persona of "Common Sense." Paine's piece took the form of a public letter to Gen. Sir Guy Carleton, now the commander in chief of British forces (and, in Brackenridge's *Death of Montgomery*, the dangler of Montgomery's corpse). Paine excelled most of the press reports on which he based his attack in treating refugees as the crown's savage pets, "trained like hounds to the scent of blood and cherished in every species of dissolute barbarity."

But it was the British themselves whom Paine saw behind all the refugees' infamies, and in particular behind Huddy's hanging, a "brutal outrage" that was "an original in the history of civilized barbarians, and . . . truly British." For if crown forces could coddle Huddy's killers, he angrily asked Carleton, "wherein do you differ from Indians either in character or conduct"? In fact, even the idea of British-Indian identity was too forgiving, since

The history of the most savage Indians does not produce instances exactly of this kind. . . . With them it is the horridness of revenge, but with your army it is the still greater crime, the horridness of diversion. . . . we whose eyes are open, who speak the same language with yourselves . . . can declare to all the world, that so far as our knowledge goes, there is not . . . a meaner or more barbarous enemy than the present British one.

An unhesitating master of the rapid-fire rhetorical attack, Paine worked continually to tear down all the things that anyone trying to buttress a war for independence had to fear—lingering affection for the British monarchy, or monarchy itself, or the British character—by discussing them in close conjunction with images of pollution and evil: disease, crime, rot, the devil, filth, rape, insurrectionary slaves, prostitution. But as his writings suggest he realized, the most useful image of all was that of Indians and Indian-style violence: burning cottages, wounded parents, relentless cruelty, and, above them all, "that barbarous and hellish power, which hath stirred up the Indians." For the more often revolutionaries could read of their compatriots "f[a]ll[ing] a sacrifice to Savage Indians and Tories, and experienc[ing] that torture in death which nothing but British and Savage cruelty could invent," the greater the sense of separation that could be made between Americans and the crown they had loved and served from a distance for more than a century.[17]

THE SPECTER of British-Indian alliances unleashed a far-reaching debate about barbarism and national character on both sides of the Atlantic. The first sign that barbarism would become an issue in the revolutionary conflict came within hours of its opening shots, when a British regular wounded in the retreat from Concord's North Bridge fell down in the road and was brained with a hatchet by a townsman. Exactly what happened to the soldier's head has been debated for centuries, but British regulars at the scene told their commanders that they had seen him "Scalped, his head much Mangled, and his ears cut off, tho' not quite Dead: a sight which struck [them] . . . with horror." This factoid set off shudders in the British ministries and media. What sort of savages were the Americans? The regular army found further proof of the rebels' "savage" predilections over the next few months, as small numbers of Stockbridge Indians—largely Mahican-descended men from a mission community in western Massachusetts—arrived at Boston Harbor to support their American neighbors in the summer's fighting. The Stock-bridges' sniping at sentries (and "turning up their backsides, to express their defiance" at Royal Navy ships) settled, to Commander in Chief Thomas Gage's satisfaction, that "[t]he Rebells . . . have brought down all the Savages they could against us," and in consequence "open'd the Door" to the use of Indian allies in the fighting ahead.

Most public attention and disapproval in Britain over the course of the war was, however, to be directed not at the rebels' Indian alliances but at those of the British themselves. Brought up endlessly in the House of Commons, they proved a long, throbbing public-relations headache. With English-speakers having spent so much ink and indignation on the cruelty of France's taking Indian allies to "come killing and scalping" on its behalf, "fleaing the Skin and Hair from [colonists'] head[s]" for a few pounds apiece, it was awkward to find one's own nation described as doing the same things to the same people. American victims had by now been so often described, in a rhetoric that was by the standards of the time so nearly perfect, as to make unbeatable foes in print.[18]

People who had no trouble defending what we now think of as far greater horrors were brought up short by their armies' "employing" Indians to fight beside them. The Anglo-Caribbean sugar planter Edward Long, for example, is now often seen as one of the eighteenth century's most loathsome writers of nonfiction. After resettling in southern England, Long assembled a thickly documented three-volume *History of Jamaica* (1774) that contained some of the most extreme thinking about African-European racial differences to see print before the 1790s, confidently proposing that Africans—though in their own way "human creatures"—were, like such other parahumans as orangutans, the products of a separate creation (and Linnaean species) from Europeans. Predictably, although in every way "a friend to mankind," Long in no way balked at slavery. It could not tarnish the honor of Britain, or his own.

But in the midst of the Revolutionary War, Long wrote a strange, conflicted book: *English Humanity No Paradox, or An Attempt to Prove that the English Are Not a Nation of Savages* (1778). Here he saw no need even to touch on slavery, but got down happily to the job of defending stage violence, the eating of beef, flogging, boxing, bullbaiting, cockfighting, hanging, gory newspaper stories about accidents, chauvinism, and street-corner harassment. But there was one subject Long visibly did not know how to defend, and that was Britain's association with Indians in the American war—an unresolved problem that colored the whole book with his disappointment at how it had put Englishmen's *"National Character . . .* in the utmost danger of being obliterated." It seemed bad enough to have hired mercenaries, or to have set slaves revolting, but the most horrific image, even for this former planter, was plainly that of Britons acting as "patrons and abettors of *Wanton Homicide,"* and *"stretching* forth *Cannibal Indians* to scalp, tomahawk, and torture, with undistinguishing fury." He shuddered for England.

It may, in short, be the ultimate testimony to the power of the rhetoric surrounding Indian war that it made even Edward Long blanch.[19]

IT WAS NOT an accident that Long's glum thoughts on Indian war appeared in 1778. That was the year of Gen. John Burgoyne's return to Britain, to face public censure and a parliamentary inquiry over the unraveling at Saratoga, New York, of a crucial campaign along the Hudson Valley the preceding fall. Burgoyne's was the most important British defeat before Yorktown. But more than any supposed cowardice, the question that dogged him at home was whether the presence in his army of Indian warriors had been humane. It quickly became clear that Burgoyne would be loathed as much for having been "cruel, savage, and sanguinary" as for losing.

Burgoyne had blundered into this indictment by the use he tried to make of Americans' fears. He knew what a terrible memory the Seven Years' War was in the countryside through which he planned to pass, and his aim—which was at least tactically shrewd—was to "spread terror without barbarity": to exploit the American dread of the Indians accompanying him to simply paralyze the rural war effort. All he wanted, as one chronicler noted, was to "revive in their minds every latent impression of fear . . . of the savages."

To this end, the general wrote out a proclamation meant "to speak daggers, but use none." Burgoyne was a practiced pamphleteer who later found success as a playwright, and it was in a real sense unlucky for him now to have such a happy way with words. The proclamation succeeded perfectly at catching the tone he was after: it was thunderously, memorably menacing. As its most quoted passage announced,

> —I have but to give stretch to the Indian forces under my direction, and they amount to thousands, to overtake the hardened enemies of Great-Britain and America . . . wherever they may lurk. . . .—The messengers of justice and of wrath await them . . . [with] devastation, famine, and every concomitant horror.

This was playing with political fire, and it would help to ensure that the Hudson Valley campaign was fought on two fronts, one in the woods and one on paper. Burgoyne worried and felt guilty about the Indians' way of war, and did what he could to hobble the fighters under his command—lecturing them about not taking scalps from women, children, "Aged men," or any but the dead once "killed by your fire and in fair opposition." It turned out, though, that what mattered most was not Burgoyne's shuffling actions but his reverberant words.[20]

The American press took up with gratification these promised horrors (as well as his curious phrasing). "Most high! most mighty!" replied the Philadelphia belle-lettrist Francis Hopkinson. "[Y]ou have collected," he wrote,

> an amiable host of savages, and turned them loose to scalp our wives and children, and to desolate our country. . . . what can we expect, but that you should in your wrath *give a stretch to the Indian forces . . . amounting to thousands, to overtake and destroy* us . . . . We humbly offer our heads to the tomahawk . . . The blood of the slain— . . . and slaughtered infants . . . call upon us in vain . . . . —Give not *a stretch* to those restorers of constitutional rights—the Indian forces under your direction.[21]

As the hip-hip-hurrahs of the regulars started to blend, in American ears, with "the Indian whoop," the effect, as rebel publicists planned, was to "jumble promiscuously, and . . . place in one point of view, the cruelties of these barbarians, and the cause in which they were exerted." A chief mechanism of this jumbling was the celebrated death of Jane (or Janey)

McCrea, a woman engaged to be married to a young Loyalist lieutenant in the garrison at Fort Edward, fifty miles up the Hudson from Albany. McCrea was mistakenly taken captive, shot, and scalped by Burgoyne's forces amid the skirmishes leading to Saratoga. Her having died at the hands of Indians under crown control was enough to completely overshadow her inconvenient attachments in the pro-revolutionary press.

Though no printed account quite accused McCrea's fiancé himself of having wanted her dead, her case was used to further prove the savage indiscriminacy of crown and Loyalist forces. Burgoyne's efforts to shield noncombatants could now be seen as bloodthirsty ploys, "sufficient to congeal the heart of humanity with horror." And, as one correspondent inevitably reported, "by what I can learn there is very little difference between the regulars and indians, for when Miss M'Crea was butchered and scalped, a large number of regulars were . . . spectators of the horrid act."

Gen. Horatio Gates, the methodical American commander, saw in McCrea's death perhaps his clearest opening of the whole campaign. He wrote at once to Burgoyne (with copies for Congress and all the Philadelphia newspapers) to express his shock. "That the Savages of America should . . . mangle and scalp," Gates noted, was nothing new. On the other hand,

> that the famous lieut. gen. Burgoyne . . . should hire the Savages of America to scalp Europeans and the descendants of Europeans; nay more, that he should pay a price for each scalp so barbarously taken, is more than will be believed in Europe, until authenticated facts shall, in every Gazette, convince mankind of the truth of the horrid tale.

Burgoyne's rejoinder, which was paired with this ringing indictment in print, read lamely beside it. The imagery—some of it from his own efforts—that had come to surround "bloody Burgoyne, and his merciless Savage allies," was by now too rich and inviting to hope to erase, no matter how accurately he might insist that the whole episode was only another of those "rhapsodies of fiction and calumny, which from the first of this contest, it has been an unvaried American policy to propagate."[22]

McCrea's death both cost Burgoyne many of his remaining Indian allies—put off by his own harsh response to the killing, whose effects he had foreseen—and helped to strip him, and Britain, of any immediate hope of holding the public high ground in the war. It is also at least possible that the McCrea story helped to rally the waves of militia who soon came smashing into Burgoyne's army. The Saratoga campaign became a double disaster.

McCrea offered a name and life history to use in further excursions into the genre that American publicists had reduced to a system during previous decades: the slow-motion pan—directing the reader's stare first this way, then that—over a landscape of mutilated families, the aftermath of an attack. "[L]o! a bloody scene salutes my eyes," one effort ran;

> *Here* lies an aged man, roll'd in his gore, . . .
> *There* lies a woman dead, all gash'd her face,
> A sucking babe just drop'd from her embrace——
> *There* lies the slaughter'd infant on a clod . . . .

Then McCrea's hairless, half-dead body could be spliced seamlessly onto the backdrop, mangled and "roll'd in blood," to effect the political transference that ended such accounts. "Is this that blooming fair? is this *M'Crea?*":

> O cruel *Britons!* who no pity feel!
> Where did they get the knife, the cruel blade?
> From *Britain* it was sent, where it was made. . . .
> . . . . . e'en from the *British throne.*

A 1778 British opposition cartoon gave McCrea the leading place in a diorama of horrors, showing acts committed by Indians working under the sponsorship of the king and his cruelest ministers (figure 8.2). An earlier atrocity from the Quebec campaign—the torture of prisoners, by roasting them while alive and stuck full of flaming pine splints (all presented as a kind of feast, which ritual torture by now practically never was)— helped to round out the panel.

And indeed, as had been true since newspapers dwelled on Carleton's sitting down to share an ox with Canadian Indians, perhaps the best way of proving British-Indian intimacy was to show them cutting apart, cooking, and eating "American flesh" together at cannibal feasts. This image from the debate over barbarism lay behind one especially startling print in 1780, "The Allies" (figure 8.3). It showed the prime minister, Lord North

8.2: *Top:* Jane McCrea meets her doom. A child is scalped, and a Hudson Valley town burns behind them. *Bottom:* American prisoners are barbecued and eaten after the Canada campaign. *Detail of "The Closet" (London, 1778). Courtesy of the Library of Congress.*

(who famously resembled George III), munching happily on colonists' body parts. The spectacle was so horrid it made even a dog vomit, while the archbishop of York hurried over with boxes full of scalping knives.

For all his nausea at Britain's war effort, Edward Long in 1778 expressed the touchingly limited hope that "in spight of our Indian Alliances, we shall never be cannibalized so far, as to regale our soldiers with the flesh of a barbecued *American* for their dinner." But he could not be quite sure.[23]

THIS WAS ALL pure gravy to the Americans. Even as they recycled the best verbiage from the British debate over Indian modes of fighting, they dismissed the debate itself, with rising confidence, as crocodile tears. "These are some of the tender mercies of the mild and amiable British," one attack report from 1782 concluded, after the fall of North's ministry—atrocities carried out under the former parliamentary opposition,

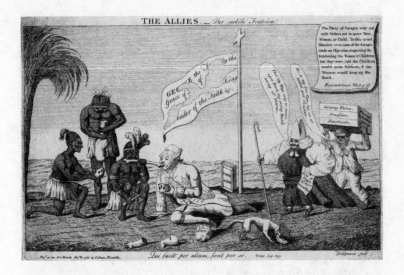

8.3: Lord North and his Indian allies eat cut-up Americans and swill their blood from skulls. *"The Allies—Par Nobile Fratrum!" (London, 1780).* Courtesy of the Lewis Walpole Library, Yale University.

whose breasts have often shuddered at the barbarities of the savage British and Tories, with their Indian allies.—Hear this, ye men of sound, who bellowed out against North and his associates in cruelty, and count the price of innocent blood which you are daily shedding with a wanton barbarism, scarcely equalled in the annals of history!

For the difference between the victims and their tormentors could not be one of political affiliations alone: it had pretty quickly become national.²⁴

Midway through the war, Franklin and the marquis de Lafayette sat down together to the task of developing concepts for "Prints to Illustrate British Cruelties." Here are some of the vignettes they came up with: a British governor receiving scalps from Indians; "Savages killing and scalping the Frontier Farmers and their Families . . . [with] English Officers mix'd with the Savages, & giving them Orders"; and—the scene without which no image of the British war effort was complete—"Prisonners kill'd and Roasted for a great festival where the Canadian indians are eating American flesh, . . . an english officer Setting at table." Franklin was as talented at evoking horror as he had been in 1764, with his narra-

8.4: *Left:* Henry Hamilton amid death's heads. *Right:* Burning a prisoner.
From John Dodge, Entertaining Narrative of the Cruel and Barbarous Treat-
ment . . . . *2nd ed. (Danvers, Mass., 1780; orig. pub. Philadelphia, 1779).*
Courtesy of the Newberry Library.

tive of the Conestoga killings, but now he had made the priorities of his
former opponents his own. This much was suggested, too, by his remarkable, forged "Supplement" to a Boston newspaper in 1782, which claimed
to reprint a captured manifest of the contents of eight bales sent to London "containing SCALPS of our unhappy Country-folks"—including
twenty-nine little scalps of fetuses, "ript out of their Mothers' Bellies."[25]

Much of this American effort at barbarizing the British centered on
Gov. Henry Hamilton, the commander of crown forces at Detroit.
Hamilton was the model for Franklin's image of a governor receiving
scalps, and in the *Entertaining Narrative of the Cruel and Barbarous Treatment and Extreme Sufferings of Mr. John Dodge During his Captivity among
the British* of 1779, Hamilton got a page and a portrait all to himself, in a
crude, skull-and-crossbones-framed woodblock print. Another, even
more straightforward cut from the same tract showed beaver-hatted regulars with tomahawks around a burning prisoner (see figure 8.4). These
images suggested how badly American visual propagandists needed their
British collaborators. But it was not hard for even primitive efforts to
show the British as receivers of American scalps, since naturally they
were. In November 1781, the Moravian missionary David Zeisberger, who
had been taken to Detroit for a forced interview with the commandant,

Maj. Arent Schuyler De Peyster, watched while at the other end of the table a Delaware war leader, Captain Pipe, offered some to De Peyster, who "himself took the scalps from him, and had them put aside."[26]

In a strange echo of indictments that the French had leveled against the British during the Seven Years' War, pro-revolutionary Americans started to discuss the British as being genetically brutish and barbarous. An anonymous essayist writing on the British national character for the Philadelphia *Freeman's Journal* in 1781 made it clear that, despite all the war's displays of "British cruelty," his contempt for Britons was more deeply rooted. "[T]heir national character" itself was to blame. And in that,

> the Britons are the same brutes and savages they were when Julius Cesar invaded them above 1800 years ago, for it is certain their mixture with the Saxons and other foreigners, has done very little towards their civilization. . . .

The idea that, long ago, the inhabitants of Britain had been blue-painted savages, more or less indistinguishable from New World Indians, had had wide currency in English-speaking culture since the sixteenth century. The comparison was always accompanied by the saving fact that since then England's cultural evolution had rocketed ahead. But now American publicists—who were skating on dangerously thin ice, given how recently they had extolled their own Englishness—started to rub away the last thousand years and collapse together the figures of naked Picts and modern Englishmen. The British were savages at heart. And even after the war was over, the writer for the *Freeman's Journal* urged, Americans should cut themselves off from so much as trading with "so bloody, so barbarous a nation." A peace might be patched up, but they could never feel friendship toward a people "whose hands *have been*, and *will yet* be dyed in [Americans'] blood." A cluster of harsh morphemes—"barbarous," "brutish," "bloody"—more and more regularly modified "Briton" in the American press. The words belonged together.

A desperate-sounding congressional address to the people, written at York, Pennsylvania, during Congress's rural exile (the British were occupying Philadelphia, ostensibly the Continental capital) was printed to drive from American minds any thought of listening to the latest British peace proposals. In its hour of need—the Continental currency collapsing, its armies shrinking daily—members of the Congress could think of no better way than the rhetoric of savagery to rally the public. British victories, they told Americans,

> have been followed by the cool Murder of Men, no longer able to resist; and those [captives] who escaped from the first Act of Carnage have been exposed . . . to become the Destroyers of their Countrymen, of their Friends, perhaps, dreadful Idea! of their Parents or Children. Nor was this the outrageous Barbarity of an Individual, but a System of deliberate Malice . . . .

As the address went more and more passionately along, growing nearly incantatory, all the dependable tropes, now decades old, rolled by:

> as if all this were insufficient to slake their Thirst of Blood, the Blood of Brothers, of unoffending Brothers, they have excited the Indians against us; . . . whole Hosts of Savages, whose Rule of Warfare is promiscuous Carnage, who rejoice to murder the Infant smiling in its Mother's Arms, to inflict on their Prisoners the most excruciating Torments, and exhibit Scenes of Horror from which Nature recoils.

Nature, perhaps, but not the American Congress. An early peace with such barbarians was plainly impossible, let alone a reunion.

Few Americans took so unforgiving a view of all Britons. After the war, far from refusing to take goods from British merchants' bloodstained hands, the new nation's citizens bought British manufactures at the fastest pace ever. But if anything the difficulty of separating Americans' hearts and habits from those of the British made the invective of revolutionary publicists more strident and blastingly inventive. If they protested too much, it was because they thought it was all still barely enough to keep their cause intact.

These dark accounts helped to advance a new American view of the British empire. The whole sphere of British activity in the world, from

Africa to Asia to America, became an extended "Scen[e] of Horror," marked by rapine, greed, and arbitrary violence. This was true whether that violence was being exercised against East Indians and Africans—and this view of the empire was closely tied to the revolutionary period's halting writings on antislavery—or by western Indians against Americans. In short, the empire was awash in blood. "—Blush! Oh Britain, blush!" as one newspaper account exclaimed; "Go on, . . . until . . . you repent in tears of blood! . . . alas! what else can wash out the stain of your East India, your West India, your American murders!"[27]

ANOTHER, PARALLEL IMAGE of empire was built up in the rhetoric of these years, one far more fair-faced and appealing: an American empire of land and liberty. When troops in a Continental anti-Iroquois force returned in 1779 from a long round of sacking empty towns in the Mohawk Valley, they were treated to a special sermon by the expedition's chaplain, a Presbyterian minister named Israel Evans. Evans's remarks sketched out in the air with luminous lines a vision of what they had done. The men were "Hero[es]," for having dared to brave "the sudden and hidden attacks of the subtile and bloody savages" to make a "just and complete conquest, of so fertile a part of the western world." When Evans looked into the future, what did he see before him?

> Methinks I see the rich lands from the Teaoga river to the banks of the
> Seneca and Cayuga lakes, and from thence to the most fruitful of lands
> on the Chenesses to the great lakes Ontario, Erie, and Huron, and from
> these to Mihigan and Superior. . . . all . . . inhabited by the independent
> Citizens of America. I congratulate posterity on this addition of
> immense wealth and extensive territory to the United States.

Where American invocations of the British empire's reach and might before the Revolution had most often been of a decidedly oceanic grandeur—of lines of power and trade extending over the world's seas—visionaries like Evans now invoked instead the sheer continental mass of the land they meant to hold. Raptures over America's future glory, expressed in Evans's gazetteer-like terms, could be found throughout revolutionary discourse. The frontispiece to Francis Bailey's *United States Magazine* for January 1779 depicted an angel winging through the air before the existing states of the American union. According to the verse caption, her flight would be a long one. *"Fame* before the vista flies," as it explained, "Rising to the western skies:"

> . . . where new states shall yet have place,
> Founded on an equal base;
> Founded far beyond the groves,
> Where the *Yochagany* roves;
> Or where *Cochnawaga* fills
> Her urn, at the *Shanduski* hills.

It paid dividends to tie the British to bloodstained savagery in their military conduct, in their choice of allies, in their national character, and at last in their empire itself. If Great Britain's Indian auxiliaries, who held these western lands, could be conquered and dismissed along with their still more savage backers, then an American counter-empire could be built. Instead of barbarian emptiness, there would be new states and a set of new beginnings for the "independent Citizens of America" who moved west to fill them, after suffering so much.[28]

IN THE FIRST YEARS of the war, Americans had made sustained efforts to recruit native allies. George Morgan, Congress's most talented Indian agent, had negotiated for the western nations' neutrality and tried unswervingly to prevent marches through the Ohio country that would turn its Indians against the United States. But by 1778 and 1779, the priorities of many policymakers had been nudged in a new direction.

At the end of September 1777, after beating Washington's army just below Philadelphia, several thousand British troops under Gen. William Howe floated unopposed over the Schuylkill—a river once again cleared of its boats, just as in the Paxton scare of 1764, with ferry ropes cut and a new bridge dismantled—to parade in triumph through the city. Some roads in the Lower Counties were littered with "hundreds of [Continental] muskets . . . which those that made off ha[d] thrown down" in their haste to flee. The city's church bells were winched to earth and carted away, and painted signs with Washington's picture were taken down.

The capital was no longer a place for rebels to linger. Gratified Loyalists had watched for days while "Carriages constantly pass[ed] with the Inhabitants going away"—and in particular as the rebel "Congress, Counsil &c [we]re flown, Boats, Carriages, and foot Padds going off all Night." After much chaotic wheeling around the countryside—most members of Congress made an evasive grand circle through New Jersey—the capitals of both the revolutionary Republic and Pennsylvania were reestablished in the heart of the countryside at York, a heavily German hamlet, and the more substantial borough of Lancaster. Divided by the Susquehanna, each of these places was about a dozen miles from the Conestoga town whose residents had been killed in December 1763. In Lancaster, assemblymen settled in for nine months of meetings at the courthouse on the central square—the building around which, just after killing the Indians confined in the workhouse at Prince and King streets later in December 1763, the original Paxton rioters had galloped away, shouting and shooting their guns in the air.

Now, as winter arrived in Lancaster fourteen years later, the exiled assemblymen's business shifted, and they found themselves more and more often listening to the echoes of those excited voices. For the first few years of the war, most petitions that they took up had been from office-seeking Philadelphians, thrusting themselves forward for every conceivable kind of patronage. Now, with the odds of the revolutionary commonwealth's continuing to exist at all having plunged, the assembly instead received many more addresses from people around it in the countryside. What these country people's hand-delivered memorials asked for, above all, was security from Indian attacks.

So the legislature—which was more sparsely attended now, as well as more heavily western in makeup—took up a long chain of addresses, like the "Three petitions from a large number of the inhabitants of Bedford county" that were all delivered to the courthouse on December 17, each "setting forth the distresses of the country from the Indian incursions." The assembly responded to these pleas by conferring with Pennsylvania's Supreme Executive Council to try and make available to the frontiers what meager resources they could command. And all the state's leaders started sending letters over the river to Congress, asking for anti-Indian expeditions and arguing that the defense of Pennsylvania's struggling back counties was a strategic—and financial—obligation of the entire United States.[29]

Always they repeated the descriptions of rural distress with which they themselves had been flooded, and always they observed that they "would not anxiously ask for [such a] . . . plan, but to satisfy the people looking up to them." This was democracy, of a sort, in action, and it got clear results. Congress approved expeditions and sent Continental soldiers to assist settlers in the region around Fort Pitt whenever it could persuade Washington to spare them.

Military and political leaders who backed a policy of conciliation along George Morgan's lines were bypassed, overruled, or replaced, as advocates of a forward policy against Indian towns wore away at their objections. Campaigns were increasingly marched into the borderlands, most notable among them the assaults on Iroquoia made in 1779 by Continental regulars under Gen. John Sullivan, and the village-destroying "squaw campaign" of autumn 1777, carried out against unaligned Ohio Delawares by militia under the Pennsylvanian Gen. Edward Hand. As in the 1760s, Hand's expedition was a noisy wrecking and plundering party that hoped to meet with little opposition. Though some defenseless villagers died, most of the damage—as on Sullivan's more sustained campaign—was to crops and whatever infrastructure of settlement could be looted or burned. In the spring of 1779, George Morgan disgustedly resigned his position as Indian agent and retired to an estate in Princeton, New Jersey, far from the western country's tortuous problems.[30]

Before about 1780, the main obstacle to organizing anti-Indian expeditions in the Pennsylvania-Virginia borderland was Col. Daniel Brodhead, Continental commander at Fort Pitt, whose innate caution and respect for the diversity of allegiances within the Delaware nation for years kept him pondering, rather than launching, attacks on the Ohio lands. But flowing up irresistibly past Brodhead in letters to his superiors were loud, united-sounding demands for westward marches and scalp bounties.

Rural commanders made their case in familiar ways, inviting the state's councilors to summon up vivid pictures of Indian attack. "The Verray Idea of a Savage enemy Comein upon defenseless famaleys," as James

Dunlap wrote hopefully in this vein, "Will be sufficient to arouse the Council in their defence." And over and over, officials were told that such horrors had "no Reale Remedy under Heaven but by Carring War in too our Savidge enemy's Cuntrey." ("[Y]ou Cant conseave the pleasure it would give me," this correspondent added, "to see it dun.") Nearly all these informants concurred that "a Defensive Warr agᵗ Savages will never doe the needfull." Gen. John Armstrong of Carlisle seemed not even particularly to care where or against which particular Indians such expeditions were sent, except that he thought it might be too difficult to march to Detroit, and so tended offhandedly to favor making a start with any Indian "Town or Towns" that might be found "in reasonable reach, on either Branch of the Susquehannah." The main thing was just to get the destruction of some Indian settlements, somewhere, underway.

In the border counties such marches sold themselves. The magnetic attraction of enormous wrecking expeditions into Indian country lay, as always, in the plunder to be had, in their safety, and in the appearance they gave of doing something definite to end the back inhabitants' suffering, even if they did as much to inflame Indian hostility as to undercut it.[31]

Promoting large-scale adventures into Indian country came close, in fact, to being the only widely popular thing that the revolutionary government was able to do at all in the countryside during the late 1770s and early 1780s. It was chronically underfunded. In 1781, the Pennsylvania government voted to pull down the decaying steeple of its own State House and sell the wood "for the highest price." Most people in the countryside resisted its efforts at gathering taxes, and many also resisted swearing oaths to it or turning out for its militias. The United States, unable to levy taxes, had no viable currency. (By late 1780, when the Congress gave up printing its fiat money in the face of unstoppable inflation, a Continental dollar was worth less than a sixtieth its value in 1777.) Its commissaries resorted more and more often to force alone in gathering forage for its dwindling, outclassed armies, armies that sometimes had fewer Americans under arms than the British forces had Loyalists. And for part of the war's first half the capital of Pennsylvania and the United States had been occupied, to the evident satisfaction of many inhabitants, by the British army.

In short, to an extent it is difficult to understand today, in the middle states—which John Adams, in York, decried as "the very Regions of Passive obedience," on every hand "benumbed with a general Torpor"—the revolutionary regime lacked the underpinnings of legitimacy. "The amazing Slowness in collecting publick Taxes hangs like a Millstone round the neck of all our publick Operations," as Joseph Reed, the president of Pennsylvania's council, explained in 1780.

> —we can scarcely command sufficient for the small & common Purposes of civil Government, & in the Predicament Congress calls daily & loudly—the Frontiers exclaim with Aunguish, & we are . . . reduced to the painful Necessity of listening to Distress we cannot releive . . . .

Rev. James Finley was sent into the Fort Pitt area as a secret agent in 1783 by Pennsylvania's council to gather information on what was contributing to apparent secessionist sentiment there. He reported back to Philadelphia that the best cure he could see for disaffection was an anti-Indian campaign. Launch one, Finley thought, and resistance to being taxed by Pennsylvania might well come to an end:

> If a Campaign should be carried on to ye westward this summer or fall in order to check ye insolence of ye savages, who have already killed & captivated many; ye people, I doubt not, will readily contribute in grain or wheat, each man his share of ye tax; & by this means will be brought into ye custom without either force or disputation.

In such circumstances, and with the knowledge that anti-Indian expeditions were one measure of the cash-strapped, legitimacy-starved government that people would actually be willing to support, wartime policy shifted in the same directions it had taken under Gov. James Hamilton during the 1760s. By 1780, President Reed was sending handbills into the countryside to announce enormous-sounding, albeit hyperinflated, scalp bounties (see figure 8.5) and to encourage "that Spirit which is so necessary in an Indian War, a Spirit of Hostility & Enterprize which will carry out young Men to their Towns.—" Reed now felt sure that during the last war scalp bounties, with the plucky little parties he thought they encouraged, had carried the day, proving far "more effectual than any Sort of

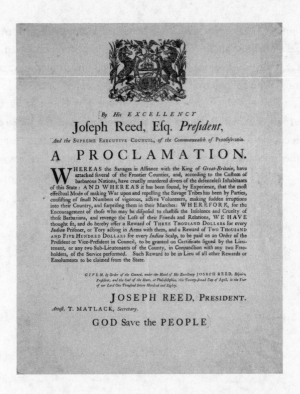

By His EXCELLENCY

Joseph Reed, Esq. *President*,

And the SUPREME EXECUTIVE COUNCIL, *of the Commonwealth of* Pennsylvania.

A PROCLAMATION.

WHEREAS the Savages in Alliance with the King of *Great-Britain*, have attacked several of the Frontier Counties, and, according to the Custom of barbarous Nations, have cruelly murdered divers of the defenceless Inhabitants of this State: AND WHEREAS it has been found, by Experience, that the most effectual Mode of making War upon and repelling the Savage Tribes has been by Parties, consisting of small Numbers of vigorous, active Volunteers, making sudden irruptions into their Country, and surprising them in their Marches: WHEREFORE, for the Encouragement of those who may be disposed to chastise the Insolence and Cruelty of those Barbarians, and revenge the Loss of their Friends and Relations, WE HAVE thought fit, and do hereby offer a Reward of THREE THOUSAND DOLLARS for every *Indian* Prisoner, or Tory acting in Arms with them, and a Reward of TWO THOUSAND AND FIVE HUNDRED DOLLARS for every *Indian* Scalp, to be paid on an Order of the President or Vice-President in Council, to be granted on Certificate signed by the Lieutenant, or any two Sub-Lieutenants of the County, in Conjunction with any two Freeholders, of the Service performed. Such Reward to be in Lieu of all other Rewards or Emoluments to be claimed from the State.

GIVEN, by Order of the Council, under the Hand of His Excellency JOSEPH REED, Esquire, *President, and the Seal of the State, at Philadelphia, this Twenty-second Day of April, in the Year of our Lord One Thousand Seven Hundred and Eighty.*

JOSEPH REED, PRESIDENT.

Attest. T. MATLACK, *Secretary.*

GOD Save the PEOPLE

8.5: A scalp bounty announced by Pennsylvania's president and council in 1780, in the free-falling Continental currency. *By His Excellency Joseph Reed . . . (Philadelphia, 1780). Courtesy of the Library Company of Philadelphia.*

defensive Operations." Writing to Brodhead that spring, he let him know that "the Savages are not to be gained or preserved on any other Principle than Fear." Writing to George Rogers Clark—the Kentuckian strategist of anti-Indian war whose volunteer expeditions attracted Congress's favor, led to the capture of Detroit, and put a seal on Brodhead's downfall—Reed assured him of whatever support he wanted from Pennsylvania.

Brodhead's reaction was understandably caustic. He tried to remind Reed that not all the Ohio Delawares were Pennsylvanians' enemies, and that ensuring the settlements' security took more than a spirit of enterprise. But like George Morgan, Brodhead was by now shouting into the wind. He was instructed to give up men and artillery under his command for the use of Clark, who was about to set off on an ill-fated expedition to the falls of the Wabash (on which, Brodhead bitterly observed, "I am told he is to drive all before him, by a supposed unbounded influence he has amongst the Inhabitants of the Western Country").[32]

Later Brodhead was relieved of his command at Fort Pitt altogether. Despite his mutterings, the course of the backcountry war from 1780 on was set. That course—one of ostensibly preventive expeditions being sent farther and farther into the western lands—proved more durable than the war itself.

Chapter 9

THE POSTWAR
THAT WASN'T

ON A SERIES OF WARM LATE APRIL EVENINGS IN 1783, LITTLE
festivals were held in cities and towns across the mid-Atlantic, with processions of virgins, pealing bells, and illuminated paper figures borne
about in the dusk. At Pittsgrove, New Jersey, "a monument of great
height" was set up on the grass, and the militia shot off a thirteen-part *feu
de joie*, with each man firing into the air in quick succession to create the
illusion of a single, sustained explosion. The next night, the people of a
neighboring town sang carols of their own composing underneath a lau-
rel bower. At Carlisle, Pennsylvania, they feasted on roasts "prepared in
the barbecue stile," before tossing off a long series of toasts, each one
punctuated by cannon fire. Then, as it grew dark, the townspeople looked
around and overhead to see candles and skyrockets flaring up in an "illu-
mination of the town, and an elegant display of fireworks."

In Philadelphia, the sheriff read a proclamation from the courthouse
steps "amid a vast concourse of people, who expressed their satisfaction
. . . by repeated shouts." The city's bells were rung, and the local artist
Charles Willson Peale put on "an agreeable display of luminous figures,
descriptive and emblematical of our rising empire" for the pleased citi-
zenry. When Peale produced another such spectacular the next year, his
glowing pictures would include Washington at the plow, Louis XVI,
Peace, Pennsylvania, a thirteen-branched tree, and all the arts and sciences. On this second occasion, the painted panels of greased paper,

behind which Peale had unwisely decided to pack a cache of fireworks, would topple and catch fire, "shooting 700 rockets at the crowds" and sending citizens shrieking through the streets in a lethal crush. But for now, all was well in Philadelphia.[1]

What made everyone so happy was peace. Congress had just ratified the preliminary Treaty of Paris with Britain, a document that would guarantee American independence and possession of all the land between Canada, the Floridas, and the Mississippi. However the residents of these towns and cities had felt during the war, they could rejoice together now that it seemed at last to be finished, and set about rebuilding their lives.

But there were no fireworks or paper arches in the western borderlands of Pennsylvania, for there the war was plainly far from over. Describing a series of attacks made the same week the peace treaty was being celebrated, the editor of the *Freeman's Journal* angrily disposed of any explanation for them except the most fundamental elements of Indian character and culture. They would, he thought, now go on hammering the back settlements regardless.

> What reason was there to expect it to be otherwise? The king of Great Britain doubtless has directed them to desist . . . . but . . . . What have these nations suffered that they should be weary of the war?

The back inhabitants' suffering would be ended only when other Americans came to realize that the Indians must be made to suffer more. "We have given them but little trouble in their towns," the *Journal* claimed;

> they have enjoyed plenty and security. What would they gain by a peace with us? . . . By war they obtain plunder from our settlements. Is not war the amusement, and the honours of it the ambition of the savage? . . . What but suffering will repress this love of pastime? . . . The people of the frontiers, who know the disposition of the savages are astonished that it should be supposed that . . . . [any]thing but a heavy campaign penetrating their country . . . can effect this.[2]

As had been true two decades before, when Pontiac's War came at the heels of the Seven Years' War, the idea of a second, perhaps indefinitely continued round of war, falling just when all had been likely at last to become peaceful, had a special power to embitter feeling against Indians in western settlements and the regional press. The Ohio and upper midwestern Indians had not been consulted at any point by Britain in its peace process. And as many contemporaries pointed out, it was impossible to see them as having been conquered by American forces, whom they had nearly always beaten.3

Nonetheless, to Americans who were ready to feel they had at last won the struggle that had consumed their societies for nearly a decade, the prolongation of warfare was peculiarly maddening. "It is hard that all the rest of the world should enjoy peace," as the *Freeman's Journal*'s report of the peace celebrations in April 1783 concluded, "while the families of the western country are murdered daily."4

After Lord Cornwallis's surrender of most of the British southern army at Yorktown, Virginia, in October 1781, a new, more narrowly anti-Indian bitterness cropped up in print. From Yorktown through 1784, with nearly all the Europeans who had supposedly egged on Indian attacks now sidelined, those Indians who kept on fighting came in for the nearly undiluted force of the war-weary revolutionaries' disappointment and disgust. Even now, some still proclaimed Britain's responsibility for all the "murders" of the war and called intently, as the only way "to put a stop to the[se] barbarities of Britons," for collective reprisal executions against British prisoners of war. (If prisoners were not killed and Indian attacks continued, one correspondent from the countryside noted, the victims' blood "will cry aloud from the vallies to Congress—RETALIATE [against the British]—the hills will resound RETALIATE—and the sound will reverbrate . . . from mountain to mountain, with increasing repetitions RETALIATE, RETALIATE, RETALIATE!")5

But blaming the British became less common, and calls for more straightforward reprisals, through government encouragement for "heavy" expeditions against Indian towns, grew shriller. "The Indians have been worse this spring than at any other time since the commencement of the war," a correspondent of the *Pennsylvania Journal* on the

Monongahela River wrote in May 1783, "killing, captivating, and burning upon all quarters." In response to this letter, the editor observed that the government should sponsor a massive punitive expedition. "It is astonishing," he wrote,

> how men in power, can hear of our poor frontiers, suffering under the barbarous hands of cruel savages, and take no measures to bring to justice a race of mankind, who glory in killing women and children.

A letter from Northumberland County, Pennsylvania, had made much the same complaints in July 1782. "Our troubles are come on again," its author reported, and so what needed to be done was to seize the next "opportunity for destroying th[e Indians'] towns."

> It is a very distressing circumstance, that our frontiers are exposed from year to year, to the enemy's butcherings, murderings, and scalpings, when we have a sufficient force in our country, willing to drive them off, and to extirpate them from the face of the earth.

This was truly exterminatory talk. And it was coming not from a soldier in time of war but from a civilian, as part of a chorus of voices—voices that rose and gained confidence as they heard each other's anger. A newly virulent anti-Indian rhetoric, which included noticeably more often the idea of their being a vicious "race of mankind," could now begin to spread.[6]

The logic of the postwar also meant that the revolutionary governments would themselves absorb some of the opprobrium of back settlers and their urban spokesmen. The governments at both the state and the confederated levels were still too weak to do much. The year 1783 was marked by multiple mutinies in the seldom-paid forces of Congress and of Pennsylvania and other states, as the revolutionary governments raced to discharge soldiers before they could mount serious insurrections. By June 1784, a bare eighty men remained on the Continental army payroll, though Congress did try to respond to the frontier's calls for help by establishing a seven-hundred-man "American Regiment" of militias. Amid the postwar collapse, calls for Indian blood would mostly be answered by local forces. They would fight—with the new governments' approval—less for wages than for plunder and revenge.

IN APRIL 1782, word arrived in Philadelphia of a volunteer action in the Ohio lands. There were no details yet, the *Pennsylvania Packet* noted in an excited account, but it did sound as if "[a] very important advantage has been . . . gained over our savage enemies on the frontiers of this state," all with the militia suffering hardly any casualties itself. But as further news came in, these reports proved too good to be true. What had taken place at the towns of Salem and Gnadenhütten (or Tents of Grace) on the Muskingum River was not a battle but a massacre, and its victims were not "savage enemies" but Moravian Indian pacifists.7

The residents of the Moravian missions at Salem, Gnadenhütten, and their neighbor settlement, Schönbrunn (or Beautiful Spring), had tried vainly throughout the war to defuse the suspicions of both the rebelling Ohio border settlers and of the Indians and British military commanders who were gathered around Detroit. The towns' missionaries had corresponded with Col. Daniel Brodhead at Fort Pitt, offering him a steady stream of information and reassurance about the Ohio Delawares' disposition, in an effort to shield their congregations from American attack. People in the settlements regularly charged that the mission Indians were, if not actually launching raids against them, at least sheltering and spying for northwestern attack parties, so this was an essential business.

Still, the missionaries were playing a counterproductive game. Neither side fully believed in their neutrality, and trying to endear their congregations to the United States further alienated the British-leaning Indians who lived close to them. By 1781, the Moravian congregations were less likely to be troubled by unruly settlers than by passing Wyandots on their way to raid the American settlements, or by other Delawares under Captain Pipe, a war captain now in the British camp. The Moravians' response was to try to appease and provide supplies to anyone, American or Indian, who passed through their towns. When Brodhead's expedition of May 1781 stopped at Gnadenhütten, its "Troops experienced great kindness from the Moravian Indians," as Brodhead observed, "& obtained a sufficient supply of meat & Corn." But the suspicions of pro-revolutionary settlers that the missions could also serve as rest stops for attack parties were correct. Often neighboring war parties brought captives to Gnadenhütten, as Zeisberger wrote in his personal journal a few months after Brodhead's visit, "and the place became a theatre of war."[8]

In time, the suspicions of the British and Wyandots grew too high, and the missionaries were plundered, stripped, and taken on a nightmarish long march with their congregations to the outskirts of Detroit. The commandant grilled them about their allegiances, and the converted Delawares were resettled on an empty plain at Upper Sandusky, with no crops in the ground. This forced migration added to the population of local Indians and pleased the anti-American Wyandot leader Pomoacan, who made a gloating speech to the new arrivals. "He said he was much rejoiced that we were now with them," Zeisberger wrote, "and that all who had the same color, were together."

But by the fall of 1781 it was clear the new settlements in this pan-Indianist's paradise could not sustain themselves. There was nothing to eat. Most of the mission Indians, trying to survive on "wild potatoes," grew malnourished and listless, with their cattle literally dropping dead around them. Returning warriors told them corn was still standing in their fields on the Muskingum. Amid incipient famine, the idea of slipping back to harvest some of it became overpoweringly tempting.[9]

When a small group left Sandusky in October 1781 to try to feed themselves from Gnadenhütten's fields, the experiment ended badly. Militiamen who had been alerted to their return imprisoned some of the Moravians for a while at Fort Pitt, including Schebosch (or John Joseph Bull), a Quaker-born European who had married a Delaware and now lived in Zeisberger's congregation. But as hunger descended at Sandusky, the fear of being attacked by patrolling militia would not be enough to keep more people from returning to the Muskingum, however dangerous it was.[10]

THE MASS KILLING at Gnadenhütten was first commemorated in 1797, when Moravians resettling the empty town site gathered the human remains they found under a wide, low mound that is still to be seen, covered with foliage. In 1872, an obelisk was raised to the "Indian Martyrs," and in time the old town became a state historic site, its grounds excavated and the houses where most of the killing took place carefully re-created, with cutaways and helpful signs. Every summer since the 1970s, tourists driving through eastern Ohio have even been able to watch the events of March 7–8 in a popular "outdoor drama."

As explanations of violent events go, the immanence of evil is never a good one. It is a confession of failure, then, to say that however much one tries to understand the events of those days and to take them apart step by step, something cold and alien—an irreducible emptiness—is likely always to remain at the core of what happened. Still, the effort at historical sympathy is, if anything, more vital in such circumstances than in everyday ones, and the massacre's outlines are not hard to understand.

A few things happened in quick succession to bring on the disaster. Through February and early March 1782, mission members had continued to flow back to the Muskingum to gather corn in the fields, until, by Zeisberger's count, there were eighty-six people of all ages and sexes at Gnadenhütten, Salem, and Schönbrunn. Many believed themselves safe from harassment as long as there was snow on the ground. Then, in mid-February, a Wyandot and Delaware raiding party killed or captured several people in the hinterland of Fort Pitt, including the wife and three children of a man named Robert Wallace.[11]

On the way back to Detroit, this attack party stopped for food in Gnadenhütten, together with their prisoners. As Zeisberger later heard, one prisoner was a man "whose wife and child [the Wyandots] killed near Gnadenhütten, and had impaled." He told the Moravians in the town that if they did not leave, they would all fall victim to the pursuers who, he claimed, were surely chasing after his captors. Then this unhappy man escaped from the war party's campsite the next night and presumably made his way back to Pittsburgh, where Zeisberger thought he must have "betrayed to them that our Indians were there."[12]

The escaped prisoner—who had seen Gnadenhütten's former residents returned and sharing supplies with a war party that had impaled his family—may be the same man described in the press as having "made his escape, and come home a few days before [March 7]" to tell the residents of the Fort Pitt area "that the Indian towns on the Muskingum had not moved, as they had been told." The people he found in the settlements, including Wallace (whose children and wife had been taken captive), had just trudged back the night before, because of poor weather, from an attempt at pursuing the war party. But when they heard that the Muskingum towns were full of Moravian Indians—and no missionary with them—the whole tenor of things changed. Perhaps 150 to 200 men now decided to set out for Gnadenhütten in a loose simulacrum of a militia unit, formed without the knowledge of Col. John Gibson, who was in command at Fort Pitt.[13]

In the *Pennsylvania Journal*'s excited telling, these men "arrived at the town in the night, undiscovered, attacked the Indians in their cabbins, and so compleatly surprised them, that they killed and scalped upwards of ninety (but a few making their escape)." So far as an account of what really happened can be put together, it depends on two young Moravian Indian men—Jacob and Thomas—who escaped from Gnadenhütten, and on the smattering of unattributed details that emerged from members of the expedition. There were not many such details. As one observer at Pittsburgh wrote after their return, "notwithstanding there seems to have been some difference amongst themselves, about that business yet they will say nothing."[14]

Like most wrecking expeditions, the Gnadenhütten volunteers went without expecting much resistance. They knew they could surprise people at the towns, and they certainly meant to take everything they had and put an end to the missions. They can have had little physical fear of Christian pacifists who had forsworn going to war decades ago, as a precondition for their towns' existence. And while it is not clear that they set out meaning to undertake a ritualized massacre, each step they took carried them closer to one.

On March 4, the volunteers swam their horses over the Ohio and elected officers at Mingo Bottom, moving on the next day toward the Muskingum. On the morning of March 7, they entered Gnadenhütten, after stopping a little outside the town to waylay Schebosch's son and two non-Moravians from Sandusky whom they found nearby. They left the scalped body of Schebosch's son lying in the road—a display that later saved the lives of most of the Indians at Schönbrunn—and narrowly missed seeing young Jacob, who hid in the bushes, "went a long way about, and observed what went on."[15]

The volunteers took everyone in Gnadenhütten prisoner without resistance, going through the fields around the town and "b[idding] them come into town, telling them no harm should befall them," news at which "they seemed to be very glad." The mission's residents, and perhaps many of the men collecting them, must have thought they would be taken back as captives to Fort Pitt, as had happened in November. And a messenger who arrived back at Sandusky on March 14, knowing only the start of events on March 7, in fact reported that all the Gnadenhütten villagers had been "taken to Pittsburg." He also said "they were bound and some killed," as Zeisberger noted, "but all of this we could not believe. But that our Indian brethren are taken to Pittsburg is the more pleasing to us, were it only all of them there, and had they again a [European] brother with them."[16]

But having been disarmed and bound, and urged to locate all their possessions for the trip ahead—they were asked a bit irritably "how it came they had no Cattle?" and "made . . . [to] bring all their hidden goods out of the bush . . . they had to tell them where in the bush the bees were, help get the honey out; other things also they had to do for them before they were killed"—as night fell, the twenty-odd congregants who had been in the fields were sorted by sex and confined in frightened groups to two buildings at the center of the settlement, the cooper's shop and the meetinghouse.[17]

When he saw the militiamen, one of the Indian ministerial assistants, John Martin, had gone over to Salem to tell the seventy or so people there about their arrival. At his calm urging, perhaps, "they all resolved not to flee." Then Martin and two other men bravely, disastrously went back to Gnadenhütten, carrying word to the militia that "there were still more Indians in Salem," and were themselves added to the cabins. As the Moravians agreed to the volunteers' taking more and more control over them—counting, disarming, binding, and sorting them and shutting them into the houses—in a useless effort to prove they were friends ("the militia themselves," Zeisberger heard, "acknowledged . . . they had been good Indians"), their danger rose steadily.[18]

That evening a "Council" was held, at which David Williamson, the militia's elected leader, "told his men that he would leave it to their choice, either to carry the Indians as Prisoners to Fort Pitt, or to kill them; when they agreed that they should be killed." This decision to kill all the prisoners does not seem to have been unanimous or quickly reached. Early reports all stressed that the volunteers had been "considering the matter" for a period of days. Regional tradition, which probably contains a kernel of truth, has a certain number of objectors—sixteen, or eighteen—stepping out of the group when Williamson put the question to them to say they would take no part in the killing. This was at most a tenth of the men present. An inquirer at Pittsburgh also reported that he had "heard it Insinuated, that about thirty or forty only of the party gave their Consent or assisted in the Catastrofy." On the whole, this seems likeliest to be a guess at the number of men who took part in the actual work of slaughter, since it is difficult, if not impossible, to imagine the killings taking place if 80 percent of the men on the expedition had been against them. The vote worked as an invitation for the objectors to absent themselves from what was going to happen, and they later sat about a hundred feet away, under the overhang of the riverbank, hidden from the sight of the cabins.[19]

Two men were sent to tell the Indians that they would all be killed the next morning. The brethren, who found themselves separated into their familiar choirs of male and female voices, started singing "Hymns & Psalms all Night . . . and kept on singing as long as there were three alive." Singing hymns helped to keep panic at bay, or channeled the urge to cry. It may have heartened some of the first victims, and it connected their coming deaths to the Christian martyrdoms they had been taught about, but it did not make them harder to kill: the sound of their trembling voices would later be described by some of the militia as war songs.[20]

When morning came, a Mahican man named Abraham was pulled out of the men's and boys' building by a cord around his neck and felled with a mallet from the cooper's shop. After this the executioner, or executioners—Zeisberger heard in April from a European captive that, at least in the first stage, "two men alone . . . accomplished the whole murder after the Indians had been bound, . . . kill[ing] them one after the other" with the mallet—moved inside for the rest of the killings, and apparently made more use of tomahawks to stove in their victims' heads.[21]

Since it would be so hard to actually brain a man at a blow with a wooden mallet, the idea behind using it at all was to restrain the victims with the cords, then stun them before at last inflicting a fatal scalping wound. With scalping substituted for throat slitting, this was the same two-step process used at harvest time to slaughter cattle. The method dominated reports and memories of the killings long after, and it was surely a basic point behind killing in this way. Killing the Moravians inside the mission buildings, "which they called the Slaughter Houses," was a way of saying that the Indians there were like dumb beasts.[22]

After the men were all slaughtered (though one scalped boy, Thomas, regained consciousness under the other bodies and managed to hide in the cellar, then get away), the women and girls in the other building were tomahawked, with "[m]any children . . . killed in their wretched mothers' arms." A Mahican woman named Christina, fluent in German and English from lessons at the Bethlehem school, threw herself at Williamson's feet and begged him not to let her die, "but got for answer that he could not help her." The victims were being ordered about angrily in a language most did not know (partly because of their missionaries' linguistic expertise). Since otherwise so few could speak intelligibly to their killers, this case stood out in observers' minds.

The killing went on in serial, with a small number of men doing the work at any moment in an agonizingly slow, abattoir-like procedure. In each house, the singing, praying victims watched one another die and be scalped for the space of perhaps a quarter hour. Thomas later said "the blood flowed in streams," following him down to the basement.[23]

Now some of the militiamen who had been taking part split up and went to Schönbrunn and Salem. At Schönbrunn, having seen Schebosch's body in the road the day before, the residents were all hiding in the woods, from which they watched the militia search their empty town. But Salem was still filled with scores of expectant people, and the Indians there—who again gathered up their belongings for the militia—were all escorted to Gnadenhütten to be readied for captivity.

By this part of the morning, the decision to kill them, and the ways of doing so, had all been thoroughly worked out. The trip to Gnadenhütten was an unmotivated deception, which the Salemites' guards may have enjoyed: with no shots fired, the Indians "did not know how it had gone with them in Gnadenhütten." But when the group reached the ford to the village, any doubt about what lay ahead dissolved. Having given up their rifles, the Salemites were disarmed even of their knives, told to strip—presumably to save their clothes and emphasize the animality of their naked bodies—and then "fetch'd . . . two or three at a time with Ropes about their Necks and dragged . . . into the Slaughter houses where they knocked them down; then they set these Two houses on Fire, as likewise all the other houses."[24]

It is hard to imagine what it was like for the victims from Salem—perhaps three-fourths of all those killed—to be hauled into the two cabins for their last moments. No one could escape the sight or sound of killing. Even the objectors, sheltering under the riverbank, watched as a young man from the Salem group who had briefly escaped—he came scrambling away from the cabins and hurtled across the river—was shot through the body. It may have been now that one man took a break from killing, saying his arm was too tired; "and he sat down and cried because he found in it no satisfaction for his murdered wife and children." Possibly this was Robert Wallace, who according to one of the objectors came over at the close of the day, trembling, bloody, and exhausted, and in "a flood of tears said: 'You know I couldn't help it!'"[25]

Despite such stories, it seems very clear the massacre was not the passionate outburst of a few of the militia. Anger over the Wallace family's abduction (or the sight of the two impaled bodies, unhelpfully left nearby by the Wyandot raiders) may have helped the men to briefly believe in a punishment justification—the analogic mirror in the mind, in which things that one does to an enemy become the enemy's actions and not one's own. This could have made it a little easier to kill at least some of the Moravian women and children; but not scores of them, and not with such incredible deliberateness—continuing over two days, and taking in two towns. Most of what the men did expressed a goal of killing Indians in general that was widely agreed upon between them.

A newspaper report written after the attack to excuse what, its author said, was unfairly being "called an horrible murder," struggled to establish the supposedly unthinking speed with which events had unfolded. In this version, Williamson's men acted spontaneously, setting off in sudden "perplexity" to stave off what they thought was an oncoming attack. At the town, a former prisoner had pointed out Indians who maltreated him during his captivity, making it clear that the Moravians were not all as innocent as they appeared. And, in this embellished version, what happened next had been not a deliberate murder but the expression of an uncontrollable—hence, crucially, forgivable—rush of emotion among a few relations of the dead, working more quickly than thought:

> A few of the men, upon seeing and hearing such things, and thinking of their wives, children or relations, that had been barbarously murdered, got inflamed, and would not be restrained, but rushed upon, and killed young and old . . . indiscriminately, notwithstanding th[at] divers persons interceded for the lives, especially of the children, and . . . fled away with tears in their eyes; and notwithstanding that the leaders of the expedition . . . had not ended their deliberations.

None of the facts supports this idea of "a fit of frenzy." And neither a desire for plunder nor their being "filled with revenge, Indignation & Sorrow for the loss of their friends, their wives & their Children"—as another palliating report expressed it—can explain the volunteers' murders on the Muskingum, murders that marked a new stage in Indian-American relations.[26]

For the mental model of Gnadenhütten, unlike that of the Paxton-era massacres, was no longer an Indian attack but a slaughterhouse. The nakedness, the binding, the being taken by ones and twos—all were deliberately chosen to make the victims' helplessness more vivid. This atrocity spoke. What it said was not about bullying, or warning away, or revenge or taking things. Mostly—over and over—it was simply about killing, on a scale that could mean eradication. It was an action that echoed through the following decade's debates. The men at Gnadenhütten were acting on a powerful postwar distaste for Indians as Indians, a feeling that in this instance was by itself so clearly pivotal and indiscriminate as to be worth labeling racist.

The militia on the Gnadenhütten expedition took a huge amount of plunder—especially furs and skins but also household pewter, tea things, honeycombs, clothes, and everything else a farming settlement held—amounting to at least eighty horseback loads of goods. (Not to mention the horses themselves, which now came eastward carrying packs instead of people.) On reemerging at Mingo Bottom, the first stop from the settlements on the western side of the Ohio, the men carefully shared out the take in a closed "vendue," or auction ("in order to prevent the inhabitants from bidding against the adventurers"), and then "divided the spoil equally between officers and men." This last action, so typical of group acts of Indian-killing, cemented their sense of collective responsibility and suggested the complexity of motives behind even such an extraordinary atrocity. The Moravian Indians' town had been rich in material possessions compared with the settlements of other Indians, probably even of some border settlers. And this wealth mattered enough to the expedition's men that they deferred killing their prisoners, for instance, till they could find out where as many possessions as possible were hidden.[27]

When they got back to Fort Pitt, they overpowered the federal soldiers guarding some American-allied Indians sheltering on an island "at the very nose" of the fort—Indians described by a sympathetic observer as "naked—almost starving—despised—in constant fears of an enraged country—cooped up in a miserable hut"—of whom they managed to kill four more. One of the survivors was Killbuck, an increasingly isolated pro-American Delaware leader, now at the end of a chain of near-misses with death that had begun with his pursuit by John Mitcheltree in 1769. Two of the dead were captains in the Continental army. The Continental fort itself was "nothing but a heap of ruins," whose drunken garrison had just agreed to mutiny for lack of pay and often spent hours in front of the tavern "playing at long bullets"—an alarming primitive form of shot-putting, in which iron balls were whizzed down streets for distance—to "the great danger [of] the lives of the children."

Fort Pitt's acting commander was Col. John Gibson, who had a child by an Indian woman, and the volunteers now defiantly sent Gibson "a message that they would also scalp him," presumably for "ha[ving] an attachment to Indians in general." It was pretty clear, in short, who was in real control of the region, and it was not Congress or its army.[28]

SOME OF THE GROUNDS for a conversion of the official mind to the militiamen's perspective were now in place. Local pressure could do a certain amount. When he returned to Fort Pitt in the aftermath of the expedition, the post's underequipped commander, Gen. William Irvine, was desperately eager not to investigate it. "No reasoning can persuade the people of this country, but that an officer who will protect an Indian at all, on any account or pretence, must be a bad man," he wrote unhappily, enjoining his wife,

> Whatever your private opinion of these matters may be . . . by all the ties of affection and as you value my reputation, that you will keep your mind to yourself, and that you will not express any sentiments for or against these deeds;—. . . No man knows whether I approve or disapprove of killing the Moravians.[29]

He found himself continually besieged by country people who were "subject," he reported, "to be clamorous, and charge continental officers with want of zeal . . . for their protection." County leaders came and demanded federal funding and troops for wrecking expeditions they dreamed of launching in all directions. He put them off, and made them agree that if any expeditions were sent off they would behave militarily. ("They . . . promise," he wrote hopefully after one such meeting, "to obey orders, etc.")[30]

But the easiest thing to do, in this wretched outpost, was to simply start agreeing, and by the second spring of Indian attacks after Yorktown, that is what Irvine did. Only a "total extirpation" of the Ohio Valley's native residents, Irvine was writing by April 1783, could bring about a peace. He was "almost persuaded," as he suggested to an unresponsive General Washington, that there would be misery and bloodshed "till the whole of the western tribes are driven over the Mississippi and the lakes, entirely beyond the American lines,—which will not now be very difficult, but would take two summers at least." Irvine said he was voicing a "temper" that was now "pretty prevalent" among the border people.[31]

In his negotiations with militia spokesmen Irvine had to stipulate that they could not use any expeditions "to extend their settlements . . . and that any conquest they might make should be in behalf and for the United States." It seems astonishing, at first, that the general should even have had to say this, but he was in fact responding to one of the largest and most important contexts for making sense of the moral disaster at

Gnadenhütten, together with nearly everything else that happened around Fort Pitt in the 1780s. For in a war to remake the fundamental sovereignty of the continent, land could be a form of plunder, too—as John Harris had already seen before the fighting began. But first its occupants had to be gone.[32]

Every day people streamed down the river and across it, into the lands that would eventually become Ohio. "Emigration and new states are much talked of," as Irvine observed warily in April 1782. The Gnadenhütten affair had at least temporarily wiped out Indian settlement on the Muskingum, and in its wake an observer at the fort observed that "the project of emigrating and settling a new State on Muskingum goes glibly down with every one." People in this borderland between Pennsylvania and Virginia had a long history of drawing and observing whatever imaginary lines around themselves best suited their needs, and now handbills were put up to announce meetings for "all who wish to become members of a new state on the Muskingum." An advertisement three years later called for a constitutional convention among everyone living west of the Ohio (with a special polling place where Gnadenhütten had been). "I do certify," its promulgator wrote,

> that all mankind, agreeable to every constitution formed in America, have an undoubted right to pass into every vacant country, and there to form their constitution, and that from the confederation of the whole United States congress is not empowered to forbid them . . . .

This urge would in time become the main problem that Congress's western policies were designed to solve. But for now it was enough, as the old Indian agent George Croghan's son found on arriving at Fort Pitt the month after the Gnadenhütten expedition, that "on this side the Mountain . . . The Country taulks of Nothing but killing Indians, & taking posession of thier lands."[33]

Often people mean what they say, and in some ways Gnadenhütten was a wrecking and clearing expedition like any other, although the "fine prize" its proponents had in mind was by now much larger than any number of horses loaded down with stolen things: as large as the Ohio lands themselves.

* * *

THE "TRAGIC SCENES of . . . killing in cold blood 95 browne or tawny sheep of Jesus Christ one by one" in "Butcher Houses or Sheds," as the Philadelphia lawyer who had defended Renatus against charges of murder two decades before described them, had a profound effect on the Moravian community and on the borderland war. After his scalping, Thomas, the boy who had survived beneath a pile of bodies, "often had fits," one of which caused his death by drowning, and Schebosch's wife became paranoid, "inclined from fear to live too much alone." A captive among the Detroit-area Indians the summer after Gnadenhütten reported that they were now joined by Moravians who, in "retaliation for the Moravian affair . . . had laid aside their Religious principles, and . . . gone to War." (This captive saw two former members of the missions "bring[ing] in scalps.") And Augustus, a Moravian Indian who had taken refuge on Province Island in 1764, decided after Gnadenhütten that the religion of white people—indeed, involvement of any kind with them— was not for him. In an angry speech to his brother Samuel, Augustus explained why:

> I was in Philadelphia, in danger of my life, and have seen with my own eyes those who made attempts upon my life . . . . On the Muskingum the white people have at last attained their purpose, murdering so many of our friends; therefore . . . no one shall take me to them; and I say to thee, nevermore will I come to you and live with you; I will hear nothing about the Saviour. . . . My forefathers have all gone to the devil; there will I go also; where they are there will I also be.

But if Augustus and other Indians had been converted to strict hostility toward all Europeans, in the next world as well as this, and if the Williamson expedition's members had conversely been acting out of a racial animus against all Indians, whatever their age, sex, or religion, their sentiments were still far from universal in Indian country or the settlements. Not everyone was convinced that all the people in the other population were part of what Edward Shippen had snarlingly described during the last postwar, in the 1760s, as "a deep plan for the extermination of us all." One of the strongest advocates of a descent on Indian towns, Col. Samuel Hunter of Sunbury, Pennsylvania, wrote disapprovingly that he thought there was "not much Honour Gained in killing Indians that would make no resistance."[34]

Colonel Williamson himself would later be elected the sheriff of Washington County, which suggests his local popularity was not too damaged by the "Catastrofy," but many observers nonetheless agreed that it became a source of "Ilwill" around Fort Pitt, with "the people . . . greatly divided in Sentiment about it." "I am Informed that you have it Reported that the Massacre of the Moravian Indians Obtain the Approbation of Every Man on this side the Mountains," a lieutenant colonel in Westmoreland County wrote earnestly to Pennsylvania's president, "which I assure your Excelency is false":

> the Better Part of the Community are of Opinion the Perpetrators of that wicked Deed ought to be Brought to Condein Punishment, that without something is Done by Government in the Matter, it will Disgrace the Annals of the United States, and be an Everlasting Plea and Cover for British Cruelty.[35]

As Franklin had first noted of the Paxton rioters in 1764, what these Indian-killers had done felt embarrassingly close to what Indians themselves had done. An outraged Congress ordered Virginia and Pennsylvania to investigate the affair. Virginia appointed a three-man commission that included Col. William Crawford, a man who would himself, by early summer, be leading another gigantic expedition against the Delaware and Wyandot towns near Sandusky. Crawford's commission soon reported brightly "that there was but one Virginian concerned in it, and that he is since dead."[36]

Officials in Pennsylvania did no better. Dorsey Pentecost, an assemblyman who visited to find out about the killings, wrote back to Philadelphia that an "Investigation may produce serious effects, and at least leave us as Ignorant as when we begon, and instead of rendering a service . . . produce a Confusion." Neither Congress nor the states pursued the matter much further than this, though Congress did later pointedly reserve the Muskingum lands for resettlement by Moravian Indians.

Still, the cool response to Gnadenhütten farther away from the fort showed that much local and official opinion was not yet ready to countenance a vision of "Exterpation of all Indians." The revolutionary self-image was still too wedded to a contrast between Americans' upstanding ways of war and the indiscriminate killing that was supposed to mark only the British and their savage allies. It would take a little more writing and thinking before the uprooting of all Indians toward which the Gnadenhütten volunteers had made such rapid strides became something close to an official policy.[37]

IN THE MEANTIME, the shadow of the killings hung for decades, not only in the minds of Moravians and Great Lakes Indians but over the Ohio Valley countryside. In August 1812, a sixteen-year-old boy in the part of Washington County from which many of the Gnadenhütten volunteers had come, thirty years before, found his town filled with streams of excited people. Volunteers were being raised again, this time to go against Indians and Tories farther afield, on the shores of Lake Erie. The day felt significant, part festival and part emergency. It was the start of another war.

Here is what he remembered most clearly of that afternoon. A pleased crowd was ringed around a drunken old man, called Uncle Sol by those closest in. Uncle Sol was singing embarrassing songs. Then someone called: "show us how they killed the Indians." At this his face changed, the boy remembered, and he started to cry. Uncle Sol began going through an elaborate series of actions, "making motions" from his memories.

At first, the boy didn't really understand what he was seeing. Uncle Sol ran forward and pretended to throw a rope over an unseen person just in front of him. Then he hauled this "imaginary object" backward by the neck. He had a stick in his hands, and he used it to club the air, "all the time howling and cursing," as the boy remembered, "like a demon." This wasn't funny. Perhaps by now the people watching him had stopped talking. After a bit, "somebody pulled him away, saying it was a shame."

When he asked, another onlooker told the boy that Uncle Sol—whose name was probably Solomon Vaile—had been at Gnadenhütten in 1782.

The horrible pantomime they had just watched was a thing he sometimes did when drunk. When he was sober, the man said, he never talked about it at all.[38]

In the wake of the war, public debates were full of sweeping proposals for reform. "R," writing late in 1782, offered a typical example. Taking literally the idea that the earth belongs to the living, why, "R" asked, should Americans keep up the "indecent and ridiculous custom" of burying their dead in the hearts of cities? Should not the graveyards of Philadelphia "be forthwith taken from the dead and appropriated to the uses of the living"? A mass exhumation and reburial in the countryside of the rotting bones of Americans' ancestors would neither be blasphemous—not to "th[e] sublime and intellectual Being" of pure reason who governed the universe—nor unprecedented. It would bring Americans' customs more in line with those of the Chinese, for one thing, and, after all, "America is a country where there is no want of ground: why then should we incumber our cities with the bodies of the departed?"[39]

Nor were corpses the only encumbrances whose removal from American ground seemed to be dictated by reason. Since its founding in 1781, the Philadelphia *Freeman's Journal* had gained a reputation for freethinking disputatiousness. The favorite editorial mode of its printer, Francis Bailey, was the exposé, especially the exposé of "snugg . . . schemes" laid against the interests of ordinary working citizens by well-born ones. ("For God's sake leave off!" one too-good-to-be-true gentleman supposedly wrote in to Bailey to complain. "I suppose before you have done our very horses will be asking us the reason why we want to ride them.") In autumn 1782, the paper ran a long, front-page rhapsody on the "rich and fertile country" of the American interior. The motive behind its publication, Bailey explained, was to alert Americans to the vast unexploited resource they could claim there, in a cornucopia of land. "We do not insert [the geographical treatise] wholly with a view to the entertainment of our readers," Bailey confessed,

but to remind them and the public what valuable lands of immense extent are now lying in a wild state of nature, possessed by indolent

Indian savages, who without all doubt ought, upon the plainest principles of reason, either to be expelled from thence as soon as it shall be in
our power, or be obliged to conform to a life of agriculture, the natural
cause of civilization, and without which there appears little or no hopes
of their ever becoming *men*, much less christians.

The policy of "expell[ing]" or culturally converting all the western
Indians, to make use of their land for the new nation's purposes, did
indeed have a clear pedigree not only among people in the lands
around Fort Pitt but in high Enlightenment thought. As a discussion
of the legal theorist Emerich de Vattel's ideas in Bailey's paper had made
clear the preceding year, since "the earth belongs to the human race in
general," any obstructive claim to land by hunting nations was inherently
absurd.[40]

But these ideas had had no perceptible currency in the mid-Atlantic
press before the postwar period. In the early 1780s, a series of disputes
over the rights to western territory of the Ohio Valley's Indians, of Virginia, of a speculative syndicate called the Indiana Company, and of the
United States spilled over into print. It made a huge difference when they
did. These disputes helped to develop an official anti-Indian discourse,
one both Congress and the United States armed forces would use to
frankly envisage the natives' total dispossession. This harsh new way of
talking built on a folk theory of sovereignty that was becoming apparent
in the postwar countryside.

THE GNADENHÜTTEN EXPEDITION had been followed in the
summer of 1782 by an expedition sent out against Sandusky under Col.
William Crawford. The raid was a panicky failure. Meeting with heavy
fighting, the expedition's members broke and fled. Crawford was left
behind in the rout and taken as a captive to Sandusky. Then—as many
observers thought was happening more and more often after the
Gnadenhütten killings, in retaliation—he was tortured to death with a
brutal ingenuity. Crawford's last hours became the stuff of horror not
only in the American settlements but among British forces at Detroit,
where, David Zeisberger reported shortly afterward, "all are much dis-

pleased" with it. Crawford was tethered, like a baited bear, to a pole beside a fire. His lower body was shot full of gunpowder, his ears were sawn off, and he was forced, by gouging with red-hot sticks, to totter around the fire on a bed of hot coals. After Crawford lay down and was scalped, probably by a lapsed Moravian, the coals were applied straight to his brainpan and he was once again poked into motion around the fire, in which, when he could no longer be made to move, he was incinerated.[41]

The new anti-Indianism of the 1780s was greatly assisted in its early stages by the rhetorical efforts of Francis Bailey's star correspondent, Hugh Henry Brackenridge, who since composing his *Death of General Montgomery* early in the war had moved west to Pittsburgh in search of opportunity. The death of Crawford offered abundant scope to a writer of Brackenridge's gifts. His play had shown him to be a master of mutilatory rhetoric, even without actual Indians to discuss. Now, in a series of articles for Bailey's paper that were quickly collected and reprinted as a pamphlet—in the same spring that Irvine, at Fort Pitt, was trying out the idea of extirpation on Washington—he worked to make Crawford's death a rallying point for outrage that could rival Montgomery's, with its target this time not the British but the innate nature of Indians. Bailey prefaced Brackenridge's sensational first installment with the hope that, "as th[e Indians] still continue their murders on our frontiers,"

> these narratives may be serviceable to induce our governments to take some effectual steps to chastise and repress them; as from hence they will see that the nature of an Indian is fierce and cruel, and that an extirpation of them would be useful to the world, and honourable to those who can effect it.

Brackenridge, who gave himself a free hand in the Crawford pieces—compressing time, rearranging events, highlighting significant details, suppressing mention of Gnadenhütten as a motive—produced what may be two of the greatest atrocity accounts in American literary history. If any stories could make Bailey's case for "an extirpation," these were the ones. The pieces summed up for a broad audience the view of all Indians' being akin to cruel animals. In the reflective closing set of "Observations on the Indians, and on their right to the Soil of the Western Country, and what ought to be our conduct towards these savages, at the final conclusion of the war" that he appended to the narratives, Brackenridge took up their implications for government policy.[42]

These "Observations" struck a fascinating balance between inciting genocide and loudly disapproving of it, perhaps because Brackenridge was operating almost exactly at the limits of the thinkable, or the printable, in post-revolutionary America. He started by making it clear that he judged the Gnadenhütten expedition's having killed any women or children to be "unjustifiable inexcusable homicide." Then, having staked out the limits of where what he was about to say might lead, Brackenridge settled comfortably into an extraordinary sustained attack on "the animals, vulgarly called Indians," a "race of men" about which, he said, posing as an unbookish longtime inhabitant of the western country, he knew "something . . . from the deeds they perpetrate daily around me." Brackenridge mocked the crack-brained idea of Indians' having an exclusive claim to the land on which they lived, which was, he insisted, a royally introduced error that free-minded Americans should now be prepared to throw off. "I would as soon admit a right in the buffaloe to grant lands," Brackenridge wrote witheringly, "as in Killbuck, the Big Cat"—the names of two real Delaware headmen—"the Big Dog, or any of the ragged wretches that are called chiefs and sachems."[43]

As Brackenridge pursued this trope of Indians' having no more title than animals to the land, from which "they . . . ought to be driven," the strong undercurrent of dehumanization in his work became explicit. "They have the shapes of men and may be of the human species," he allowed,

> but certainly in their present state they approach nearer the character of Devils: take an Indian is there any faith in him? . . . Can you trust his word or confide in his promise? When he makes war upon you, when he takes you prisoner and has you in his power will he spare you?

Obviously the answer was supposed to be no, and here—by extending the logic behind his atrocity stories to all Indians—Brackenridge drove inexorably toward the final point. "[A]re not the whole Indian nations," he asked, murderers? Many of them may have not had an opportunity of putting prisoners to death, but the sentiment which they entertain leads them invariably to do this . . . : these principles constitute them murderers, and . . . . [t]he tortures which they exercise on the bodies of their prisoners, justify extirmination. . . . I do not know but . . . that even reforming from these practices, they ought not to live: These nations are so degenerate from the life of man, so devoid of every sentiment of generosity, so prone to every vicious excess of passion, so faithless, and so incapable of all civilization, that it is dangerous to the good order of the world that they should exist in it.

Here the language of Indian attack's being the same as murder, so central to anti-Indian discourse since the 1750s, came to its fulfillment. Murderers, a group into which Brackenridge now swept "the whole Indian nations," were punished with death. Even Indians trained up in colonial schools would keep this murderous "temper of their race," he noted, carefully closing a loophole: they were too much given to assassination to deserve any other fate themselves. And at the very least,

This being the character of these men, shall we not wish to dispossess them of the goodly lands . . . to the westward, which they have so long made a scene of horror by their practices[?] At the termination of the present war . . . it will be easy to drive them beyond the lakes: Instead of forming treaties . . . I would simply let them know that they are no longer to show themselves below the heads of the great rivers . . . : [in this way] they may be reduced to more distant bounds, until driven to the cold snows of the north west, where darkness reigns . . . , their practices shall be obscured, and the tribes gradually abolished.

America was to be a new world, and who could say it would not need new men to live in it? Before this, there was no statement half so complete anywhere in the corpus of mid-Atlantic letters of what it would mean to "abolish" or "extirminat[e]" all the Indians, or of why doing so would be, in Bailey's idealistic words, "useful to the world." But despite their relative novelty, one of the most striking things about Brackenridge's and Bailey's statements was how confidently the language of exterminatory anti-Indianism that they promoted seemed to be springing forth, all of a piece and with little criticism from other public writers.44

Brackenridge said he was simply picking up and retransmitting from his western neighbors a new desire to kill all Indians. In his thoughts on land title, he may also have been writing in response to an emerging sense that all of the bloodshed the frontier inhabitants had suffered had given them a new kind of title to contested lands. In the past, communities had used Indian attack as a reason to claim exemption from taxes. Now some groups moved to claim the land itself on the same basis. An agent for settlers in the Wyoming Valley, who were living there under licenses granted by Connecticut, petitioned Pennsylvania in January 1783 for confirmation of their title to the valley's lands. To be sure, he allowed, Congress had thrown out Connecticut's pretensions to the territory, and the Wyoming people could offer no conventional reason why their claims should be regarded.

But they had one charter, the Yankees felt, that Pennsylvania was bound to respect: a charter of blood. Whatever the previous rights and wrongs of the case, their sufferings on this tract of land had ended by making it theirs. "[T]he richest blood of our neighbour's and friend's children, husbands and fathers," their petition read, "has been spilt in the general cause of their country, and we ourselves have suffered every danger this side death" from Indian and Loyalist marauders. After such suffering, there should be some forgiveness. "Our houses are desolate, many mothers childless, widows and orphans multiplied, our habitations destroyed . . . which exhibits a scene most pitiful," the plea went, "and deserving of mercy." In comparison with these things, the small tract of earth under those ruined homes was something no feeling person could deny them. They had suffered enough for it to make it theirs.45

LIKE THIS CONCEPT of sovereignty through suffering, another idea became steadily stronger in the postwar talk of border settlers: sovereignty through popular conquest. In time, Congress squashed their efforts to set up new separatist states in the newly "conquered" parts of Indian country by claiming all western land as its own, and such projects were channeled into the restraints of the 1787 Northwest Ordinance. But during the early 1780s, as General Irvine had seen, the founding of new states by conquest was still a grassroots program.

Such talk was driven into the realm of public policy by a dispute over what groups could properly lay claim to the Ohio country. In this debate, the place of the so-called Indiana Company—a name chosen in tribute to the Indian deeds on the basis of which its proprietors, British and colonial men of influence, had in 1775 been on the verge of winning royally confirmed title to an enormous quantity of western land—was pivotal. The company's main antagonist was Virginia, which had vast claims of its own. But the result of their legal struggle was unexpected by either side. Resentment of both Virginia's claims and the Indiana Company's Indian-derived ones was probably what did most to popularize the idea that the new nation's citizens had the right to override existing titles and claim all Indian land.

One pivotal voice in the postwar debate over Indian land titles belonged to an imaginary ancient Briton, "painted blue with many singularities," by the name of Caractacus. (Paine devoted a special number of the "Common Sense" series just to answering this figment's essays.) In 1782, the friendly blue man had stepped out of midair "to reveal a few things necessary to be known at this time." As channeled by an anonymous writer for the *Freeman's Journal* in a long-running series, Caractacus' message for Americans was one of hope. The war debts to which they were still adding might be vast, but the western lands were vaster.

The men who feared that the state and national bills could be paid only with taxes so steep as to "mak[e] even our children slaves" were wrong. They "know little of the geography of the country . . . . The words, lakes, back lands, Ohio, and Mississippi, they have heard, but have no ideas of the value of the country." And this ignorance of their western birthright's sheer size and splendor left American farmers easy prey for tricksters—tricksters like the Indiana Company's members, who were at that moment trying to worm their way into the confidences of Congress, so as to win the right to parcel out wholly owned new colonies to American settlers. Such "pretended proprietors" were petitioning, planning, litigating, and, above all, trumping up "indian deeds" in the service of a single end: their "base plots, to rob the United States of their lands."[46]

Caractacus' pieces met every requirement of the muckraking genre so dear to Francis Bailey's editorial heart. The articles were built around the detection of *"dirty Indian business,"* connived at by a combination of luke-warm but influential Americans like Samuel Wharton, a Quaker mer-chant of uncertain political loyalties, and *"big* people" in England. They wanted to make it seem as if Indian titles should fence the nation in. Per-haps it was his own experience as a savage, himself subdued and chased from his lands by another, earlier empire, that gave Caractacus the right to pronounce for the *Journal*'s readers on Indian rights. Whatever it was, he felt able to roundly announce that

> all lands, especially on this side of Ohio, were taken from the savages by force of arms last war, and at the expence both of blood and treasure; and therefore any thing done at treaties was mere policy, to quiet the minds of the savages, being the cheapest way of getting peaceable possession . . . . Great Britain paid no regard to Indian deeds, neither ought America.

The most determined answer to all this for the Indiana Company came from Samuel Wharton. It is doubtful Wharton's writings did much to sway the popular mind, since his pamphlets were almost unbelievably bad—less works of original intellection than relentless, long-winded pas-tiches of every authority, legal, historical, or constitutional, that he had to hand, so that quotations from *Paradise Lost* jostled with those from early eighteenth-century Indian conferences. But the changing nature of the sources Wharton chose to cite showed what he thought he was up against.

Writing at the start of the war, in 1776, Wharton had generally con-tented himself with reproducing the minutes of closely relevant legal opinions and Indian negotiations. In the early 1780s, by contrast, Whar-ton's citations betrayed a growing anxiety over the safety of relying on the idea of Indians' being people like any others, with rights to property, and he tried for the first time to undertake an analysis of basic principles. He quoted discussions of the "glaringly absurd" fifteenth-century papal grants that had pretended to sign away whole continents—surely Ameri-cans were by now beyond such sweeping dispossessions?—and, touch-ingly, he quoted the Declaration of Independence, as if that malleable document would make his compatriots see that because "ALL MEN ARE CREATED EQUAL," it must follow "as a necessary and final conclusion, that [Indians] have an indefeasible right freely to sell, and grant [their land] to any person whatsoever."[47]

But his was a losing battle, at least in the first half of the 1780s. The new national state was so powerless and poor that hoping it would keep from trying to sell the Indian lands to which the Treaty of Paris had given it a theoretical claim—once the conflicting claims of the states could be adjudicated, and the way cleared for the creation of a national domain—was like hoping a drowning man would not seize a life preserver. As Caractacus had sensed, many Americans found the new nation's spectacular debt load quite frightening, having never known anything like it before. Some means had to be found, too, of satisfying the republic's unpaid armies. In the sale of western lands, the founding generation saw a tantalizing chance to literally pay for the American Revolution on the backs of the few thousand Indians against whom they had spent most of the war fighting. In neither war nor politics do such opportunities—or, for that matter, such desperate needs—often offer themselves, let alone dovetail so neatly.

IN OCTOBER 1783 the Confederation Congress heard a report from a special committee on Indian affairs, chaired by James Duane. The members of Duane's committee—addressing a marginal, poorly attended house that now found itself in Princeton, the country town to which it had recently fled from Philadelphia, when mutinying Continental soldiers encircled the State House to demand their pay at the point of bayonets—laid out the reasons for a harsh new policy. The essential point was that the United States had pledged "to grant portions of the uncultivated lands as a bounty to their army," which, as Congress needed no reminding, was now mutinying regularly, while "the public finances do not admit of any considerable expenditure to extinguish the Indian claims." Whatever the United States did in the middle western lands, Indians could have no reasonable basis for complaint. They had been the "aggressors in the war, without even a pretence of provocation"; their "wanton barbarity" had brought the "utter ruin . . . of thousands of families, . . . desolat[ing] our villages and settlements"; and the Indians had "abandoned" the western lands—a useful bit of legal make-believe—once "the war, at a vast expence . . . was carried into their own country."

Whole families and villages had bled for the land at Indian hands, as passive sufferers and as conquerors, and now that land was theirs. Duane's committee recommended a policy startlingly like the one Brackenridge had just described. Instead of holding complicated negotiations, the United States should simply notify the northern Indians that they had already lost the sovereignty over their country with Britain's loss, and that although America might now by right exile them all beyond the Great Lakes, they would only have to withdraw behind a distant line, running from the mouth of the Great Miami River (on the present-day border of Indiana and Ohio) in a steep line northward to Lake Erie. This would create a vast new European reserve, "within which they the Indians shall not come," the committee specified, "but for the purposes of trading, treating or other business equally unexceptionable." In the course of debate, draft language about even warning American squatters in the new reserve "to abstain from acts of violence" against Indians was struck down.[48]

Over the next three years, the United States acted directly on these brusque recommendations, sending out soldiers to dictate treaties to all the main groups of Indians above the Ohio. In 1784, 1785, and 1786, influential Wyandots, Delawares, Ottawas, Chippewas, and Shawnees were flatly told that, since the ratification of the Treaty of Paris, the land they lived on was not their own. Unless they wanted to go back to war—and for now, at least, most of these nations were nearly as fractured and economically strained as the United States—they had to accept the right of Congress to "allot" them limited reserves.

Asserting that all of the land for which the United States might otherwise be negotiating already belonged to it, congressional delegations took on a tone of superbness that did not improve Indian relations. As they testily explained to the Six Nations at Fort Stanwix in 1784, "The King of Great Britain ceded to the United States *the whole*, [and] by the right of conquest they might *claim the whole.*" Before proceeding to the business of "allot[ting] . . . lands within their territory to live and hunt upon," the United States accordingly required that each Indian nation "acknowledge the United States to be the sole and absolute sovereign of all the territory" signed over at Paris. And if all this was not persuasive, the Americans turned by reflex—even in these debates with Indians—to the right of sovereignty by suffering. "[T]his country belongs to the United States," recalcitrant Shawnees at the mouth of the Great Miami in 1786 were told; "—their blood hath defended it."⁴⁹

But by 1786, the repudiation of these treaties by many Indian nations and the outbreak of fresh violence was revealing the greatest weakness of a hard line: the United States did not want more fighting, either, and could not afford it. The Northwest Ordinance of 1787, which built on earlier enactments to sketch an expansive vision of controlled and (so far as possible) self-governing settlement in the new lands by free citizens, settling at a stroke the problem of how to divide sovereignty in the governance of imperial territories that had helped to start the Revolution, also marked a turning point in American policy toward the western Indians. They would not, of course, have any place in the orderly grids of settlement to be drawn across the West, with townships and schools planted like pieces on checkerboards for giants amid a vast system of mighty-sounding new states—Metropotamia, Pelisipia, Polypotamia—that Jefferson had seen in mind's eye when drafting the act. (Neither would African slaves, who were barred from the territories.) But the ordinance also included language of a kind that had been struck from Duane's report in 1783, on the importance of observing "the utmost good faith . . . towards the Indians." And it went further. The Indians' rights and landed property, Jefferson specified in a charter of fundamental principles by which territorial citizens were forever to be bound, "never shall be invaded or disturbed" without their consent.⁵⁰

This new emphasis was in tune with a complete reversal of congressional policy toward Indians that emerged in the summer of the Constitutional Convention, as the members of Congress became more willing to acknowledge the weaknesses of the existing confederation. Confronted with a renewal of war, they were forced to balance the problem of not having enough money to pay the national debt against another, more immediate, problem: the meta-difficulty of not having enough money to pay an army to fight for the land they wanted to sell to pay that debt. After a report in July by Henry Knox, the secretary of war, that pointed out Congress's powerlessness to respond to recent Indian attacks—with the United States' finances "render[ing] them utterly unable to maintain an Indian war with any dignity or prospect of success"—in August a new committee recommended dropping the pretense of allotting land to Indians, together with the "language of superiority and command," in favor of negotiations "more on a footing of equality." Even with this belated adjustment, it would take years more of war in the Northwest—and important victories by the army of the new national government under the Constitution—before peace was regained.[51]

THE ANTI-INDIAN RODOMONTADES of the early 1780s did not set the national course in Indian policy for all time, then, or even very long. Instead of rising steadily, ideologies can arrive and evaporate unpredictably, like fog banks, especially at the starts and ends of wars. The Confederation Congress was a different animal—a starved, dying one— from Congress under the Constitution. And it had become clear by 1787 that the Confederation's preferred method of lashing out against the northern and middle Indians was disastrously counterproductive, not to mention capable of "fix[ing] a stain," in Secretary Knox's words, "on the national reputation of America."[52]

But the anti-Indian policy that briefly controlled the Confederation's councils during the postwar did reflect the priorities of the increasing numbers of people who lived on the receding borders of Indian country. Anti-Indianism's rise was the result not of a realistic calculation of the national interest but of a vacuum of policies and power at the federal level. Amid popular demands, that vacuum came to be filled by dreams of Indian treachery and American suffering—dreams that always returned to the prospect of vast new lands, and even new republics, in the Ohio country.

The revolutionary era had produced a polity that was, in many ways, an anti-Indian localist's paradise, where if Congress could do little more than weakly encourage frontier people to fight for the land they sought, it could also never stop them from doing so (or tax them after they had it). This disorderly, short-lived republic was everything that the Constitution's framers most feared and disliked. The prospect of a borderland forever afire with tax revolt, separatism, and war was precisely what the Northwest Ordinance was written to prevent, and successive Federalist administrations would soon decisively apply the Constitution's powers in the West.[53]

In the debate over the new national Constitution, it came naturally to Federalists to cast Anti-Federalists as unenlightened rural bigots—the sort of people who had gone on the Gnadenhütten expedition in 1782. A satiric fantasy in the *Pittsburgh Gazette* in 1788, for instance, described the discovery in the Ohio country of "Political Springs," flowing out of the side of a hill. "These springs rise with a beautiful white sand . . . commodiously situate for baths, and prove to be a sovereign remedy for all political disorders," the piece reported:

> although the water is warm, they tend to cool the head. An experiment was tried with three of Mr. S——'s congregation (they were three of those choice spirits who killed ninety-six Moravian Indians, without the loss of a single man) who were so far gone with an antifoederal complaint, that it had penetrated their brain and communicated with the animal spirits to such a degree, that they were determined to oppose the new constitution with force and arms . . . but upon binding some of the sand to their eyes, ears, and the fore part of their heads . . . they became so far relieved . . . as to pronounce that the union would be much safer to adopt it . . . .

But before the Constitution, with no effective national government, there were few restraints or cures of any kind for the actions of state regimes, like the strange but highly democratic state the Revolution had made in Pennsylvania. And, to the extent that the United States had any common policy in the West, it fitted the preferences of "Mr. S——'s congregation."[54]

CONCLUSION

Borne along in part by the strain of trying to make sense of what had happened at Gnadenhütten, during the troubled decade of the 1780s the mid-Atlantic's reformers discovered and started to describe something they found at once repellent and, as an idea, surprisingly useful. That new concept was the power of prejudice over people's minds. As a teenaged oratorical sensation from Columbia College named David Schuyler Bogart explained, this was a force both widely spread (*"Prejudice* . . . . is perhaps of all other vices the most universal. . . . stain[ing] the minds of the literati as well as those of the vulgar") and stubbornly rooted in the human psyche. Prejudice could now be recognized as the supreme agent for embittering groups of people against one another, setting off all the "most cruel persecutions and inhuman barbarities that have existed." "Read the histories of nations," Bogart directed, "and you will find . . . [that] bloodshed and cruelty in every age of the world . . . . proceeds from Prejudice."

In their efforts to denounce this deep-set stain, if not actually to erase it—for "[t]o exterminate Prejudice from the mind," as Bogart noted with regret, "appears next to an impossibility"—post-revolutionary reformers brought to maturity the central arguments of the previous decades: arguments over bigotry and persecution, over the worth and instincts of ordinary people, and over the proper goals of an American government.[1]

* * *

ANTHONY BENEZET, an elderly Philadelphia Quaker who may have been the most influential eighteenth-century American agitator against the slave trade, published a pamphlet on Indian affairs in 1784, a year before his death. After reading with disgust Hugh Henry Brackenridge's atrocity stories and his "Observations on Indians" the preceding spring, Benezet wanted to give the Gnadenhütten Indians a pamphlet of their own. He had to write it, he said, because of the glaring need to fight against not only the "wicked disposition . . . for denying to the Natives a right of acknowledgement for their lands" but "the prevaling prejudice in the back settlements against all indians . . . [which is] so strongly incentive to the[ir] utter extirpitation."[2]

Reformers like Benezet thought that the central problem of Indian affairs was an inward sin: that individual hearts could chart the course of intercultural relations. Benezet was drawing an unconscious analogy. Though Gnadenhütten had jolted him out of his usual antislavery track, he would carry over to his pro-Indian efforts some favorite ideas. Most of all, he felt sure that he saw in recent events a controlling taint of skin-color prejudice. Used as he was to discussing what Africans' coloring might have to do with their fitness for freedom, it seemed to Benezet that what he had here, in essence, was more of the same. The idea had been in the air at least since 1764, when Franklin—influenced by Montesquieu's commonsensical proposition, in The Spirit of the Laws, that for slaveholders it must be "natural to think that color constitutes the essence of humanity"—had ridiculed defenders of the Paxton riots for presumably loathing Indians' color, in the same illogical way that anyone who wanted to kill all red-haired people would have to loathe theirs.[3]

The premise of Benezet's new book was that such rising prejudices might be countered, if he simply refused "to flatter those of his own colour by acknowledging that they are superior to the tawney Indian." Instead, he would make them face up to what white people had done at Gnadenhütten. By showing how sympathetic the Indians who died there were, Benezet hoped to "giv[e] the necessary information, to many otherwise weldisposed who are under inconsiderate & mistaken prejudices." His detailed narrative put it beyond question that the Moravians had died "as Lambs," martyrs to Christian nonresistance. Despite Brackenridge's claims, then, Indians were not naturally cruel. If his readers could only see past such "erronious ideas" and "superficial prejudices . . . and be convinced, that it is not the colour of our skins" that governed human worth, but one's changeable inner awareness of God, a great many things would get better.[4]

The shock of Gnadenhütten could be put to work against the stain of prejudice. As prejudice was blotted out from individual minds, Europeans would treat Indians better, and the shadow of violence would lift from the countryside. Benezet was happy to promise that this return to "friendly intercourse" could lead, in turn, "not only [to] the civilization of these uncultivated people" through their embrace of Christianity, but also to a readier colonization of Indians' lands. Since respectful settlers would enter more smoothly "on lands belonging to . . . our Indian neighbours," with an improvement in attitudes they would, in fact, probably "have more land upon very easy terms as fast as we should be ready to settle it." This vision had less to recommend it from most Indians' point of view than Benezet must have hoped.[5]

After Gnadenhütten, like-minded reformers entrenched the notion of color prejudice as one of the main grounds for combating anti-Indian behavior (as well as slavery). As this attractively simple explanation spread for the unhappy history of Indian-European relations, talk about toleration moved decisively past the question of what different European religious groups owed to one another, a subject that could—in a revolution little remarked at the time—safely be treated as settled. Instead, the question became what Europeans owed to Indians and Africans, as thinkers confronted the challenge of dilating the *"Circle of the social and benevolent Affections"* (as one illustration in a postwar magazine diagrammed it) beyond the limiting ring of "NATIONS OF THE SAME COLOUR."[6]

But color prejudice could not give a very good account of how or why animosity had risen to the level shown at Gnadenhütten. Perhaps the thing most conspicuous by its absence in eighteenth-century Europeans' anti-Indian talk and behavior was simply any real concern with their skin color. Treacherousness, a culture of revenge, a desire to mutilate bodies, a fearful aptitude for fighting—these things, by contrast, were all very much part of the anti-Indianists' account of what made Indians worth disliking. But the reflexive response to skin color that Franklin and Benezet both decried came to fill the reformers' thoughts, perhaps not least because it was so easy to argue against.7

For an entire generation, the Americans of the mid-Atlantic had mulled over not prejudice or diversity as such but one another's religious clannishness and political disloyalties. Now, however, it seemed there could be few tasks so urgent as simply battling prejudice. If this was a misreading of events, it was a misreading shared by many people who tried to confront the terrible vista that the postwar had opened.

SINCE PREJUDICE was so deeply seated and pervasive, it could be a paralyzing concept. Prejudice demanded its due. Benezet was hopeful that with time it could be educated out of people, but even so, prejudice seemed to require, for instance, not the quick emancipation of slaves (he thought there would be far too much danger "as well to themselves, as to the whites") but the slow improvement of their condition, followed in time by their physical removal. And in the case of Indians, explaining the ugly events of previous decades only in terms of a thing so intangible, and so slow to change, left a strangely narrow, rueful set of policy choices.

For the uprooting of prejudice could reasonably be expected to go on for a long time—if not forever—without many visible results for Indians. Benezet does not seem to have intended his writing to lead to any great public measure on the order of new Indian land claims. Because he thought that the basic intercultural problem was one of psychic animosities flaring up at the edges of settlement, his more modest goal was to erode the "prevaling prejudice," and to keep frontier people from acting so nastily. This guaranteed an inward-looking program, plucking most Indian matters out of the realm of relations between nations and making them into relations between individuals. In the place of political problems, it left a race problem. It took as a given most of the framework of legal norms that the federal and state governments evolved after the Revolution, with Indians living on carefully bordered parcels of land and one direction for change: toward the sale (never leasing) of further land to a single buyer, the state.[8]

More isolated from electoral politics after the Revolution than at any previous time, Friends were about to intensify their involvement in Indians' lives, including their first attempts at missionary work. And most reformers and missionaries—Quakers or not—came during these years to favor the same things as the post-revolutionary state. Indians could learn to thrive only by farming for the market and living soberly, as the best Europeans did. Segregation on reservations would be the solution: albeit reservations that were small enough to rule out hunting, and a segregation, too, that should slowly make itself unnecessary, as Indians' adoption of steady habits wore away at Europeans' prejudices.[9]

But it was exactly when Indians were sandwiched between European farming territories in reservations that were large enough to covet and infiltrate, but too bounded and small to launch attacks from (or plausibly threaten to) and retreat back onto again, that they faced the worst pressures. Even living on town-sized reservations was better—so long, at least, as there were other Indians somewhere around for Europeans to fear. As the wartime survival of the Moravian mission at Goshen had shown, self-interested fear could win concessions from European neighbors that fellow feeling never did. Fear was functional. But segregation and removal dried up any dread of retaliation.[10]

Benezet's lesson about prejudice seemed most meaningful if one emptied out all the specific contexts within which friction between Indians and Europeans actually arose. He was half right: the murders at Gnadenhütten could not have happened without some Americans' believing, and daring to say, that Indians warranted killing simply as Indians, and that there was something brutal and animal-like in them, never to be changed. But, amid the chaos of a civil war for sovereignty, the murders had depended as well on the tempting availability of the Muskingum River lands for settlement and a new state.

As this suggested, any solution to intercultural problems that accepted the repartitioning of the landscape—turning its attention inward, instead, to the unending riddle of prejudice's influence over European hearts and minds—was doomed to fail, again and again. Even if it was simpler to know how to be tolerant than to be just, struggling toward color-blindness could do little to change what was happening.

EUROPEANS STILL fought off prejudice among themselves, though with growing self-satisfaction. It had never been so unacceptable, so clearly beyond the bounds of reasonable discourse, to run down other groups for their religion or language. Though there was much de facto religious persecution during the Revolution, it never dared to speak its name. Instead, Whigs doggedly, painfully defended even the most obvious anti-Quaker or anti-Loyalist measures as being needed to defend—never to oppress—other groups' rights of conscience.

In a way, democracy had flourished with the war. The Pennsylvania constitution of 1776 required that the assembly's doors be always open, and that proposed bills, with weekly reports of the house's debates, be printed for the people to read. The requirements for voting were loosened, so that in theory nearly all free adult men could vote. The dream of ethnic and denominational equality grew stronger, overlapping with demands for "equal liberty" in other forms. German voters were again wooed urgently, this time by the revolutionaries, who decried their maltreatment at the old order's hands. (When a hot by-election was fought in spring 1776, supporters of independence were able to make "some small disturbance among the Dutch" by denouncing a moderate gentleman for supposedly sneering "that except they were naturalized, [the Germans] had no more right to a vote than a Negro or Indian.")[11]

The rhetoric of a suffering people, all bound into one body and forming a single interest, free of religious or national bigotry, was trumpeted as never before. A leaflet passed out in 1776 to demand an end to the Pennsylvania house, which had "held us up as sacrifices to a bloody-minded enemy," and the calling of a convention by "the AUTHORITY of the PEOPLE" (including, of course, all "those German inhabitants . . . who are now incorporated with us in one common stock"), looked forward eagerly to making Americans, at last, one people "without regard either to country or profession of religion . . . [and] perfect liberty of conscience . . . [for] all men, rich and poor." The preamble to the new constitution enshrined it as fundamental law that public life should be carried on "without partiality for, or prejudice against, any particular class, sect, or denomination."[12]

But policing dissent would be a central occupation for Pennsylvania's revolutionaries. A Patriotic Association sprang up to monitor the lukewarm, and especially Quakers. Its public-spirited activities included chivvying the capital's Quakers to dig up from their graveyard the "stinking flesh" of a treasonous Friend. Punitive taxes, confiscations, and disfranchisement—supposedly for life—buffeted Friends who refused to take Continental currency, take pro-revolutionary oaths or affirmations, and serve in the militia or pay fines for its support. Speech crimes were prosecuted, and seventeen Quaker merchants—including, inevitably, Israel Pemberton—were deported to Virginia for internment. The fear of disloyalty was strongest at the edges of Indian country. In 1780, men from some Quaker families in Northumberland County were bludgeoned with a tomahawk and jailed while the militia pillaged their houses and farms. The reason was that "their names was said," groundlessly, "to be on a paper found Among the Indians as such who were attached to the King."[13]

Repeated test acts and loyalty oaths purged tens of thousands of people from citizenship, among them—quite satisfactorily, to many revolutionaries' minds—nearly all observant Friends and many German sectarians. By the 1780s some places, like the town of Byberry, just outside Philadelphia, were left without enough citizens to fill their own offices. Although one of the world's most radically democratic states had been made—a place where, as John Armstong of Carlisle approvingly noted, "'tis the general Sufferages of the people that fills the Sails of Government & carries the Vessel Successfully through," underneath the waterline the ship of state had an astoundingly narrow, tippy hull.[14]

Crucially, though, one thing that no one ever did in defending the revolutionary repressions was to admit that they might amount to unfair burdens on one kind of people. This was shown most clearly in the actions of the Philadelphia militia, who usually served less as troops than as political police. For these militiamen, fining and bullying pacifist Quakers to extract war taxes from them in no way trampled on their liberty of conscience—which was "so sacred a Thing that it ought ever to be preserved inviolate." On the contrary. It was their withholding of war taxes that would "be an Invasion of *our* Liberty of Conscience," by forcing people from other denominations to undergo the "grievous Sufferings" of defeat by a ruthless enemy.[15]

Such tortured arguments were typical of a deeply divided society, where all sides were nonetheless grimly determined to act as if they were tolerant toward other Europeans. With the coming of a long peace, that collective pretense had a chance to become genuine.

TIME AND FORGETFULNESS did their work. The mid-Atlantic countryside, full of "lawns and groves, fields of grain and interjacent meadows, ... thick trees . . . . [and] shaded seats," came to seem a safe and agreeable place. Outside the city, popular pleasure grounds were established for Philadelphians—one with a thundering waterfall to provoke their wonder, rock grottoes wreathed in shuddering mists, and a brigade of gardeners to shape and reshape vistas of artless-seeming natural grandeur.

Even at once fearful places like the site of Braddock's defeat, the bones and half-crushed skulls that had littered the landscape for years were all grown over now, buried and forgotten. After rowing up the Monongahela while a companion played quietly on a flute, a picnicker at Braddock's Field observed, "[t]he prospects around here are most charming . . . , and the walks pleasant beyond description. I had often heard of the celebrated fortress of Du Quesne in my youth—what is it now; a little irregular ground, a few graves, and the fosse of the Fort are only visible." Engravings of places that had been notorious for violence came gradually, in the decades after the Revolution, to depict only willow branches, lowing cows, and cloud shadows passing over the undulating ground. The shock waves of the exterminatory warfare that had been waged there faded, in European imaginations, to little more than a few delicious shivers.[16]

As the middle states embarked on the long boom of the 1790s, to many observers they came to seem some of the happiest and most enlightened places on earth. Facing exile from the England of the younger Pitt, the chemist and political freethinker Joseph Priestley chose for his new home not Paris but the Susquehanna-side hamlet of Northumberland, Pennsylvania. Lafayette's brother-in-law founded a little colony for French and Haitian émigrés, in flight from their own countries' revolutions—naming it, simply, Asylum—next to the site of Wyalusing, Papunhang's abandoned town. The young English poets Robert Southey and Samuel Taylor Coleridge likewise dreamed of moving on to the banks of the Susquehanna to start a pantisocracy, a commune where all inhabitants would hold equal power. They felt a tug at the thought of all that cheap territory, lying in the heart of a nation devoted to unimpeded liberty (where, moreover, "literary Characters make money"); especially after a land agent whom Coleridge met in a pub told him of the riverine land's "excessive Beauty, & it's security from hostile Indians."[17]

And so what was still left of a wretched, ripped-apart society came to see itself as a shining model of toleration and broad-mindedness. With the rise of such hopeful visions of the mid-Atlantic region—even of hopes for the regeneration there of all human society—one can start to see clearly the roots of something beautiful growing out of something ugly. A generation that was constantly haunted by war, and shaped by the moments of fear it provided, had remade Americans' beliefs in toleration, in the desirability of overcoming intergroup prejudice, and in the democratic sovereignty of the people. The crises of Indian war had tilted public life toward the celebration of a suffering people, creating a new politics that was harsh and ruthless, if recognizably democratic.

These changes helped along and, given the war-strapped finances of the new nation that they made, even demanded a series of strange displacements in the landscape. Where there had been Indian towns, there would be voting places on the Muskingum River; a Haitian plantation mistress playing the piano at Wyalusing; German barns, with their distinctive thatched roofs, lining the Tulpehocken Valley.

Most of the people in these places, one way or another, were after their own ideas of equal liberty. Many were determined to tolerate one another's differences. And by now at least some of them—like the Irish farmer near Tioga, who told a visitor that one would have "no reason to complain of them as neighbours"—probably believed they were ready enough to welcome Indians, too, if any happened by.[18]

APPENDIX

To SUGGEST how much more common it became during the Seven Years' War for mid-Atlantic Europeans to read about "white people," in contexts contrasting this group with the supposedly solid front of Indians assaulting it, chart 1 shows the results of a computerized trawl for the word "white" used as an adjective for people in a fifty-year run (1734–83) of one mid-Atlantic newspaper, the *Pennsylvania Gazette*. Using three overlapping geographic areas (the world in general, the mainland colonies, and the mid-Atlantic colonies), it traces great upward spikes in the number of discrete articles each year mentioning "white" people in the *Gazette*, spikes that coincided with the start of the Seven Years' War in the mid-Atlantic colonies (see 1755–56); the Cherokee War, at the middle of that war (1760); Pontiac's War, at its close (1764); Dunmore's War (1774); and, to a diminished extent, the Revolution.[1]

Finer sorting of the evidence from the mainland North American colonies alone, in chart 2, confirms that midcentury spikes in newspaper talk of people's being "white" were driven almost wholly by Indian matters. This chart shows, as a shaded background, the totals for the mainland colonies from chart 1, then overlays them with lines showing the number of reports that contrasted and juxtaposed "white" people directly with Indians, or—making a fairly low and stable baseline by comparison—with Africans or African Americans. As it shows, years during which the word surged were remarkable for the high rate at which "white" people were being contrasted with Indians: in 1756, for instance, 77 percent of news items derived from the middle colonies using the term did so in order to distinguish "white" people from Indians; the next year, 92 percent did; and in 1764, a year dominated by news of Pontiac's War, the rate was 88 percent.[2]

Less statistical evidence suggests that the rise of "the white people" as a rubric might have been assisted by the power of national-group consciousness. Before the war, reported treaty minutes had been full of Indian and European speakers' accounts of the offenses that natives and the "English" had committed against each other, with the Irish and Germans seldom separated out. Thus for a time even Germans unable to speak a word of English tended awkwardly to call themselves English, too. In 1759, when two German-speaking girls escaped from the Delawares in the Ohio country and reached the riverbank opposite Fort Pitt, the bedraggled, Indian-clothed foreigners had one last problem:

> the people in the boat made many difficulties, they took us for Indians and wanted us to stay on the other side that night . . . . But after we had convinced them we were English captives who had run off from the Indians . . . we were taken up.

But because of the conspicuously poor fit that "English" made, even as a convenient blanket term, in many such cases where people sought to draw a clear contrast between Indians and themselves, as the war went on it seems to have lost ground to the word "white."[3]

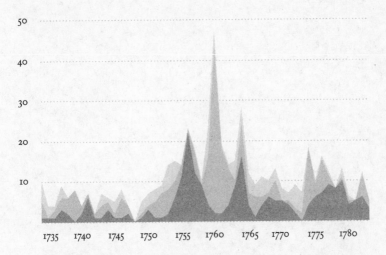

1: Reports mentioning "white" people in the *Pennsylvania Gazette* from all places (light gray area); from only the mainland North American colonies (medium gray area); and from only the mid-Atlantic colonies (dark gray area)

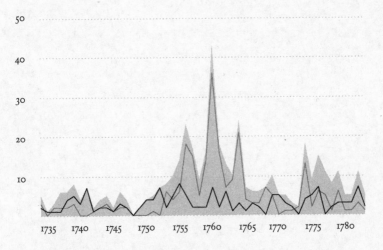

2: Reports mentioning "white" people in the *Pennsylvania Gazette* from the mainland North American colonies (gray area), with breakdowns for contrasts with Indians (gray line) and Africans or African Americans (black line)

ABBREVIATIONS

AHR
American Historical Review

Allinson Papers
Allinson Family Papers, Quaker Collection, Haverford College Library, Haverford, Pa.

"Annals"
John F. Watson, "Annals of Philadelphia, or Facts illustrative of the History of the City of Philada. . . . ," 2 boxes, L.C.P.

Am. Weekly Mercury
American Weekly Mercury

A.P.S.
Library of the American Philosophical Society, Philadelphia

AQ
American Quarterly

Barton Diary
Thomas Barton Diary, 1758, Diaries and Letterbooks Collection, H.S.P.

Benezet Papers
Anthony Benezet Papers, Quaker Collection, Haverford College Library, Haverford, Pa.

Bethlehem Vicinity MSS
Miscellaneous MSS, Bethlehem and Vicinity, 1741–1849, H.S.P.

Bouquet Papers
The Papers of Henry Bouquet, ed. Sylvester K. Stevens and Donald H. Kent, 19 unnumbered vols. (Harrisburg, Pa., 1940–43). Cited by series number, part (if applicable), and page.

Burd-Shippen Papers
Burd-Shippen Papers, 1708–1792 (Series I: Correspondence, 1740–1792), A.P.S.

Cadwalader-Croghan Papers
Cadwalader Family Papers, George Croghan Papers, 1744–1782, H.S.P.

Chew Papers
Chew Family Papers, Benjamin Chew Papers, H.S.P.

Cont. Cong. Journals
Journals of the Continental Congress, ed. Worthington C. Ford et al., 34 vols. (Washington, D.C., 1904–37)

Doc. Hist. N.Y.
The Documentary History of the State of New-York . . . , ed. E. B. O'Callaghan, 4 vols. (Albany, N.Y., 1850–51)

Docs. Rel. Col. Hist. N.Y.
Documents Relative to the Colonial History of the State of New-York . . . , ed. E. B. O'Callaghan, 15 vols. (Albany, N.Y., 1853–87)

Edward Shippen Correspondence
Edward Shippen Correspondence, 1753–1761, A.P.S.

Edward Shippen Papers
Papers of Edward Shippen Sr., 1727–1789, A.P.S.

Elder Papers
Elder Family Papers (Group MG 70), Historical Society of Dauphin County, Harrisburg, Pa.

Etting-Pemberton Papers
Pemberton Papers, 1654–1806, Frank M. Etting Collection, H.S.P.

F.H.L.
Friends Historical Library, Swarthmore College, Swarthmore, Pa.

Franklin Papers
The Papers of Benjamin Franklin, ed. Leonard W. Labaree et al., 37 vols. to date (New Haven, Conn., 1959–)

Friendly Assoc. Minutes (hard)
Friendly Association Minutes, 1755–1757 (really 1758; hardbound), Miscellaneous Indian Papers collection, H.S.P.

Friendly Assoc. Minutes (soft)
Friendly Association Minutes, 1756–1759 (softbound), Friendly Association Papers, Cox-Parrish-Wharton Papers, H.S.P.

Friendly Assoc. Papers (Haverford)
Papers Relating to the Friendly Association, Quaker Collection, Haverford College Library, Haverford, Pa.

Friends and Enemies, ed. Pencak and Richter
Friends and Enemies in Penn's Woods: Indians, Colonists, and the Racial Construction of Pennsylvania, ed. William A. Pencak and Daniel K. Richter (University Park, Pa., 2004)

Heckewelder, *Indian Nations*
John Heckewelder, *History, Manners, and Customs of the Indian Nations Who Once Inhabited Pennsylvania and the Neighbouring States,* ed. William C. Reichel, rev. ed. (Philadelphia, 1876)

Horsfield Letterbook
Timothy Horsfield Letterbook, 1754–1755, H.S.P.

Horsfield Papers
Timothy Horsfield Papers, A.P.S.

H.S.P.
Historical Society of Pennsylvania

Hunter, *Pa. Forts*
William A. Hunter, *Forts on the Pennsylvania Frontier, 1753–1758* (Harrisburg, Pa., 1960)

Ind. Affairs Papers
Indians, 1682–1900 and n.d., Indian Affairs Papers, Society Miscellaneous Collection, H.S.P.

Indian and Military Affairs MSS
Indian and Military Affairs of Pennsylvania Manuscripts, 1737–1775, A.P.S.

Irvine Correspondence
Washington-Irvine Correspondence: The Official Letters Which Passed between Washington and Brig.-Gen. William Irvine and between Irvine and Others concerning Military Affairs in the West from 1781 to 1783, ed. C. W. Butterfield (Madison, Wisc., 1882)

JAH
Journal of American History

JEH
Journal of Economic History

JER
Journal of the Early Republic

JIH
Journal of Interdisciplinary History

JSH
Journal of Southern History

Johnson Papers
The Papers of Sir William Johnson, ed. Alexander C. Flick, Milton W. Hamilton, et al., 14 vols. (Albany, N.Y., 1921–65)

Jordan, *White over Black*
Winthrop D. Jordan, *White over Black: American Attitudes toward the Negro, 1550–1812* (Chapel Hill, N.C., 1968)

Joseph Shippen Letterbook (A.P.S.)
Letterbook of Joseph Shippen Jr., 1763–1773, A.P.S.

Joseph Shippen Letterbook (H.S.P.)
Joseph Shippen Letterbook, 1754–1755, Shippen Family Papers, H.S.P.

Lamberton Scotch-Irish Papers
Papers of Scotch-Irish Settlements, Cumberland County, 1734–1786, collected by J. F. P. Lamberton, H.S.P.

Lancaster Co. Papers
Miscellaneous Papers, 1724–1772, Lancaster County Papers, H.S.P.

L.C.P.
Library Company of Philadelphia

Loskiel, *History*
George Henry [Georg Heinrich] Loskiel, *History of the Misssion of the United Brethren among the Indians in North America*, trans. Christian Ignatius La Trobe [Latrobe] (London, 1794; orig. pub. Leipzig, 1789)

Loudon, *Interesting Narratives*
Archibald Loudon, *A Selection of Some of the Most Interesting Narratives of Outrages Committed by the Indians in Their Wars with the White People*, 2 vols. (Carlisle, Pa., 1808–11)

McCusker and Menard, *Economy of British America*
John J. McCusker and Russell R. Menard, *The Economy of British America, 1607–1789, with Supplementary Bibliography* (Chapel Hill, N.C., 1991)

Mag.
Magazine

Merrell, *Into the American Woods*
James H. Merrell, *Into the American Woods: Negotiators on the Pennsylvania Frontier* (New York, 1999)

Merritt, *At the Crossroads*
Jane T. Merritt, *At the Crossroads: Indians and Empires on a Mid-Atlantic Frontier, 1700–1763* (Chapel Hill, N.C., 2003)

Morav. Recs.
Records of the Moravian Mission among the Indians of North America from the Archives of the Moravian Church, Bethlehem, Pennsylvania, 40 microfilm reels (New Haven, Conn., 1970). Cited by box and folder or by box, folder, and item.

Mühlenberg Journals
The Journals of Henry Melchior Muhlenberg, trans. and ed. Theodore G. Tappert and John W. Doberstein, 3 vols. (Philadelphia, 1942–58)

MVHR
Mississippi Valley Historical Review

Northampton-Bethlehem Papers
Bethlehem and Vicinity Papers, Northampton Co. Papers, H.S.P.

Northampton Co. Papers
Northampton County Papers, Miscellaneous MSS, 1727–1851, H.S.P.

N.Y. Gazette
Gaine's *New-York Gazette, and the Weekly Mercury*

N.Y. Mercury
Gaine's *New-York Mercury*

N.Y. Journal
New-York Journal, or the General Advertiser

OED
Oxford English Dictionary, 2nd ed.

Pa. Arch.
Pennsylvania Archives . . . , ed. Samuel Hazard et al., 9 series (Harrisburg, Pa., 1832–1935). Cited by series, volume, and page.

Pa. Archaeologist
Pennsylvania Archaeologist

Pa. Chronicle
Pennsylvania Chronicle and Universal Advertiser

Pa. Col. Recs.
Minutes of the Provincial Council of Pennsylvania . . . , 16 vols. (Harrisburg, Pa., 1818–32; stamped "Pennsylvania Colonial Records" on spine)

Pa. Eve. Post
Pennsylvania Evening Post

Pa. Gazette
Pennsylvania Gazette

Pa. Hist.
Pennsylvania History

Pa. Journal
Pennsylvania Journal and Weekly Advertiser

Pa. Mercury
Story and Humphrey's *Pennsylvania Mercury and Universal Advertiser*

Pa. Packet
Pennsylvania Packet, or the General Advertiser

Parrish-Pemberton Papers
Pemberton Papers, Parrish Family Papers, H.S.P.

Pa. Staatsbote
Henrich Millers Pennsylvanischer Staatsbote

Pemberton Papers
Pemberton Family Papers, 1641–1880, H.S.P.

Penn Official Correspondence
Official Correspondence, Penn Papers, H.S.P.

PMHB
Pennsylvania Magazine of History and Biography

Proceedings of the A.P.S.
Proceedings of the American Philosophical Society

Q.C.
Quaker Collection, Haverford College Library, Haverford, Pa.

Reynell Letterbook
John Reynell Letterbook, H.S.P.

Richter, *Ordeal of the Longhouse*
Daniel K. Richter, *Ordeal of the Longhouse: The Peoples of the Iroquois League in the Era of European Colonization* (Chapel Hill, N.C., 1992)

Shippen Papers
Shippen Family Papers, 1701–1856, H.S.P

Shippen Military Letterbook
Joseph Shippen Military Letterbook, 1756–1758, Shippen Family Papers, H.S.P

Shippen Misc. Correspondence
Miscellaneous Correspondence, 1727–1781, Papers of Edward Shippen Sr., 1727–1789, A.P.S.

Shippen-Shippen Correspondence
Correspondence of Edward and Joseph Shippen, 1750–1778, Papers of Edward Shippen Sr., 1727–1789, A.P.S.

Silver, "Indian-Hating"
Peter Rhoads Silver, "Indian-Hating and the Rise of Whiteness in Provincial Pennsylvania" (Ph.D. diss., Yale Univ., 2001)

Silverman, *Cultural History*
Kenneth Silverman, *A Cultural History of the American Revolution* (New York, 1976)

Smith, *Essay on Variety*
Samuel Stanhope Smith, *An Essay on the Causes of the Variety of Complexion and Figure in the Human Species, to Which Are Added, Strictures on Lord Kaims's Discourse on the Original Diversity of Mankind* (Philadelphia, 1787)

Votes
Votes and Proceedings of the House of Representatives of the Province of Pennsylvania, 6 vols. (Philadelphia, 1752–76)

W. Pa. Hist. Mag.
Western Pennsylvania Historical Magazine

Weiser Correspondence
Conrad Weiser Correspondence, 1741–1766, H.S.P.

White, *Middle Ground*
Richard White, *The Middle Ground: Indians, Empires, and Republics in the Great Lakes Region, 1650–1815* (New York, 1991)

WMQ
William and Mary Quarterly, 3rd series

Wöch. Phila. Staatsbote
Wöchentliche Philadelphische Staatsbote

Zeisberger, *Diary*
Diary of David Zeisberger, a Moravian Missionary among the Indians of Ohio, ed. and trans. Eugene F. Bliss, 2 vols. (Cincinnati, 1885)

NOTES

INTRODUCTION

1. James Kenny to Israel Pemberton Jr., 2nd mo. 12, 1759, Friendly Assoc. Papers (Haverford) 2:431; "On the late defeat at Te[c]onderoga," *New American Mag.* (Woodbridge, N.J.), Aug. 1758, p. 201.

2. Rev. Andrew Burnaby, *Travels through the Middle Settlements in North-America, in the Years 1759 and 1760* . . . . 2nd ed. (London, 1775), p. 158. Edmund Burke's cousin William took it for granted in a popular account of Pa. that enlightened readers would know what he meant by referring to the "evil" of "the diversity which prevails [there], and would by all human and honest methods endeavour to prevent it" (*An Account of the European Settlements in America*, 2 vols. [London, 1757], vol. 2, chap. 12, pp. 192–93). Defined simply as places with more different sorts of Europeans than New England, but fewer slaves than the South, the middle colonies have often been used to ask whether and exactly how, in the absence of religious unity and widespread slavery, an American colonial society could be cemented. For the mid-Atlantic as a region, see Wayne Bodle, "The 'Myth of the Middle Colonies' Reconsidered: The Process of Regionalization in Early America," *PMHB* 113 (1989): 527–48; and esp. Michael Zuckerman, "Puritans, Cavaliers, and the Motley Middle," in *Friends and Neighbors: Group Life in America's First Plural Society*, ed. Zuckerman (Philadelphia, 1982), chap. 1.

3. For the so-called contact hypothesis, see H. D. Forbes, *Ethnic Conflict: Commerce, Culture, and the Contact Hypothesis* (New Haven, Conn., 1997); and Miles Hewstone and Ed Cairns, "Social Psychology and Intergroup Conflict," in *Ethnopolitical Warfare: Causes, Consequences, and Possible Solutions*, ed. Daniel Chirot and Martin E. P. Seligman (Washington, D.C., 2001), pp. 319–36.

4. See Philip Gleason, "Identifying Identity: A Semantic History," *JAH* 69 (1983): 910–31; and Patrick Griffin's thoughtful introduction to *The People with No Name: Ireland's Ulster Scots, America's Scots Irish, and the Creation of a British Atlantic World, 1689–1764* (Princeton, N.J., 2001).

5. See Stephen Cornell, "Discovered Identities and American Indian Supratribalism," in *We Are a People: Narrative and Multiplicity in Constructing Ethnic Identity*, ed. Paul Spickard and W. Jeffrey Burroughs (Philadelphia, 2000); and, for essential overviews, Nancy Shoemaker, *A Strange Likeness: Becoming Red and White in Eighteenth-Century North America* (New York, 2004), chap. 6; Gregory Evans Dowd, *A Spirited Resistance: The Native American Struggle for Unity, 1745–1815* (Baltimore, Md., 1992), chap. 2; and Daniel K. Richter, *Facing East from Indian Country: A Native History of Early America* (Cambridge, Mass., 2001), pp. 180–82, 190, and 193–99. Almost certainly because it focuses on the period after the 19th century, Cornell's empirical work on Indian identities (e.g., in "Land, Labour, and Group Formation: Blacks and Indians in the United States," *Ethnic and Racial Studies* 13 [1990]: 368–88), tends—from an early American perspective, at least—to misapply his very useful theoretical categories, concluding that Indians did not discover themselves as a coherent category or conceive pan-Indian movements until the 20th century. This book finds in 18th-century pan-Indianism a set of cultural events that not only long predate but practically invert the European-to-Indian transmission of racial identities Cornell would posit.

6. For thoughtful cautions, see Benjamin Braude, "Primary Colors," a review of Roxann Wheeler, *The Complexion of Race: Categories of Difference in Eighteenth-Century British Culture* (Philadelphia, 2000) in *WMQ* 59 (2002): 742–46; and George M. Fredrickson's warnings against the historical dead end of "find[ing] a vague and undifferentiated attitudinal racism almost everywhere" in his "Reflections on the Comparative History and Sociology of Racism," *Race Traitor* 3 (1994): 83, as reprinted in *Racial Classification and History*, comp. E. Nathaniel Gates (New York, 1997), p. 51.

7. This book's interpretive energy is directed mostly at uses made of Indians within European-American society, since—despite a 20-year outpouring of excellent Indian history—the tensions and diversity within European settler society have tended to remain a historiographical backwater. It shows not how the proximity of Europeans affected Indian economies, religion, and politics but how Indians' presence within and around provincial societies fed back influences in the opposite direction. At present far more is known about the Indian than the European side of this story, where a few threadbare truisms—nearly all misleading or wrong—can often still be found accounting for European responses to contact and violence with Indians (Indian-hating; the rise of racism; hardy, viciously effective riflemen; a laager-like spirit of unity). This study's first lines of inquiry—esp. its account of changing beliefs about human differences, of diverse communities coming grudgingly together under attack, and of the religiously expressed revitalizations that contact with very different peoples could inspire—were suggested simply by reapplying some of the interpretive models behind the best new Indian history, and expanding them to take in Europeans. In this way the new Indian history can be made to shine a sharp, unexpected light back onto the histories of colonial Europeans. For what such interpretive enlargements have to offer, see James H. Merrell, "American Nations, Old and New: Reflections on Indians and the Early Republic," in *Native Americans and the Early Republic*, ed. Frederick E. Hoxies, Ronald Hoffman, and Peter J. Albert (Charlottesville, Va., 1999), pp. 346–49. Merrell, *Into the American Woods*, and Merritt, *At the Crossroads*, have taken up Indian interac-

tions with Europeans (esp. intercultural go-betweens and Moravians) in provincial Pa. In comparison with both works, this study finds wider European-American culture to be less uniformly given over to Indian-hating (esp. outside the realm of print, with fear apparently controlling most responses to Indians and Indian war in the countryside), and less precocious in anti-Indian racial thinking. In tracing Indian war's transforma-tive shocks on a European settler culture, Jill Lepore's project in *The Name of War: King Philip's War and the Origins of American Identity* (New York, 1998) resembles this one, though the mid-Atlantic differed sharply from early New England. Roiling religious and national-group divisions—absent in European New England—drove the 18th-century middle colonies toward far sharper internecine political uses for the rhetoric of Indian war, and may have delayed a meaningfully racialized discourse on Indians longer (until late in the Revolution). The anxiety Lepore finds among New Englanders over their own barbarization—or loss of Englishness—through war is for the most part also missing here; mid-Atlantic colonists proved adept, above all, at confining such compar-isons to their enemies.

8. For thoughts on the racial limits to 18th-century pluralism, see Ned Landsman, "Plu-ralism, Protestantism, and Prosperity: Crèvecoeur's American Farmer and the Founda-tions of American Pluralism," in *Beyond Pluralism: The Conception of Groups and Group Identities in America*, ed. Wendy F. Katkin, Landsman, and Andrea Tyree (Urbana, Ill., 1998), chap. 5; for a general account (rather remarkably finding little real diversity before the 19th century), see William R. Hutchison, *Religious Pluralism in America: The Contentious History of a Founding Ideal* (New Haven, Conn., 2003), chap. 1; and for a theologically inflected essay on religious liberty's growth (perhaps overstating ecu-menism's appeal at midcentury and during the Revolution), Chris Beneke, "Beyond Toleration: The Religious Origins of American Pluralism" (Ph.D. diss., Northwestern Univ., 2001).

9. Even the most determined nationalists long hardly dared to talk of a "national" gov-ernment, preferring instead the less threatening word "federal." See, above all, John M. Murrin, "A Roof without Walls: The Dilemma of American National Identity," in *Beyond Confederation: Origins of the Constitution and American National Identity*, ed. Richard Beeman, Stephen Botein, and Edward C. Carter II (Chapel Hill, N.C., 1987), pp. 333–48; and Lance Banning, "Republican Ideology and the Triumph of the Consti-tution, 1789 to 1793," *WMQ* 31 (1974): 167–88. As David Waldstreicher has put this idea, Americans after the Revolution "practiced a divisive politics and a unifying nationalism at the same time" (*In the Midst of Perpetual Fetes: The Making of American Nationalism, 1776–1820* [Chapel Hill, N.C., 1997], p. 2).

10. Perhaps because the Revolutionary War was forwarded only by a small, if deter-mined and well-armed, minority of the middle colonies' residents (most of whom opposed it), once the fighting was over, its political and cultural legacy came into dis-pute—together with the anti-Indian policies it had enabled. (In private moments, the revolutionary president of Pennsylvania was ready to admit that "[w]hatever we may say . . . a great majority of the people are in the British interest in sentiment and affection . . . at least from New York downwards inclusive. It is by the activity, zeal, and bravery of the comparative few that many have been kept under"; Joseph Reed to Gen.

Nathanael Greene, Nov. 1, 1781, in William B. Reed, *Life and Correspondence of Joseph Reed,* 2 vols. [Philadelphia, 1847], vol. 2, p. 372.)

11. As a rule it was likely true, as one frustrated settler wrote, that on the fringes of European settlement "[t]he man that is strong and able to make others afraid of him seems to have the best chance"; William Crawford to George Washington, Mar. 15, 1772, in *The Washington-Crawford Letters . . .* , ed. C. W. Butterfield (Cincinnati, Ohio, 1877), p. 25. See the excellent brief account of Greathouse and Creap's murders in Michael N. McConnell, *A Country Between: The Upper Ohio Valley and Its Peoples, 1724–1774* (Lincoln, Nebr., 1992), pp. 268–79 (and, for less cynical views of Greathouse and Cresap, in White, *Middle Ground,* pp. 356–65). Similarly, the realm of anti-Indian rhetoric, which proved such a durable part of American culture, was dominated by a few especially loud and skillful voices. At midcentury the Rev. William Smith, first provost of the College of Philadelphia, did infinitely more through his pamphlets and students to shape anti-Indian culture than any other person, in or out of America (see chaps. 3 and 7). In the 1780s the partnership of the author Hugh Henry Brackenridge and the Lancaster printer Francis Bailey would do much the same (see chap. 9).

12. I have not changed the spelling or punctuation of quotations from manuscript sources, except to lower superscript letters and transcribe thorns as *th*'s, macroned *m*'s as *mm*'s, and initial *ff*'s as capital *F*'s. Thorns and superscripts are left intact in quotations from printed sources. Quotations follow the so-called rigorous method laid out in *The Chicago Manual of Style,* 15th ed. (Chicago, 2003), secs. 11.62–65, except that (following the 14th edition, sec. 10.61) ellipsis points do not precede or follow run-in quotations; nor do they precede block quotations, or follow them unless they fail to end in grammatically complete sentences. Translations from German are mine, with word choices often influenced by *The New and Complete Dictionary of the German and English Languages . . .* , ed. John (or Johannes) Ebers, 3 vols. (Leipzig, 1796–99). If the original wording of part or all of a German quotation is itself of possible interest, it is provided in the notes (with completely literal translations omitted); if a source's title does not make it obvious that it is in German, I add "(in German)" to the first reference. The dates of documents from before the British adoption of calendar reform in 1752 have not been adjusted. In the text, but not the notes, the year is always taken to begin on Jan. 1. Since the older practice of starting the year in March became especially confusing when coupled with the Quaker practice of using numbers rather than names for months (so that "tenth month" was sometimes January; see "An Act to prevent Disputes about the Dates of Conveyances . . . ," *Pa. Arch.* 1:2:69), the notes keep whatever nomenclature makes it easiest to find the documents cited.

Chapter 1
AN UNSETTLED COUNTRY

1. Mittelberger, *Reise nach Pennsylvanien im Jahr 1750 . . .* (orig. pub. Stuttgart, 1756), ed. Jürgen Charnitzky (Sigmaringen, 1997), pp. 135, 137, 139 ("sehr dicht voller Feuerkäferlein fliegt, daß es scheint, es schneie Feuer"), and 180; also in Mittelberger, *Journey to*

Pennsylvania, ed. and trans. Oscar Handlin and John Clive (Cambridge, Mass., 1960), pp. 56, 57, 59, 61, and 92. For bells and "the peace of near, well-defined horizons" (p. 97), see Alain Corbin, *Village Bells: Sound and Meaning in the Nineteenth-Century French Countryside,* trans. Martin Thom (New York, 1998), chap. 4; see also Richard Cullen Rath, *How Early America Sounded* (Ithaca, N.Y., 2003), chap. 2.

2. Mittelberger, *Reise nach Pennsylvanien,* pp. 167 ("dem ruchlosen Leben einiger Leute in diesem freien Land"), and 123–24 and 163 ("Sonderlich die Jugend . . . gleich den alten Einwohnern oder Wilden aufgezogen"); also in Handlin and Clive's edition, pp. 84, 48, and 80. Cf. pp. 88–89 and 166–67 (pp. 22 and 83 in Handlin and Clive's edition). Mittelberger liked the peaceableness and lack of contention in Pennsylvania's public life almost as much as he disliked the slipping away of orthodox Lutheran values he thought he saw there.

3. Penn, *Englands Present Interest Discovered . . . ,* 2nd ed. (London, 1676), p. 39. In Penn's overly hopeful view—grounded in the pragmatic, results-oriented arguments that were usual before "toleration" quite existed as a coherent ideal—tolerating multiple denominations would not only promote settlement and prosperity (see, e.g., Penn, *Considerations Moving to a Toleration, and Liberty of Conscience . . .* [London, 1685], no. 8, pp. 4–5), but somehow neutralize religiously motivated civil contention. For mid-Atlantic toleration and pluralism, see esp. Zuckerman, "Puritans, Cavaliers, and the Motley Middle"; Jack P. Greene, "Coming to Terms with Diversity: Pluralism and Conflict in the Formation of Colonial New York" (1977–78), in *Interpreting Early America: Historiographical Essays* (Charlottesville, Va., 1996), chap. 10; Sally Schwartz, *"A Mixed Multitude": The Struggle for Toleration in Colonial Pennsylvania* (New York, 1987), which understates intergroup conflict; Joyce D. Goodfriend, *Before the Melting Pot: Society and Culture in Colonial New York City, 1664–1730* (Princeton, N.J., 1992); and Ned C. Landsman, "Roots, Routes, and Rootedness: Migration, Diversity, and Pluralism in the Middle Colonies," *Early American Studies* 2 (2004): 267–309. For 17th-century disputes over toleration, see Andrew R. Murphy, *Conscience and Community: Revisiting Toleration and Religious Dissent in Early Modern England and America* (University Park, Pa., 2001), esp. chap. 5.

4. See Henry Gemery, "European Immigration to North America, 1700–1820: Numbers and Quasi-Numbers," *Perspectives in American History,* n.s., 1 (1984): 283–342; Aaron S. Fogleman, "Migrations to the Thirteen British North American Colonies: New Estimates," *JIH* 22 (1992): 691–709, and his *Hopeful Journeys: German Immigration, Settlement, and Political Culture in Colonial America, 1717–1775* (Philadelphia, 1996); Patrick Griffin, *The People with No Name: Ireland's Ulster Scots, America's Scots Irish, and the Creation of a British Atlantic World, 1689–1764* (Princeton, N.J., 2001), chap. 3; and Marianne S. Wokeck, *Trade in Strangers: The Beginnings of Mass Migration to North America* (University Park, Pa., 1999). The population of New England was doubling about every 28 years, and that of the Chesapeake every 25, but Pa.'s European inhabitants doubled every 20; McCusker and Menard, *Economy of British America,* pp. 228–29.

5. Computed from Robert Proud, *The History of Pennsylvania . . . Written principally between the Years 1776 and 1780,* 2 vols. (Philadelphia, 1797), 2:273–74; *Am. Weekly Mercury,* Nov. 6–13, 1729, p. 1; Hugh Boulter, archbishop of Armagh, to duke of Newcastle, Nov. 23, 1728, quoted in Wayland F. Dunaway, *The Scotch-Irish of Colonial Pennsylvania*

(1944; reprinted Hamden, Conn., 1962), p. 36; for an overview, see R. J. Dickson, *Ulster Emigration to Colonial America, 1718–1775,* new ed. (Belfast, 1988), including G. E. Kirkham's introduction.

6. See David Hempton and Myrtle Hill, *Evangelical Protestantism in Ulster Society, 1740–1890* (London, 1992), and Peter Brooke, *Ulster Presbyterianism: The Historical Perspective, 1610–1970* (Dublin, 1987).

7. Marianne Wokeck, "The Flow and the Composition of German Immigration to Philadelphia, 1727–1775," *PMHB* 105 (1981): 249–78; Farley Grubb, "German Immigration to Pennsylvania, 1709 to 1820," *JIH* 20 (1990): 417–36.

8. Mittelberger, *Reise nach Pennsylvanien,* pp. 92 and 77 ("Dampf, Grauen, Erbrechen, . . . Ruhr, . . . Mundfäule [scurvy] und dergleichen"; also in idem, *Journey to Pennsylvania,* ed. Handlin and Clive, pp. 25 and 12); *Pa. Gazette,* Feb. 15, 22, 1732.

9. The percentage of single men in the German and Irish migrations as a whole never came anywhere near equaling that among English voyagers. Grubb, "German Immigration," pp. 420–22, 431–33, 435; cf. Bernard Bailyn, *Voyagers to the West: A Passage in the Peopling of America on the Eve of the Revolution* (New York, 1986); and see Marianne S. Wokeck, "German and Irish Immigration to Colonial Philadelphia," *Proceedings of the A.P.S.* 133 (1989): 130–31. For farms and ideas of economic security, see James A. Henretta, "Families and Farms: *Mentalité* in Pre-Industrial America," *WMQ* 35 (1978): 3–32, and Richard Lyman Bushman, "Markets and Composite Farms in Early America," *WMQ* 55 (1998): 351–74.

10. See A. G. Roeber, *Palatines, Liberty, and Property: German Lutherans in Colonial British America* (Baltimore, Md., 1993), chap. 2, and Fogleman, *Hopeful Journeys,* chaps. 1–2. These voyagers were only part of a huge, long-range shift of the German-speaking population (mostly directed toward other lands of opportunity in eastern Europe): perhaps about 115,000 of 900,000 total migrants over the 18th century (Hans Fenske, "International Migration: Germany in the Eighteenth Century," *Central European History* 13 [1980]: 344–47, cited in Fogleman, *Hopeful Journeys,* p. 223).

11. See Eric Hinderaker, *Elusive Empires: Constructing Colonialism in the Ohio Valley, 1673–1800* (New York, 1997), pp. 106–10.

12. "Scheme of a Lottery For One Hundred Thousand Acres of Land . . . ," July 12, 1735, Friendly Assoc. Papers (Haverford); Samuel Blunston to Thomas Penn, Mar. 3, 1737/8, Lancaster Co. Papers, p. 33. Early American squatting has not received as much systematic study as it demands, but see David L. Preston, "Squatters, Indians, Proprietary Government, and Land in the Susquehanna Valley," in *Friends and Enemies,* ed. Pencak and Richter, chap. 10. Neither squatting, nor Indian attacks, nor panicky refugeeism was confined to the backwoods; some of the most striking midcentury events, like the so-called Paxton killings in 1763, were in part interesting because they happened so far from the frontier of settlement. This study looks not so much at the "backcountry" (a word without real currency before the 1780s, at least beyond S.C.) as at the farmed countryside in general, surprisingly much of which was molded by Indians' presence—constant or intermittent, real and dreaded—for most of the century. This makes it simpler to see the connections between rural and urban ways of experiencing and imagining Indian war—whose back-and-forth mutual reshapings have often been

slighted as much in frontier historiography as in more nearly intellectual histories (e.g., Robert F. Berkhofer Jr., *The White Man's Indian: Images of the American Indian from Columbus to the Present* [New York, 1978]).

13. Delaware Indians to Gov. George Thomas, Jan. 3, 1741, Chew Papers. This led to a scolding reply from Thomas, who reminded them of the 1737 Walking Purchase (Mar. 24, 1741, Chew Papers 12:3), and a treaty conference held with the Iroquois at Philadelphia in July 1742 "to squelch the Delawares at the forks": the Delawares, of necessity declaring themselves satisfied with the Six Nations' mediation, accepted Iroquois urging to settle at the Wyoming Valley and Shamokin on the upper Susquehanna, where Nanticokes and Delaware-speakers from the Minisinks and northern N.J. joined them (William N. Fenton, *The Great Law and the Longhouse: A Political History of the Iroquois Confederacy* [Norman, Okla., 1998], p. 410).

14. James Hendrix to Edward Shippen, Oct. 27, 1740, Burd-Shippen Papers.

15. The usual division was into Minisinks, or Munsees; northern Unami-speakers at the forks of the Delaware, always referred to in English as Forks Indians but calling themselves Lenni Lenape—a name, meaning roughly "the ordinary people," later applied to all Delawares; and southern Unami-speakers, closer to Philadelphia; see Ives Goddard, "Delaware," in *Handbook of North American Indians,* ed. Bruce G. Trigger (Washington, D.C., 1978), vol. 15, *The Northeast,* pp. 213–39; Paul A. W. Wallace, *Indians in Pennsylvania,* 2nd ed. rev. by William A. Hunter (Harrisburg, Pa., 1986), p. 52. For Iroquois claims, see Richter, *Ordeal of the Longhouse.*

16. Wallace, *Indians in Pennsylvania,* p. 116; Barry C. Kent, *Susquehanna's Indians* (Harrisburg, Pa., 1984), p. 105 (the first "Conestogas" were resettled Susquehannocks, another Iroquoian group; see Silver, "Indian-Hating," pp. 27–29). Because the Susquehanna had also long been the main corridor that Iroquois raiding parties followed southward, and their Catawba and Cherokee opponents northward, in carrying war to one another (Fenton, *Great Law and the Longhouse,* p. 404), Pa. tried at its first direct treaty (1732) with the Six Nations to push this path, and the friction along it between European settlers and provision-seeking war parties, farther west.

17. David Brainerd's Journal, 1745, Sept. 13, 1745, p. 30, A.P.S.

18. Blunston to Thomas Penn, Mar. 18, 1734, Apr. 9, 1735, and Mar. 25, 1738, Lancaster Co. Papers, pp. 3, 19, and 31. The best analysis of the Penns' antisquatting expeditions (stressing that they feared that squatters would lease from Indian landlords as much as they feared their embittering them) is Preston, "Squatters, Indians, Proprietary Government, and Land," pp. 194–99.

19. "Report of Richard Peters . . . of the Proceedings against sundry Persons settled in the unpurchased Part of the Province," July 2, 1750, *Votes* 4:142, 141, and 138.

20. Ibid., p. 141.

21. *Votes* 4:204 (Feb. 3, 1752); Logan to J. Chalmers, Sept. 26, 1727, quoted in Dunaway, *Scotch-Irish,* p. 37; Logan to unspecified, Nov. 23, 1727, quoted in Henry Jones Ford, *The Scotch-Irish in America* (Princeton, N.J., 1915), p. 264; Logan to John Penn, 1729, quoted in Dunaway, *Scotch-Irish,* p. 37.

22. For a Scots-Irish "architecture of impermanence," see David Hackett Fischer, *Albion's Seed: Four British Folkways in America* (New York, 1989), esp. p. 662. For the wild-Irish-

as-Indians comparison, see James Muldoon, "The Indian as Irishman," *Essex Institute Historical Collections* 3 (1975): 267–89, as well as Nicholas Canny, "The Ideology of English Colonization: From Ireland to America," *WMQ* 30 (1973): 575–98.

23. *The Carolina Backcountry on the Eve of the Revolution: The Journal and Other Writings of Charles Woodmason, Anglican Itinerant,* ed. Richard J. Hooker (Chapel Hill, N.C., 1953), pp. 4, 42; 60, 50, 14; and 52, 11, 56 (entries written between Aug. 1766 and Sept. 1768).

24. See the several days' worth of angry exchanges reprinted in *Pa. Gazette,* May 22, 1755; "Petition of Germans in Philadelphia, 1754," *Pa. Arch.* 1:2:217; *Votes* 4:121 (9th mo. 22, 1749); Lewis Evans, report on the causes of Palatine fever (1754), fols. 1–5, Material Pertaining to Pennsylvania Indian Affairs, A.P.S.

25. *Votes* 4:171 (11th mo. 15, 1750); MS Minutes of Philadelphia Monthly Meeting, Mar. 27, 1730, vol. 2, p. 185, as quoted in Frederick B. Tolles, *Meeting House and Counting House: The Quaker Merchants of Colonial Philadelphia, 1682–1763* (Chapel Hill, N.C., 1948), p. 232.

26. *Votes* 4:175 (11th mo. 23, 1750).

27. Though Europeans here could live to an unprecedented extent on widely spaced solo farmsteads, in the absence of true self-sufficiency, only a tiny proportion of mid-Atlantic farmers had no contact with the world outside; Lemon, *The Best Poor Man's Country: A Geographical Study of Early Southeastern Pennsylvania* (Baltimore, Md., 1972), pp. 102–9. For sectarians' being "unable to procure . . . contiguous tract[s]," see (against its author's emphases) C. Lee Hopple, "Spatial Development of the Southeastern Pennsylvania Plain Dutch Community to 1970: Part I," *Pennsylvania Folklife* 21 (1971): 22. The settlement of the Pa. countryside has long been imagined as one of sequential assignment to ethnic sectors. But the idea of Cumberland and the westernmost counties as a Scots-Irish "shield" for the rest of Pa. will not hold up: the Irish were "not unduly concentrated on the frontier," and half lived in the southeasternmost counties or what is now imagined as Pa. Dutch country (Thomas L. Purvis, "Patterns of Ethnic Settlement in Late Eighteenth-Century Pennsylvania," *W. Pa. Hist. Mag.* 70 [1987]: 119). The disproportionate number of Germans in their supposed hearthland also occurred within an overall context of very even intermixture: the "Indices of [residential] Dissimilarity" calculated for Pa. by Aaron Fogleman, e.g. (.431 for the Germans, .394 for the Dutch, .410 for the Swedes, .308 for the Scots-Irish, .368 even for the French), all fall within a strikingly low, narrow band—while western Md., by comparison, with a German–English dissimilarity index of .709, might genuinely have felt segregated (*Hopeful Journeys,* p. 82). Whatever their ethnic majorities at the level of the county, tax list after tax list showed the townships of the mid-Atlantic interior to be substantially divided between English, Irish, and German names. (See esp. the excellent charts in Lemon, *Best Poor Man's Country,* pp. 82–83.)

28. Christoph Saur, "Ein Gespräch zwischen einem Neukommer und einem Einwohner . . . ," in *Der Hoch-Deutsch Americanische Calender auf das Jahr . . . 1751 . . .* (Germantown, Pa., 1750), unpaginated back matter ("ich . . . kan mich noch nicht drein finden"), a source mentioned in Fogleman, *Hopeful Journeys,* p. 98, within a larger discussion of German immigration that does much to direct my analysis here.

29. Franklin to Peter Collinson, May 9, 1753, *Franklin Papers* 4:484. For speculations about hostility to Germans, see Liam Riordan, "'The Complexion of My Country: The German as 'Other' in Colonial Pennsylvania," in *Germans and Indians: Fantasies, Encounters, Projections,* ed. Colin G. Calloway, Gerd Gemünden, and Susanne Zantop (Lincoln, Nebr., 2002), pp. 97–120.

30. *Eine Andere Anrede an die Deutschen Freyhalter der Stadt und County Philadelphia . . . ,* bound with *Eine Anrede an die Deutschen Freyhalter der Stadt und County Philadelphia* (Philadelphia, 1764), p. 8, and *Votes* 3:583–85. See William T. Parsons, "The Bloody Election of 1742," *Pa. Hist.* 36 (1969): 290–306, and Norman S. Cohen, "Philadelphia Election Riot of 1742," *PMHB* 92 (1968): 306–19.

31. *Votes* 4:172 (11th mo. 16, 1750), and pp. 118 and 122 (description of voting sticks from Lancaster Co., 8th mo. 16 and 9th mo. 22, 1749).

32. Blunston to Thomas Penn, Sept. 8 and Oct. 21, 1736, Lancaster Co. Papers.

33. David Crantz, *The History of Greenland: Containing . . . a Relation of the Mission . . . ,* 2 vols. (London, 1767), 2: 123–25.

34. Ibid., pp. 266, 354, and 267.

35. The German-speaking Moravians had been ready to imagine and set about building enormous empires of the spirit since the time of their pansophistic forerunner Jan Amos Comenius. But the similarity of the Moravians' global vision—at least in scope—to that of the Pietist movement at Halle (which produced the pivotally important Lutheran missionary Heinrich Melchior Mühlenberg, discussed below) invites further study of what in 1740s German culture led to the hatching of these extraordinary efforts at religious empire building.

36. Wallace, "Revitalization Movements," *American Anthropologist* 58 (1956): 265, 269, and 267. Wallace's model is expounded and reapplied in *Reassessing Revitalization Movements: Perspectives from North America and the Pacific Islands,* ed. Michael E. Harkin (Lincoln, Nebr., 2004).

37. Zeisberger, Lagundo Utenünk (Friedenstadt) Diary (in German), July 11, 1770, *Morav. Recs.* 137:1 ("*Schwonnaks* [weiße Leute]"); idem, Goschgoschünk Diary (in German), Jan. 26, 1769, ibid. 135:2; Zeisberger, Lagundo Utenünk Diary, July 11, 1770, ibid. 137:1. Since Anthony F. C. Wallace's foundational work on Delaware revitalizations ("Revitalization Movements" and "New Religions among the Delaware Indians, 1600–1900," *Southwestern Journal of Anthropology* 12 [1956]: 1–21), see esp. Gregory Evans Dowd, *A Spirited Resistance: The North American Indian Struggle for Unity, 1745–1815* (Baltimore, Md., 1992), chap. 2, Alfred A. Cave, "The Delaware Prophet Neolin: A Reappraisal," *Ethnohistory* 46 (1999): 265–90, Daniel K. Richter, *Facing East from Indian Country: A Native History of Early America* (Cambridge, Mass., 2001), chap. 6, and Merritt, *At the Crossroads,* chap. 3. Duane Champagne stresses the specific political context of French defeat in "The Delaware Revitalization Movement of the Early 1760s: A Suggested Reinterpretation," *American Indian Quarterly* 12 (1988): 107–26.

38. Merritt, *At the Crossroads,* p. 90; "John Hays' Diary and Journal of 1760," *Pa. Archaeologist* 24 (1954): 76–77, as quoted in Charles E. Hunter, "The Delaware Nativist Revival of the Mid-Eighteenth Century," *Ethnohistory* 18 (1971): 42; Dowd, *Spirited Resistance,* p. 37; and Heckewelder, *Indian Nations,* p. 294.

39. Michael N. McConnell, *A Country Between: The Upper Ohio Valley and Its Peoples, 1724–1774* (Lincoln, Nebr., 1992), p. 220; Hunter, "Delaware Nativist Revival," p. 46; "Journal of James Kenny, 1761–1763," *PMHB* 37 (1913): 188; "A Narrative of the Captivity of John M'Cullough, Esq.," in Loudon, *Interesting Narratives* 1:332.

40. Heckewelder, *Indian Nations*, p. 292; *The Siege of Detroit in 1763: The Journal of Pontiac's Conspiracy and John Rutherford's Captivity Narrative*, ed. Milo Milton Quaife (Chicago, 1958), pp. 14–15. For cleansing by war: the best account of Pontiac's War is Gregory Evans Dowd, *War under Heaven: Pontiac, the Indian Nations, and the British Empire* (Baltimore, Md., 2002), chap. 9.

41. For spiritual cross-fertilization between Moravians and Indians in colonial Pa., see Merritt, *At the Crossroads*.

42. *A Treaty Held at the Town of Lancaster, in Pennsylvania . . . in June, 1744* (Philadelphia, 1744), p. 23; message from the Shawnees to Gov. James Hamilton, Feb. 8, 1752, in *Early American Indian Documents: Treaties and Laws, 1607–1789*, ed. Alden T. Vaughan, vol. 2, *Pennsylvania Treaties, 1737–1756*, ed. Donald H. Kent (Frederick, Md., 1984), p. 262. Europeans before the 1780s had nothing to match this polygenist talk (see chap. 5 below), and often tried to rebut it. In 1776, e.g., when U.S. commissioners still hoped most Indians could be kept neutral in the Revolutionary War, they tried to insist to their Ohio-country "brothers" that they were together "the same people though of different Complexions" (council at Pittsburgh, Oct.–Nov. 1776, ibid., vol. 18: *Revolution and Confederation*, ed. Colin G. Calloway [1994], pp. 129 and 132).

43. *A Compendious Extract Containing the . . . Most Remarkable Transactions of Count Lewis of Zinzendorf . . .* (Philadelphia, [1742]), p. 10n. For summaries of the early conferences, see *Authentische Relation von dem Anlass, Fortgang und Schlusse der . . . Versammlung einiger Arbeiter derer meisten Christlichen Religionen . . .* (Philadelphia, [1742]).

44. *Mühlenberg Journals* 1:154; *A Protestation of the Several Members of the Protestant Lutheran and Reformed Religions . . .* (Philadelphia, 1742).

45. *Compendious Extract*, p. 12.

46. Marilyn J. Westerkamp, *Triumph of the Laity: Scots-Irish Piety and the Great Awakening, 1625–1760* (New York, 1988)—which traces Presbyterian back-to-basics enthusiasm from its seedbeds on the Firth of Clyde and North Channel across the Atlantic —rightly sees Whitefield as an unwitting beneficiary of the established Scots-Irish popular revival tradition. But the revivals overseen by ministers associated with the Tennent family's Neshaminy, Pa., "Log College" among the middle colonies' Presbyterians were only some of the best-known episodes in this nearly universal course of early 18th-century religious contests and clarifications, so enormous that it is almost hard to see—in which, far from "watch[ing] . . . in perplexed silence," even the Quakers took part with brio (Jon Butler, "Enthusiasm Described and Decried: The Great Awakening as Interpretative Fiction," *JAH* 69 [1979]: 311). Ned Landsman's classic study of Presbyterian revival in Freehold, N.J., exemplifies how such a process could work; with years of congregational squabbling running along an angry, invisible line of Anglo-Scottish division, as revival proceeded, Scots and Presbyterians became ever more identified, so that its revivals became "the culmination of the process of unifying, or Presbyterianizing" local Scots more tightly than they could have been in Britain.

Landsman, "Revivalism and Nativism in the Middle Colonies: The Great Awakening and the Scots Community in East New Jersey," *AQ* 34 (1982): 161; and *Scotland and Its First American Colony, 1683–1765* (Princeton, N.J., 1985).

47. Timothy L. Smith discusses the "sharpening of the religious boundaries of ethnic association" as one of New World migration's most reliable effects in "Religion and Ethnicity in America," *AHR* 83 (1978): 117; and since revivals, as Perry Miller observed, often prompt groups to ask themselves whether they are living up to the ideal of a unified Christian community—stirring hopes of "redeeming communities en bloc"—the limits of the communities within which revivals unfolded had terrific importance, because those boundaries would be sanctified by their progress; Miller, *The Life of the Mind in America from the Revolution to the Civil War*, bks. 1–3 (New York, 1965), p. 11.

48. Mühlenberg became the first head of the united Lutheran ministerium in Pa., and literally laid the cornerstone for Zion Lutheran Church, German Pa.'s grandest, at its construction in 1766.

49. Ibid. 1:30, 31, and 35. The Salzburgers' emigration is chronicled in Mack Walker, *The Salzburg Transaction: Expulsion and Redemption in Eighteenth-Century Germany* (Ithaca, N.Y., 1992).

50. *Mühlenberg Journals* 1:85. Bernard Bailyn beautifully evokes this strange sectarian landscape in his *Peopling of British North America: An Introduction* (New York, 1986), chap. 3, as does Elizabeth W. Fisher in "'Prophesies and Revelations': German Cabbalists in Early Pennsylvania," *PMHB* 109 (1985): 299–333.

51. *Mühlenberg Journals* 1:381 and 185; and see, e.g., pp. 70, 79, 109, and 446.

52. Ibid. 1:297; 2:308, 1:118 (and see Aaron Spencer Fogleman, "Jesus Is Female: The Moravian Challenge in the German Communities of British North America," *WMQ* 60 [2003]: 295–332); cf. Franklin to Peter Collinson, May 9, 1753, *Franklin Papers* 4:484, and, e.g., *Mühlenberg Journals* 1:261, 238, and 154.

53. Ibid. 1:193, 725, 197, and 213; cf. p. 85.

54. Ibid. 1:129; 2:302, 2:256, and 1:651; cf. 1:218, 2:183 (report of a sermon by Provost Carolus von Wrangel), and 1:453. During an epidemic in 1748, Mühlenberg even saw Exodus-like signs that God had put a difference between German congregants and the English, singling out his people for preservation while "snatch[ing] away" their neighbors (ibid. 1:178–79).

55. Ibid., 1:310 and 2:89–90; Saur to Conrad Weiser, Sept. 6, 1755, trans. J. Daniel Rupp, in *The Life of Rev. Michael Schlatter . . .* , ed. H. Harbaugh (Philadelphia, 1857), pp. 293–95 n. 1; *Mühlenberg Journals* 1:437.

56. *Mühlenberg Journals* 1:299.

57. Ibid. 1:449. In short, accommodations at the level of individuals were unavoidable (in the peculiarly colonial brand of mutual borrowing and lending of traits between cultures over time, in ways both small and large, that is often studied as "creolization"); but at least during the early decades, once such de facto forms of convergence were filtered through the pens and sermons of worried cultural leaders at the level of whole groups, they could actually help to drive their attitudes toward one another further apart (cf. H. D. Forbes, *Ethnic Conflict: Commerce, Culture, and the Contact Hypothesis* [New Haven, Conn., 1997], pp. 146, 167, and 169). Martin E. Lodge, "The Crisis of the

Churches in the Middle Colonies, 1720–1750," *PMHB* 95 (1971): 195–220, remains perhaps the best description of the mid-Atlantic culture brokers' panic.

58. Beatty, *Journals of Charles Beatty, 1762–1769,* ed. Guy Soulliard Klett (University Park, Pa., 1962), Aug. 22, 1766, p. 47; Beatty, *The Journal of a Two Months Tour . . . among the Frontier Inhabitants of Pennsylvania . . .* (London, 1768), p. 18; *Journals of Beatty,* Aug. 25, 1766, p. 48.

59. Beatty, *Journal of a Two Months Tour,* pp. 13, 24, and 14.

60. Tennent, *The Danger of an Unconverted Ministry . . .* (Philadelphia, 1740); to Rev. Jonathan Dickinson, Feb. 12, 1742, in Richard Webster, *A History of the Presbyterian Church in America . . .* (Philadelphia, 1857), p. 189; and see Milton J. Coalter, "The Radical Pietism of Count Nicholas Zinzendorf as a Conservative Influence on the Awakener, Gilbert Tennent," *Church History* 49 (1980): 35–46.

61. Samuel Finley, *Satan Strip'd of His Angelick Robe . . .* (Philadelphia, [1743]), p. iii; [Creaghead], *A Renewal of the Convenants . . .* ([Philadelphia], 1748; orig. pub. 1743), p. 76 (this was preceded by similar denials of the "out-landish Lutheran" William III; the popish James III; the backsliding Charles II; the compromising Cromwell; and the reformation-thwarting Charles I; ibid., pp. 72–76); Finley, *Satan Strip'd,* p. viii.

62. [Creaghead], *Renewal of the Covenants,* pp. xxi and i; pp. xxix, xxvi, and lvi; pp. 66–67; and pp. xii and 69. For mockery see, e.g., Samuel Blair, *Animadversions on the Reasons of Mr. Alex. Creaghead's Receding . . .* (Philadelphia, [1742]), p. 7n.

63. Joseph Smith, *Old Redstone, or Historical Sketches . . .* (Philadelphia, 1854), pp. 153–54; Gilbert Tennent, "The Duty of Self-Examination Considered . . . ," in *Sermons on Sacramental Occasions . . .* (Boston, 1739), p. 143; and ibid., pp. 78–79 and liii; pp. 79 and iv; p. 76; and p. iv. For the inherited model of large-scale outdoor communion services established in early 17th-century Ulster and southwest Scotland, see Westerkamp, *Triumph of the Laity,* pp. 30–34, 161–64, and Leigh Eric Schmidt, *Holy Fairs: Scottish Communions and American Revivals in the Early Modern Period* (Princeton, N.J., 1989).

64. Samuel Blair, *A Short and Faithful Narrative, of the Late Remarakable Revival of Religion in the Congregation of New-Londonderry . . .* (Philadelphia, [1744]), p. 11. In short, to the considerable degree that the religious revivals most discussed in Pa. and N.J., especially during the 1740s, actually took place within Presbyterian congregations, and with help from Presbyterian mass communions, they can profitably be examined as expressions of Irish religious renewal.

65. "The Christian Orator on hearing Samuel Fothergill preach in Philadelphia———," 1756, Pemberton Papers 34:30. Fothergill's tour lasted from 1754 to 1756; his father, John, had made similar American speaking tours in 1706, 1722, and 1737. See [Samuel Fothergill], *Two Discourses and a Prayer, Publickly Delivered . . . the Whole Taken down in Characters, by a Member of the Church of England . . .* (Philadelphia, [1767?]), for examples of Fothergill's preaching style, which reverberates with painful word pictures, exclamations, "lively force and heart-felt energy" (ibid., p. iv). For meeting sizes, see evidence assembled by Isaac Sharpless in Rufus Jones, *The Quakers in the American Colonies* (London, 1911), p. 523 (a study that, like Frederick B. Tolles, "Quietism versus Enthusiasm: The Philadelphia Quakers and the Great Awakening," *PMHB* 69 [1945]: 20–49, to some extent falls prey to self-stereotyping by 20th-century Friends historians

on the subject of "quietism"). Even in unfriendly Boston, Fothergill gathered 2,000 listeners in 1743; a Providence meeting may have drawn 5,000 (Fothergill Journal, 8th mo., 2, 1743, quoted ibid., p. 130; Edmund Peckover's estimate quoted ibid., p. 129n). For "reformation," see Jack D. Marietta's *Reformation of American Quakerism, 1748–1783* (Philadelphia, 1984).

66. For 18th-century Quakers as pivoting against (and beginning to undermine) the whole Western moral inheritance as they found it, see David Brion Davis, *The Problem of Slavery in Western Culture* (New York, 1999), chap. 10. See Sydney V. James, *A People among Peoples: Quaker Benevolence in Eighteenth-Century America* (Cambridge, Mass., 1963), and Jean R. Soderlund, *Quakers and Slavery: A Divided Spirit* (Princeton, N.J., 1985), which also stresses Quaker reformers' interest in erecting testimonies to fence themselves off from surrounding groups, in the belief "that slavery—and perhaps the slaves themselves—polluted their religion and Delaware Valley society" (*Quakers and Slavery*, pp. 174; see also esp. pp. 143–44, 161, 177). I would interpret much of Soderlund's evidence as overriding her division between idealists and purity-minded "tribalists," since the reasons for both tendencies seem to have been tied together with tail-biting tightness.

67. Isaac Whitelock to Israel Pemberton, 6th mo. 6, 1760, Friendly Assoc. Papers (Haverford) 3:475.

68. Or (nearly always the same thing) if they were married under the care of a non-Quaker church. In the mid-1710s, cases of marrying in the wrong way came to the attention of the meetings in one group outside Philadelphia perhaps seven times each year, but 30 years later, the rate of disciplinary action for irregular marriage had risen by 800 percent, and in just another 5 years, in 1749–51, by nearly another 50 percent (Marietta, *Reformation of American Quakerism*, p. 51).

69. Elizabeth Wilkinson Journal, pp. 78–79, as quoted ibid., p. 64; table 3: "Exogamous Marriages," ibid., p. 63.

70. West, *A Treatise Concerning Marriage* . . . (London, 1707; reprinted Philadelphia, 1730 and 1738, and eventually again in London, 1761), title and pp. 14 and 31 (citing 1738 ed.); Reynell to Michael Lee Dicker, Dec. 21, 1739, and Mar. 19, 1740/41, James Reynell Letterbook, 1738–41, H.S.P.

71. Henry Drinker to James Thornton, 8th mo. 31st, 1788, Richard T. Cadbury Collection, Q.C., as quoted in Marietta, *Reformation of American Quakerism*, p. 93 n. 48.

72. Woolman, *A Journal of the Life* . . . , in *Works* (Philadelphia, 1774), p. 142; Benezet to Morris Birbeck, 10th mo. 16, 1781, Misc. MSS, F.H.L., as quoted in Marietta, *Reformation of American Quakerism*, p. 85 n. 28. Woolman's perception that the unjust stewardship of world resources caused war was what led him, with earnest abruptness, to this new expression of inward purity: recounting the effects on his spirit, e.g., of thinking about the distresses caused by Indian war—"with the miseries of many of my fellow-creatures . . . some suddenly destroyed; some wounded, and . . . [made] cripples"— Woolman wrote, without seeing the need for an explicit transition, "Thinking often on these things, the use of hats and garments dyed with a dye hurtful to them . . . grew more uneasy to me" (*Journal*, p. 140).

73. *Mühlenberg Journals* 2:370; 1:131 and 661. Even a cheap digest of English grammar

from the 1740s, marketed explicitly for Pa.'s "German lovers of the English language," was careful to give no hint that learning English was something its readers should feel driven to do, so "that there may be none who . . . by all too much practice in English, neglect and forget their consummate German mother-tongue, or speak it ashamedly" (*Grammatica Anglicana Concentrata* . . . [Philadelphia, 1748], foreword, pp. [1], [6] [in German]).

74. A Tradesman of Philadelphia [Benjamin Franklin], *Plain Truth* . . . ([Philadelphia], 1747), p. 10; council minutes, June 9, 1748, and dep. of Edmund Liston, Jul. 27, 1747, *Pa. Col. Recs.* 5:271 and 117. For the startling events set off in these same years by fear of war and invasion in another city, see Jill Lepore, *New York Burning: Liberty, Slavery, and Conspiracy in Eighteenth-Century Manhattan* (New York, 2005).

75. [Franklin], *Plain Truth,* pp. 22; title, 20, and 19; and 20–21.

76. Tennent, *The Late Association for Defence, Encourag'd* . . . (Philadelphia, [1748]), p. 5, and *The Late Association for Defence, Farther Encourag'd* . . . (Philadelphia, [1748]), p. 41 (arrow image from Deut. 32:41–42). Tennent was also much given to the use of imperative perception verbs (See! Hark! Behold! Hear!) to help in imagining scenes of destruction, à la Sodom, for the morally or militarily careless. For the "Form of Association" signed by the volunteers, see *Franklin Papers* 3:205–12.

77. As Mühlenberg continually announced to friends and parishioners, the "[c]onditions in this land, I often think, are like those in ancient Israel" between the Hebrews' entry into Canaan and the rise of the Davidic monarchy: Pa. was "an undisciplined country . . . [with] things going as they did in the Book of Judges . . . 'In those days there was no king in Israel, but every man did that which was right in his own eyes.'" *Mühlenberg Journals* 1:376 and 2:97.

78. Ibid., p. 27; Tennent, *The Late Association for Defence Farther Encouraged . . . In a Reply to Some Exceptions against War* . . . (Philadelphia, 1748), p. 1. For this maneuver's theology, see Silver, "Indian-Hating," pp. 72–76 and 126–30.

79. Tennent, *Sermon Preach'd at Philadelphia, January 7. 1747–8* . . . (Philadelphia, 1748), pp. 25 and 33 (image from Zech. 2:5); *A Treatise Shewing the Need We Have to Rely upon God* . . . (Philadelphia, 1748), p. 17.

80. Tennent, *Late Association for Defence Farther Encouraged . . . In a Reply to Some Exceptions,* p. 2 and 72.

81. For Pa. lawmaking, see John M. Murrin, "Political Development," in *Colonial British America: Essays in the New History of the Early Modern Era,* ed. Jack P. Greene and J. R. Pole (Baltimore, Md., 1984), p. 439.

82. For the Seven Years' War, see Fred Anderson's grand history, *Crucible of War: The Seven Years' War and the Fate of Empire in British North America, 1754–1766* (New York, 2000), now handily condensed (albeit around what may be an overstated form of the thesis that events were controlled, as early as the 1750s, by widespread anti-Indian racism among Europeans) in *The War That Made America: A Short History of the French and Indian War* (New York, 2005); for Pontiac's War see Dowd, *War under Heaven.*

83. "A Dream of — in the year 1757 Concerning Philadelphia and Repeated again by Dream about Eleven years after . . . ," in the notebook "Prophecy and Dream," H.S.P.

Chapter 2
FEARING INDIANS

1. Smith also changed the play—and showed off more of his students—by deciding to "leave out all the Womens Parts, or put their Words into other Mouths" (although he did recruit girls to sing some of the piece's songs, to full musical accompaniment; see *Pa. Gazette,* Jan. 20, 1757, and following three issues).

2. *Life and Correspondence of the Rev. William Smith, D.D. . . . ,* comp. Horace Wemyss Smith (Philadelphia, 1879), 1:56n.

3. *Pa. Gazette,* Feb. 10, 1757.

4. N. A. M. Rodger, "Sea-Power and Empire, 1688–1793," in *The Oxford History of the British Empire,* ed. Wm. Roger Louis, vol. 2: *The Eighteenth Century,* ed. P. J. Marshall (Oxford, 1998), chap. 8. One of William Hogarth's anti-Gallican engravings could call up this standardized set of fears simply by showing a French priest on an invasion beach, gloating over a little coffin-like box full of fetters and spikes; see Hogarth, "France," pl. 1 from *The Invasion of France & England* (London, 1756).

5. George Stevenson to Richard Peters, Sept. 17, 1756, Indian and Military Affairs MSS, p. 165; "De Roche," *A Letter from Quebeck . . .* (Boston, 1754), pp. 7, 5, and 8.

6. *Am. Weekly Mercury,* Mar. 26–Apr. 4, 1745, p. 2 (extracting *London Mag.,* Sept. 1744).

7. When Europeans displayed the mutilated corpses from such attacks for their own cultural purposes (see chap. 3 below), their task was made simpler because the Indian attackers who displayed the corpses in the first place had already tried to imbue them with lessons about a frightening cruelty and indiscriminacy. As well as more specific lessons: for mutilatory wit in war—specifically a 17th-century Algonquian "aesthetic of war," filled with irony, inversion, and contempt in the treatment of corpses—see Frederic W. Gleach, *Powhatan's World and Colonial Virginia: A Conflict of Cultures* (Lincoln, Nebr., 1997), pp. 47–51; and see Jill Lepore, *The Name of War: King Philip's War and the Origins of American Identity* (New York, 1998), pp. 95–96 and 104–5, for lessons staged in the destruction of animals, buildings, and Bibles; Merritt, *At the Crossroads,* pp. 179–80 and 184–85, for a view of genital mutilation as aimed at "eras[ing] a common humanity" between Indians and Europeans (p. 182); and, for a 1791 instance of the pointed manipulation of European corpses (stuffing their mouths with Ohio country soil), see Alan Taylor, *The Divided Ground: Indians, Settlers, and the Northern Borderland of the American Revolution* (New York, 2006), p. 259. Putting bodies in roads helped the overall goal of cutting communications between forts emphasized in Dowd, *War under Heaven* (though I would add rural depopulation as an Indian war aim).

8. Horsfield to Gov. Robert Hunter Morris, Nov. 27, 1755, Horsfield Letterbook; Franklin to Peter Collinson, Dec. 19, 1756, *Franklin Papers* 7:51–52. Some contemporaries saw the tactics of mid-Atlantic attacks in the 1750s and 1760s as a replay of the methods used by New England Indians in King Philip's War (for which see Patrick M. Malone's elegant *Skulking Way of War: Technology and Tactics among the New England Indians* [Lanham, Md., 1991]; see "Dissertation on the Indians Murdering the White People" [ca. July–late Oct. 1755], Ind. Affairs Papers 11c:5). This was partly a stereotyped view of Indian war, since even besieging forts, with continual gunfire and the setting

alight of outbuildings, was well within the Delawares' power, as the 1756 capture of Fort Granville and many events in Pontiac's War showed (cf. Craig S. Keener, "An Ethnohistorical Analysis of Iroquois Assault Tactics Used against Fortified Settlements of the Northeast in the Seventeenth Century," *Ethnohistory* 46 [1999]: 777–807).

9. Col. James Burd, "A Proposition for the better securing . . . Pennsylvania from the Inroads of the Indians," *Pa. Arch.* 1:3:99–104, at p. 102. For a detailed account of this system in practice, see Job Chillaway's account in [Lewis Weiss] to unknown, Nov. 19, 1763, *Morav. Recs.* 124:6:15.

10. Col. Thomas Hartley to Pa. Board of War, Aug. 9, 1778, *Pa. Arch.* 2:6:689.

11. William Trent to Col. James Burd, Oct. 4, 1755, *Pa. Col. Recs.* 6:641; "The Captivity of Charles Stuart, 1755–57," ed. Beverly W. Bond Jr., *MVHR* 13 (1926): 58–81 (regroupings described pp. 60–61). The war leaders were Shingas and John Peter, respectively. Stuart described the whole reunited "company of Delware Mingo & Shawnese Indians" involved as being "ab^t 90" (pp. 60, 59). From the number of horses the amalgamated group could lead along ("ab^t 110"), it seems reasonable to conclude that their entire expedition, which depopulated at least three distinct areas of settlement and alarmed the entire western countryside, had no more than those 90 members.

12. *A Narrative of the Sufferings and Surprizing Deliverances of William and Elizabeth Fleming* . . . (Boston, 1756), pp. 5, 3, 8, and 7. The Hickses' house proved to have been already abandoned in panic when they burst in. The acting out of Hicks's death agonies was part of a culture of mimesis surrounding Indian war-making. The gestural dances performed by 18th-century Delaware men before going to war or—with "terrific looks and gestures"—around captives slated for torture similarly had the intent of "strik[ing] terror in the beholders": each knife-, club-, or tomahawk-holding dancer, according to one observer, "strikes, stabs, grasps, pretends to scalp, to cut, to run through" an imaginary enemy; another described how Mingo men, dancing shortly after the Revolution, "threw themselves . . . into the various Postures of dodging . . . chasing & Murdering a flying Enemy" (Heckewelder, *Indian Nations,* p. 209; Allinson Papers 8:100:3).

13. Collins to Israel Pemberton, 2nd mo. 13, 1756, Pemberton Papers 11:49; Burd, "Proposition for the better securing . . . Pennsylvania," p. 102. Many printed firsthand reports of home invasions, in particular, summoned up each terrifying instant of the experience in sequence, like unhappy hallucinations, showing all the hallmarks of so-called flashbulb memories of violence—especially the dilation of time, as well as "weapon focus" and other signs of attentional narrowing, with perception drilling in upon and magnifying the central features of each attack. In a sense, such accounts were simply embedding artificial traumatic memories of Indian attacks in a mass of people who had never undergone them, stirring in readers (in a commonsense converse of the idea of "state-dependent memory") a backwash of the sensations of stress and fear amid which they had first been formed. For state-dependent and mood-congruent retrieval, to which Ken Norman kindly introduced me, see Daniel L. Schachter, *Searching for Memory: The Brain, the Mind, and the Past* (New York, 1996), pp. 60–64 and chap. 7.

14. *Am. Weekly Mercury,* Aug. 17–24, 1727, p. 4 (for the death of the preceding king, Wequeala—he was hanged by N.J. for murder—see *Pa. Col. Recs.* 3:330 and discussion in Wallace, *King of the Delawares,* pp. 197–200); petition to Gov. Patrick Gordon, Apr.

29, 1728, *Pa. Arch.* 1:1:209–10; petition of May 10, 1728, ibid., pp. 213–14.

15. See Arthur Cecil Bining, *Pennsylvania Iron Manufacture in the Eighteenth Century* (Harrisburg, Pa., 1938), appendix A and chaps. 2 and 6; and Bernard Bailyn, *Voyagers to the West: A Passage in the Peopling of America on the Eve of the Revolution* (New York, 1986), pp. 245–54.

16. Gordon to assembly, May 15, 1728, *Am. Weekly Mercury,* May 23–30, 1728, p. 1; *Pa. Col. Recs.* 3:303 (May 15, 1728). The encounter of which Gordon first heard exaggerated accounts was a case of forced hospitality gone wrong—imposed on local residents by a scouting party of Shawnees from near the Durham Iron Works (*Pa. Col. Recs.* 3:309 [May 20, 1728]; and Gordon to Shawnees, May 21, 1728, *Pa. Arch.* 1:1:223). Rumors of imaginary attacks and damage seem to be most likely when intense popular fear of danger from a specific source creates a "need for action . . . [seen as] so compelling that some people spread information and misinformation indiscriminately out of a sense of responsibility"; Ralph H. Turner, "Rumor as Intensified Information Seeking: Earthquake Rumors in China and the United States," in *Disasters, Collective Behavior, and Social Organization,* ed. Russell R. Dynes and Kathleen J. Tierney (Newark, Del., 1994), p. 250. For rumors in Indian country as intercultural trial balloons used to test out intentions, see Gregory Evans Dowd, "The Panic of 1751: The Significance of Rumors on the South Carolina–Cherokee Frontier," *WMQ* 53 (1996): 527–60.

17. Despite all this bashing, the second woman may not have been dead until Roberts finished her with another ax stroke the next morning (Winters' confessions, *Am. Weekly Mercury,* July 4–11, 1728, p. 3). Despite Gov. Gordon's assuming that the man killed was the familiar local Delaware named Tacocolie, this seems unlikely, since the Winters' accounts left him unnamed while they spoke of finding another victim "in Tacoolie's Cabin" (e.g., examination of Walter Winter, May 12, 1728, *Pa. Arch.* 1:1:219).

18. Winters' confessions, *Am. Weekly Mercury,* July 4–11, 1728, pp. 2–3. Gov. Gordon's exasperated summary—"from the Reports in the Countrey of the Indians having Killed some white men, they thought they might lawfully Kill any Indian"—corroborates this account: they believed they were at war; *Pa. Col. Recs.* 3:304 (May 15, 1728).

19. Proclamation, May 16, 1728, *Am. Weekly Mercury,* May 23–30, 1728, p. 3 (correcting text first printed in issue of May 16–23, 1728, p. 1); charge at Philadelphia quarter sessions, June 3, 1728, ibid., May 30–June 6, 1728, p. 2.

20. For difficulty in signing up men for fort duty, and mutinies if guarantees of fort-free duty offered to recruits were infringed, see Peter Spycker to Gov. William Denny, June 24, 1757, Weiser Correspondence 2:61; and Capt. Joseph Shippen Jr. to Maj. James Burd, May 31 and June 7, 1757, Shippen Military Letterbook, fols. 56v–58r and 62r–v.

21. Joseph Shippen Jr. to Edward Shippen, Sept. 3, 1756, Shippen Military Letterbook, fol. 21v.

22. John Van Etten (Johannes Vannetten) Diary, Apr. 25 and June 2, 1757, H.S.P. The scouting calculation is complicated by allowances for bad weather, which wipes out several months for comparative purposes, and gaps in Vannetten's attendance, but I make the average time between recorded scouts 2.2 days in Dec., with a modal interval of 1 day, and 4.3 days in May, with a modal interval of 5 days. The quantity of (more static) guarding and in-fort exercising that Vannetten's men did also rose steadily.

23. William Trent, Journal at Fort Pitt, Aug. 27, 1763, fol. 38v, H.S.P. (in orderly-book section of the journal, upside down at back); July 27, 1763, fol. 22r (in diary section at front).

24. *Wöch. Phila. Staatsbote,* June 25, 1764, p. 3 ("man hört die Indianer oft auf ihre fürchterliche art zwischen den bergen heulen"); Heckewelder, *Indian Nations,* p. 217; William Trent, Journal at Fort Pitt, June 1, 1763, p. 6, H.S.P. (e.g., July 1, 1763, p. 16); *Pa. Packet,* Sept. 5, 1778.

25. A fort's presence could comfort country people even when they were not inside it. In 1766, generalizing from the experience of Pontiac's War (which started with attacks on forts), Sir William Johnson noted that "Frontier Inhabitants . . . [derive] Encouragem^t. . . . [from the forts' being] in a War . . . the first objects of the Inds. attention & . . . prevent[ing] them from fall^g like a Torrent on the Settleme^{ts}" (to Gen. Thomas Gage, Jan. 7, 1766, *Johnson Papers* 5:3); for primitive forts, see Hunter, *Pa. Forts,* chap. 5 (Steel's meetinghouse at p. 176).

26. Mortimer, "Diary of the Indian congn. at Goshen on the river Muskingum, commencing with the month of May 1812," Sept. 18, 1812, fol. 19v, *Morav. Recs.* 173:9.

27. "Some Account of Prisonrs. to be sent to Pitt's burgh, 1762," Friendly Assoc. Papers (Haverford) 4:343.

28. John Campbell to Baynton, Wharton, and Morgan, Aug. 1, 1769, microfilmed *Baynton, Wharton, and Morgan Papers in the Pennsylvania State Archives,* ed. George R. Beyer (Harrisburg, Pa., 1967), roll 3, frames 934–36; Wyoming Indians to Gov. Morris, Nov. 9, 1755, *Pa. Col. Recs.* 6:752.

29. On the revolutionary glorification of rural riflemen as Indian-fighters, see, e.g., Rhys Isaac, *The Transformation of Virginia, 1740–1790* (Chapel Hill, N.C., 1982), chap. 11. For a prime specimen of the genre (describing William Tell–like marksmanship), see *Pa. Mercury,* Aug. 18, 1775, p. 3.

30. *Wöch. Phila. Staatsbote,* Sept. 5, 1763, p. 2 (in German).

31. Adam Hoops to Gov. Morris, Nov. 3, 1755, *Pa. Arch.* 1:2:462; Potter to Richard Peters, Nov. 3, 1755, *Pa. Col. Recs.* 6:674.

32. Hosterman to Col. Winter, June 10, 1778, and Col. Thomas Hartley to Pa. executive council, Sept. 1, 1778, *Pa. Arch.* 1:6:589–90 and 729.

33. Fleming, *Narrative of the Sufferings,* p. 5 (this was the same boy, Hicks, who was later killed before him).

34. Hosterman to Winter, June 10, 1778, *Pa. Arch.* 1:6:591.

35. [Murray], "The Druid, No. II," *Pa. Journal,* Mar. 14, 1781, pp. 1–2 (italics in original).

36. Dispatches from Fishkill, N.Y., Aug. 8, 1782, *Pa. Gazette,* Aug. 14, 1782.

37. Most theorists considered the laws of war, taken as a subset of the law of nations, to be "[s]o close" to the natural law that "even non-European 'barbarian' societies might [properly] be subject" to their dictates (Vitoria, *Political Writings,* ed. Anthony Pagden and Jeremy Lawrence [Cambridge, 1991], pp. xv, xvi); natural law and, below it, human law were both thought to be progressively more elaborate (and culturally specific) descendants of divine law—from whose ineluctable principles, like an architect's spidery plans or a few stars in the night sky, a universe of laws could be deduced.

38. [Emerich] de Vattel, *The Law of Nations . . .* , trans. from French (Dublin, 1787), 3.5, §72, p. 482, and 3.8, §145, p. 524 (citing by book and chapter, section number, page). This is virtually a repeat of Grotius's arguments in *Of the Rights of War and Peace . . .* , trans. from Latin, 3 vols. (London, 1715), bk. 3, chap. 11, §§8–16, pp. 189–202.

39. Assembly to Gov. Denny, May 3, 1758, *Pa. Col. Recs.* 8:109. It followed for Vattel from the principle of not attacking those who cannot resist that, in general, prisoners should be treated well and not killed (Vattel, *Law of Nations*, 3.8, §140, pp. 519–20)—except when fighting enemies who had themselves set the laws of war at nought (3.8, §141, p. 520). Similarly, nations like the Indians that "rather over-r[u]n than inhabi[t]" their too extensive lands might well "deserve to be exterminated as savage and pernicious beasts" (1.7, §81, p. 67; cf. 3.3 §34, pp. 457–58). (Vattel, in fact, returned frequently to the idea that "the Indians of North America had no right to appropriate all that vast continent to themselves" [2.7, §97, p. 265]; a theory whose attractions for the post-revolutionary generation were shown by a front-page essay in the Philadelphia *Freeman's Journal*, Aug. 15, 1781; see chap. 9 below).

40. Vattel, *Law of Nations*, 3.8, §155, p. 533; 3.13, §193, and 3.9, §167, pp. 570, 545.

41. Vitoria, "On Dietary Laws, or Self-Restraint," in *Political Writings*, p. 210. As Ruth Richardson has found, with a popular belief in the importance of bodily wholeness to the knitting together and reanimation of the decomposed dead at resurrection running deep, to many early moderns dissection may have seemed a "deliberate . . . destruction of identity, perhaps for eternity"; *Death, Dissection, and the Destitute* (London, 1987), pp. 29 and 76. Cremation was also viewed with horror—and illegal—in the English-speaking world before sanitary crusades during the 1880s; see Stephen Prothero, *Purified by Fire: A History of Cremation in America* (Berkeley, Calif., 2001).

42. John Van Etten (Johannes Vannetten), Journal kept at Ft. Hyndshaw, 1756–57, Apr. 26, 1756, H.S.P.; Parsons to Conrad Weiser, Oct. 31, 1755, Lancaster Co. Papers, and Parsons to Richard Peters, Oct. 31, 1755, *Pa. Arch.* 1:2:443–45 (two states of the same letter).

43. This was truer in the 1750s and 1760s, when substantial groups of Indians still lived within easy traveling distance of the longest-settled parts of Pennsylvania and northern New Jersey, than it was in the 1770s and 1780s.

44. *Pensylvanische Berichte, oder Sammlung*, Sept. 16, 1755, p. 3 ("in Eyrisch und teutscher Sprache"; "man solt die Hunde alle todt schiessen, sie sind Verräther und Schelmen"); [Murray,] "The Druid, No. II," *Pa. Journal*, Mar. 14, 1781, p. 2.

45. Henry Geiger to Timothy Horsfield, Sept. 5, 1763, Bethlehem Vicinity MSS, p. 125.

46. John Brodhead and Samuel Gonsalus to Johnson, Apr. 6, 1766, *Johnson Papers* 5:150.

47. Dep. of Lemuel Barret, Mar. 6, 1766, *Johnson Papers* 5:52–54; see W. G. Aitchison Robertson, "Bier-Right," *Juridical Review* 44 (1932): 361–73. When Gov. John Penn wrote after this to Virginia Gov. Francis Fauquier, hoping for his help in finding Jacobs, Fauquier airily replied (for which see chap. 4 below) that there was no prospect of success, since in his back counties the killing of Indians "is looked on as a meritorious action, and [killers] are sure of being Protected" (Gov. Francis Fauquier to Penn, Dec. 11, 1766, *Pa. Col. Recs.* 9:349–50). Things were evidently different in Jacobs's part of Cumberland County. For another, more successful experiment with bier right the fol-

lowing year in Bergen County, N.J.—this time performed on a slave, suspected of killing a Dutch neighbor—see *N.Y. Journal,* Oct. 1, 1767, p. 2 (he was burned to death in Hackensack; ibid., Oct. 29, 1767, p. 2).

48. Dep. of Conrad Reiff, Nov. 1, 1763; dep. of Sgt. Lawrence McGuire, Oct. 15, 1763; and dep. of John Lischer, Oct. 18, 1763 (in German), *Morav. Recs.* 124:6.

49. The shaky case against Renatus was itself premised, after all, on the popular belief that Indian revenge would follow local Indians' killings as surely as night followed day; Weiss to assembly, Dec. 23, 1763, *Morav. Recs.* 124:6:16.

50. *Wöch. Phila. Staatsbote,* June 25, 1764, p. 3 (in German); Weiss, memorandum for Renatus's defense, *Morav. Recs.* 124:6:11.

51. See *Morav. Recs.* 124:6:22–23 (and incidental accounts of Renatus in Philadelphia in Rev. Bernhard Adam Grube's 1764 mission diaries, cited chap. 6 below). A more optimistic interpretation would be that the jurors were frightened enough of Indian attack not to resist considering the evidence of Renatus's innocence fairly, so that they were frightened equally of European and Indian retaliations.

52. Mortimer, "Diary of the Indian congn. at Goshen," Aug. 23, 1812.

53. "Account of the Face of the Country of the Borders of Pennsylvania," *Pa. Col. Recs.* 7:445.

54. "Report of Richard Peters . . . of the Proceedings against sundry Persons settled in the unpurchased Part of the Province," July 2, 1750, *Votes* 4:141. The sense of a sharp-sided hollow set among mountains goes back no farther than the 18th century (see *OED,* s.v. "cove").

55. John Armstrong to Gov. Morris, Nov. 2, 1755, *Pa. Arch.* 1:2:452.

56. John Harris to Gov. Morris and petition from west of the Susquehanna, both Oct. 20, 1755, *Pa. Col. Recs.* 6:645–46 and 647–48.

57. *Wöch. Phila. Staatsbote,* Aug. 13, 1764, p. 2 ("man befürchte, ein so weit in dem besetzen theil des landes gethaner streich der Indianer werde die einwohner veranlassen von ihren platzen zu weichen").

58. Joseph Shippen Jr. to Edward Shippen Sr. ("on the Road to Philad:a or at Philadelphia"), Nov. 1, 1755, Shippen Family Papers; Harris to Conrad Weiser (next forwarded by Weiser to Gov. Morris), June 30, 1755, *Pa. Col. Recs.* 6:457; Edward Shippen Sr. to Brig. Gen. John Stanwix, Aug. 23, 1759, Edward Shippen Correspondence, p. 192.

59. John Potts et al. to Gov. Morris, Oct. 31, 1755, Horsfield Papers 1:33. [James Burd] to [James Hamilton], [1760], Shippen Family Papers 5:123; Joseph Shippen Jr. to Edward Shippen Sr., Aug. 26, 1756, Shippen Military Letterbook. Most Indian news was carried not by regular post riders—who galloped across the countryside in peacetime with distinctively sealed letter bags, gaily sounding posthorns—but by less obvious special expresses (see Franklin's "Post Office Instructions and Directions" [ca. 1753], *Franklin Papers* 5:161–77). Express riders still seem to have been easy to identify and intercept—as with the sword- and gun-bearing Bucks Co. man who stopped one and broke open his letters ("tr[ying] to read [them] Which he cou'd not Very well"; Timothy Horsfield to Gov. Morris, Dec. 1, 1755, Horsfield Papers 1:77). For speed of travel, see Alberto E. Minetti, "Efficiency of Equine Express Postal Systems," *Nature* 426 (2003): 785–86.

60. Harris to Col. James Burd, Dec. 19, 1763 (for subscriptions see Harris to James Burd,

Apr. 28, 1767), and Joseph Shippen Jr. to Edward Shippen Sr., May 15, 1756, Shippen Family Papers.

61. Rev. John Elder to Col. Joseph Shippen, Nov. 5, 1763, *Pa. Arch.* 1:4:133; William Parsons to Richard Peters, Oct. 31, 1755, *Pa. Arch.* 1:2:444; Smith to George Bryan, July 12, 1778, *Pa. Arch.* 1:6:632; William Maclay to Pa. Council of State, July 12, 1778, *Pa. Arch.* 1:6:634; Barton to Peters, Feb. 6, 1756, *Pa. Arch.* 1:2:568.

62. Rhoda Barber, Journal of Settlement at Wright's Ferry (ca. 1830), H.S.P.; and petitions in *Votes* 4:420 (Jul. 31, 1755). These estimates of the size and duration of panics come from collating press reports of the surprisingly sparse raids made in Pa. and N.J. during 1763 with the accounts of the staggering refugee movements that they set off (everywhere outside the southeasternmost halves of Bucks, Philadelphia, and Chester counties, where there were no evacuations). The figures of 50 miles and 25–30 miles are impressions based on many accounts (the former's being, e.g., the distance between Ft. Bedford and Shippensburg in July 1763, or between Penn's Creek and Tulpehocken in Oct. 1755; the latter's being the distance between Carlisle and the attacks the same month on Tuscarora Creek; *Pa. Gazette*, July 28, 1763).

63. William Parsons to Richard Peters, Oct. 31, 1755, *Pa. Arch.* 1:2:444; Hugh Mercer to James Burd, July 10, 1757, Shippen Family Papers; William Trent to Peters, Feb. 15, 1756, *Pa. Arch.* 1:2:575; Parsons to Peters, Oct. 31, 1755, *Pa. Arch.* 1:2:444; *Pa. Journal*, Nov. 6, 1755, p. 2 (original all in italics); Franklin to Gov. Morris, Jan. 14, 1756, *Franklin Papers* 6:357; Arthur St. Clair to Gov. John Penn, June 12, 1774, *Pa. Arch.* 1:4:514.

64. George Stevenson to Rev. William Smith, Nov. 5, 1755, *Pa. Arch.* 1:2:466; *Pa. Gazette*, July 28, 1763, p. 3; Bartram Galbraith to George Bryan, July 14, 1778, *Pa. Arch.* 1:6:642; Pres. Joseph Reed to Gen. John Armstrong, Dec. 4, 1780, *Pa. Arch.* 1:8:636. Selfish herds were introduced by W. D. Hamilton in "Geometry for the Selfish Herd," *Journal of Theoretical Biology* 31 (1971): 295–311.

65. Franklin to Morris, Jan. 14, 1756, *Franklin Papers* 6:357; *Pa. Gazette*, July 28, 1763, p. 3; dep. of Conrad Reiff, Nov. 1, 1763, *Morav. Recs.* 124:6; *Pa. Gazette*, July 28, 1763, p. 3; Hugh Mercer to James Burd, July 10, 1757, Shippen Family Papers.

Chapter 3
WOUNDS CRYING FOR VENGEANCE

1. *Pa. Packet*, Jan. 17, 1782 (dispatches from Poughkeepsie, N.Y., Dec. 31, 1781), p. 3.

2. For the sovereign people, see chap. 7 below and, in general, Edmund S. Morgan's *Inventing the People: The Rise of Popular Sovereignty in England and America* (New York, 1988), esp. chaps. 3 and 11; and—for "the people" in revolutionary Pa., whose 1776 constitution's unicameral and radically unmixed "approach to simplicity," trumpeted by Paine though loathed by moderates, put it at the heart of debates over ordinary people's political potential—Gordon S. Wood, *The Creation of the American Republic, 1776–1787* (Chapel Hill, N.C., 1969), pp. 333–39 (quotation from Benjamin Rush, *Observations upon the Present Government of Pennsylvania, in Four Letters to the People . . .* [Philadelphia, 1777], p. 7).

3. Charles to Mary Pemberton (his mother), 8th mo. 24, 1762, Pemberton Papers; journal of Frederick Post at Lancaster treaty, 1762, *Pa. Arch.* 1:4:98; for taunting, see chap. 5 below, Friendly Assoc. Minutes (soft), Oct. 26, 1756, p. 20n, and Friendly Assoc. Minutes (hard), Nov. 10, 1756. For treaties as human occasions, see Merrell, *Into the American Woods*, chap. 7.

4. Israel Pemberton to Dr. John Fothergill, 5th mo. 30, 1757, Etting-Pemberton Papers 29:23 (township name from proprietary minutes: May 18, 1757, *Pa. Col. Recs.* 7:538).

5. [Adam] Hoops to Gov. Robert Hunter Morris, Nov. 6, 1755, *Pa. Arch.* 1:2:474–75, and "Memorial from Inhabitants of Northampton Co.," Sept. 1, 1763, ibid. 1:4:120.

6. *Pa. Journal,* Sept. 5, 1754, pp. 2–3.

7. Ibid., Dec. 18, 1755, p. 2, and Reynell to James Shirley, Dec. 16, 1755, John Reynell Letterbook, 1754–56, H.S.P. Interviewed in old age, the Philadelphian Thomas Bradford reminisced about seeing this body display as a boy of about six: "I saw . . . in the State house yard the Corps of a German Man, woman & their Son (about 20) who were all Killed & Scalped by the Indians in Shearmans Valley . . . —the People there . . . hired a Man to put these bodies in a waggon & bring them to the city & to place them thus before the eyes of the People" (Annals 1:48).

8. [Smith], *A Brief View of the Conduct of Pennsylvania . . .* (London, 1756), p. 88 (for this pamphlet, see chap. 7 below). For Gov. Morris's and the assembly's accounts of this encounter, see Morris to Thomas Penn, Nov. 28, 1755, *Franklin Papers* 6:279–84, and *Votes* 4:524 (Nov. 26, 1755); see also Arthur D. Graeff, *The Relations between the Pennsylvania Germans and the British Authorities, 1750–1776* (Norristown, Pa., 1939), chap 7.

9. *Wöch. Phila. Staatsbote,* June 6, 1763, p. 2 ("Wir hören alle stunden von Scalpen"), and *Pa. Gazette,* July 28, 1763, p. 3 (innumerable newspaper articles referred in this way to seeing someone killed, but managing nonetheless to "sav[e] his Scalp"; ibid., July 14, 1757, p. 3). Europeans were not alone in placing such stress on scalping's avoidance: after battles, fallen Delawares were whenever possible carefully concealed, exactly "so that the enemy may not get their scalps" (Heckewelder, *Indian Nations,* p. 276; cf. David Zeisberger's manuscript "History of the North American Indians" [ca. 1780], ed. and trans. Archer Butler Hulbert and William Nathaniel Schwarze, *Ohio Archaeological and Historical Society Publications* 19 [1910]: 104).

10. *Pa. Journal,* Jan. 8, 1756, p. 2.

11. *Pa. Mercury,* Sept. 29, 1775, p. 2.

12. I have most in mind the case of Friedrich Stump (see chap. 5 below), who in Jan. 1768 suddenly stove in the heads, scalped, and hacked away at the bodies of ten Indians who had been staying near him at Middle Creek, off the upper Susquehanna, then incinerated some of their bodies in a cabin. Even if Stump's behavior verged on the psychopathic, the analogic aspect to such anti-Indian acts was perhaps the most important key to their reception. For their defenders, the things that Europeans like Stump and the first two sets of Paxton rioters (discussed in chap. 6 below) did to Indians hardly existed as isolated acts: instead, they formed a mental counterpoint, as retaliations or preemptions, to images of what Indians themselves might do. This logic made almost any action into a reaction. Many mutilations—above all, scalping—in fact neared the status of rituals, with meanings (esp. something like *since this is what Indians do, this is*

what they deserve) packed into every wound: see Natalie Zemon Davis, *Society and Culture in Early Modern France* (Stanford, Calif., 1975), chap. 6, esp. pp. 156–57, 164, 167–68, 179. Early photographs of scalping victims (like William S. Soule's "Morrison, A Wolf Hunter, Killed near Ft. Dodge, 1868," Photographs of Soldiers, Cheyenne, Apache, and Arapaho Indians in Indian Territory, Beinecke Library, Yale University) offer a starting point for understanding how body displays might have looked. As Soule's photograph suggests, the scalping wound—like a horrible, bloody cap pulled down low and tight across the victim's forehead—very much told a story. It would have been hard to look at without thinking uncomfortably of the specific way the scalped person died. (The visual sign of a red hemisphere atop the head plainly made a lasting impression on Indian observers, too: Maj. Robert Rogers told, e.g., of seeing young Indian men painted for war with their bald heads carefully smeared all in red down to the ears; Rogers, *A Concise Account of North America . . .* [London, 1765], p. 227.) For scalping's basic techniques, see James Axtell, "The Unkindest Cut, or Who Invented Scalping?" in *The European and the Indian: Essays in the Ethnohistory of Colonial North America* [New York, 1981], pp. 16–35.

13. *Pa. Journal,* Dec. 25, 1755, p. 3.

14. Historical preamble (ca. 1758) to Friendly Assoc. Minutes (hard). As the Pa. assembly observed, the pages of mid-Atlantic newspapers were soon "filled with continual Accounts of the bleeding and distressed Situation of our Frontiers"; Isaac Norris and Pa. assembly to Gov. William Denny, Sept. 30, 1757, *Votes* 4:751.

15. Orndt, "A List of the Peoble which where Killed and Takin Presoners by the Indians from Lichy River and Eastwards," Dec. 16, 1757, transcriptions folder, Northampton-Bethlehem Papers; *Pa. Journal,* Dec. 18, 1755, p. 2; and *Pa. Gazette,* Aug. 4, 1757, p. 3. Printing body lists was an old rhetorical tactic, dating back to the early 17th century in colonies (like Va.) that had already undergone Indian war; see, e.g., back matter to Edward Waterhouse's appeal, *A Declaration of the State of the Colony and Affaires in Virginia . . .* (London, 1622).

16. *Pa. Journal,* Feb. 5, 1756, p. 2.

17. *Copy of a Letter from Charles Read, Esq. . . . ,* 3rd ed. (Philadelphia, 1764), pp. 3–4; *Pa. Gazette,* Aug. 18, 1757, p. 3 (the eastern Delaware leader Teedyuscung attended the inquest and concurred in this verdict). Some descriptive passages were especially long-lived and influential, turning up in quotations, summaries, and allusions, for years to come (see esp. Capt. Asher Clayton's 1763 burial expedition to the Wyoming Valley, *Pa. Gazette,* Oct. 27, 1763, p. 3).

18. *Pa. Journal,* Aug. 21, 1755, p. 1; *Pa. Gazette,* Oct. 13, 1763, p. 2; *Pa. Journal,* Feb. 5, 1756, p. 2; ibid., Dec. 18, 1755, p. 2.

19. *Pa. Journal,* Dec. 25, 1755, p. 2 (the second "wounds" is probably a printer's error for "mouths"); *Pa. Gazette,* July 21, 1763, p. 2.

20. Harris to Conrad Weiser, June 30, 1755, *Pa. Col. Recs.* 6:456; *Pa. Gazette,* July 21, 1763, pp. 3 and 2.

21. William Parsons to Conrad Weiser, Oct. 31, 1755, Lancaster Co. Papers; *Pa. Journal,* Aug. 28, 1755, p. 1. The logic that could underlie invocations of legitimating feeling is thoughtfully unpacked in Nicole E. Eustace, "'Passion Is the Gale': Emotion and Power

on the Eve of the American Revolution" (Ph.D. diss., Univ. of Pennsylvania, 2001), chap. 4.

22. Shippen to Charles Thomson, Apr. 2, 1755, Joseph Shippen Letterbook (H.S.P).

23. A succession of critics has charted the steadily rising stock of sincerity and passion over the 18th century, in a complex of cultural developments that laid the basis for the Romantic movement. Of infinite references, see John Mullan, *Sentiment and Sociability: The Language of Feeling in the Eighteenth Century* (Oxford, 1988), and Marshall Brown, *Preromanticism* (Stanford, Calif., 1991). The literature of sensibility grew more luridly psychological as sublime discourse contracted from the sublime of the beautiful and the grand to the pathetic—a movement away from the expression of moral emotions (esp. "greatness of soul," or the natural world's vastness or wildness) toward pure sentiment, esp. the pain of individuals and love or sorrow within the family. The discourse on the sublime was, in short, shifting (in Peter de Bolla's phrase) from "an ethico-aesthetic enquiry into a psychology of the individual" at about the time the mid-Atlantic's scenes of Indian war became available for rewriting (*The Discourse of the Sublime: Readings in History, Aesthetics, and the Subject* [Oxford, 1989], p. 42).

24. Despite obvious continuities in subject matter, this anti-Indian writing of the 18th century differed sharply from that of other regions, exposed earlier to Indian war, in the 17th (for which see, e.g., Mary Rowlandson, *The Soveraignty & Goodness of God* . . . , 2nd ed. [Cambridge, Mass., 1682], the greatest captivity narrative of King Philip's War in New England). The 17th-century New England school had been deeply concerned with the differences between the material and esp. the spiritual circumstances of Indians and English—rendering attacks as simulacra of hell, Indian raiders as "atheisticall . . . diabolicall" anti-Christians, and making narratives be at bottom about "the Lords doings . . . and dealings" with his people (ibid., preface, p. [4]; and subtitle). Authors using the anti-Indian sublime, by contrast, bent their efforts toward manipulating, not spiritual feelings, but emotions of the heart; the grand lessons they pointed were far likelier to be political than divine; and they showed greater sophistication (at least by the new tastes of their era) about how to stage the shocking images of Indian assault— and, in particular, how to script the supposedly artless interruptions of overpowering emotion by the narrator in response to those images that taught readers what to make of them. Stylistically the anti-Indian writing of midcentury in fact came closest to prefiguring the Gothicized crime narratives of Federal and Victorian America (for which see Karen Halttunen, *Murder Most Foul: The Killer and the American Gothic Imagination* [Cambridge, Mass., 1998], chap. 3).

25. John Elder to Gov. James Hamilton, Oct. 25, 1763, Pa. Arch. 1:4:127. The idea that pools of innocent blood cried out for vengeance was brought up endlessly, plainly drawing on God's dressing-down of Cain in Gen. 4:10; for *compositio loci*, see Louis L. Martz's *Poetry of Meditation: A Study in English Religious Literature of the Seventeenth Century*, rev. ed. (New Haven, Conn., 1962).

26. As Edmund Burke theorized, certain mannerisms and ready-made word sets—the "modes of speech that mark a strong and lively feeling"—were at least as important in

prose that hoped to awaken emotion as the things that were actually said (*A Philosophical Enquiry into the Origin of Our Ideas of the Sublime and Beautiful,* 2nd ed. [London, 1759], pt. 5, §7, pp. 339–40).

27. Ibid., pt. 1, §7, p. 58, and §14, pp. 72–74; and pt. 1, §7, p. 74. As he concluded, "terror is in all cases whatsoever, either more openly or latently the ruling principle of the sublime" (pt. 2, §2, p. 97). This idea's artistic implications were obvious: it should be possible to induce terror and delight, as a chain of novelists after Horace Walpole's *Castle of Otranto* (1765) tried to do, by describing "the real misfortunes and pains of others"—along with a long list of other, vaguely dangerous things first enumerated in Burke's *Enquiry,* including darkness, "The cries of Animals," nasty smells, and loud noises (ibid., table of contents). Shippen, for one, was well versed in these ideas: writing to his relations about a trip to the Indian town of Aughwick, he noted that "a Description of the Road from the inhabited Part of the Country to that Place . . . would appear like a romantick Scene, & excite in you an Idea of Horror" (Shippen to William Shippen Jr., Jan. 13, 1755, Joseph Shippen Letterbook [H.S.P.]). Reading over the bloodstained corpses, savage rites, lonely settings, and dismembered families and romantic units in a good Gothic novel—like Matthew Lewis's *The Monk* (1797)—alongside those in this period's anti-Indian prose makes their connections clear; for the Gothic, see esp. E. J. Clery's *Rise of Supernatural Fiction, 1762–1800* (Cambridge, 1995).

28. *Pa. Journal,* Aug. 28, 1755, p. 1; Weiser et al. to Gov. Morris, rec. Nov. 24, 1755, *Pa. Arch.* 1:2:511–12. The Indian superintendent Sir William Johnson speculated that Indian observers were especially upset when families, as opposed to single men, squatted on debatable lands, for "Familes . . . [they] know[,] will encrease . . . when once a beginning is made" (to Gen. Thomas Gage, Apr. 5, 1766, *Johnson Papers* 5:145). In this sense, by attacking or capturing women and children, raiders deliberately undercut the basis of European expansion. For women and children in the laws of war, see chap. 2 above.

29. Reid to Col. Henry Bouquet, July 26, 1764, *Bouquet Papers* 21650:2:45; George Cockings, *War: An Heroic Poem . . .* , [2nd ed.] (Portsmouth, N.H., 1762; orig. pub. London, 1760), bk. 3, p. 14, col. 1. Otherwise, because it was a hybrid creature—part corpses, part poignancy—the anti-Indian sublime's physical and familial halves were in some tension. Theorists would later decide that bloody imagery by itself was only horrible, lacking the fine touch that set heartstrings atremble: overpowering and "entirely fill[ing]" minds with inward-turning terror, it was not about sympathy but about shock. (Could one even "chang[e] places in fancy"—the basis for all sympathy, for Adam Smith—with a corpse?) Gruesomeness could be made less stunning by dwelling on other people's responses to mutilation (as with the reactions of body buriers, or of narrators themselves, whose exclamations over their inability to describe such sights made them key characters in their own texts); Burke, *Philosophical Enquiry,* pt. 2, §2, p. 96; Smith, *The Theory of Moral Sentiments,* 2nd ed. (London, 1761), pt. 1, §1, chap. 1, p. 3 (and pp. 8–10). By the 1770s, writers of the rising generation felt one might otherwise be "less moved at the description of an Indian tortured . . . than with the fatal mistake of the lover in the Spectator, who pierced an artery in the arm of his mistress"; John and Anna Laetitia Aikin (later Barbauld), "An Enquiry into Those Kinds of Distress Which Excite

Agreeable Sensations," in *Miscellaneous Pieces, in Prose* (Belfast, 1774; orig. pub. London, 1773), p. 96.

30. [Smith], *Brief View of the Conduct of Pennsylvania,* p. 56.

31. Franklin, *Narrative of the Late Massacres . . .* (Philadelphia, 1764), pp. 6 and 27 (see chap. 7 below for discussion).

32. John Bartram to J. Eliot, Feb. 12, 1753 (*sic;* on internal evidence this badly misdated letter should be assigned to late July 1755), and to Peter Collinson, Feb. 21, 1756, Bartram Papers, vol. 1, sect. 1, pp. 34 and 44, H.S.P. For a different discussion of the second letter (within a broader account of Bartram, illustrated by these letters, as a committed Indian-hater, with which I would cautiously disagree), see Thomas P. Slaughter, *The Natures of John and William Bartram* (New York, 1996), p. 24.

33. Hopkinson, "The Treaty: A Poem," in *The Miscellaneous Essays and Occasional Writings . . .* , 3 vols. (Philadelphia, 1792), 3:121–22 and 124.

34. Davies, "[Frontier Warfare]" and "Verses on Gen. Braddock's Defeat," in *Collected Poems,* ed. Richard Beale Davis (Gainesville, Fla., 1968), pp. 170–71 and 219. The debt Davies owed to the gorier parts of Pope's translations of Homer (see Davies, *Miscellaneous Poems . . .* [Williamsburg, Va., 1751], p. vi) was obvious, as was a connection to his religious verse. There, too, Davies was given to inviting readers to form horrific pictures of bleeding corpses, although they represented the victims of sin, or the dying Jesus, instead of farm families (Davies, "Early Piety recommended . . . ," in *Miscellaneous Poems,* pp. 7–8; and see esp. "The universal Lamentation," pp. 31–39). In its overpourings of emotion, the anti-Indian sublime had clear affinities with the urgent tone of revival rhetoric, a kinship with which not all writers were as much at ease as Davies: the Anglican William Smith struggled to distinguish the "noble, manly, and rational Enthusiasm" one should feel at Indian attacks from the lowlier enthusiasm behind revivals; Smith, "The Christian Soldier's Duty . . ." (1757), *Discourses on Public Occasions in America,* 2nd ed. (London, 1760), p. 92.

35. Silverman, *Cultural History,* p. 238. Though his play was performed in Philadelphia, Cockings himself was a Boston customs man who seems to have written the *Conquest* while in Newfoundland (though, following a curt and hostile entry in the *Dictionary of National Biography,* Silverman calls Cockings English [p. 237]; his works were self-published in London before being reprinted here, but bibliographers usually list him as an American author).

36. Cockings, *War: An Heroic Poem . . .* , [2nd ed.] (Portsmouth, N.H., 1762; orig. pub. London, 1760), bk. 3, p. 14, col. 1. Cockings ratcheted the emotional tone equally high in his overstuffed footnotes, one of which swerved unstoppably into the most frothy-mouthed invective: at the surrender of Ft. William Henry in 1757, Cockings explained, French-allied Indians fell on the capitulating regulars "with their wives and children, and began to knock down, strip, and butcher, men, women, and children, promiscuously! . . . glut[ting] themselves, in plundering, scalping, ripping womens bodies, and dashing children['s] brains out!" (ibid., bk. 3, p. 14n, col. 2; original all in italics—or anyway, "if all this was not done there," he ended by conceding lamely, "it was done at other places several times").

37. Ibid., bk. 6, p. 26n, col. 1 (original all in italics); Cockings, *The Conquest of Canada*

... (Albany, N.Y., 1773; orig. pub. London, 1766), act 4, scene ii, p. 46; *War*, bk. 6, p. 25n, col. 2 (original all in italics).

38. Jackson, ode in "An Exercise . . . on Occasion of the Peace" (1763), in Nathaniel Evans, *Poems on Several Occasions . . .* , ed. William Smith (Philadelphia, 1772), p. 79; and Godfrey, "Epistle to a Friend; from Fort Henry," in *Juvenile Poems . . .* (Philadelphia, 1765), pp. 20n and 21.

39. Ernst H. Kantorowicz, *The King's Two Bodies: A Study in Mediaeval Political Theology* (Princeton, N.J., 1957), pp. 419–37, at p. 429; and Ralph E. Giesey, *Royal Funeral Ceremony in Renaissance France* (Geneva, 1960). The English used them, too; hence a 1612 funeral effigy for Charles I's older brother had posable limbs that "moved to sundry actions" (Nigel Llewellyn, *The Art of Death: Visual Culture in the English Death Ritual, c. 1500–c. 1800* [London, 1991], p. 55). This idea pervaded English law into the 18th century: as Pa.'s assembly declared in an argument over taxation, the monarch (and, by analogy, whichever Penn was proprietor of the colony) "has two Bodies, of which the one is a Body natural, consisting of natural Members, as every other Man is; the other is a Body politic, and his Members thereof are his Subjects" (assembly to Gov. Morris, Aug. 19, 1755, *Votes* 4:445).

40. Burd, "A Proposition for the better securing . . . Pennsylvania from the Inroads of the Indians," *Pa. Arch.* 1:3:103; and Henry R. Schoolcraft, *Notes on the Iroquois . . .* (New York, 1846), p. 29, as quoted in Richter, *Ordeal of the Longhouse*, p. 66. What happened in the middle colonies—a community's showing off the damaged bodies of its own members—was unlike nearly every other instance of early modern European corpse display. It was infinitely more common to show off the mutilated bodies of a community's enemies than of the people themselves (Roy Porter, *Bodies Politic: Disease, Death, and Doctors in Britain, 1650–1900* [Ithaca, N.Y., 2001], pp. 47–49; Davis, *Society and Culture in Early Modern France*, p. 179; Edward Muir, *Mad Blood Stirring: Vendetta and Factions in Friuli during the Renaissance* [Baltimore, Md., 1993], chap. 4, and *Ritual in Early Modern Europe* [Cambridge, 1997], pp. 106–8). The exception was a few British antidissection riots, which also used the carting around of mutilated cadavers to rally an outraged sense of victimization and betrayal, depicting the dissection as "a crime against the whole community, demanding public retribution" (Ruth Richardson, *Death, Dissection, and the Destitute* [London, 1987], pp. 91–92; and cf. esp. p. 228). Philadelphia's only anatomist, Dr. William Shippen Jr.—who published denials of "taking up [any] Bodies from . . . the burying Ground belonging to any Denomination of Christians whatever" (*Pa. Chronicle*, Jan. 8, 1769, pp, 410–11)—seems, by cutting up criminals' corpses, to have avoided more than minor troubles.

41. Pemberton to Sir Charles Hardy, 4th mo. 26, 1756, Friendly Assoc. Minutes (hard), f. 8v; petition of William Moore to Gov. Denny, Oct. 19, 1757, *Pa. Gazette*, Dec. 1, 1757.

42. *OED*, s.v. "bleeding" sense 2a. The corpse-carrying processions of colonial Pa. served a purpose exactly analogous to that of the radicalizing "funerals for liberty" held in Philadelphia and many other cities in the Stamp Act crisis and Revolution. Always focused on the effigy or coffin of a murdered American Liberty, in these marches columns of mourners bore Liberty's body through public places to climaxes that could include effigy-burning, grief-stricken eulogies, and the political body's burial in the

ground (though sometimes at the last moment Liberty revived). See Philip Davidson, *Propaganda and the American Revolution, 1763–1783* (Chapel Hill, N.C., 1941; reprinted New York, 1973), pp. 176–77, esp. n. 9; Edmund S. Morgan and Helen M. Morgan, *The Stamp Act Crisis: Prologue to Revolution,* new rev. ed. (New York, 1963), pp. 247–48, 257–58; and Peter Shaw, *American Patriots and the Rituals of Revolution* (Cambridge, Mass., 1981), pp. 180–82. For pre-revolutionary effigies embodying the public's enemies instead of the public itself, see ibid., pp. 177–80, 184–85, and 215–22, and Robert Blair St. George, *Conversing by Signs: Poetics of Implication in Colonial New England Culture* (Chapel Hill, N.C., 1998), pp. 250–62.

43. For related thoughts on revolutionary self-images (seeing an iconographic role esp. for dismembered female bodies), see Nancy Isenberg, "Death and Satire: Dismembering the Body Politic," in *Mortal Remains: Death in Early America,* ed. Isenberg and Andrew Burstein (Philadelphia, 2003), chap. 4.

Chapter 4

THE SEVEN YEARS' WAR
AND THE WHITE PEOPLE

1. *Pa. Arch.* 1:3:230; *Pa. Gazette,* Jan. 29, 1756, p. 2. The crackle of several guns going off in succession was so closely associated with attack that it could reliably set off panics; at Goshen, N.Y., in Aug. 1763, e.g., men out hunting flushed some partridges, "at which 4 Guns were discharged, three of them pretty quick after each other; this being an uncommon Accident . . . was mistaken by some of the Inhabitants . . . for the firing of Indians.— . . . which produced an amazing Pannick and Confusion among the People, near 500 Families; some for Haste cut the Harness of their Horses from their Plows and Carts, and rode off with what they were most concerned to preserve—Some who had no Vessels to cross the River, plunged thro', carrying their Wives and Children on their Backs; some, we have already heard, proceeded as far as New-England, spreading the Alarm as they went, and how far they may go is uncertain" (*N.Y. Mercury,* Aug. 22, 1763, p. 3). In the first autumn of attacks, James Wright wrote of how he "saw the whole Country so full of Smoke that we can scarce breathe in it (which we can Attribute to Nothing but the Number of Houses Barns and Grain that are burning as we cannot learn the Woods are anywhere on Fire)"; Wright to unspecified, Nov. 6, 1755, Du Simitière Papers Yi–966, L.C.P. (now held at H.S.P.), as cited in Anthony F. C. Wallace, *King of the Delawares: Teedyuscung, 1700–1763* (Philadelphia, 1949), p. 72.

2. William Parsons to Richard Peters, Oct. 31, 1755 (describing events of Oct. 27), *Pa. Arch.* 1:2:443. Such useless marching and shooting was, Parsons added, also "the Case with almost all the others, being about 500 in different parts of the Neighbourhood" (ibid., pp. 443–44). Firing off guns to celebrate when summiting peaks may have been an 18th-century habit (as when Rev. Thomas Barton and an officer on the 1758 expedition against Ft. Duquesne climbed "a very high Mountain": "We reach'd the Summit

with much Difficulty," Barton noted. "—A very extensive Prospect opens to our View . . . —We fir'd each of us a Gun, & then return'd"; Barton Diary, Aug. 30, 1758).

3. In fall 1763, e.g., when an attack struck Craig's Settlement, in Northampton Co., Pa., a "Company of Gentlemen" at once crossed the river to Bethlehem and not only "vehemently laid the Charge of the Murders committed, to the Bethlehem Indians"—pacifist Christian converts living in a tightly controlled commune—but "insinuated too," by modern expectations much more surprisingly, "as if the Bethlehem [European] People had likewise a Hand in it" (dep. of Conrad Reiff, Nov. 1, 1763, *Morav. Recs.* 124:6:12). Cf. Kai Erikson's application of the idea of the traumatic worldview (see *A New Species of Trouble: Explorations in Disaster, Trauma, and Community* [New York, 1994], esp. pp. 226–42) to the Yugoslav civil wars: attacks seen as abetted by people "within one's own surround"—"especially when those other people had been considered . . . members of the same general community"—had extraordinary effects on the subjects' trust in most human institutions, and esp. their readiness to denounce internal "betrayers" ("War Comes to Western Slavonia: Voices from Pakrac," faculty seminar paper, Princeton Univ., Mar. 24, 2000, p. 22).

4. Weiser to Gov. Robert Hunter Morris, Nov. 19, 1755, Weiser Correspondence 1:34; see also Weiser, Emanuel Carpenter, and Adam Simon Ruhm to Gov. Morris, ca. Nov. 24, 1755, *Pa. Arch.* 1:2:511.

5. The specter of an Indian-Catholic axis had by itself been enough to help touch off multiple revolts in 17th-century Maryland; see Lois Green Carr and David William Jordan, *Maryland's Revolution of Government, 1689–1692* (Ithaca, N.Y., 1974).

6. "Extracts from the Diary of Daniel Fisher, 1755," ed. Mrs. Conway Robinson Howard, *PMHB* 17 (1893): 274; John Potts to Conrad Weiser, July 22, 1755, Weiser Correspondence; Henry Harvey et al. to Gov. Morris, July 23, 1755, *Pa. Col. Recs.* 6:503; and reward notice, *Pa. Gazette,* Dec. 25, 1760, reprinted in Edgar A. Musser, "Old St. Mary's of Lancaster, Pa.: The Jesuit Period, 1741–1785," *Journal of the Lancaster Historical Society* 71 (1967): 121. The Pa. militia act of 1757 duly provided for the seizure of any "Military Accoutrements" found in the possession of "all Papists, and reputed Papists" (*Pa. Arch.* 1:3:131, 121). See also Joseph J. Casino, "Anti-Popery in Colonial Pennsylvania," *PMHB* 105 (1981): 279–309.

7. Biddle to James Biddle, Nov. 16, 1755, *Pa. Col. Recs.* 6:705 (the expresses had brought detailed, imaginary accounts of large-scale fighting with Indians 15 miles from the city).

8. James Read et al. to Gov. Morris, Oct. 31, 1755, Horsfield Papers 1:33.

9. [Pemberton], prefatory remarks, Friendly Assoc. Minutes (hard), fol. 1r.

10. Rules (1749), in Minutes of the St. Andrews Society, A.P.S.; and *Die Regeln der Teutschen Gesellschaft . . .* (Germantown, 1766), p. [2]. See *Constitution and Rules of the St. Andrew's Society . . .* (Philadelphia, 1769); *Die erste Frucht der Teutschen Gesellschaft . . .* (Germantown, 1765); Records of the Corporation for Relief (Presbyterian Ministers' Fund), Presbyterian Historical Society, Philadelphia; William Smith, *Some Account of the Charitable Corporation . . .* , 2nd ed. (Philadelphia, 1770); Society of the Friendly Sons of St. Patrick Papers, 1771–97, H.S.P.; *Rules and Constitutions of the Society of the Sons of St. George* (Philadelphia, 1772); and Carl and Jessica Bridenbaugh, *Rebels and Gentlemen: Philadelphia in the Age of Franklin,* 2nd ed. (New York, 1961), pp. 236–43.

11. *Mühlenberg Journals* 1:676 and 2:36; Minutes of the St. Andrew's Society, Nov. 21, 1753 (expansion of definition) and passim. Despite its specialized name, the Presbyterian Ministers' Fund, in particular, became an all-purpose vehicle for backcountry relief.

12. Christoph Saur to Israel Pemberton, 4th mo. 25, 1756, Friendly Assoc. Papers (Haverford) 1:127.

13. Articles of the New-Jersey Association for Helping the Indians, Apr. 16, 1767, Allinson Papers, p. 2.

14. Annals 1:57. For Pemberton's composition draft, see Friendly Assoc. Papers (Haverford) 1:64–65; quotations from "Conference held in the House of Israel Pemberton between Frds. and Several Indian Chiefs . . . ," Pemberton Papers (Swarthmore), later edited as *Several Conferences between Some of the Principal People amongst the Quakers in Pennsylvania, and . . . the Six Indian Nations . . .* (Newcastle-upon-Tyne, 1756).

15. "Conference . . . in the House of Israel Pemberton," fols. 6v ("all true Quakers") and 4r ("we shall now Arise"); fols. 4v–5r.

16. Thomas and Richard Penn to Friendly Assoc., Sept. 5, 1760, Friendly Assoc. Papers (Haverford) 4:15; e.g. Frederick Post to Pemberton, May 20, 1763, ibid. 3:521.

17. "Journal of James Kenny, 1761–1763," *PMHB* 37 (1913): 165, 13, and 169; Kenny to Pemberton, 6th mo. 19, 1759 (during an earlier stay near Ft. Pitt, for the Friendly Assoc.; his later stay was sponsored by the assembly), Friendly Assoc. Papers (Haverford).

18. *A Journal of the Life . . .* , in *Works* (Philadelphia, 1774), chap. 8, pp. 154, 163, 162, 154–55, 152, and 164. Woolman wrote happily that the town's leader said, of one of his messages given without translation in the shared tongue of the spirit, "in substance . . . 'I love to feel where words come from'" (p. 163; see Edward C. Gray, *New World Babel: Languages and Nations in Early America* [Princeton, N.J., 1999], pp. 53–54, for early New Englanders' similar faith in untranslated prayer). Anthony Benezet went still further afield for spiritual instruction, admiring the "divine reason & strength contained in Confusius's maxims" and looking forward to seeing the Chinese sage in heaven (to George Dillwyn, 9th mo. [1783], Benezet Papers). By comparison, even a sometime Moravian missionary like the go-between Christian Frederick Post was much less sanguine about the spiritual condition of Indians in the woods, decrying their "l[o]st condessions . . . whan one come in thear contry, wear the Devell has his sea[t] amongst them . . . it is som wad worser then to go in hoeal" (to Pemberton, Aug. 8, 1761, Friendly Assoc. Papers [Haverford] 4:187).

19. Christian Frederick Post to Israel Pemberton, May 20, 1760, and Gov. James Hamilton to Papunhang and Wyalusing Indians, Oct. 12, 1761, Friendly Assoc. Papers (Haverford) 3:521 and 4:233; for baptismal date (in 1763), Loskiel, *History*, pt. 2, chap. 15, p. 206. Had Woolman gotten to Wyalusing just a month earlier, before David Zeisberger's first visit—after the Moravian bustled there on "report[s] of a remarkable awakening in those parts" among the Indians—it might have led to Quakers' first successful missionization of native peoples (see Loskiel, *History,* pt. 2, chap. 15, pp. 203, 205–6; and for Zeisberger's speeding past Woolman on the path, Woolman, *Journal,* p. 152). The postdating of Papunhang's baptism to 1760 in his Moravian biography seems to be a scribal error; *Lebenslauf* of Papunhang, May 14, 1775, *Morav. Recs.* 141:6, as printed in Merritt, *At the Crossroads,* appendix A, p. 318. In fall 1760, Papunhang was still discussing the

Bible and Christianity as an interested outsider (Nathaniel Holland to Israel Pemberton, 10th mo. 16, 1760, Friendly Assoc. Papers [Haverford] 4:43).

20. Christian Frederick Post to Israel Pemberton, May 20, 1760, Friendly Assoc. Papers (Haverford) 3:521; *An Account of a Visit Lately Made to the People Called Quakers in Philadelphia, by Papoonahoal, an Indian Chief* . . . (London, 1761), p. 3; Pemberton to Benjamin Hersey et al., 1st mo. 14, 1761, Friendly Assoc. Papers (Haverford) 4:263; *Lebenslauf* of Papunhang, Merritt, *At the Crossroads,* p. 317; "Some Remarks made by a Person who accompanied Papunahoal and the other Indians from Philadelphia on their Way home as far as Bethlehem," n.d., Indian Affairs Papers.

21. Israel to Mary Pemberton, 8th mo. 4, 1761, Friendly Assoc. Papers (Haverford) 4:153; Pemberton et al., "Report of the Trustees of the Friendly Association who Attended the Indian Treaty at Easton," 8th mo. 12, 1761, ibid. 4:139; Israel to Mary Pemberton, 8th mo. 7, 1761, ibid. 4:163.

22. Christian Shultze to Israel Pemberton, Aug. 29, 1760, Friendly Assoc. Papers (Haverford) 4:11 (for same information sent to Lancaster Co. Mennonites, see Pemberton to Benjamin Hersey et al., 1st mo. 14, 1761, ibid. 4:263); Papunhang and Job Chilloway (by David Owens) to Pemberton, Sept. 15, 1761, ibid. 4:191; "Substance of . . . Conversation with Paponahoal," Pemberton Papers 13:23. Shultze wrote back later to note his thrill at getting a copy of Papunhang's remarks, which he had translated into German and redistributed (to Pemberton, Dec. 1, 1760, Friendly Assoc. Papers [Haverford] 4:59).

23. Pemberton (by Robert White) to Tonquakena, 10th mo. 31, 1761, ibid. 4:56; Anthony Benezet to George Dillwyn, 9th mo. [1783], Benezet Papers.

24. [Pemberton], "Minutes of the Proceedings of the People called Quakers . . . ," Nov. 10, 1756, Friendly Assoc. Minutes (hard), fol. 18v (a section most of which was wisely crossed out); Conrad Weiser quoted in [Richard Peters], "Observations on printed Remonstrance of Quakers," 1757, Weiser Correspondence 2:81; "Minutes of the Proceedings of the People called Quakers," Nov. 15, 1756, Friendly Assoc. Minutes (hard), fol. 21r.

25. Benjamin Chew, Diary of the Treaty at Easton, Oct. 8 and 17, 1758, fols. 7v and 17v, H.S.P.; statement of William Peters and Jacob Duché Jr. (fall 1757), *Pa. Arch.* 1:3:274. Quaker-Indian preparations for treaty sessions could go quite far, with full-scale dress rehearsals; see Pemberton et al., "Report of the Trustees," Friendly Assoc. Papers (Haverford) 4:139, and Silver, "Indian-Hating," p. 317.

26. William Logan to James Pemberton, Dec. 12, 1761, Pemberton Papers. The proprietary men's target in "the Quakers" could vary opportunistically between Quaker politicians in the assembly—in a pronounced minority after 1755, when several withdrew—and the Friends reform community outside it. But examining how the assembly spent £100,000 (Pa. currency) levied for war-related expenses, Apr. 1760–Nov. 1763, suggests surprisingly well how a perception arose that more was being spent on Indians than on Europeans. Of £10,000 that did not go directly to military recruiting and supplies, the assembly spent ca. £4,000 on Indians' expenses and ca. £400 on all European captives and refugees' expenses (less than it spent to clean the State House clock). These sums do not include poor relief or religious charities, but neither do they include the large budget of the Friendly Assoc. (accounts, Sept. 22, 1764, *Votes* 5: 369–71).

27. See Samuel Parrish, *Some Chapters in the History of the Friendly Association . . .* (Philadelphia, 1877), and Theodore Thayer, "The Friendly Association," *PMHB* 67 (1943): 356–76; and cf. articles of New-Jersey Association for Helping the Indians, Allinson Papers, pp. 7–8 (Quakers only). For counsel to abandon the association, see Dr. John Fothergill to its trustees, 9th mo. 8, 1760, Friendly Assoc. Papers (Haverford) 4:23.

28. *A Letter from Batista Angeloni . . .* ([Philadelphia], 1764), pp. 7–8. For a manuscript version, differing very slightly, see Shippen Papers 6:115.

29. *Merry Andrew's Almanack . . . for the Year of Our Lord 1762* (Philadelphia, [1761]), observations for June. Of 11 fairs usually listed in Pa. almanacs at mid-century, 4 were in the Lower Counties (modern Del.), and 3 in southern N.J.; the Pa. fairs were at Philadelphia, Chester, Marcus Hook (another Delaware-side town), and Lancaster. The fair mentioned for Reading, Pa., in James W. Lemon, *The Best Poor Man's Country: A Geographical Study of Early Southeastern Pennsylvania* (New York, 1976), chap. 5, seems to be a phantom. For discussion of how an array of other events had probably failed to provide the same experience of coming together in truly diverse crowds—including elections and revival preaching (since preachers with mass drawing power, like George Whitefield and Gilbert Tennent, tended to preach on the most traveled north–south thread of the seaboard and often in places—like Nottingham, Pa., or the Tennent family's own base of Neshaminy—that lay at the heart of the Presbyterian community as well)—see Silver, "Indian-Hating," pp. 175–78.

30. Manuel Gonsales and James Hyndshaw to Anderis Dingman, Aug. 14, 1763, Northampton Co. Papers 2:153; Timothy Horsfield et al. to Northampton Co. inhabitants, Nov. 24, 1755, Horsfield Papers 1:65.

31. George Stevenson et al. to Gov. Morris, Nov. 1, 1755, *Pa. Arch.*, 1:2:448; Franklin to Morris, Jan. 14, 1756, *Franklin Papers* 6:359. A striking want of arms, of which several interior townships in Pa. complained months before any attack, added to the sense of crisis (e.g., petitions from Lurgan, Cumberland Co., Aug. 1, 1755, and Paxton, Derry, and Hanover, July 22, 1754; *Pa. Col. Recs.* 6:533 and 132). Even in Oct. 1763, Col. James Burd encountered this shortage in Northampton, a village "crouded with men, Women, & Children, flying before the Enemy whome they said was within a few miles of the Town killg all before them and burning the houses . . . I Collected the Men of the Town together . . . but found only four Guns in the Town," two of them broken (to William Allen, Jan. 10, 1764, Shippen Family Papers). The exaggerated account of rural gunlessness in Michael A. Bellesiles, *Arming America: The Origins of a National Gun Culture* (New York, 2000), should not discourage further study.

32. Edward Shippen Sr. to William Allen, July 4, 1755, *Pa. Col. Recs.* 6:460; Shippen to Joseph Shippen Jr., July 25, 1763 (and see also same to same, July 21, 1763), Shippen-Shippen Correspondence. For Harris's prediction, see, e.g., Harris to Conrad Weiser, June 30, 1755, ibid., p. 457.

33. Conrad Weiser to Gov. Morris, Oct. 30, 1755, Weiser Correspondence 1:30; Weiser to James Read, Oct. 26, 1755, *Pa. Col. Recs.* 6:651 (when eastern Delawares wanted to stress to Col. James Burd how sincerely on his side they were in late 1757, Burd reported, they used precisely this image: "that they were determined to live & dye with me, &

that we should be put in the same Grave"; Burd, "Continuation of Colonel Burd's Journal . . . ," Oct. 21, 1757, fols. 2r–3r, Shippen Family Papers, James Burd Journals, 1757 and 1758, H.S.P.); for Kurtz, see *Mühlenberg Journals* 1:192, 211, 200, 101, and 173.

34. Conrad Weiser to Gov. Morris, Oct. 30, 1755, *Pa. Col. Recs.* 6:658.

35. William Buchanan to George Croghan, Nov. 2, 1755, Shippen Family Papers; Timothy Horsfield to Gov. Morris, Nov. 27, 1755, Horsfield, Letterbook; *Pa. Journal*, Dec. 4, 1755; Augustus Spangenberg to Horsfield, Dec. 17, 1755, Horsfield Papers 1:97.

36. Weiser to Morris, Oct. 30, 1755, Weiser Correspondence, and to William Allen, Oct. 30, 1755, *Pa. Col. Recs.* 6:660.

37. Edward Shippen Sr. to unknown, Oct. 29, 1755, Horsfield Papers 1:31; and see R. S. Stephenson, "Pennsylvania Provincial Soldiers in the Seven Years' War," *Pa. History* 62 (1995): 196–212.

38. Weiser to James Read, Oct. 26, 1755, *Pa. Col. Recs.* 6:651; unknown writer, July 8, 1758, Indian and Military Affairs MSS, p. 597.

39. [Timothy Horsfield], "Memorandum of an acct. the Indians Nicodemus and Jo Peepe have given . . . ," June 30, 1756, Horsfield Papers 1:145 (Horsfield, consistently writing "white People" as he took down their account, at one point crossed out the phrase in tidying up this draft and corrected it to "English," evidently to make the style sound more standard); speech of Ogagradarisha, Oct. 18, 1756, *Pa. Col. Recs.* 7:299. An investigation by Nancy Shoemaker suggests use of "white" in New England and the middle colonies may have been the result of its propagation northward, with concomitant time lag, from an origin in the cultures of 17th-century southern slavery (*A Strange Likeness: Becoming Red and White in Eighteenth-Century North America* [New York, 2004], chap. 6, esp. pp. 129). But as the appendix below suggests, perhaps because residents of the middle colonies faced different demographic conditions from the less heterogeneous, slavery-filled Southeast, Indian war, not slavery, was demonstrably the main spur to the phrase's popularity there. Even in the mid-Atlantic, the original authorship of the phrase was not necessarily Indian ("white people" does not literally translate the Delaware *shuwánakw,* either a term of abuse—"sour" or "bitter people"; see Heckewelder, *Indian Nations,* pp. 242–43—or a reference to "saltwater people" from over the sea; and cf. Shoemaker, *Strange Likeness,* p. 132). But this in no way affects the point that the starting place for the middle colonies' explosion of interest in talk of "white" people was the language habitually used in Indian contexts, and in Indian diplomatic speech that had been translated into English—sources in which at first "the white people" turned up as an Indian-hand's term of art, much like "the young men" (who were for their part always blamed in treaty discourse for peacetime offenses). In statistical terms, the proportion of news items in the *Pa. Gazette* referring to "white" people that literally took the phrase from Indians' own mouths—by quoting or paraphrasing Indian speech—was 26 percent during the war decade, 1754–64. (In 1760, during a surge in accounts of the Cherokee war, the proportion was 44 percent.)

40. Beatty, *The Journal of a Two Months Tour* [in 1766]; *with a View of Promoting Religion among the Frontier Inhabitants of Pennsylvania* . . . (London, 1768), p. 33n, and Beatty to Rev. John Erskine, Feb. 27, 1768, ibid., pp. 90–91. See, similarly, Georg Hein-

rich Loskiel's footnote in his 1789 history of the Moravian missions, glossing his first use of "the white people": "Thus the Europeans and their descendants are called in America, to distinguish them from the Indians" (Loskiel, *History*, pt. 1, chap. 1, p. 3).

41. As work by James Axtell, esp. "The White Indians of Colonial America," *WMQ* 32 (1975): 55–88, and such studies as John Demos's *Unredeemed Captive: A Family Story from Early America* (New York, 1994) have made familiar. Wholehearted absorption, as opposed to harsh servitude and a lingering sense of cultural difference, may even have been more common for European captives than for Indian ones: see Richter, *Ordeal of the Longhouse*, pp. 73–74.

42. Samuel Stanhope Smith, *Strictures on Lord Kaims's Discourse on the Original Diversity of Mankind* (Philadelphia, 1787), bound together with Smith, *Essay on Variety*, p. 5.

43. Smith, *Essay on Variety*, pp. 60–61; Ruth L. Woodward and Wesley Frank Craven, *Princetonians, 1784–1790* (Princeton, N.J., 1991), pp. 442–52, s.v. "White Eyes, George Morgan"; William Trent, Journal at Ft. Pitt, June 5, 1763, p. 7, H.S.P.; "Reexamination of Garshum Hicks" by Capt. William Grant, Apr. 19, 1764, *Bouquet Papers* 21651:8.

44. See, above all, William G. McLoughlin's brilliant "Note on African Sources of American Indian Creation Myths" (1976) and "Red Indians, Black Slavery, and White Racism: Interracial Tensions among Slaveholding Indians" (1974), in McLoughlin, *The Cherokee Ghost Dance: Essays on the Southeastern Indians, 1789–1861* (Macon, Ga., 1984); and McLoughlin and Walter H. Conser Jr., "'The First Man Was Red'—Cherokee Responses to the Debate over Indian Origins, 1760–1860," *AQ* 41 (1989): 243–64. Whether the pervasiveness of their polygenist thinking made the mid-Atlantic Indians' outlook more racialist than Europeans' own is a vexed question, not least because of the difficulty of squeezing contemporaries' categories into those of the modern notion of race.

45. Kames, *Sketches of the History of Man*, 2nd ed., 4 vols (Edinburgh, 1778; orig. pub. Edinburgh, 1774), "preliminary discourse," 1:76. But just what was one to make of the Mosaic creation account—with the different accounts in its first and second chapters, and its implausible flood? Could it really include America? The intellectual landscape of 16th- and 17th-century Europe was littered with sad reminders of scholars who stumbled over these obstacles, like Giordano Bruno, an exuberant proponent of local creations "in [the] various continents" of different orders of mankind, including Indians; in 1600 he was immolated by the Inquisition. Before his killing, Christopher Marlowe had been charged by a police informer with disbelieving that Genesis could account for Indians' existence; and in the 1650s, the Huguenot Isaac De Peyrère flatly suggested there had been a pre-Adamic creation of all the world's gentiles, including Indians, with Genesis describing only the Hebrews. His book was banned and burned before De Peyrère himself was converted forcibly to Catholicism and made to publish a self-denunciation. Despite his disclaimers, Kames would be widely seen as a skeptic when—relying partly on evidence from Pa. correspondents—he made his book's centerpiece a functional equivalent for Bruno's old heresy. But Kames's muffled, carefully orthodox version of polygeny (making clever use of the Babel story; *Sketches*, ibid., p. 78) proved remarkable through the 1790s mostly for the fury with which it was rebutted. His cousin David Hume was less bold. Under fire, Hume simply cut from later print-

ings of his essay "Of National Characters" a parenthetical observation, inserted in the 1750s, that there were four or five human "species," all "naturally inferior to the whites." The writer most immune to pressure was beyond doubt Voltaire, who several times proposed that there were separate human species. In a teasing essay, he serenely suggested one of the reasons for believing this to be true: the Indians themselves thought so. "The savage . . . is not more ignorant in this respect than we," Voltaire proposed, "and reasons much better." I am grateful to Anthony Grafton for discussion of these points. Bruno, *Spaccio de la bestia trionfante . . .* (1584), III, ii, as trans. and cited in Jean Jacquot, "Thomas Harriot's Reputation for Impiety," *Notes and Records of the Royal Society* 9 (1952): 171; Aaron Garret, "Hume's Revised Racism Revisited," *Hume Studies* 26 (2000): 171–77; Voltaire, "Relation concerning a White Negro . . . ," in *Works,* trans. Tobias Smollett, 4th ed. (Dublin, 1772–73), 9:257–60; and "Reflections on the Population of America," *Dublin Mag.* (1764), vol. 1, p. 94.

46. *Encyclopædia Britannica,* 2nd ed., 10 vols. (Edinburgh, 1778–83), 1:302 and 300, s.v. "America"; "History of the Rise and Fall of the British Empire in America," *Britannic Mag. . . . ,* 12 vols. (London, 1794–1807), 3:171; Joseph Robson, *An Account of Six Years Residence in Hudson's-Bay . . .* (London, 1752), p. 48; Goldsmith, *An History of the Earth . . . ,* 8 vols. (London, 1779), 2:241, 236, and 242.

47. Smith, *Essay on Variety,* pp. 59n, 114, 56, 20, 25, 26, 12, 126, and 64n.

48. Smith, *Strictures on Lord Kaims's Discourse,* bound with *Essay on Variety,* p. 3; *Pa. Arch.* 1:4:96; *Mühlenberg Journals* 2:203–5 (the episode moved Mühlenberg to compare the effects of a Lutheran education to "the Egyptian arcanum, by which they embalmed their dead bodies so that they remained undecayed for many hundreds of years").

49. Elizabeth Tell: *Pa. Journal,* Oct. 31, 1754, p. 2; for disoriented returnees, see *Pa. Gazette,* May 8 and July 3, 1760, and Mar. 17, 1763; advertisement for amnesiac captives, *Pa. Gazette,* Feb. 21, 1765 (cf. the notice ibid., Sept. 9, 1762). For impostors, see, e.g., ibid., Oct. 14 and 23, 1762.

50. Smith, *Essay on Variety,* p. 36n. For a survey of environmentalism (the doctrine of human difference's being determined by external causes rather than birth), see Jordan, *White over Black,* chap. 14; see also John Wood Sweet, *Bodies Politic: Negotiating Race in the American North, 1730–1830* (Baltimore, Md., 2003), chap. 7. To be sure, the environmentalist view of human difference was not ultra-tolerant, since most observers assumed it was in civilized, well-fed life in the northern temperate zone that the best-developed people would always be found.

51. *"A* brief Disquisition *concerning the Original and Transportation of the* American Indians," *American Magazine . . .* (Philadelphia, 1758), 1:196, 250, and 249. In particular, the theory that Indians were lapsed members of one of Israel's ten lost tribes had astonishing durability. The trader James Adair proved in obsessive detail 23 ways that southeastern Indians were just like Jews; Charles Beatty, the Presbyterian backwoods evangelist, similarly thought Indian and Hebrew rituals too much alike for coincidence: see Adair, *The History of the American Indians . . .* (London, 1775), and Beatty, *Journal of a Two Months Tour.*

52. *Strictures on Lord Kaims's Discourse,* bound with *Essay on Variety,* p. 16n (by Smith's time this was not necessarily an entirely unadmiring discourse—just as the discourse on

Indians was not all unadmiring; he saw westerners becoming like Indians not only in social and bodily "habits" and appearance but in supposed hardihood and activity). In close agreement were the speculations about Indian-European differences of Benjamin Rush, revolutionary Philadelphia's most intellectually adventurous physician, who thought that diet—especially the presence or absence of constant hunger—and way of life combined to produce nearly every human trait. Rush's imagined Indians were by no means admirable specimens; but removed from the wild and properly managed, they would be. Rush, "An Account of the Vices Peculiar to the Indians of North America," in *Essays, Literary, Moral, and Philosophical . . .* (Philadelphia, 1798), pp. 257–62.

53. [Rev. William Smith], *An Historical Account of Colonel Bouquet's Expedition . . .* (Philadelphia, 1765), p. 29.

54. Capt. David Hay to Col. Henry Bouquet and Timothy Green to Bouquet, both Oct. 4, 1764, *Bouquet Papers* 21651:13.

55. *A Declaration and Remonstrance of the Distressed and Bleeding Frontier Inhabitants of the Province of Pennsylvania . . .* ([Philadelphia], 1764); see chap. 7. For body displays, see chap. 3 above.

56. "Speech of Ackowanothio . . . ," Sept. 1758, Indian and Military Affairs MSS, p. 681; James Pemberton to Richard Partridge, 10th mo. 23, 1755, Pemberton Papers 11.

Chapter 5
ATTACKING INDIANS

1. *Tom Quick, or the Foundation and Capstone: Pioneer Enterprise and National Independence,* comp. A[braham] S. Gardiner (Chicago, 1889; a collection of clippings and program notes from the unveiling, assembled by its impresario); William Westfall, "Pike County," in *An Illustrated History of the Commonwealth of Pennsylvania, Civil, Political, and Military . . . ,* comp. William H. Egle (Harrisburg, Pa., 1876), pp. 1051–52; and *Harper's New York and Erie Rail-Road Guide Book,* 8th ed. (New York, 1855–56), p. 91. See also esp. James Eldridge Quinlan, *Tom Quick, the Indian Slayer, and the Pioneers of Minisink . . .* (Monticello, N.Y., 1851), and the modern history-of-folklore account in Vernon Leslie, *The Tom Quick Legends* (Middletown, N.Y., 1977). After the monument's tablets were smashed in the 1990s, it was removed for renovation and never reinstalled.

2. Bernard to Teedyuscung (by Moses Tetami and Isaac Stelle), June 25, 1758, Allison Papers 8:100.

3. *Pa. Gazette,* Dec. 4, 1755, p. 2, and Jan. 29, 1756, p. 2; Horsfield to Gov. [James Hamilton], Sept. 5 and Sept. 3, 1761, Horsfield Papers 2:445 and 441–42. Despite 19th-century mythmaking, no source suggests the younger Quick was present (or had to scramble away from Indian bullets across the iced-up Delaware, a detail probably supplied from *Uncle Tom's Cabin*).

4. Quinlan, *Tom Quick,* chap. 5. Maudlin's death, described in the Quick corpus with more specificity than any other case, seems to be the only one to leave a trace in any contemporary source. Given the detectable ripples such killings set off—the fear they stirred in neighbors, and the care with which governments in both N.J. and Pa. fol-

lowed up other cases (posting rewards, trading letters, calling conferences of condolence and reassurance, holding trials if possible)—Quick's career is far more likely to have started and ended with Maudlin than to have run on, undiscussed and undetected, through decades and scores of victims more.

5. Gov. Hamilton to Horsfield, Oct. 10, 1763, Horsfield Papers 2:491. Herman Melville's still influential portrait of Indian-hating in chaps. 25–27 of *The Confidence-Man* (1857) was fed by a rich Victorian substratum of pulp fiction on Indian-haters, esp. James Hall's *Sketches of History, Life, and Manners in the West,* 2 vols. (Philadelphia, 1835); for a census see Roy Harvey Pearce, "Melville's Indian-Hater: A Note on a Meaning of 'The Confidence-Man,'" *PMLA* 67 (1952): 942–48, esp. p. 943 n. 3.

6. *Ponteach* 1.2.30; ll. 31–44; and ll. 45–46. The play's other high points included a prolonged torture, the tossing of bloody scalps across the boards, and even a full production number (3.3.285–86), with singing Indians flourishing scalping knives as they danced about ("The Edge is keen, the Blade is bright, / Nothing saves them but their Flight").

7. *Ponteach* 1.2.65–66, 86, and 78–80. These were the squalid details that made the play an artistic flop—one critic complained that everyone in it came off simply "as devils incarnate, mutually employed in tormenting one another"—but also made it so revealing; *Gentleman's Mag.* 36 (Feb. 1766): 90. The play was produced in London as part of a successful effort by Rogers to win notoriety and advancement.

8. *Ponteach* 1.2.48–49.

9. Shippen, Journal at Ft. Augusta, 1757–58, Jan. 10, 1758, Shippen Papers; Shippen to Maj. James Burd, Jan. 20, 1758, Shippen Military Letterbook; Shippen, Journal at Ft. Augusta, Feb. 15, 1758; ibid., Mar. 11 and Mar. 10, 1758. For Indian hunting, see, e.g., [Caleb] Graydon and [Samuel] Hunter at Ft. Augusta to Mrs. Burd, Sept. 30, 1761, Shippen Papers (where Graydon laments the departure of "the Indian Hunters about this place" for a treaty, "so that I fear we shall be obliged to kill the other Cow").

10. Hugh Mercer to James Burd, July 10, 1757 (a damaged letter), Shippen Papers.

11. Gage to Sir William Johnson, Aug. 5, 1756, *Johnson Papers* 13:89; the relish-filled report of Edward Shippen Sr. to Capt. Joseph Shippen Jr., Oct. 6, 1759, Shippen Papers. "I have ordered The Head to be buried, & wish every Thing relating to this Affair could be buried with it," Gage wrote worriedly; but because, as his superior, Lord Loudoun, wrote, Jerry had evidently been drinking and "owning all the People he had Murderd . . . and braging no Man Dared to tutche him for it" before his death, Gage need not have worried much about official fallout (draft of Loudoun to Johnson, Aug. 8, 1756, ibid. 10:499).

12. Charles Thomson and Christian Frederick Post to Pa. Gov. William Denny and Gen. John Forbes, June 18, 1758, Friendly Assoc. Papers (Haverford) 2:27; "Court of Enquiry held at Fort Augusta" on Sgt. McManes (1756), Shippen Papers.

13. "Information of . . . John Nicholas Widerhold Captain," Aug. 6 (i.e., 11), 1756, Horsfield Papers 2:253; Capt. George Reynolds to Timothy Horsfield, Aug. 12, 1756, Horsfield Papers 2:261 (and see *Pa. Arch.* 1:2:754–55, and Capt. George Reynolds to Conrad Weiser, ca. Aug. 10, 1756, Northampton Co. Papers, p. 53). The accounts of this case are complicated almost beyond untangling by the participants' drunkenness and many

mutual accusations, furious denials, and countercharges (including charges of having slept with the Indian women, which the lieutenant and some men, possibly including Weyrick, had done).

14. Capt. John Stewart to Col. Henry Bouquet, June 28, 1764, *Bouquet Papers* 21650:1:203; Bouquet to Col. James Burd, Aug. 26, 1758, Shippen Papers; William Trent, Journal at Fort Pitt, June 24, 1763, H.S.P., p. 11 (diary section); John Hughes to Bouquet, July 11, 1763, Amherst to Bouquet, July 16, 1763, Bouquet to Amherst, June 25, 1763, and Amherst to Bouquet, June 29, 1763, as printed in Bernhard Knollenberg, "General Amherst and Germ Warfare," *MVHR* 41 (1954): 492, 493, and 491 (Bouquet seems to have meant that Indians were inhumane, not inhuman). See Elizabeth A. Fenn, *Pox Americana: The Great Smallpox Epidemic of 1775–82* (New York, 2001), suggesting attempts were surprisingly often made (or thought to have been made) at spreading smallpox among European opponents as well.

15. Reid to Bouquet, Sept. 3, 1764, *Bouquet Papers* 21650:2:117–118.

16. See Philip D. Morgan, *Slave Counterpoint: Black Culture in the Eighteenth-Century Chesapeake and Lowcountry* (Chapel Hill, N.C., 1998), pp. 271–72; and Jordan, *White over Black*, pp. 231–32. Some British officers had an unfortunate taste for calling Indians "dogs" (with connotations of slavery) to their faces (see Gregory Evans Dowd, *War under Heaven: Pontiac, the Indian Nations, and the British Empire* [Baltimore, Md., 2002], p. 63).

17. Stevenson to Sir William Johnson, Dec. 18, 1770, *Johnson Papers* 7:1040. British views of French treacherousness were serious enough to help bring about the forcible "extirpation," or uprooting from their Acadian lands, in 1755 of 7,000 French-speakers (as well as the internal dislocation of 11,000 more, with perhaps 10,000 accompanying deaths), in America's first wholesale campaign of ethnic cleansing for the sake of land seizure before the Creek, Seminole, and Cherokee removals in 1836–39, some 80 years later (see John Mack Faragher, *A Great and Noble Scheme: The Tragic Story of the Expulsion of the French Acadians from Their American Homeland* [New York, 2005]).

18. Some such killings (discussed by social scientists as "opportunistic" private vengeance) follow many wars, without requiring perceived racial—or even ethnic or national—boundaries; see Charles Tilly, *The Politics of Collective Violence* (New York, 2003), chap. 6.

19. *Pa. Journal*, p. 2, and *Pa. Gazette*, Feb. 5, 1756, p. 2; Rev. Thomas Barton to Rev. Richard Peters, Feb. 6, 1756, *Pa. Arch.* 1:2:568; Gov. Robert Hunter Morris to Pa. Indian commissioners, Apr. 8, 1756, *Pa. Arch.* 1:2:617; Sir William Johnson to Gov. John Penn, June 7, 1765, *Pa. Arch.* 1:4:227; Killbuck to [James Burd], Jan. 10, 1769, Shippen Papers 6:2:221; Joseph Shippen Jr. to Burd, Feb. 23, 1769, Shippen Papers 7:1:1. An anonymous narrative collected in the semireliable Loudon, *Interesting Narratives*, adds local traditions about the death of Hugh Mitcheltree's wife (2:184).

20. *Pa. Gazette*, Oct. 10, 1765 (inn location); council minutes, Mar. 9, 1756, *Pa. Col. Recs.* 7:59.

21. Friendly Assoc. Papers (soft), Oct. 26, 1756, p. 20n; Friendly Assoc. Papers (hard), Nov. 10, 1756, f. 19v, and 11th mo. 15, 1756, f. 21r; Gov. Denny to Timothy Horsfield, Apr. 26, 1757, Horsfield Papers 2:332.

22. Conrad Weiser to Richard Peters, July 22, 1755, Weiser Correspondence 1:53 (the surveyor George Gabriel's opinion).

23. Edward Shippen Sr. to Gov. Morris, Apr. 19, 1756, *Pa. Arch.* 1:2:634; Conrad Weiser, quoting John Shickellamy (Tachneckdorus), Feb. 22, 1756, *Pa. Col. Recs.* 7:51; speech of Scarouady, Apr. 10, 1756, ibid., p. 80.

24. Lt. Francis Gordon to Col. Henry Bouquet, Aug. 1, 1762, *Bouquet Papers* 21648:2:34; *Pa. Col. Recs.* 7:57 (Mar. 4, 1756; for "good mind to Scalp," see previous note).

25. Edward Shippen Sr. to Joseph Shippen Jr., Sept. 15, 1763, Shippen–Shippen Correspondence.

26. Robert Strettell to Timothy Horsfield, Apr. 14, 1758, Horsfield Papers 2:421; Conrad Weiser, quoting John Shickellamy (Tachneckdorus), Feb. 22, 1756, *Pa. Col. Recs.* 7:51.

27. "Journal of the Proceedings of Conrad Weiser with the Indians at John Harris's Ferry," Jan. 31, 1756, *Pa. Col. Recs.* 7:34–35.

28. N.J. Gov. Thomas Boone to Gov. Hamilton, Aug. 24, 1761, Pa. Arch. 1:4:67. For Indians' expectations of hospitality after land sales, see Alan Taylor, *The Divided Ground: Indians, Settlers, and the Northern Borderland of the American Revolution* (New York, 2006), pp. 37, 132, and 196; and for Europeans' uneasiness over hosting them, Merrell, *Into the American Woods,* pp. 141–42.

29. "Dissertation on the Indians Murdering the White People," Ind. Affairs Papers 11c:5.

30. Grube, "Diarium des Indianer-Gemeinleins in Weequetank," Sept. 3, 1763, *Morav. Recs.* 124:4; Sept. 20, 1763 ("war sehr aufgebracht über uns. Indianer, und sagt, . . . wenn nur ein Mann dißeit der *Lecha* umgebracht werden solte, so würde . . . das ganze *Irishe Settlement* . . . uns überfallen u. umbringen"); Capt. Jacob Wetterholt, ranging journal (for colonel-magistrate Timothy Horsfield), Sept. 22, 1763, Northampton Co. Papers 2:161.

31. Grube to Timothy Horsfield, Oct. 13, 1763, Horsfield Papers 2:503; Grube, "Diarium . . . in Weequetank," Oct. 9, 1763, *Morav. Recs.* 124:4 (in German).

32. Mortimer, "Diary of the Indian congn. at Goshen on the river Muskingum, commencing with the month of May 1812," Aug. 5, 1812, fol. 5r; Aug. 29, 1812, fol. 10r; Aug. 21, 1812, fol. 11v; July 26, 1812, fol. 3v; and Aug. 31, 1812, fol. 11r, *Morav. Recs.* 173:9.

33. Ibid., Nov. 15, 1812, fol. 41r; Sept. 1, 1812, fol. 12v; Sept. 1, 1812, fol. 12r; Sept. 21, 1812, fol. 25r; Sept. 20, 1812, fol. 24v.

34. Ibid., Aug. 9, 1812, fols. 6v–7r. Cf. the events of Sept. 28 (fol. 32v).

35. Ibid., Sept. 19, 1812, fol. 21r (no plans for murder); Sept. 20, 1812, fol. 22v; and Sept. 21, 1812, fol. 24v.

36. Ibid., Sept. 20, 1812, fols. 22v and 23r. It helped that Mortimer could adduce as proof the ominous "example before us of . . . Green-town," Ohio, whose Indians had had to flee, and on which the attacks that triggered the crisis at Goshen had fallen, he asserted, as retaliation (ibid., same date, fol. 22v).

37. Ibid., Sept. 25, 1812, p. 32r, and Oct. 3, 1812, fol. 35v.

38. Ibid., Sept. 25, 1763 ("wenn es sollte geshehen, daß weise leute uns umbringen wolten, so werde ich mich gar nicht wehren"—adding, "but the savages [den wilden] I will resist as much as I can"); see entry for Sept. 11, where Grube exhorts his congre-

gants "that no one should give in and flee this place by themselves, we must all hold out with one another until the end."

39. Mortimer, "Diary of the Indian congn. at Goshen . . . ," July 22, 1812, fol. 2v (Kaschates); Aug. 4, 1812, fols. 4r–4v (Ska); dep. of Charles Cunningham, [1764], as printed in [Rev. Thomas Barton], *The Conduct of the Paxton-Men* . . . (Philadelphia, 1764), p. 19n; for Europeans' own threatening stories, see Mortimer, "Diary of the Indian congregation at Goshen on the river Muskingum from 1 Decr. 1799 . . . ," Apr. 27, 1800, p. 34, *Morav. Recs.* 171:6 (after an episode of mutual threatening between Ska and an American neighbor who falsely pretended to have been present at Gnadenhütten, for which see chap. 9 below). For other complaints and threats about Kaschates, see Mortimer, "Diary of the Indian congn. at Goshen . . . ," Aug. 14, 1812, fols. 7r–8r.

40. Council minutes, Apr. 4, 1770, *Pa. Col. Recs.* 9:663; dep. of Sgt. Leonard McGlashan et al., Aug. 20, 1765, *Pa. Arch.* 1:4:236; dep. of William Nimens, Jan. 25, 1771, ibid., p. 387; dep. of Aaron Van Campen, Jan. 11, 1771, *Susquehannah Co. Papers* 4:152.

41. Daniel Claus to Sir William Johnson, July 3, 1772, *Johnson Papers* 8:526; for execution position, see, e.g., Heckewelder, *Indian Nations,* p. 299 (and cf. pp. 105–6).

42. *The Jesuit Relations and Allied Documents: Travels and Explorations of the Jesuit Missionaries in New France, 1610–1791,* ed. Reuben Gold Thwaites, 73 vols. (Cleveland, Ohio, 1896–1901), 22:241 (Barthelemy Vimont, describing the Hurons in 1642), as cited in Peter C. Mancall, *Deadly Medicine: Indians and Alcohol in Early America* (Ithaca, N.Y., 1995), p. 75 (for forgiveness of violence, see ibid., pp. 79–82); Lt. James Irvine (Ft. Augusta) to unknown, Jul. 13, 1762, Horsfield Papers; and [Johnson], "Review of . . . Affairs in the Northern District . . . ," in *Collections of the Illinois State Historical Library,* vol. 16 (British Series, vol. 3), *Trade and Politics, 1767–1769,* ed. Clarence Walworth Alvord and Clarence Edwin Carter (Springfield, Ill., 1921), p. 36.

43. Gov. Morris to John Ross, Mar. 8, 1755, *Pa. Arch.* 1:2:595; Heckewelder, *Indian Nations,* p. 336. That killing a sleeping victim is a classic tactic of the weak suggests how some such Europeans saw the waking relationship between themselves and their victims. It also suggests how deeply they had taken on the idea of drink as an all-purpose Indian incapacitant (often in the context of fraud and the fur trade), together with a specific archetype of being able to kill large numbers while stuporous: by the 1790s, e.g., a tale of killing everyone in an Ohio Indian war party that became "all completely drunk, and began to sleep" was even added to the Baron Munchausen canon; *A Sequel to the Adventures of Baron Munchausen* . . . (London, 1792), pp. 195–96. For alcohol-related killing and the diplomacy surrounding later 18th-century murders, see White, *Middle Ground,* pp. 342–43 and 346–47.

44. Report of Vannetten (John Van Etten), July 22, 1756, *Pa. Arch.* 1:2:720–21.

45. As Lewis Weiss noted for the defense in Renatus's 1764 murder trial (see chap. 2 above), Indians to whom evil was intended would "very often . . . [be] tempted by white People to taste the first dram & then not being able to bear much are easily futtled"; memorandum, n.d., *Morav. Recs.* 124:6:11.

46. This many shots from five men suggests it was common not only to load multiple projectiles, as with Vannetten's swan shot (birdshot), but for those who could afford it to carry two rifles at once; cf. William Stewart's "having two Guns" in a fight at the

Wyoming Valley (dep. of William Nimens, Jan. 25, 1771, *Pa. Arch.* 1:4:388).

47. David Rittenhouse to Rev. Thomas Barton, Feb. 16, 1764, *Memoirs of the Life of David Rittenhouse . . .* , ed. William Barton (Philadelphia, 1813), pp. 147–48 n. 47 (these were Paxton rioters, streaming past the scientist's Norriton workshop); Devereux Smith to unknown, June 11–13, 1775, *Pa. Arch.* 1:4:631 (shaking stick, thrusting muzzle); dep. of Sgt. Leonard McGlashan et al., Aug. 20, 1765, ibid., p. 236 (thumbs); dep. of George Aston, Aug. 24, 1774, ibid., p. 572 (cocking); dep. of Charles Foreman, Feb. 7, 1775, ibid., p. 604 (pushing); Robert Hanna to Gov. Penn, Feb. 8, 1775, ibid., p. 606 (catching hold). For Fleming, see chap. 2 above.

48. Jones, *Journal of Two Visits Made to Some Nations of Indians . . .* (Burlington, N.J., 1774), p. 58.

49. "Remarks on Dr. Connollys Proceedings," June 25, 1774, *Pa. Arch.* 1:4:528; speech of White Eyes, July 23, 1774, ibid., p. 552.

50. Sir William Johnson to Henry Moore, Sept. 1, 1769, *Johnson Papers* 7:154; *Votes* 6:185 (Sept. 25, 1769); "Minutes of a Conference . . . ," Aug. 21, 1769, *Pa. Col. Recs.* 9:614; Court Papers, 1769—Cumberland Co., R.G. 33, Division of Archives and Manuscripts, P.H.M.C., as quoted in Alden T. Vaughan, "Frontier Banditti and the Indians: The Paxton Boys' Legacy, 1763–75" (1984), in *Roots of American Racism: Essays on the Colonial Experience* (New York, 1995), p. 93 (proclamation). For a vividly seen, quite different account of the same event, see Merrell, *Into the American Woods,* pp. 302–15. For Indians' actively preferring diplomatic to judicial resolutions in similar cases, see Taylor, *Divided Ground,* pp. 30ff., 236, and 245.

51. Sir William Johnson to Gen. Thomas Gage, Apr. 17, 1766, *Johnson Papers* 12:74; Gov. Franklin to Johnson, Apr. 15, 1766, ibid. 12:72–73 (non-English-speaking, no property); Abraham Van Campen to Gov. William Franklin, Apr. 3 and 11, 1766, ibid. 5:169–71 (anxiety, vagabond, plunder); *N.Y. Mercury,* Jan. 12, 1767, p. 1.

52. Dep. of Samuel Davis and Johannes Decker, Apr. 9, 1766, *Johnson Papers* 5:171; Franklin to Col. Cornelius Low Jr., Dec. 9, 1766, ibid. 5:421; *N.Y. Mercury,* Jan. 12, 1767, p. 1 (murmur); Francis J. Swayze, "Historical Sketch of Sussex County, New Jersey," in *Sussex County Sesqui-Centennial . . .* , ed. Jacob L. Bunnell (Newton, N.J., 1903), pp. 20–74, at p. 44 (first hanging); Sir William Johnson to Minisink magistrates, Sept. 8, 1766, and Col. Cornelius Low Jr. to Gov. Franklin, Dec. 4, 1766, both *Johnson Papers* 5:419 (widow). Even so, shortly afterward three more Oquaga Iroquois paid a threatening visit at Minisink and told one of the J.P.'s "& his Neighbours that since the White People trifled so with them . . . there were Eighty Warriors . . . who had resolved to take revenge for the Indians Death"—on which, inevitably, several families fled and all "the Inhabitants," it was reported, "were in great Terror" (ibid.). As this suggests, Seamor's conviction may have been another example of a trial—like Renatus's (chap. 2 above)—that was shaped by Europeans' fear of how a powerful group of neighboring Indians would respond to the wrong verdict. For Gov. Franklin's impatience with the Europeans of Sussex, who all, he felt sure, "let what will happen to them . . . have only themselves to blame," see Franklin to Low, Dec. 9, 1766, ibid. 5:421–22; but cf. his own far more upbeat assessment of at least "the People of Substance on the Frontiers" (who, being "much alarm'd . . . it may be productive of another Indian War . . . will be active

in their Endeavours to bring [Seamor] to Justice"; to Johnson, Apr. 15, 1766, ibid. 12:72). The trial was held in Sussex, not Burlington, and there is no sign that David Ray's manslaughter case, tried the same day, was related to Seamor's (cf. Vaughan, "Frontier Banditti," p. 96); for condolence proceedings in the case, May 24, 1766, see *Johnson Papers* 12:95.

53. Bishop Augustus Gottlieb Spangenberg to Gov. Morris, May 2, 1756, *Pa. Col. Recs.* 7:119; see "Muster Roll of . . . Captain John Nicholas Wetterholt . . . ," July 18–Aug. 24, 1763, Weiser Correspondence 2:191, for soldiers' descriptions.

54. Col. James Burd Journal, Feb. 27, 1758, Papers of the Provincial Council, Division of Public Records, P.H.M.C., Harrisburg, as quoted in Hunter, *Pa. Forts*, p. 248 (for closure of forts, see ibid., pp. 214–16 and 265); Lewis Klotz (of Macungie) to Timothy Horsfield, July 17, 1763, Northampton Co. Papers 2:157; Lt. James Hyndshaw (of Nazareth) to Horsfield, Aug. 17, 1763, Bethlehem Vicinity MSS, p. 107.

55. Jacob Wetterholt, ranging journal, Oct. 7, 1763, Northampton Co. Papers 2:161; Nicholas Wetterholt to Horsfield, Sept. 13, 1763, ibid. 2:171.

56. Nicholas Wetterholt to Horsfield, Sept. 2 and Oct. 4, 1763, Northampton Co. Papers 2:169 and 171; Nicholas Wetterholt, ranging journal (for Horsfield), Oct. 5, 1763, Northampton Co. Papers 2:165.

57. Nicholas Wetterholt, ranging journal, Aug. 5, 1763, Northampton Co. Papers 2:163; Dodge to Horsfield, Aug. 5, 1763, Bethlehem Vicinity MSS, p. 95. Besides the four rifles (valuable if in good repair), Dodge admitted to ending up with 13 (presumably short-haired, summer) deerskins weighing 31 lbs.: their cash value in Philadelphia in 1763 was ca. £4 8s. Pa. currency (ca. 11¼ dollars specie); a lieutenant's salary was 6s. per day and a private's 1s. 6d. For deerskin values, see William Trent, Miscellaneous Papers on Indian Losses, H.S.P., accounts of Alexander Lowry, Robert Callender, and John Gibson (Apr.–Aug. 1766, describing losses of spring 1763), pp. 3–5 and 39–40.

58. [Lewis Weiss], paraphrase (possibly prepared for use in court) of Nicholas Wetterholt to Weiss, Oct. 12, 1763, *Morav. Recs.* 124:6:10. For a similar case from Schenectady, N.Y., of a Indian's gun and skins being stolen at a tavern, see John Baptist Van Eps to Sir William Johnson, May 19, 1772, *Johnson Papers* 7:489–90.

59. Nicholas Wetterholt to Horsfield, Sept. 27, 1763, Northampton Co. Papers 2:171; [Weiss], paraphrase of Wetterholt to Weiss, Oct. 12, 1763, *Morav. Recs.* 124:6:10. Immediately after this discovery, Indians headed through with furs from Wyalusing began fording the river three miles above the fort, in the most precipitous section of the Lehigh gorge, "for fear of the soldiers" (Grube, "Diarium . . . in Weequetank," Sept. 14, 1763, *Morav. Recs.* 124:4; in German).

60. Dodge to Horsfield, Sept. 16, 1763, Northampton Co. Papers 2:187; Jacob Warner to Horsfield, Sept. 16, 1763, Bethlehem Vicinity MSS, p. 129.

61. Nicholas Wetterholt to Horsfield, Sept. 27, 1763, Northampton Co. Papers 2:171; Warner to Horsfield, Sept. 16, 1763, Bethlehem Vicinity MSS, p. 129. In 1756, e.g., a small number of pro-English Delawares at Tioga reportedly "did not know which way to come away from the Rest for they foresaw that the Others . . . would . . . follow & kill them"; "Memorandum of Sundry Questions asked Augustus . . . ," May 23, 1756, Bethlehem Vicinity MSS, p. 35.

62. Deps. of Oblinger (Nicholas Ablinger) and Moses Beer, Sept. 5, 1763, Bethlehem Vicinity MSS, p. 115.

63. Horsfield, memorandum of soldiers' allegations, Oct. 7, 1763, Bethlehem Vicinity MSS, p. 135; Duncan Smith to Rev. Dr. Smith, June 19, 1774, Wharton-Willing Papers, 1769–1887, box 3, H.S.P.

64. *N.H. Gazette, and Historical Chronicle,* July 25, 1766, p. 2 (strollers); *Pa. Gazette,* July 10, 1766; *N.Y. Mercury,* Aug. 11, 1766, pp. 2–3.

65. *N.Y. Mercury,* July 28, 1766, p. 3, and Aug. 11, 1766, p. 3. As Sir William Johnson at once wrote to London, "this seems to be the opinion of all the common people" (to Board of Trade, Aug. 20, 1766, *Docs. Rel. Col. Hist.* N.Y. 7:852); for parallel skepticism about the accuracy of this assessment, see Dowd, *War under Heaven,* p. 206.

66. Gov. Francis Fauquier to Penn, Dec. 11, 1766, *Pa. Col. Recs.* 9:349–50.

67. Wills Hill, 1st earl of Hillsborough, to Gov. John Penn, Aug. 13 and Mar. 12, 1768, *Pa. Arch.* 1:4:306 and 296; *N.Y. Gazette,* Feb. 15, 1768, p. 2 (fleeing); Penn, instructions to John Allen and Joseph Shippen Jr., Mar. 31, 1768, *Pa. Col. Recs.* 9:494–95 (goods); *Pa. Gazette,* Mar. 17, 1768 (descriptions). It is useful to understand how leaky all judicial custody was, and not simply because of group rescues—of which there were nonetheless very many ("Our Gaol is of no use," as the founder of Hanna's Town noted sadly; "the worst Raskel is set at Liberty"; *Pa. Col. Recs.* 10:234–35). On Jan. 23, 1768, e.g., a Chester Co. farmer recorded in his even-keeled diary that "David," either his son or hired boy, was "sent to Chester Goal——"; and then, under Mar. 7, observed simply that "David got out Chester Goal over the Walls & came home last Night was in there 6 Weeks & one Day. . . . cool & Sharp this Day" (Gibbons Diary, 1760–69, Gibbons Family Papers, H.S.P.). Cf. G. S. Rowe, "The Frederick Stump Affair, 1768, and Its Challenge to Legal Historians of Early Pennnsylvania," *Pa. History* 49 (1982): 276, part of Rowe's body of work on lawlessness in the mid-Atlantic.

68. "A List of the names of the Indians killed," Jan. 1768, Shippen Papers 6:2:195 (and cf. Gov. Penn to Great Island and Wyalusing Indians, Jan. 23 and 28, 1768, *Pa. Col. Recs.* 9:428–29 and 436–37); Lt. James Irvine to unknown, July 13, 1762, Horsfield Papers (liquor seller); dep. of William Blyth, Jan. 19, 1768, Penn Official Correspondence 10:124 (and *Votes* 6:24; hole in ice, fire); James Galbreath and Jonathan Hoge to Penn, Feb. 29, 1768, *Pa. Col. Recs.* 9:487–88 (corpse downriver).

69. Dep. of William Blyth, Jan. 19, 1768, Penn Official Correspondence 10:124 (and *Votes* 6:24). Stump was one of a small category of lone binge killers, who killed several Indians at once while socializing drunkenly with them or watching them sleep. (One near Ft. Niagara in 1772, David Ramsay, said that being drunk while killing "did not disable me, but rather made me more furious and alert"; P[atrick] Campbell, *Travels in the Interior Inhabited Parts of North America . . .* [Edinburgh, 1793], p. 241; for Ramsay, see *Johnson Papers* 8:482–86, 496–97, and 512–14; and ibid. 12:964.) These murders took place in isolated settings: a cabin outside the purchased lands of Pa.; campfires deep in the woods; a claustrophobic fur trader's cabin, snowed in for months with a few residents "drunk and mad all winter" (Campbell, *Travels in the Interior,* p. 236; one such trader vividly described being alone with a partner in "Lethargy" for "the whole Winter [who] sat at the fire side with his Elbow on his knee & his Chin on his hand picking his nose

without speaking a Word . . . 13 or 14 weeks"; Ferrall Wade to Sir William Johnson, Apr. 6, 1771, *Johnson Papers* 8:65). In such places—as Johnson put it, "as well out of the protection as the Eye of Government" (to George Etherington, June 7, 1772, *Johnson Papers* 8:512)—some killers saw the tempting if unrealistic prospect of killing so completely that news of their crimes need never reach other Indians, or officials. The most horrifying binge killer was David Owens, a deserter and longtime go-between who in 1764 killed his Delaware wife, her father, their two children, and other relations at a campsite—scalping all but the children, then using the scalps as a passport to return and assume a position as interpreter in the European armies before they struck the Ohio country (see Benjamin Franklin to unknown, Apr. 12, 1764, *Franklin Papers* 11:163–64; also *Pa. Gazette*, Apr. 19, 1764). Even after his killings were known, Owens was able to play a key role as mediator between Delawares and Europeans (for one tradition about this, see Loudon, *Interesting Narratives* 2:177). Sir William Johnson's verdict may be right: "As he was always much attached to Indians, I fancy he began to fear he was unsafe amongst them, and killed them, rather to make his peace with the English, than from any dislike . . . to them" (to Gov. Penn, June 18, 1764, *Pa. Col. Recs.* 9:190; for his role as interpreter, see ibid., p. 228 [Nov. 11, 1764]; and for earlier activity, including at Wyalusing, e.g., *Pa. Arch.* 1:4:61 and Nathaniel Holland to Israel Pemberton Jr., 8th mo. 21 and 9th mo. 12, 1760, Friendly Assoc. Papers [Haverford] 4:3 and 27).

70. *Pa. Gazette*, Feb. 11, 1768 (capture); dep. of James Cunningham, Feb. 4, 1768, *Votes* 6:36 (hands); see Patterson to Gov. Penn, Jan. 23, 1768, *Pa. Col. Recs.* 9:453–54. Patterson was raised to the magistracy within weeks (council minutes, Feb. 19, 1763, ibid. 9:470); and beyond two dubious snippets of politicized Philadelphia hearsay (assembly adherents seized on the affair as establishing Pa.'s ungovernability under the Penns), there is no support for the assertion he fled the county (in Rowe, "Stump Affair," p. 271).

71. Gov. Penn to sheriffs of Cumberland, Lancaster, and Chester, Feb. 2, 1768, *Pa. Col. Recs.* 9:441–42; Penn to Cumberland magistrates, Jan. 19, 1768, ibid. 9:417.

72. *Pa. Gazette*, Mar. 3, 1768; Edward Shippen Sr. to James Tilghman, Feb. 2, 1768, Shippen Papers 6:2:196; Sheriff John Holmes to Gov. Penn, Feb. 7, 1768, *Pa. Col. Recs.* 9:464.

73. John Armstrong et al. to Chief Justice William Allen, Jan. 27, 1768, *Votes* 6:32 (expected trial); two deps. of James Cunningham, both Feb. 4, 1768, *Votes* 6:35–37 and *Pa. Col. Recs.* 9:451–451, and Sheriff John Holmes to Gov. Penn, Feb. 7, 1768, ibid. 9:464 (visit and rescue); *Pa. Gazette*, Mar. 3, 1768 (jostled).

74. John Armstrong to Gov. Penn, Feb. 26, 1768, *Pa. Col. Recs.* 9:484; Armstrong et al. to Chief Justice William Allen, Jan. 27, 1768, *Votes* 6:33.

75. John Armstrong to Gov. Penn, Jan. 24, 1768, *Votes* 6:32; same to same, Feb. 7, 1768, *Pa Col. Recs.* 9:462; Edward Shippen Sr. to James Tilghman, Feb. 2, 1768, Shippen Papers 6:2:196.

76. Penn to John Armstrong, Feb. 3, 1768, Pa. Col. Recs. 9:446; *Conductor Generalis, or the Office, Duty, and Authority of Justices of the Peace . . .* , 2nd ed. (New York, 1749), p. 385 (see "Trial" and "Guide to Juries," ibid., pp. 307 and 377–411, and esp. pp. 383–85, on juries' discretion in murder trials)—a source for which I am indebted to Barbara Clark Smith, "Beyond the Vote: The Limits of Deference in Colonial Politics," *Early American Studies* 3 (2005): 341–62. When in 1774 Parliament's "Murder Act" provided for

troops' criminal trials being held in Britain, this disregard for the rights as Englishmen of American subjects helped directly to bring on the formation of the Continental Association (David Ammerman, *In the Common Cause: American Response to the Coercive Acts of 1774* [Charlottesville, Va., 1974], p. 9); and cf. Peter D. G. Thomas, *The Townshend Duties Crisis: The Second Phase of the American Revolution, 1767–1773* (Oxford, 1987), p. 117.

77. *Pa. Gazette,* Apr. 7, 1768; John Armstrong to Gov. Penn, Jan. 24, 1768 (postscript), *Votes* 6:32; *Pa. Gazette,* Mar. 3, 1768; John Armstrong to Gov. Penn, Feb. 7, 1768, *Pa. Col. Recs* 9:463.

78. *Pa. Gazette,* Feb. 11, 1768 (half the company); John Armstrong to Gov. Penn, Feb. 7, 1768, *Pa. Col. Recs* 9:463 (confined); Sheriff John Holmes to Gov. Penn, Feb. 7, 1768, ibid. 9:464 (gentlemen); *Pa. Gazette,* Apr. 7, 1768 (large numbers).

79. *Pa. Gazette,* Feb. 11, 1768 (convinced); ibid., Mar. 3, 1768 (willing, permitted; cf. John Armstrong to Gov. Penn, Feb. 26, 1768, *Pa. Col. Recs.* 9:484); dep. of James Cunningham, Feb. 4, 1768, *Votes* 6:36 (deadline). In late February, Stump was thought to have been spotted crossing Bucks Co. with another man, heading toward New England; that winter the county put Stump's forfeited property up for auction and divided it among his creditors (Joseph Shippen Jr. to Giles Knight, Mar. 5, 1768, Joseph Shippen Letterbook; *Pa. Gazette,* Jan. 5, 1769).

80. Dep. of Lt. Charles Grant, ca. June 1765, *Pa. Arch.* 1:4:221 (prisoners); Gen. Thomas Gage to Gov. John Penn, June 16, 1765, *Pa. Col. Recs.* 9:267 (rebellion); Lt. Col. John Reid to Gage, June 1, 1765, ibid. 9:268 (bugger); Capt. William Grant to Reid, Nov. 25, 1765, *Pa. Arch.* 1:4:247 (Ft. Loudoun). Over 20 men were indicted for taking part in Stump's rescue; in a decade with more than one indicted riot per average year in Cumberland Co., 8 of these 20 rescuers were brought to trial (about the average ratio for all accused rioters; although, like 90 percent of Cumberland rioters who did face juries, they were acquitted; Rowe, "Stump Affair," pp. 270 and 274). Events surrounding the Black Boys would in time be immortalized as patriotic precursors of the Revolution in one of the worst early John Wayne vehicles, *Allegheny Uprising* (1939).

81. James Smith, *Account of the Remarkable Occurrences in the Life and Travels . . .* (Lexington, Ky., 1799), p. 62 (civil law); William Smith to Lt. Charles Grant, June 22, 1765, *Pa. Arch.* 1:4:229 (authority); William Smith, travel pass, May 20, 1765, ibid. 1:4:220 (subjects); dep. of Lt. Charles Grant, 1765, ibid. 1:4:221 (passes); and *Pa. Gazette,* Oct. 5, 1769 (begging), and see Smith, *Account of the Remarkable Occurrences,* pp. 68–73. In baiting soldiers and setting the legality of army orders against civil authority, the rioters were striking at the doubt-ridden heart of all officers who tried to suppress crowd actions, as well as playing on a widespread distrust of the army itself (especially an army of Scots); see Tony Hayter, *The Army and the Crowd in Mid-Georgian England* (London, 1978), pp. 20–21 and 52–53. See Dowd, *War under Heaven,* pp. 205–10, for a similar stress on the legalism of Smith's followers.

82. Certainly concern over trial-venue privileges had not been merely a pretense for someone like John Armstrong—as exhaustive inquiries established (council minutes, May 12, 1768, *Pa. Col. Recs.* 9:512–13); or for the sheriff, magistrates, and lawyers at the court sessions whose opinions were recorded; or for the clergymen who tried to prevent

Stump's rescue (see esp. Rev. George Duffield's defense, *Pa. Gazette,* Apr. 7, 1768); or for William Patterson and his neighbors; or for the first group of would-be rescuers, who were put off with constitutional assurances; or, indeed, for anyone who spoke up at the two large conferences held during Feb. in Shearman's Valley. As rhetoric, in short—even when Indian-killers were involved, and even though in time Armstrong decided with self-blaming exasperation that "the grand Reason" for Stump's escape was simply "unwillingness that White Men should be brought to the Risque of Life for Killing Indians . . . when War is expected" (to Penn, Feb. 26, 1768, *Pa. Col. Recs.* 9:485)— this constitutional concern was demonstrably never "altogether sham" (E. P. Thompson, *Whigs and Hunters: The Origin of the Black Act* [New York, 1975], p. 267). An assembly-party handbill in 1764 usefully reproduced some of the language used in decrying attempts at changing venues (in this case, against Lewis Weiss's attempt to move the murder trial not of a European but of the Indian Renatus, discussed in chap. 2): they "call it," he observed, "disfranchising the People!" (*To the Freemen of Pennsylvania . . .* [Philadelphia, 1764], p. 1). For juries as a form of representation, see esp. Smith, "Beyond the Vote."

83. For related observations about metropolitan diehards (in this case, British "armchair patriots," who were happy to imagine a ruthless American empire from a safe distance), see Eliga H. Gould, *The Persistence of Empire: British Political Culture in the Age of the American Revolution* (Chapel Hill, N.C., 2000), pp. 57–61 and 66–71. The safer Europeans felt from Indians—whether because they lived far away from them, or were in the midst of large armies—the freer their feelings toward them were to vary, from benevolent humanitarianism all the way to genocidal hatred. Alan Taylor perceptively suggests that "fear and hatred [might be treated] as alternating emotional currents affecting the same people *depending on circumstances,*" so that provided country people were out of harm's way, they "could indulge in hate when and if they felt they could get away with it"; I would simply tend to stress how seldom most country people felt themselves to be safe, and to assume indifference instead of hatred to have been most people's psychological resting state (personal communication, Nov. 30, 2005).

Chapter 6
A SPIRIT OF ENTERPRISE

1. Council minutes and proclamation, Apr. 14, 1756, *Pa. Col. Recs* 7:88; Hamilton to Gov. Morris, Dec. 25, 1755, ibid. 6:764; James Pemberton to Samuel Fothergill, 7th mo. 4, 1757, Pemberton Papers 34:57 (forts).

2. The scalp-bounty paradox was discovered in the 1950s, to his surprise, by Pennsylvania's senior archivist; see Henry J. Young, "A Note on Scalp Bounties in Pennsylvania," *Pa. History* 24 (1957): 211 (Samuel Murray's scalps, discussed just below, accounted for three from this total of eight). A small number of other scalps brought back by soldiers on official military expeditions—as opposed to private subjects, acting as freelancers—were bought; Col. John Armstrong's raid against Kittanning in 1756 returned with seven others. Though the very large bounties in Md. were cited as a model by Hamilton and

other would-be hard-liners, Md.'s experience was no different: of £4,000 set aside for bounties, the assembly could disburse no more than £230 before letting it lapse into a slush fund; Gov. Horatio Sharpe to assembly, Dec. 6, 1757, *Proceedings and Acts of the General Assembly of Maryland*, ed. J. Hall Pleasants, vol. 55 (Baltimore, Md., 1938), pp. 309–10. See also ibid., pp. xliv–xlv. New England in the 1720s may have differed from the listless mid-Atlantic picture, but by the Seven Years' War successful scalp-taking there seems to have been "a rare thing," too; John Grenier, *The First Way of War: American War Making on the Frontier, 1607–1814* (New York, 2005), pp. 64–65, and see pp. 42–43 and 50–51 for earlier successes.

3. *Pa. Gazette*, July 1, 1756, p. 2; and proclamation in *N.Y. Mercury*, Apr. 26, 1756, p. 3. In Pa. currency, the bounty would have amounted to about £60 per killer.

4. Morris to Sir William Johnson, Apr. 24, 1756, *Pa. Col. Recs.* 7:98. Morris (who canceled the hostilities within three weeks) was invoking the people's rage as an excuse, while backing away from his own decision to issue bounties—to which Johnson had reacted with angry amazement, in view of his ticklish negotiations with the eastern Delawares. See Morris to Johnson, Apr. 24, 1756, ibid. 7:98; and Johnson to Gov. William Shirley, Apr. 24, 1756, ibid. 7:117.

5. Joseph Shippen Jr. to John Elder, July 12, 1763, Elder Papers 2:15 (influence); Elder to Gov. James Hamilton, Aug. 4, 1763, Elder Papers 2:17 (sunk, evacuated); Hamilton to Elder, Aug. 11, 1763, Elder Papers 2:18 (surprise); Elder to Hamilton, July 29, 1763, Elder Papers 2:16 (won't enlist); Edward Shippen Sr. to Joseph Shippen Jr., June 13, 1763, Shippen-Shippen Correspondence (guard Paxton; Elder had claimed this would free up people around Paxton to "assist . . . to save" the Ft. Augusta garrison, farther upriver, but since the refrain of all his reports until Aug. 1763 was a lack of recruits, this was almost certainly an effort to save face). A war party that struck in Northampton Co. on Oct. 8, 1763, had also sacked the Conn. settlement at Wyoming on its way north; but this was ca. 100 miles from the European towns on the middle Susquehanna (*Pa. Gazette*, Oct. 27, 1763, p. 3; see below). When Europeans killed Conestogas near Lancaster in Dec. 1763, it would be the first attack during Pontiac's War made on any settlement—European or Indian—within 60 or 70 miles.

6. Thomas McKee to Col. James Burd, July 9, 1763, Shippen Papers 6:1:41 (the men's prediction reached Philadelphia and its newspapers perhaps a day before their scalps; *Pa. Gazette*, July 21, 1763). For other wishful Indian predictions of phantom attacks against Ft. Augusta by forces hundreds strong, see "Intelligence of Ogaghradarishah," Oct. 11, 1756, *Pa. Col. Recs.* 7:281; Hunter, *Pa. Forts*, p. 487 (in Mar. 1757); and Gen. John Stanwix to Gov. Denny, June 19, 1757, *Pa. Col. Recs.* 7:603.

7. Thomas McKee to Col. James Burd, July 9, 1763, Shippen Papers 6:1:41 (about double the bounty Gov. Hamilton did eventually award).

8. Joseph Shippen Jr. to Col. James Burd, July 24, 1763, Shippen Papers 6:1:45 (shot by Murray "a fortnight ago"); Gov. Hamilton to Edward Shippen Sr. and James Wright, July 23, 1763, Burd-Shippen Papers (reward, encouragement); Hamilton to Edward Shippen Sr., Aug. 10, 1763, Burd-Shippen Papers (enterprise); Edward Shippen Sr. to Joseph Shippen Jr., July 21, 1763, Shippen–Shippen Correspondence (quelling); same to same, July 25, 1763, Shippen–Shippen Correspondence (leading man); same to same,

Aug. 15, 1763, Shippen–Shippen Correspondence (so right, posthaste); [Rev. Francis Alison; my attribution], "The Apology of the Paxton Voluntiers addressed to the candid & impartial World" (a pamphlet composition draft marked up but not printed, cataloged at H.S.P. as Am .283), as transcribed in *The Paxton Papers,* ed. John R. Dunbar (The Hague, 1957), p. 193 (commonwealths); Hamilton to Timothy Horsfield, Oct. 10, 1763, Horsfield Papers 2:491; Rev. John Elder to Hamilton, Oct. 25, 1763, Elder Papers 2:26 (no safety). For Wyalusing, see chap. 4 above.

9. Bouquet to Harris, July 19, 1764, *Bouquet Papers* 21650:2:32 (Bouquet noted that he was "So much disgusted at the Backwardness of the Frontier People in . . . taking Revenge of the Savages who murder them daily with Impunity, that I hope this will be the Last Time I Shall Venture my Reputation and Life for their Sake"; ibid., pp. 32–33); *Votes* 5:264–65, 297 (Sept. 17, 1763, and Jan. 11, 1764; petitions from Great Cove); anonymous narrative in Loudon, *Interesting Narratives* 2:185 (friendly).

10. *Pa. Gazette,* Sept. 8, 1763 (prudent, spirits); anonymous narrative in Loudon, *Interesting Narratives* 2:203 (retreat); anonymous narrative ibid., pp. 186–88 (other details). They had gone the wrong way down the leg of the Great Warriors Path between Ft. Augusta and Nescopeck; ibid., p. 186; see Paul A. W. Wallace, *Indian Paths of Pennsylvania* (Harrisburg, Pa., 1965), pp. 72–74. The Indian man who fled without his scalp— George Allen—had only been shot in the arm, but slathered his torso in blood; wearing a hat of wet moss, he made his way to the Great Island and recovered to tell this story later to other Europeans. The affair later became a scandal; see Charles Read, *Copy of a Letter from Charles Read, Esq. . . .* (Philadelphia, 1764), p. 5, and rejoinder in *A Declaration and Remonstrance of the Distressed and Bleeding Frontier Inhabitants . . .* (Philadelphia, 1764), pp. 14–15.

11. Edward Shippen Sr. to Joseph Shippen Jr., Sept. 26, 1763, Shippen–Shippen Correspondence (brave boys); Loudon, *Interesting Narratives* 2:203 (Snake); *Pa. Gazette,* Sept. 8, 1763 (first fire); Rev. John Elder to Gov. Hamilton, Sept. 13, 1763, Elder Papers 2:21 (adventurers); Shippen to Shippen, Sept. 3 (skill) and Aug. 31, 1763 (high spirits), Shippen–Shippen Correspondence; *Pa. Gazette,* Oct. 27, 1763 (battering, auction); C[aleb] Graydon to Col. James Burd, Oct. 12, 1763, Shippen Papers 6:1:53 (starved); Elder to Hamilton, Sept. 30, 1763, Elder Papers 2:22 (favor); Edward Shippen Sr. to Gov. James Hamilton, Oct. 29, 1763, Shippen Misc. Correspondence (lively); Harris to Col. James Burd, Nov. 20, 1763, Shippen Papers 6:1:61 (bounties, weather). Harris acted as paymaster in dividing the profits of the trip; see Harris, Journal, Papers of John Harris, H.S.P. (e.g., account with Moses Carson, Mar. 26, 1765, p. 63). The fourth scalp is a mystery, likely with much the same solution.

12. Gov. Hamilton to Timothy Horsfield, Sept. 1, 1763, Horsfield Papers 2: 483 (illegal); *Pa. Gazette,* Oct. 13, 1763 (public spirit); Hamilton to assembly, Oct. 15, 1763, *Votes* 5:281; Gen. Sir Jeffery Amherst to Sir William Johnson, Oct. 16, 1763, *Votes* 5:282 (tamely); *Pa. Gazette,* Oct. 27, 1763 (terror); Hamilton to Horsfield, Oct. 10, 1763, Horsfield Papers 2:491 (patience); Lewis Weiss to Horsfield, Aug. 1, 1763, Bethlehem Vicinity MSS, p. 95 (protection); Hamilton to Papunhang et al., Oct. 22, 1763, *Pa. Col. Recs.* 9:68 (revenge; in fact, the Lancaster Co. expedition to Wyoming followed Hamilton's injunctions to leave Wyalusing alone). For rage, see George Cockings, *War: An Heroic Poem . . . ,* [2nd

ed.] (Portsmouth, N.H., 1762; orig. pub. London, 1760), p. 10, col. 2 (gen'rous); Francis Dobbs, *The Patriot King, or Irish Chief* . . . (London, 1774), p. 48 (glorious). Cf. *OED*, s.v. "rage," senses 8–9; and, for a possible earlier transition in the word's status, Nicole E. Eustace, " 'Passion Is the Gale': Emotion and Power on the Eve of the American Revolution" (Ph.D. diss., Univ. of Pennsylvania, 2001), chap. 3.

13. Hamilton to Timothy Horsfield, Sept. 20, 1763, Horsfield Papers 2:487 (that subject); Papunhang (by David Owens) to Israel Pemberton Jr., Sept. 15, 1761, Friendly Assoc. Papers (Haverford) 4:191 (wampum; cf. another such effort, Papunhang to Hamilton, Sept 17, 1763, *Pa. Col. Recs.* 9:45); Newoleka (via Papunhang) to Gov. John Penn, Dec. 1, 1763, ibid. 9:78–79 (so strong); Henry Geiger to Horsfield, Sept. 5, 1763, Bethlehem Vicinity MSS, p. 125 (goods).

14. Grube, "A true Copy of the Originall of my Journall kept in the german Language" (Sept. 3–Oct. 11, 1764; prepared for use by the defense in Renatus's murder trial), Sept. 12, 1763, *Morav. Recs.* 124:4 (with details not reported in Grube's German "Diarium des Indianer-Gemeinleins in Weequetank," Sept. 12, 1763, ibid.; for Grube's self-editing, see Silver, "Indian-Hating," p. 220 n. 211).

15. Philip Vickers Fithian, *Journal, 1775–1776* . . . , ed. Robert Greenhalgh Albion and Leonidas Dodson (Princeton, N.J., 1934), pp. 63 (July 19, 1775), 81 (July 31, 1775), 71 (July 26, 1775), and 82–83 (July 31); Robert Honyman, *Colonial Panorama, 1775: Dr. Robert Honyman's Journal for March and April,* ed. Philip Padelford (San Marino, Calif., 1939), p. 16 (for this delegation, see *Pa. Arch.* 1:4:615 [Mar. 11, 1775] and *Votes* 6:573 [Mar. 7, 1775]).

16. *Pa. Gazette,* May 24, 1764. The women were doing their best to observe the custom of "mourning over the corpse," described in the 1760s as "a ceremony that cannot be dispensed with" in Delaware-speaking towns. On the deaths of important residents, mourners would walk from house to house wailing out the news until "the village resounds from one end to the other with the loud lamentations of the women," who often keened by the corpse in shifts all day and night (Heckewelder, *Indian Nations,* pp. 275 and 269–70).

17. *Votes* 5: 284 (Oct. 21, 1763); "Extract of a letter from Philadelphia, Aug. 22," *London Chronicle,* Oct. 20–23, 1764, p. 7.

18. "Petition of Us Inhabitants in Lower Smithfield Township," before Oct. 22, 1763, *Morav. Recs.* 124:7:6. Far from being a Moravian put-up job, this address was organized and hand-delivered to the governor by Carl Solomon Friederici, a chronically underemployed Lutheran catechist in Lower Smithfield who had himself fled to Philadelphia with the petition, his family, and little else; *Mühlenberg Journals,* Oct. 22, 1763.

19. *Pa. Gazette,* Mar. 28, 1781; see also leasing and sale notices and descriptions ibid., Feb. 20, 1770, Dec. 22, 1763, and Aug. 15, 1753, and Nicholas Scull and George Heap, *A Map of Philadelphia and Parts Adjacent* . . . (Philadelphia, 1752). Besides farmhouses and barns, the island held the port's lazaretto, in which unhealthy immigrants could be put up until their fevers ran their course.

20. Bernhard Adam Grube, "Diarium des Indianer-Gemeinleins in Weequetank [and Philadelphia]," Nov. 11, 1763 ("Alle lästerreden, Spott u. Hohn musten wir hören"; "aufgerieben"; "die Jungens machten ein gros Geshrey"), *Morav. Recs.* 127:1:1.

21. The sojourn in Philadelphia was in fact every Moravian missionary's nightmare scenario: living with one's converts amid a large, corrupting population of Europeans without proper farm work to do. Grube, "Diarium der Indianer-Gemeine auf Province-Island am flüß der Dellawär . . . ," Dec. 7, 1763 (milking), and Dec. 4, 1763 (where the mention of shopping came in the context of Grube's requesting that they call it off for a while, since the city people seemed to him "exasperated anew again"), *Morav. Recs.* 127:1:1; idem, "Diarium des Indianer-Gemeinleins in Weequetank [and Philadelphia]," Nov. 27, 1763; Nov. 28, 1763 ("sehr freundshafftl."); and Nov. 13, 1763 ("machten . . . eine Stöhrung"). For worries over drinking, see ibid., Dec. 20, 1763. Papunhang was now a Moravian-baptized Christian of six months' standing.

22. Grube, "Diarium der Indianer-Gemeine in den *Barracks* zu Philadelphia," Feb. 26, 1764 ("Nichts *charm*iert die leute mehr"), Sept. 20, 1764 (gypsies), and May 10, 1764 (handiworks); cf. entry for May 1), *Morav. Recs.* 127:2; idem, "Diarium des Indianer-Gemeinleins auf der Pilgershafft," Jan. 16, 1764, ibid. 127:1:2.

23. Da[vid] Henderson to Joseph Galloway, Dec. 17, 1763, Friendly Assoc. Papers (Haverford) 4. For Conestogas, see chap. 1 above (as well as H. Frank Eshleman, *Lancaster County Indians: Annals of the Susquehannock . . .* [Lancaster, Pa., 1908], an exhaustive source collection).

24. Barber, Journal of Settlement at Wright's Ferry (ca. 1830), H.S.P.; Sheehays et al. to Gov. John Penn, Nov. 30, 1764, *Pa. Col. Recs.* 9:89. According to Barber, the two local caretakers were "a person of the name of Hare a german" (i.e., Herr; a family that in 2000 still had a farm near the massacre site) and James Wright of Hempfield (supported in Edward Shippen Sr. to Joseph Shippen Jr., Jan 5, 1764, Shippen–Shippen Correspondence); but for official purposes they seem to have been Robert Beatty and John Miller, who may have devolved their everyday responsibilities onto Herr and Wright (Beatty and Miller to Gov. Penn, Dec. 28, 1763, *Pa. Arch.* 1:4:151–52). For trading at ironworks, see Shippen to Gov. Penn, Dec. 14, 1763, *Pa. Col. Recs.* 9:89. By spring, the empty town site was already being squatted on, with new log houses rising up in the ruins, by two European refugee families from 50 miles upriver; Edward Shippen also found there an elderly couple, the Maggintys, "living in an Indian Wigwam" that had managed, unlike its owners, to survive (Shippen to Gov. Penn, Mar. 24, 1764, Edward Shippen Papers).

25. Edward Shippen Sr. to Gov. Penn, Dec. 14, 1763, Pa. Col. Recs. 9:89–90 (scalped); "Journal of the Proceedings of Conrad Weiser with the Indians at John Harris's Ferry," Jan. 31, 1756, ibid. 7:34–35 (deeper within; see chap. 5 above); Shippen to Rev. John Elder, Dec. 16, 1763, Shippen Misc. Correspondence (protection); Shippen to Joseph Shippen Jr., Jan. 5, 1764 (weather), and Dec. 19, 1763 (corpses, revenge), Shippen–Shippen Correspondence; Slough and 14 jurymen, inquisition verdict, Dec. 14, 1763, *Pa. Arch.* 1:4:147–48; Gov. Penn, proclamation, Dec. 22, 1763, *Pa. Col. Recs.* 9:95–96. Barber's perception that the killers were not from the neighborhood is likely to be accurate (if they had made reconnoitering visits, they probably would not have attacked when most of Conestoga's residents were gone).

26. Da[vid] Henderson to Joseph Galloway, Dec. 17, 1763, Friendly Assoc. Papers (Haverford) 4 (jail, jailer, hallooing); Shippen to Gov. Penn, Dec. 27, 1763, *Pa. Col. Recs.*

9:100 (prevail); Sheriff John Hay to Penn, Dec. 27, 1763, ibid., 103–4 (victims' identities); Shippen to Joseph Shippen Jr., Jan. 5, 1764, Shippen–Shippen Correspondence (other details). For scalping or severing of hands or feet on some bodies, see memories of the town boy William Henry (perhaps seven at the time), n.d., in I. Daniel Rupp, *History of Lancaster County* . . . (Lancaster, Pa., 1844), pp. 358–59; for killing in the yard, see [Rev. Thomas Barton], *The Conduct of the Paxton-Men* . . . (Philadelphia, 1764), p. 22.

27. Edward Shippen to Joseph Shippen Jr., Dec. 19, 1763, Shippen–Shippen Correspondence; Henderson to Joseph Galloway, Dec. 17, 1763, Friendly Assoc. Papers (Haverford) 4.

28. Rev. John Elder to Joseph Shippen Jr., Feb. 1, 1764, Elder Papers 2:29 (meetings); "Fragments of a Journal Kept by Samuel Foulke, of Bucks County, while a Member of the Colonial Assembly of Pennsylvania, 1762–3–4," ed. Howard M. Jenkins, *PMHB* 5 (1881): 69 (Feb. 3, 1764; routes); anonymous letter from Lebanon, Pa., Dec. 31, 1763, *Pa. Arch.* 1:4:156; Susanna Wright to Isaac Whitelock, Jan. 16, 1764, Parrish-Pemberton Papers.

29. Henderson to Joseph Galloway, Dec. 17, 1763, Friendly Assoc. Papers (Haverford) 4; Foulke, "Fragments of a Journal," p. 66 (Jan. 3, 1764; banditti); Gov. Penn to assembly, Feb. 4, 1764, and assembly to Penn, Jan. 20, 1764, *Votes* 5:312 and 306. To give some suggestion of how intimidating it was to learn such news, during the Stump affair (chap. 5 above) in 1768, William Johnson Jr.—the half-Irish, half-Mohawk son of Sir William Johnson—was studying in Lancaster as a pupil of Rev. Thomas Barton. On hearing of the killings, his tutor reported, young William at once plunged into depression and tried to leave Pa. completely: "he got so uneasy at the violent Proceedings in these Parts, that he apprehended himself in Danger indeed no Wonder!" (Barton to Sir William Johnson, Mar. 25 and May 1768, *Johnson Papers* 6:170–71 and 238).

30. Anonymous letter from Lebanon, Pa., Dec. 31, 1763, *Pa. Arch.* 1:4:156 (harbor); petition of Philadelphia overseers of the poor, Jan. 6, 1764, *Votes* 5:295–96. See John Harris's petition from Paxton for reimbursement and its rejection (Jan. 25 and 29, 1763); the similar petitions (Sept. 17 and 20, 1763, and Jan. 11, 1764) by inhabitants of the Great Cove and Conococheague, including one David Scott, who had "rashly g[i]ve[n] his Bond to pay and maintain Twenty-seven Men" during summer 1763; and the similar petition (Jan. 9, 1764) by inhabitants of six townships in upper Northampton Co.—all ibid., pp. 239, 241, 264–65, 266, 296–98 (tax cuts and Scott: p. 297). Poverty rates in Philadelphia had doubled since the war began; see Gary B. Nash, "Poverty and Poor Relief in Pre-Revolutionary Philadelphia," *WMQ* 33 (1976): 3–30, table 1 (at p. 9).

31. Foulke, "Fragments of a Journal," p. 67 (ca. Jan. 7, 1764); Elder to Joseph Shippen Jr., Feb. 1, 1764, Elder Papers 2:29. The classic account of this ideological strand is Richard Richard L. Bushman, *King and People in Provincial Massachusetts* (Chapel Hill, N.C., 1985), chap. 5. For a view of these events as expressions of rage by "small patriarchs" (p. 208) in the context of wartime assaults on households, see Krista Camenzind, "Violence, Race, and the Paxton Boys," in *Friends and Enemies*, ed. Pencak and Richter, chap. 11.

32. Grube, "Diarium . . . auf Province-Island," Dec. 29, 1763 (rebels), and Jan. 2, 1764 (Nantucket), *Morav. Recs.* 127:1:1; Lewis Weiss to assembly, Jan. 3, 1764, *Votes* 5:293; ibid.,

pp. 294–95 (Jan. 4, 1764). For reaction to the bill, see Foulke, "Fragments of a Journal," p. 67 (ca. Jan. 7, 1764, noting that it "Occasion'd such a Clamour in ye House & out-a-doors that the house thought proper to let it lye"); for extralocal trials, see the Stump case, chap. 5 above.

33. Grube, "Diarium . . . auf der Pilgershafft," Jan. 5, 1764 ("Zieml. wild, und sonderl. plagten sie unsere junge Weibes leute"), *Morav. Recs.* 127:1:2.

34. Grube, "Diarium . . . auf der Pilgershafft," Jan. 5, 1764 ("Der Zulauft von Menshen wurde sehr starck, so daß wir uns Kaum durch drängen Konten"), *Morav. Recs.* 127:1:2; Franklin to Penn, Jan. 12, 1764, *Votes* 5:300–301 (Jan. 16, 1764); Grube, "Diarium . . . auf der Pilgershafft," Jan. 8, 1764 ("mußten sich zieml. mustern laßen"), and Jan. 7, 1764 (Princeton), *Morav. Recs.* 127:1:2; Grube, "Reiße-Diarium des Indianer Gemeinleins," Jan. 18, 1764 ("ein boshafftiger Mensh, mit einem Stock, . . . stieß die Elisabeth in ihre Seite, so daß sie in ohnmacht fiel"), ibid. Elizabeth was the name of Grube's wife, so that the poking victim seems more likely to have been his own European spouse than one of the Indians.

35. Colden to Penn, Jan. 10, 1764, *Votes* 5:301 (Jan. 16, 1764). By contrast, Colden was inclined to see the Iroquois as hardy Romans in the rough; see the preface to his *History of the Five Indian Nations . . .* (New York, 1727, with expanded and slightly retitled editions in 1750 and 1755; in this view Colden much resembled Gen. James Edward Oglethorpe, the founder of Georgia, to whom he dedicated his history's later editions).

36. Dep. of Benjamin Kendall, Jan. 28, 1764, *Pa. Col. Recs.* 9:126; *Mühlenberg Journal* 2:18; *Votes* 5:308 (Jan. 27, 1764).

37. *Votes* 5:311 (Feb. 6–8, 1764); *Mühlenberg Journals* 2:16 (sleighing); "Information given Isaac Wayne," 2nd mo. 3–8, 1764, Pemberton Papers 17:10 (cold, wind). For streets, see, e.g., Carl and Jessica Bridenbaugh, *Rebels and Gentlemen: Philadelphia in the Age of Franklin*, 2nd ed. (New York, 1961), p. 11; for ferries, petition of James Coultas (keeper of the Market St. ferry), *Votes* 4:107 (6th mo. 8, 1749), and *An Historical Account of the Late Disturbance . . .*, p. 4 (adding that boats were sunk and ferry ropes cut down).

38. James Pemberton to Dr. John Fothergill, 3 mo. 7, 1764, Pemberton Papers 34:125–28; Grube, "Diarium . . . in den *Barracks* zu Philadelphia," Feb. 5, 1764 ("sprach ihnen Muth zu, und war sonderl. freundl. gegen die Kinder"), *Morav. Recs.* 127:2; Pemberton to Fothergill, 3 mo. 7, 1764, Pemberton Papers 34: 125–28; *Mühlenberg Journals* 2:19 (ringing); *The Paxton Boys: A Farce . . .*, 2nd ed. (Philadelphia, 1764), pp. 2–3 (expresses, watchmen). The moon had set at nine that night, and was in any case only a thin paring, barely past new.

39. *Mühlenberg Journals* 2:64 and 20 (bells, small boys). According to a special meeting committee appointed to investigate their "unstiddyness," only 32 of the Quakers in arms were underaged and "unacquainted with the grounds of Friend's Testimony" on arms-bearing (Hannah Harris to Rachel Pemberton, July 10, 1764, Pemberton Papers; and Philadelphia Monthly Meeting Minutes, Feb. 22, 1765, and July 27, 1764, F.H.L.). There were no disownments, but members' differing interpretations of the peace testimony—with a small group feeling that "[t]his doctrine of non-resistance does not stand upon the same ground as other doctrines"—later led to purges in the Revolution (Samuel Wetherill, *An Apology for the . . . Free Quakers . . .* [Philadelphia, 1798], pp. 32–33).

40. Israel Pemberton Jr. to John Pemberton, 2nd mo. 27, 1764, Pemberton Papers 17:11 (Berks and Lancaster groups); *Mühlenberg Journals* 2:20–21.

41. James Pemberton to Dr. John Fothergill, 3 mo. 7, 1764, Pemberton Papers 34:125–28 (the assemblyman was likely Isaac Wayne of Chester Co., a key news broker in the crisis; cf. council minutes, Feb. 4, 1764, *Pa. Col. Recs.* 9:132, and "Information given Isaac Wayne," 2nd mo. 3–8, 1764, Pemberton Papers 17:10); *Votes* 5:316–18 (Feb. 17, 1764; later printed in *A Declaration and Remonstrance of the Distressed and Bleeding Frontier Inhabitants . . .* [Philadelphia, 1764]). This first complaint must have been written before the marchers reached Whitemarsh, most likely in or around Lancaster; so that despite suspicions of its being readied in Philadelphia by Penn family partisans and "furnish'd" to the rioters, it likely offers the best look available at what they originally thought they were doing (Israel Pemberton Jr. to John Pemberton, 2nd mo. 27, 1764, Pemberton Papers 17:11). I would doubt two candidates' authorship: Rev. Thomas Barton (on stylistic grounds) and Rev. John Elder (for its treatment of the Conestogas' killings—cf. Elder to Gov. Penn, Dec. 16, 1763, Elder Papers 2:27—though otherwise Elder is an ideal suspect).

42. James Pemberton to Dr. John Fothergill, 3 mo. 7, 1764, Pemberton Papers 34:125–28.

43. *Mühlenberg Journals* 2:22–23. Elder had recommended Armstrong as an intermediary a few days before (to Joseph Shippen Jr., Feb. 1, 1764, Elder Papers 2:29).

44. *Mühlenberg Journals* 2:23. The first statement of grievances also touched on the Lancaster Co. massacres' bad press in Philadelphia—what Elder, in Paxton, bitterly called "the manner of the Quakers resenting these things . . . [by] charg[ing Presbyterians] in bulk" with them and calling them unparalleled barbarities (to Joseph Shippen Jr., Feb. 1, 1764, Elder Papers 2:29). Elder was goaded, above all, by one stinging response to the killings—Franklin's anonymous *Narrative of the Late Massacres . . .* (Philadelphia, 1764)—and a desire to somehow answer back in public was one spur to the march, which at least some of its backers seem to have imagined would better the image of "frontier people."

45. John Harris to Col. James Burd, Mar. 1, 1764, Shippen Papers (see the city); "Information given Isaac Wayne" (as summarized by a Pemberton), 2nd mo. 3–8, 1764, Pemberton Papers 17:10 (ragged, taken notice of); Foulke, "Fragments of a Journal," p. 71 (Feb. 7, 1764; shabby gang); *Paxton Boys, A Farce . . .* , p. 4 (ragged); Grube, "Diarium . . . in den *Barracks* zu Philadelphia," Feb. 9, 1764 ("sahen sich dieselben genau an, kanten aber keinen"; this was probably "Smith"); Feb. 12, 1764 (getting rest); and Apr 2, 1764 (pamphlets), *Morav. Recs.* 127:2. For musical evenings, see, e.g., ibid., May 22, 1764.

Chapter 7
THE QUAKERS UNMASKED

1. Bingham to John Gibson, May 4, 1764, Shippen Papers; *Mühlenberg Journals* 2:167–68. By *Harlekin* Mühlenberg meant a "Merry Andrew," or clowning barker used to drum up business. The Merry Andrew whom Mühlenberg saw selling this broadside (namely

[Isaac Hunt], *A Conference between the D[evi]l and Doctor D[ov]e . . .* [Philadelphia, 1764]) was later described in another pamphlet: "a little Fellow with a Bee-hive-Wig, on a dapple Powny, with *Jenny's* Apple bobbing, [who] hawk'd [Dove] and [his] Friend the Devil, yesterday, about the Streets; and sold [them] both for Six-pence" ([Hunt], *A Continuation of the Exercises in Scurrility Hall, No. II* [Philadelphia, 1765], p. 5).

2. For Smith, see Albert Frank Gegenheimer, *William Smith, Educator and Churchman, 1727–1803* (Philadelphia, 1943); Charlotte Goldsborough Fletcher, *Cato's Mirania: A Life of Provost Smith* (Lanham, Md., 2002); and esp. *Life and Correspondence of the Rev. William Smith, D.D. . . .* , comp. Horace Wemyss Smith, 2 vols. (Philadelphia, 1879–80).

3. [Smith], *A Brief State of the Province of Pennsylvania,* 3rd ed. (London, 1756; orig. pub. 1755 and written Dec. 1754), pp. 31, 17, 32, 30–31, 35, and 17. Pa.'s few Catholics were viewed with enough alarm in wartime by officials as well as country people that in 1757 a special census was undertaken, Gov. William Denny "thinking it necessary to know the exact Number of Roman Catholics." According to figures provided by Philadelphia's resident Jesuit, there were a bare 1,365 Catholic communion takers in Pennsylvania, which had a population in 1757 of about 160,000. A great preponderance, probably 70 percent, of these were German-speakers (*Pa. Col. Recs.* 7:447–48).

4. [Joseph Galloway], *A True and Impartial State of the Province of Pennsylvania* (Philadelphia, 1759), p. 40; Smith, "A Letter Concerning the Office and Duty of PROTESTANT MINISTERS . . . in Times of Public Danger . . . ," in his *Discourses on Public Occasions in America,* 2nd ed. (London, 1762), pp. 14–15 (Smith was writing here against what he called unfair Quaker attacks on his anti-Catholic sermons as being "of a biggoted and persecuting Spirit"; Smith to archbishop of Canterbury, Oct. 22, 1755, *Life and Correspondence* 1:119); message of Isaac Norris and Pa. assembly to Gov. Robert Hunter Morris, Sept. 29, 1755, *Votes* 4:464; [Galloway], *True and Impartial State,* pp. 29–30.

5. [Benjamin Franklin or Richard Jackson], *An Historical Review of the Constitution and Government of Pennsylvania . . .* (London, 1759), pp. 191, 299; "Fragments of a Journal Kept by Samuel Foulke, of Bucks County, while a Member of the Colonial Assembly of Pennsylvania, 1762–3–4," ed. Howard M. Jenkins, *PMHB* 5 (1881): 73; *A Receipt to Make a Speech by J[oseph] G[alloway] . . .* (Philadelphia, 1764). This well-established vein of political rhetoric, whether focused on constitutionalism or questions of power and liberty (jointly mapped by Jack P. Greene, "Political Mimesis: A Consideration of the Historical and Cultural Roots of Legislative Behavior in the British Colonies in the Eighteenth Century," *AHR* 75 [1969]: 337–60, and Bailyn, *The Ideological Origins of the American Revolution* [Cambridge, Mass., 1967], esp. chap. 3), was about to be put in the shade as a form of argument by the rhetorical innovations that Indian war unleashed. For the origins in preceding decades of an orderly sphere of printed debate, see John Smolenski, "Friends and Strangers: Religion, Diversity, and the Ordering of Public Life in Colonial Pennsylvania, 1681–1764" (Ph.D. diss., Univ. of Pennsylvania, 2001), chap. 5 (and, for a view of the 1764 print war as embedded within that Quaker public culture, chap. 8).

6. [Smith], Supplement to *N.Y. Mercury,* Oct. 27, 1755, p. 2; Smith to Thomas Penn, May 1, 1755, Penn Official Correspondence 7:29, as quoted in *Franklin Papers* 6:52 n. 5;

Joseph Shippen Jr. to Charles Thomson, May 14, 1755, Joseph Shippen Letterbook ("I hope," he plaintively wrote, "the next Londn. Vessel will bring over more of them, that I may purchase one to keep by me . . . . I have heard a great Character of that Piece"). The same week Quakers thanked an English correspondent for dispatching "two or three of those Scandalous Pamphlets" to them in Philadelphia, so that they could see for themselves how they were talked of "on your Side of the Water" (Israel Pemberton Jr. to Dr. John Fothergill, May 19, 1755, *Franklin Papers* 6:52).

7. Barton, *Unanimity and Public Spirit: A Sermon Preached at Carlisle . . . Soon after General Braddock's Defeat . . .* (Philadelphia, 1755), pp. 1 and 8; [William Smith], *A Brief View of the Conduct of Pennsylvania . . .* (London, 1756; written Dec. 1755), p. 42.

8. [Smith], *Brief State*, p. 27, and *Brief View*, p. 4 and title.

9. Flemings' advertisement, *Pa. Gazette*, Feb. 19, 1756; *A Narrative of the Sufferings and Surprizing Deliverances of William and Elizabeth Fleming . . .* (Boston, 1756).

10. [Smith], *Brief View*, p. 46; *Pa. Journal*, Sept. 25, 1755, p. 1 (in note); [Smith], Supplement to *N.Y. Mercury*, Oct. 27, 1755, p. 2.

11. [Smith], *Brief View*, pp. 87, 6, 17, 24, 58, 54, 58, 77, 23, 60, 70n, 60, and 53–54; *Pa. Journal*, Sept. 12, 1754.

12. [Franklin or Jackson], *Historical Review*, p. 236; [Galloway], *True and Impartial State*, pp. 5, 120; Morris to assembly, Aug. 13, 1755, *Votes* 4:333; assembly to Morris, Sept. 29, 1755, 4:463: to the assemblymen's ears Morris's speeches sounded like leftover bits from Smith's pamphlets, "serv'd . . . up as a cold Hash" (Humphrey Scourge, *Tit for Tat, or the Scourge Wip'd Off* [New York, 1758; written Nov. 1755], p. 1). As the son of Lewis Morris, a central agitator in the Cosby-Morris controversy that wracked New York politics in the 1730s—with the writings by members of his faction against Gov. William Cosby bringing about the celebrated libel trial of John Peter Zenger, their printer— Robert Hunter Morris had already spent his teenaged years in a world of printed political combat. See Michael Warner, *The Letters of the Republic: Publication and the Public Sphere in Eighteenth-Century America* (Cambridge, Mass., 1990), pp. 49–58; and Alan Tully, *Forming American Politics: Ideals, Interests, and Institutions in Colonial New York and Pennsylvania* (Baltimore, Md., 1994), pp. 94–106 (the most complete synthesis of either Pa. or N.Y. politics).

13. [Franklin or Jackson], *Historical Review*, pp. 366, 277, 235, 277, 234, 294, 356, 359, 356, 359, and 277.

14. Ibid., pp. 439 and 235.

15. *Votes* 4:495 (Nov. 5, 1755; see address of Moore to Gov. Denny, *Pa. Gazette*, Dec. 1, 1757, for petition wording); *Votes* 4:502–3 (Nov. 12, 1755).

16. [Smith], *Brief View*, p. 72, and Smith to Thomas Penn, Nov. 27, 1755, as quoted in Gegenheimer, *William Smith*, p. 131; [Franklin or Jackson], *Historical Review*, pp. 292; [Galloway], *True and Impartial State*, p. 153.

17. Address of Moore to Gov. Denny, *Pa. Gazette*, Dec. 1, 1757; *Votes* 4:781 (Jan. 25, 1758). In the course of these controversies Smith married Moore's daughter.

18. *Remarks on the Quaker Unmask'd . . .* , p. 2 (impossible); Charles Read, *Copy of a Letter from Charles Read, Esq. . . .* , p. 5 (bravery; cf. [Benjamin Franklin], *A Narrative of the Late Massacres in Lancaster County of a Number of Indians . . .* , pp. 29–31); *The Author of*

Quaker Unmask'd Strip'd Start Naked . . . , p. 10 (spirited); "The Paxton Expedition, Inscribed to the Author of the Farce . . ." (grog; and cf. *The Paxton Boys: A Farce* . . . , p. 14, and the carefully impartial instant history *An Historical Account of the Late Disturbance* . . . , to whose author the Quakers' being "prepared with Arms like *Spartans* brave, striding forth with Gigantic Pace to defend their Laws and Liberty," seemed worthy of being "Recorded in the Annals of after Ages in LETTERS of GOLD" [p. 4]). Unless otherwise noted, publications quoted in this chapter were printed at Philadelphia in 1764; the sequence in which they are discussed as having been printed is reconstructed from internal evidence.

19. Read, *Copy of a Letter,* p. 3; *A Dialogue between Andrew Trueman and Thomas Zealot* . . . , pp. 3–5 (the reply, of course, was that "we did not let them fecht Us").

20. [Franklin], *Narrative of the Late Massacres,* pp. 21–22 and 27; see chap. 3 above.

21. Ibid., p. 13; for skin-color prejudice, see conclusion below.

22. [Isaac Hunt], *A Looking-Glass, &c., No. II* (bound in his collected *A Looking-Glass for Presbyterians*), p. 15.

23. *A Letter from a Gentleman at Elizabeth-Town* . . . , p. 5.

24. *A Declaration and Remonstrance of the Distressed and Bleeding Frontier Inhabitants* . . . ; [David James Dove], *A Battle! A Battle! A Battle of Squirt* . . . , p. 8.

25. [Dove], *A Battle!* p. 6 (bereft); [Rev. Thomas Barton], *The Conduct of the Paxton-Men* . . . , pp. 16, 9, 5, 28, and 3; *Remarks on the Quaker Unmask'd,* p. 7 (mob, Slemish). John Harris similarly insisted from the Susquehanna-side that what he was referring to, by March, as "the General Cause" of "the Good People of this Province" had been supported by "the Inhabitants of this Province on all Roads from Paxton to Philada:"— all of whom, he could (not surprisingly) report, had treated the armed column of "Volonteers Well . . .—& no Person Offer'd to Insult them" (Harris to Col. James Burd, Mar. 1, 1764, Shippen Papers).

26. *Dialogue Containing Some Reflections on the Late Declaration* . . . , p. 4; *The Address of the People Call'd Quakers* . . . , p. 3; *Dialogue Containing Some Reflections,* pp. 10, 3, and 2.

27. *Quaker Unmask'd Stripped Start Naked,* p. 9; back cover of [David James Dove], *The Quaker Unmask'd, or Plain Truth* . . . , 2nd ed.; title page of *A Serious Address to Such of the Inhabitants* . . . ("To which is now added, *A Dialogue between Andrew Trueman and Thomas Zealot* . . ."), 4th ed; William Murrell, *A History of American Graphic Humor,* 2 vols. (New York, 1933–38), 1:12–13; *The Paxton Boys: A Farce,* p. 6. Some such ephemera survive, in the collection of the L.C.P., thanks mainly to the artist and curiosity-collector Pierre Eugène du Simitière, who amassed as many imprints as he could—stooping to gather some from Philadelphia's streets—and carefully noted their dates of first issuance.

28. [Hunt], *Looking-Glass, &c., No. II* (bound in collected *Looking-Glass for Presbyterians*), p. 14.

29. [Dove], *Quaker Unmask'd,* pp. 12 and 5.

30. Ibid., pp. 9–10 and 10–11. The image of violent Quakers was popularized in [Dove], *A Battle!* p. 6, and an accompanying engraving by James Claypoole Jr. (see below), which made as much as possible of the image of Quaker hats interpenetrated by bristling guns.

31. [Barton], *Conduct of the Paxton-Men*, p. 30.

32. Ibid., pp. 17 and 4; *An Address to the Rev. Dr. Alison . . . Being a Vindication of the Quakers . . .* (1765), p. 33.

33. [Barton], *Conduct of the Paxton-Men*, p. 32. See esp. [Hugh Williamson], *The Plain Dealer . . . No. III*, which sifted all the records of dissension at earlier treaties between the Friendly Assoc. and executive officials to find proof that Quakers had "persuaded the Indians ... they ought to scourge the white people who live on the frontiers. In other words, plunder, tomahawk and burn them" (p. 11).

34. Johnson to Croghan, Oct. 24, 1762, Cadwalader-Croghan Papers.

35. [Dove], "King Wampum, or Harm Watch, Harm Catch," in *A Battle!* pp. 19–20.

36. [Barton], *Conduct of the Paxton-Men*, pp. 29–30. According to a hostile report, Pemberton "alarmed the whole Family where he lodged [in flight from the marchers in N.J.] with his Cries—*'They are coming; They are coming to kill me;'* being terribly frightened by the . . . Fall of a Bag of Straw" ([Isaac Hunt], *Now in the Press . . . The Life and Adventures of a Certain Quaker Presbyterian Indian Colonel* [1766]).

37. [Dove], *A Battle!* p. 8.

38. [Hunt], *Life and Adventures of . . . Quaker Presbyterian Indian Colonel* (shame; by this time, in 1766, Pemberton had also come out against the assembly's move to put Pennsylvania under crown control, and Hunt, easily the most passionate pro-Quaker publicist, also felt at liberty to lay into him for "sen[ding] Messages to, and h[o]ld[ing] a Correspondence with the Natives in the Time of open War"); *The Quaker Vindicated . . .* (Philadelphia, 1764), p. 9 (lenity); *Address to the Rev. Dr. Alison . . .* , p. 5 (absurd conduct).

39. *An Answer to the Pamphlet Entituled the Conduct of the Paxton Men . . .* , p. 28 (ulceration); [Isaac Hunt], *A Letter from a Gentleman in Transilvania . . .* , pp. 4 and 6; *Address to the Rev. Dr. Alison,* pp. 11 (task) and 13 (defame); [Isaac Hunt], *The Scribler . . .* , p. 14 (reflections, priests); *Author of Quaker Unmask'd Strip'd Start Naked,* p. 5 (bigoted). The harsher light on Presbyterianism was partly owing to contemporaries' misattribution, over several months, of *The Quaker Unmask'd* to Rev. Francis Alison, an Edinburgh-educated Ulsterman (his authorship was the sole premise of *Author of Quaker Unmask'd Strip'd Start Naked*). The attacks also fitted neatly into the view of Presbyterians and Presbyterianism that had controlled English letters at least since the publication of Samuel Butler's doggerel epic *Hudibras,* in the wake of England's civil war. An archetypal Presbyterian—cruel, persecuting, bigoted, unhappy with anything shy of absolute mastery, somehow at once bloodthirsty and ridiculous—drew those writers who opposed the rioters as if by gravitational attraction (as, indeed, did the meter of *Hudibras* itself, most blatantly in *The Paxtoniade: A Poem*).

40. *Author of Quaker Unmask'd Strip'd Start Naked,* p. 6 (enemies); [Isaac Hunt], *The Substance of a Council . . .* , printed as appendix to *Looking-Glass, &c., No. II,* in collected *Looking-Glass for Presbyterians,* p. 34 (extirpating); *Address to the Rev. Dr. Alison . . .* , pp. 17–18 and 7–8 (power, pleasure). For the ministers' supposed desire for a Presbyterianized province, see *Substance of a Council,* p. 28.

41. *Address to the Rev. Dr. Alison . . . Being a Vindication of the Quakers . . .* , p. 14. The closest Hunt ever dared come to criticizing his opponents' reflexive recourse to the anti-

Indian sublime was once to charge Presbyterian ministers who had preached charity sermons in Ireland with having made it a practice wave before crowds fluttering little objects "as Proofs, declaring they were the Skins of their Heads that were barbarously . . . torn off by the wild *Indians*" in Pa.—when in fact, Hunt claimed, they were only "a Parcel of Squirrel Scalps" (*Looking-Glass, &c., No. II*, in collected *Looking-Glass for Presbyterians*, p. 18). Williamson was of Ulster Presbyterian descent, and the other most effective writer on the anti-Quaker side, Rev. Thomas Barton, was also from Ulster, though himself an Anglican. Hunt, an embittered former student of Alison's at the college, was almost certainly working on a salary from the assembly side.

42. [Hugh Williamson], *The Plain Dealer, or a Few Remarks upon Quaker Politicks . . . Numb. I*, pp. 16, 8, 18, and 9–10; *Address to the Rev. Dr. Alison . . . Being a Vindication of the Quakers . . .*, p. 17.

43. Before this stage of appealing to the Germans as fellow sufferers was arrived at, one representatively ham-fisted early anti-Quaker effort had even gone out of its way to insult them (*A Letter from Batista Angeloni . . .*, p. 8).

44. [Williamson], *Plain Dealer, . . . Numb. I*, pp. 7, 18, 9, and 11.

45. [Franklin], *Cool Thoughts on the Present Situation of Our Public Affairs . . .*, pp. 6, 10, 9, and 21–22.

46. Assembly resolves, Mar. 24, 1764, *Votes* 5:337–339; [Williamson], *Plain Dealer . . . No. III*, p. 4; [Franklin], *Explanatory Remarks on the Assembly's Resolves . . .*, p. 1; *An Address to the Freeholders and Inhabitants . . . in Answer to a Paper Called the Plain Dealer*, p. 7 (bleed on).

47. [Williamson], *Plain Dealer . . . No. III*, p. 4; *To the King's Most Excellent Majesty . . .* (the petition for royalization), p. 1.

48. [Galloway], *True and Impartial State*, p. 153 (numbers, the whole people); [Williamson], *Plain Dealer . . . No. III*, p. 4. It was esp. difficult to make such a shift for Galloway, who continually forgot that the campaign for royalization was supposed only to be a reflection of the people's sovereign will. At one point, Galloway let himself be lured (by William Smith, now back in Philadelphia and running the press war) into all but admitting the program's unpopularity: "[T]ho' Millions and Mountains oppose," Galloway grandly announced, the assembly would nonetheless push it through, as royalization was the right thing for the people whether or not they knew it (*The Speech of Joseph Galloway, Esq. . . .*, p. 35). This idea (like Galloway) did not have a long future in Pa.

49. *Votes* 5:320, 321 (petitions; Feb. 25 and 29, 1764), and 325 (denial; March 6, 1764); [Smith], *An Answer to Mr. Franklin's Remarks . . .*, p. 4 (yeas, accountable); *Pa. Gazette*, Dec. 27, 1764 (tribunal).

50. *Observations on a Late Epitaph . . .*, p. 4 (harmony); *New-Year Verses of the Printers Lads . . .* (1765). For political lectures, see, e.g., [Isaac Hunt], "An Election Ballad . . . ," in *The Birth, Parentage, and Education of Praise-God Barebone . . .* (1766), p. 15n, and *An Address of Thanks to the Wardens of Christ Church . . .*; and for free distribution of prints, [Hunt], *Continuation of the Exercises in Scurrility Hall, No. II*, p. 4. For the broadening of political life of which the election was part, see generally Richard R. Beeman, *The Varieties of Political Experience in Eighteenth-Century America* (Philadelphia, 2004), chaps. 8–9. For broader narratives focused on Pa., see esp. Tully, *Forming American Poli-*

tics, chaps. 7 and 10; and James H. Hutson, *Pennsylvania Politics, 1746–1770: The Movement for Royal Government and Its Consequences* (Princeton, N.J., 1972); also see Alison Olson, "The Pamphlet War over the Paxton Boys," *PMHB* 123 (1999): 31–56.

51. [Christoph Saur], *Anmerckungen über Ein noch nie erhört und gesehen Wunder Thier . . . ,* p. 10 ("sie . . . T'schentelmänner heissen darff, sondern die Arrestanten an den Schweif seines Pferdes binden, und sie nach trollen machen").

52. *An Die Freyhalter und Einwohner Der Stadt und County Philadelphia, deutscher Nation,* p. 1 ("Heerde"). See Franklin, "Observations concerning the Increase of Mankind, Peopling of Countries, &c." (1751), *Franklin Papers* 4:234. Franklin left this essay in manuscript until agreeing to its publication just before war's onset in 1755.

53. *Eine Andere Anrede an die deutschen Freyhalter . . . ,* bound in *Eine Anrede an die Deutschen Freyhalter der Stadt und County Philadelphia,* p. 5 ("daß Englische Wort Boors hat keine weitere Bedeutung, dann Bauren")]; [Williamson], *What Is Sauce for a Goose . . . ,* p. 4. Another weak early line of defense was to pretend, in English, that the German-language attacks had literally claimed "boors" meant "boars" (as in *The Plot, by Way of a Burlesk . . .*).

54. [Saur], *Anmerckungen über Ein noch nie erhört und gesehen Wunder Thier,* pp. 10 and 15 ("sie so schwärmen, sich Heerdenweise vermehren, und bey ihrer Sprache und Grobheit bleiben").

55. *Getreue Warnung gegen die Lockvögel . . . ,* p. 11 ("laß sie nur brav voran gehen, wo die Gefahr am grösten ist . . . . O! es sind nur Teutsche und Eyrische").

56. *Der Lockvögel Warnungsgesang vor den Stoßvögeln,* p. 3. One remarkable feature of the new election in the German press was the repeated printing of all the names in a coherent opposition slate, to be handed in together on ballot papers at the courthouse—a slate that included two Germans, whose candidacy was endorsed at an election-day meeting of all Philadelphia Lutherans, called by St. Michael's Lutheran Church council. Mühlenberg furiously told an assembly deputation sent to remonstrate over the Lutheran role in backing this "New Ticket," "I approved it because we German citizens are not bastards but His Majesty's . . . naturalized children" (*Mühlenberg Journals* 2:192). See Dietmar Rothermund, "The German Problem of Colonial Pennsylvania," *PMHB* 84 (1960): 3–21; and Wolfgang Splitter, "The Germans in Pennsylvania Politics, 1758–1790: A Quantitative Analysis," *PMHB* 122 (1998): 39–76.

57. Robert J. Dinkin, *Voting in Provincial America: A Study of Elections in the Thirteen Colonies, 1689–1776* (Westport, Conn., 1977), table 9, pp. 158–59; Charles Pettit to Joseph Reed, Nov. 3, 1764, in William B. Reed, *Life and Correspondence of Joseph Reed* (Philadelphia, 1847), 1:36–37 (steps, litters); [Henry Dawkins, with verses by Isaac Hunt], "The Election, a Medley . . ." (saving grace); *Mühlenberg Journals* 2:123; Franklin to Richard Jackson, Oct. 11, 1764, *Franklin Papers* 11:397; unknown artist, "The Counter-Medley . . ." (boors); [James Biddle], *To the Freeholders and Electors . . .* (1765; jealous). The next fall, in 1765, there would be even more voters—4,332—and in 1766 the total for Philadelphia Co. was still 3,019. The precise participation rates for 1761, 1764, and 1765 were 11.1 percent, 42.2 percent, and 46.1 percent; Dinkin thinks rates of participation for 1765 in Bucks and Lancaster also approached 50 percent.

58. Samuel Wharton to Benjamin Franklin, Oct. 13, 1765, *Franklin Papers* 12:317; Burd to

Purviance, Sept. 17, 1764, Shippen Papers; Purviance to [James Burd], Sept. 20, 1765, Shippen Papers. Saur's handbill: *Wertheste Landes-Leute . . . !* (Germantown, 1765).

59. [John Dickinson], MS "Observations on Mr. Franklin's Remarks," in *The Writings of John Dickinson,* ed. Paul Leicester Ford (Philadelphia, 1895), 1:163, as quoted in *Franklin Papers* 11:448 n. 4; letter from Philadelphia, Nov. 23, 1764, *N.C. Mag. . . . for 1764,* pp. 226–27, as quoted in J. Philip Gleason, "A Scurrilous Colonial Election and Franklin's Reputation," *WMQ* 18 (1961): 83; John Dickinson et al., *A Protest Presented to the House of Assembly . . . ; Franklin, Remarks on a Late Protest . . . ,* p. 3; [Smith], *An Answer to Mr. Franklin's Remarks . . . ,* p. 14.

60. For one such printed update to the *"GENTLEMEN"* of the voting public (on the militia bill, and probably by Franklin, see *Franklin Papers* 11:360–65), *To the Freemen of Pennsylvania . . . .*

61. *Pa. Journal,* Sept. 20, 1764; [Franklin], preface to *Speech of Joseph Galloway,* p. xxxii.

Chapter 8
BARBARISM AND THE AMERICAN REVOLUTION

1. Dixon and Hunter's *Va. Gazette,* Aug. 24, 1776, p. 8.

2. Harris to Biddle, July 29, 1776, *Pa. Arch.* 1:4:789.

3. In the South, in spring 1776 the crown's superintendent of Indian affairs was still intentionally misinterpreting direct instructions from his commander in chief to recruit Indian allies: "I could not construe this to mean an indiscriminate attack upon the Frontier Inhabitants," as he wrote, which "would induce a Coalition of all parties for repelling a Common Enemy" (John Stuart to Gen. Henry Clinton, Mar. 15, 1776, quoted in Philip M. Hamer, "John Stuart's Indian Policy during the Early Months of the American Revolution," *MVHR* 17 [1930]: 362 n. 38). For Morgan's actions, see Max Savelle, *George Morgan, Colony Builder* (New York, 1932), and Gregory Schaaf, *Wampum Belts and Peace Trees: George Morgan, Native Americans, and Revolutionary Diplomacy* (Golden, Colo., 1990).

4. *Pa. Mercury,* Aug. 18, 1775, p. 4; "A Speech of the Chiefs and Warriors of the Oneida Tribe of Indians . . . ," *Pa. Mag., or American Monthly Museum,* supplement for 1775, pp. 601–2.

5. As Colin G. Calloway observes, "most [Indian] people fluctuated in their sentiments, and participation in the fighting was often relatively brief" (*The American Revolution in Indian Country: Crisis and Diversity in Native American Communities* [Cambridge, 1995], p. 32). See White, *Middle Ground,* chap. 10, for an influential account of such assassinations; and for the devastation of the revolutionary economy, Richard Buel Jr., *In Irons: Britain's Naval Supremacy and the American Revolutionary Economy* (New Haven, Conn., 1998).

6. *In Congress, July 4, 1776: A Declaration . . .* (Philadelphia, 1776).

7. *Berrow's Worcester Journal,* July 22, 1779, and *Morning Chronicle and London Advertiser,* Mar. 31, 1778, both quoted in Stephen Conway, "From Fellow-Nationals to Foreigners: British Perceptions of the Americans, circa 1739–1783," *WMQ* 59 (2002): 65–100.

8. In the southern colonies, by contrast, Lord Dunmore's declaration of freedom for the slaves of rebels who took up arms against their masters helped almost at once to make the image of murderous Africans into a useful tool for abhorring the British cause.

9. *An Oration in Memory of General Montgomery . . .* (Philadelphia, 1776), pp. 18, 19, 28, and 31. Descriptions: Smith, *Correspondence* 1:545; Silverman, *Cultural History*, p. 314; Smith to Jasper Yeates, Feb. 13, 1776, *Correspondence* 1:544 (music).

10. *Pa. Eve. Post,* Mar. 2, 1776, pp. 111–12; and *Common Sense . . . and a Dialogue between the Ghost of General Montgomery . . . and an American Delegate in a Wood, Near Philadelphia . . .* (Philadelphia, 1776), pp. 14–15; *Death of General Montgomery* (Philadelphia, 1777), p. 7. In the course of the war, Brackenridge changed his middle name from Montgomery to Henry.

11. Freneau and Brackenridge, *A Poem on the Rising Glory of America . . .* (Philadelphia, 1772), ll. 51–52 and 314–15.

12. *Pa. Eve. Post,* Dec. 26, 1775, p. 595 (pipe of wine); and *The Death of General Montgomery . . .* (Philadelphia, 1777), 1.1.24–33 (offspring; verse references are to act, scene, and line); p. 10n (tyranny); unpaginated key to frontispiece; 4.2.218–26, 230–34, and 237 (groaning, sight deplorable); 5.4.1 s.d.; 5.5.91–93 (skull); 5.4.10–11 (behold) and 38–40.

13. Hunt, *The Political Family . . .* (Philadelphia, 1775), pp. 31 and 28.

14. "[T]he circular letter sent to the Committees of the different counties . . ." (May 21, 1776), *Pa. Eve. Post,* June 13, 1776, pp. 295–96.

15. *Pa. Staatsbote,* Aug. 12, 1778, p. 1 (bloodbath); *Pa. Packet,* July 30, 1778, pp. 1–2 (perished); *Pa. Gazette,* Aug. 29, 1781 (Aug. 20 dispatches from Poughkeepsie, N.Y.; more savage); Piper to Pres. Thomas Wharton, May 4, 1778, Pa. Arch 1:6:470. For the refugees, cf. *Extracts from the Diary of Christopher Marshall . . .* , ed. William Duane (Albany, N.Y., 1877), p. 192 (July 18, 1778).

16. *Pa. Packet,* May 6, 1778 (published from exile in Lancaster; horrid design), p. 3; *Pa. Packet,* July 30, 1778, p. 2 (Terry). Paine had to confront this problem directly in *Common Sense,* where he argued somewhat desperately that the language of the "mother country" (for whose implications see Edwin G. Burrows and Michael Wallace, "The American Revolution: The Ideology and Psychology of National Liberation," *Perspectives in American History* 6 [1972]: 167–306) was an attempt to mislead Americans about the nature of the Anglo-American relationship, which was not that between parent and child but between "monster" and victim: "Even brutes do not devour their young, nor savages make war upon their families; . . . the phrase parent or mother country hath been jesuitically adopted by the king and his parasites, with a low papistical design of gaining an unfair bias on the credulous weakness of our minds" (*Collected Writings,* ed. Eric Foner [New York, 1995], p. 23).

17. *N.J. Gazette,* Apr. 24, 1782, pp. 2–3 (taskmasters); [Paine], "To Sir Guy Carleton," May 31, 1782, in *Collected Writings,* pp. 334–37; ibid., p. 35; *Pa. Journal,* May 23, 1781, p. 2.

18. David Hackett Fischer, *Paul Revere's Ride* (New York, 1994), pp. 216–18 and 406–7 n. 49; "A Circumstantial Account of an Attack . . . on the 19th of April 1775, on his Majesty's Troops . . ." (1776), in *Theatrum Majorum: The Cambridge of 1776 . . .* , ed. Arthur Gilman (Cambridge, Mass., 1876), p. 104 (mangled); Calloway, *American Revolution in Indian Country,* pp. 92–93 (backsides, open door); *The Cruel Massacre of the*

Protestants in North America, Shewing How the French and Indians Join together to Scalp the English . . . (London, [1756]), pp. 2–3 (flaying), a peculiar little production. As the Mass. Loyalist exile Peter Oliver was happy to at least be able to note—in the course of a pained reply to "american Complaints, about the scalping Knife & Indian Savages"—"I never heared of an Englishmans scalping an Englishman, untill the Battle of *Lexington* told the savage Tale" (Peter Oliver's *Origin and Progress of the American Revolution: A Tory View,* ed. Douglass Adair and John A. Schutz, 2nd ed. [Stanford, Calif., 1967], pp. 132–34).

19. Long, *The History of Jamaica, or General Survey of the Antient and Modern State of That Island* . . . , 3 vols. (London, 1774), bk. 3, chap. 1 ("Negroes"), p. 390 (orangutans); idem, *Candid Reflections upon . . . What Is Commonly Called the Negroe-Cause* . . . (London, 1772), p. 74 (see p. 55n for his sneering at the "laughable" fantasies behind agitation against the slave trade); idem, *English Humanity No Paradox* . . . (London, 1778), pp. 85, 84, 81, and 82. This effort cannot be understood in isolation from the anti-British discourse, depicting the English national character as one of "barbarism," that had flowered in French (especially in state-sponsored organs) during the Seven Years' War—or from the stunning indictment in *The Savages of Europe* (1764), to which the first parts of Long's book read like a direct reply (see Robert Martin Lesuire, *The Savages of Europe,* from the French, trans. James Pettit Andrews [London, 1764], and David A. Bell, *The Cult of the Nation in France: Inventing Nationalism, 1680–1800* [Cambridge, Mass., 2001], pp. 84–106).

20. *Address to the Rulers of the State* . . . (London, 1778), p. 14 (sanguinary); Burgoyne, *A State of the Expedition from Canada* . . . (London, 1780), p. 7 (terror); *The Annual Register . . . for the Year 1777* (London, 1778), p. 146 (revive); *The Substance of General Burgoyne's Speeches* . . . (London, 1778), pp. 6–7 (daggers); Burgoyne, proclamation, July 2, 1777, *Pa. Eve. Post,* Aug. 21, 1777, p. 438; Thomas Anburey, *Travels through the Interior Parts of America* . . . , 2 vols. (London, 1789), 1:286–87 (aged); and cf. *Annual Register . . . for the Year 1777,* p. 146, and defense testimony (June 1, 1779) in *State of the Expedition,* pp. 48–50.

21. Hopkinson, "An Answer to General Burgoyne's Proclamation" (1777), in *The Miscellaneous Essays and Occasional Writings* . . . , 3 vols. (Philadelphia, 1792), 1:146 and 148–50; [Wheeler Case], "St. Clair's Retreat and Burgoyne's Defeat," in *Poems on Several Occurrences in the Present Grand Struggle for American Liberty,* 5th ed. (Chatham, N.J., 1779), p. 8 (shrieks). An exultantly vicious poem in the *Pa. Packet,* Aug. 26, 1777—probably written by the governor of N.J., William Livingston (see Silverman, *Cultural History,* p. 659 n. 10)—also explicated the violent subtext of Burgoyne's announcement.

22. Burgoyne, *State of the Expedition,* p. 61 (whoop); *Annual Register . . . for 1777,* p. 156 (jumble); *Pa. Eve. Post,* Aug. 12, 1777, p. 423 (congeal); *Pa. Journal,* Aug. 13, 1777, p. 2 (spectators); Gates to Burgoyne, Aug. 30, 1777, and Burgoyne to Gates, Sept. 2, 1777, *Pa. Eve. Post,* Sept. 16, 1777, pp. 1–2; Pa. Gazette, Aug. 13, 1777 (bloody Burgoyne).

23. [Case], "The Tragical Death of Miss Jane M'Crea . . . ," in *Poems on Several Occurrences,* pp. 17–18 (throne); *Cont. Cong. Journals* 5:536 (July 10, 1776; sensation); Long, *English Humanity,* p. 82 (cannibalized). See James Austin Holden, "Influence of the Death of Jane McCrea on the Burgoyne Campaign," *Proceedings of the N.Y. State His-*

torical Association 12 (1913): 249–94; and June Namias, *White Captives: Gender and Ethnicity on the American Frontier* (Chapel Hill, N.C., 1993), chap. 4. Congress's account of pine-splint tortures at the Cedars appeared in the newspapers of Philadelphia (and from them, most American cities) later in July 1776. For a related account see Linda Colley, *Captives: The Story of Britain's Pursuit of Empire and How Its Soldiers and Civilians Were Held Captive by the Dream of Global Supremacy* (London, 2002), pp. 220–22, 225, and 227–31.

24. *Pa. Gazette*, July 28, 1782 (men of sound).

25. Franklin and Lafayette, "Ideas for the Prints / List of British Cruelties," *Franklin Papers* 29:591–92 (designs); and ibid. 37:186–90 (forged "Supplement"); see Luther S. Livingston, *Franklin and His Press at Passy . . .* (New York, 1914). The "Supplement" was reprinted uncritically in a monthly London anthology of news and cheap print about the war, the *Remembrancer or Impartial Repository of Public Events* (1775–84), by the indefatigable bookseller John Almon (a red-hot Americophile, to whom "the American writers constantly sent . . . their pamphlets and papers to be re-printed in England"; *Memoirs of a Late Eminent Bookseller . . .* [London, 1791], p. 33). Almon's *Remembrancer* also printed the cartoon, "The Allies" (discussed above), and the morsels of news that were its source.

26. Dodge, *Entertaining Narrative . . .* , 2nd ed. (Danvers, Mass., 1780; orig. pub. Philadelphia, 1779), pp. 25 and 21; Zeisberger, *Diary* 1:37 (Nov. 9, 1781). De Peyster, a New York Loyalist in the regular army, would go on to have a splendidly improbable life in the mainstream of British imperial culture, eventually rediscovering the tiny South Pacific island chain of Tuvalu as commander of the London brigantine *Rebecca* in 1819. For Hamilton's significance, see Bernard W. Sheehan, " 'The Famous Hair Buyer General': Henry Hamilton, George Rogers Clark, and the American Indian," *Ind. Mag. of Hist.* 79 (1983): 1–28.

27. *Freeman's Journal*, Sept. 19, 1781, p. 4 (Caesar); *An Address of the Congress to the Inhabitants of the United States of America* (York, Pa.—as well as Annapolis, Baltimore, Providence, Hartford, Boston, and Exeter, N.H.—1778; scenes of horror); *Pa. Gazette*, Aug. 4, 1779 (a dispatch from Fishkill, N.Y.; blush). For the French analogue to American barbarization of the British—which was very exact—see notes to discussion of Edward Long, above. For the postwar surge in British imports, see McCusker and Menard, *Economy of British America*, chap. 17; and Gordon C. Bjork, "The Weaning of the American Economy: Independence, Market Changes, and Economic Development," *JEH* 24 (1964): 541–60.

28. Evans, *A Discourse, Delivered at Easton . . . and to Be Distributed among the Soldiers— Gratis!* (Philadelphia, 1779), pp. 19, 18, and 22; and *The United States Mag., a Repository of History, Politics, and Literature* (Philadelphia), Jan. 1779, p. 6. For a valuable discussion, see Peter S. Onuf, *Jefferson's Empire: The Language of American Nationhood* (Charlottesville, Va., 2000), chap. 1.

29. Elizabeth Sandwith Drinker, *The Diary of Elizabeth Drinker*, ed. Elaine Forman Crane et al., 3 vols. (Boston: Northeastern University Press, 1991), 1:229–30 and 232 (Sept. 12, 15, and 19, 1777), and see ibid., pp. 232 and 234–35 (Sept. 20 and 24–25); Da[vid] Henderson to Joseph Galloway, Dec. 27, 1763, Friendly Assoc. Papers (Haverford) 4 (rioters); *Journals of the House of Representatives of the Commonwealth of Pennsylvania*

. . . (Philadelphia, 1782), p. 174 (Dec. 17, 1774; Bedford). For Congress's route, see John to Abigail Adams, Sept. 30, 1777, *The Book of Abigail and John: Selected Letters of the Adams Family, 1762–1784,* ed. L. H. Butterfield et al. (Cambridge, Mass., 1963), pp. 193–94; and for Congress's cultural history in this undignified period, see Benjamin Hylton Irvin, "Representative Men: Personal and National Identity in the Continental Congress, 1774–1783" (Ph.D. diss., Brandeis Univ., 2004). Until it decided in late summer 1776 that a general jail delivery was befitting an "even[t] of such importance" as the "total change of government" the Revolution had brought about, the assembly had also faced a glut of petitions from imprisoned debtors; *Journals of the House,* pp. 59–60 (Aug. 1, 1776). For frontier defense costs to be paid by the U.S., see, e.g., Pa. assembly to Congress, Apr. 2, 1778, *Journals of the House,* pp. 204–5.

30. Pa. council to Pres. of Congress Henry Laurens, May 2, 1778, *Pa. Arch.* 1:6:461; Fon W. Boardman Jr., *Against the Iroquois: The Sullivan Campaign of 1779 in New York State* (New York, 1978); and Savelle, *George Morgan.*

31. Dunlap to Jonathan Hoge, June 22, 1778, *Pa. Arch.* 1:6:611; Col. James Potter to Pa. vice president George Bryan, July 25, 1778, ibid. 1:6:666 (pleasure); Harris to Pa. Pres. Thomas Wharton, Jan. 29, 1778, ibid. 1:6:211; Armstrong to Pres. of Congress Henry Laurens, July 22, 1778, and to George Bryan, June 23, 1778, ibid. 1:6:657 and 612 (later Armstrong was able to pin his suggestion down to "a certain small town, the name of which I have not yet learned, but where the perpetrators of some of the late murders are said to reside"; to Congress, n.d., 1778, ibid. 1:6:614); John Carothers to Pa. Pres. Thomas Wharton, May 28, 1778, ibid. 1:6:560.

32. Resolution of the general assembly, Apr. 2, 1781, *Pa. Arch.* 1:9:52 (price); John to Abigail Adams, Sept. 30, 1777, *Book of Abigail and John,* p. 194; same to same, Oct. 28, 1777, *Adams Family Correspondence,* ed. L. H. Butterfield et al., 7 vols. to date (Cambridge, Mass., 1963–), 2:361–62; Pa. Pres. Joseph Reed to Rev. Joseph Montgomery, Apr. 8, 1780, *Pa. Arch.* 1:8:170; Finley to Pa. Pres. John Dickinson, Apr. 28, 1783, ibid. 1:10:41 (for Finley's mission, see Robert L. Brunhouse, *The Counter-Revolution in Pennsylvania, 1776–1790* [Harrisburg, Pa., 1942], pp. 127–28); Reed to Montgomery, Apr. 8, 1780, *Pa. Arch.* 1:8:170 (enterprise); Reed to Col. Samuel Hunter, Apr. 7, 1780, ibid. 1:8:167 (effectual); Reed to Brodhead, Apr. 29, 1780, ibid. 1:8:218; Brodhead to Reed, May 18, 1780, ibid. 1:8:250; same to same, Feb. 25, 1781, ibid. 1:8:743. Reed's bounty, in place three and a half years, was paid on six scalps; see Henry J. Young, "A Note on Scalp Bounties in Pennsylvania," *Pa. History* 24 (1957): 217. For inflation and Loyalist numbers, see Robert A. Becker, "Currency, Taxation, and Finance, 1775–1787," in *A Companion to the American Revolution,* ed. Jack P. Greene and J. R. Pole (Malden, Mass., 2000), p. 390, table 1, and Paul H. Smith, "The American Loyalists: Notes on Their Organization and Numerical Strength," *WMQ* 25 (1968): 259–77.

Chapter 9
THE POSTWAR THAT WASN'T

1. *Pa. Gazette,* Apr. 23 and May 14, 1783; *Freeman's Journal,* Apr. 23, 1783, p. 3; Silverman, *Cultural History,* pp. 425–26.

2. *Freeman's Journal*, Apr. 23, 1783, p. 3.

3. See White, *Middle Ground*, p. 408; and cf. James H. Merrell, "Declarations of Independence: Indian-White Relations in the New Nation," in *The American Revolution: Its Character and Its Limits*, ed. Jack P. Greene (New York, 1987), pp. 197–223.

4. *Freeman's Journal*, Apr. 23, 1783, p. 3.

5. "A Farmer on Juniata," *Pa. Packet*, Aug. 22, 1782, p. 3, and Nov. 7, 1782, p. 3.

6. *Pa. Journal*, June 21, 1783, p. 3; ibid., Aug. 28, 1782, p. 3; ibid., June 21, 1783, p. 3. For an important account of the mid-Atlantic revolutionary experience (finding at the core of the whole war a commandingly unifying, skin-color-based racial thinking among Europeans), see Gregory T. Knouff, *The Soldier's Revolution: Pennsylvanians in Arms and the Forging of Early American Identity* (University Park, Pa., 2003). For overviews of the war in the countryside, see *Beyond Philadelphia: The American Revolution in the Pennsylvania Hinterland*, ed. John B. Frantz and William Pencak (University Park, Pa., 1998).

7. *Pa. Packet*, Apr. 6, 1782, p. 3.

8. Brodhead to Pa. council president Joseph Reed, May 22, 1781, *Pa. Arch.* 9:161; Zeisberger, *Diary* 1:7 (Aug. 20, 1781).

9. Zeisberger, *Diary* 1:20 (Oct. 3, 1781), 60 (Jan. 10, 1782), and 66 (Feb. 20, 1782).

10. Ibid. 1:31 (Oct. 30, 1781).

11. Ibid. 1:78–79 (Mar. 23, 1782); *Pa. Eve. Post*, Apr. 16, 1782, p. 38; for the gathering up of remains, see Benjamin Mortimer, "Diary of the Indian congregation at Goshen on the river Muskingum from 1 Decr. 1799 . . . ," Apr. 12, 1800, pp. 26–27, *Morav. Recs.* 171:6.

12. Zeisberger, *Diary* 1:82 (Mar. 23, 1782).

13. *Pa. Journal*, Apr. 17, 1782, p. 3. But since this prisoner is described in the press as having been taken in the fall, it may represent a conflation of John Carpenter, who escaped from his captors months before, with the prisoner whose family was impaled; for Carpenter, see William M. Farrar, "The Moravian Massacre," *Ohio Archaeological and Historical Quarterly* 3 (1891): 287–89, an essential local investigation, recording some testimony from participants' families. The unnamed prisoner's family—the sight of which greeted the militia when it approached Gnadenhütten—was persistently confused in early accounts with Wallace's, which had in fact been buried (for which see ibid., p. 289–91; Farrar did not see Zeisberger and treats the impaled family as a fiction).

14. *Pa. Journal*, Apr. 17, 1782, p. 3; Dorsey Pentecost to Pa. council president William Moore, May 8, 1782, *Pa. Arch.* 1:9:540.

15. Zeisberger, *Diary* 1:80 (Mar. 23, 1782).

16. Frederick Lineback, "Relation of what Frederick Lineback was told by two of his Neighbours, living near Delaware River above Easton, who were just returned from the Monaungahela" (Apr. 1782), *Pa. Arch.* 1:9:524; Zeisberger, *Diary* 1:73 (Mar. 14, 1782).

17. Lineback, "Relation," p. 524; Zeisberger, *Diary* 1:80 (Mar. 23, 1782).

18. Zeisberger, *Diary* 1:80–81 (Mar. 23, 1782). Some of these steps—agreeing to be disarmed and gathered into one building, so as to help establish a mission group's harmlessness—were proposals of which Rev. Benjamin Mortimer would passionately resist any hint at the Goshen mission in autumn 1812 (see chap. 5 above). He had learned from Gnadenhütten that surrendering control over weapons and persons made anti-Indian violence more, rather than less, likely.

19. Lineback, "Relation," p. 524–25; Brig. Gen. William Irvine to George Washington, Apr. 20, 1782, *Irvine Correspondence,* p. 99 (considering); Dorsey Pentecost to Pres. Moore, May 9, 1782, *Pa. Arch.* 1:9:540 (consent); Farrar, "Moravian Massacre," p. 294.

20. Lineback, "Relation," p. 524–25 (hymns); *Pa. Packet,* Nov. 7, 1782, p. 2 (war songs).

21. Zeisberger, *Diary* 1:79 (Mar. 23, 1782) and 85 (Apr. 7, 1782).

22. Lineback, "Relation," p. 525. The hammers for making most barrels were not outstandingly heavy or large. For cooper's tools, and binding and stunning in slaughtering cattle, see Denis Diderot, *A Diderot Pictorial Encyclopedia of Trades and Industry . . . Selected from L'Encyclopédie . . .* , ed. Charles C. Gillespie, 2 vols. (New York, 1959), vol. 2, plates 458 (item g) and 387 (narrated s.v. "tonnelier" and "boucher" in the *Encyclopédie*). The few non-Moravian men found at the village, suspected of being warriors, seem to have been led away from the huts for outdoor tomahawkings that must have been imagined as more warlike. It is at about this point that one's comprehension can start to bridle; but as Inga Clendinnen usefully points out, simply setting out to understand just how things were done can, with care, bring an inquirer almost as close as many participants ever got to understanding why they were done; Clendinnen, *Reading the Holocaust* (Cambridge, 1999), p. 89.

23. Brig. Gen. William Irvine to Anne Callender Irvine, Apr. 12, 1782, *Irvine Correspondence,* p. 343; Zeisberger, *Diary* 1:80 (Mar. 23, 1782); John Heckewelder, *A Narrative of the Mission of the United Brethren among the Delaware and Mohegan Indians . . .* (Philadelphia, 1820), p. 323 (blood).

24. Zeisberger, *Diary* 1:80 (Mar. 23, 1782); Lineback, "Relation," p. 525.

25. Farrar, "Moravian Massacre," p. 294–95 and 299 (objectors); note by J. T. Holmes (son of Obadiah Holmes, who told his son he was an objector), Joseph Doddridge, *Notes on the Settlement and Indian Wars of the Western Parts of Virginia and Pennsylvania,* 3rd ed. (Pittsburgh, 1912; orig. pub. 1824), p. 203 (cried); Farrar, "Moravian Massacre," p. 295.

26. *Pa. Gazette,* Nov. 2, 1782; Brig. Gen. William Irvine to George Washington, Apr. 20, 1782, *Irvine Correspondence,* p. 99 (frenzy); Dorsey Pentecost to Pres. Moore, May 9, 1782, *Pa. Arch.* 1:9:540 (loss of friends); *Pa. Journal,* Apr. 17, 1782, p. 3 (40 warriors).

27. *Pa. Gazette,* Apr. 17, 1782 (spoil); Maj. William Croghan to Va. war secretary William Davies, July 6, 1782, *Irvine Correspondence,* p. 345 n. 3 (robbing scheme).

28. Brig. Gen. William Irvine to Anne Callender Irvine, Apr. 12, 1782, *Irvine Correspondence,* pp. 343–44 (nose); *Pa. Journal,* May 22, 1783, p. 3 (cooped up); petition of John Bradley et al. to Irvine, May 29, 1782, and order of Irvine, May 31, 1782, *Irvine Correspondence,* pp. 290–91 n. 3 (long bullets); Capt. John Finley to Irvine, Feb. 2, 1782, ibid., p. 351 (mutiny); Irvine to Anne Callender Irvine, Apr. 12, 1782, ibid., p. 344 (Gibson).

29. Irvine to Gen. Benjamin Lincoln, July 25, 1782, and to Anne Callender Irvine, Apr. 12, 1782, *Irvine Correspondence,* pp. 179 and 344.

30. Irvine to Gen. Benjamin Lincoln, July 1, 1782, ibid., p. 175; Irvine to Pres. Moore, July 5, 1782, ibid., p. 250. For local leaders' requests, see, e.g., Irvine to Lincoln, July 1, 1782, ibid., p. 175.

31. Irvine to Gen. Benjamin Lincoln, Apr. 16, 1783, ibid., p. 149; Irvine to Washington, Apr. 16, 1783, ibid., p. 149.

32. Irvine to George Washington, May 21, 1782, ibid., p. 113

33. *Pa. Journal,* May 22, 1783, p. 3, col. 2; Irvine to George Washington, Apr. 20, 1782, *Irvine Correspondence,* p. 109; John Emerson, "Advertisement," Mar. 12, 1785, ibid., p. 198 n. 2; and William Croghan to Barnard and Michael Gratz, Apr. 26, 1782, Gratz-Croghan Papers, Frank M. Etting Collection, H.S.P.

34. Lewis Weiss to Charles Thomson (secretary of Congress), Apr. 7, 1782, *Pa. Arch.* 1:9:523; Zeisberger, *Diary* 1:281 (Jun. 30, 1786; Thomas) and 368 (Sept. 8, 1787; Schebosch's wife); Brig. Gen. William Irvine to Pres. Moore, July 5, 1782, *Pa. Arch.* 1:9:576 (principles); Zeisberger, *Diary* 1:296 (Oct. 7, 1786; Augustus); Shippen to Joseph Shippen Jr., June 13, 1763, Shippen–Shippen Correspondence (extermination); Hunter to Pa. council vice president James Potter, Apr. 17, 1782, *Pa. Arch.* 1:9:529 (honor).

35. Dorsey Pentecost to Pres. Moore, May 8, 1782, and May 9, 1782, *Pa. Arch.* 1:9:540–41; Lt. Col. Edward Cook to Pres. Moore, Sept. 2, 1782, ibid. 1:9:629.

36. *Official Letters of the Governors of the State of Virginia,* ed. H. R. McIlwaine (Richmond, Va., 1929), 3:200; James Hayes's *Virginia Gazette, or the American Advertiser,* Aug. 17, 1782, p. 3.

37. Pentecost to Pres. Moore, May 9, 1782, *Pa. Arch.* 1:9:541.

38. The story was collected and put in this order by Farrar, "Moravian Massacre," p. 296; for identity, see Doddridge, *Notes on the Settlement and Indian Wars,* p. 201 n. 1.

39. *Freeman's Journal,* Dec. 11, 1782, p. 1 ("R" may well have been the physician Benjamin Rush).

40. Ibid., Apr. 24, 1782, p. 2; ibid., Sept. 4, 1782, p. 1; ibid., Aug. 15, 1781, p. 1.

41. Zeisberger, *Diary* 1:121 (Nov. 6, 1782); for the lapsed Moravian, Joseph, see also ibid., pp. 431 (Aug. 2, 1788) and 123 (Nov. 20, 1782). Details of the torture come from Brackenridge's account, discussed just below.

42. *Freeman's Journal,* Apr. 30, 1783, p. 1 (extirpation). Installments ran ibid., Apr. 30–May 28, 1783; collected as Brackenridge, *Narratives of a Late Expedition . . .* (Philadelphia, 1783). For narrative changes, see Parker B. Brown, "The Historical Accuracy of the Captivity Narrative of Doctor John Knight," *W. Pa. Hist. Mag.* 70 (1987): 53–67.

43. Brackenridge, *Narratives of a Late Expedition,* pp. 31, 32, and 35.

44. Ibid., pp. 35–38.

45. *Pa. Journal,* Feb. 1, 1783, p. 2.

46. *Freeman's Journal,* Apr. 3, 1782, p. 2.

47. Wharton, *Plain Facts: Being an Examination into the Rights of the Indian Nations of America, to Their Respective Countries . . .* (Philadelphia, 1781), pp. 3, 25, and 28. His earlier effort: Wharton, *View of the Title to Indiana, a Tract of Country on the River Ohio . . .* (Philadelphia, 1776).

48. *Cont. Cong. Journals* 25:682, 683, 686, and 689 (Oct. 15, 1783).

49. "Treaty of Fort Stanwix, in 1784," in *The Olden Time,* ed. Neville B. Craig (Pittsburgh, Pa., 1848; reprinted Cincinnati, Ohio, 1876), 2:426, as quoted in Reginald Horsman, "American Indian Policy in the Old Northwest, 1783–1812," *WMQ* 18 (1961): 38 (conquest); *Articles of a Treaty, Concluded at the Mouth of the Great Miami . . .* (New York, 1786; allotting); "Journal of General [Richard] Butler," in *Olden Time,* ed. Craig,

2:521–24, as quoted in Horsman, "American Indian Policy," p. 39 (protect). For conquest theory, see Stuart Banner, *How the Indians Lost Their Land: Law and Power on the Frontier* (Cambridge, Mass., 2005), chap. 4. For an overview see Horsman, *Expansion and American Indian Policy, 1783–1812* (East Lansing, Mich., 1967).

50. *An Ordinance for the Government of the Territory of the United States* . . . (New York, 1787), p. 2, art. 3.

51. *Cont. Cong. Journals* 33:388, 480, and 479 (July 21 and Aug. 9, 1787).

52. Ibid. 33:389 (July 21, 1787).

53. See esp. Andrew R. L. Cayton, "Radicals in the 'Western World': The Federalist Conquest of Trans-Appalachian North America," in *Federalists Reconsidered*, ed. Doron Ben-Atar and Barbara Oberg (Charlottesville, Va., 1998), pp. 77–96; and Peter Onuf, *Statehood and Union: A History of the Northwest Ordinance* (Bloomington, Ind., 1987).

54. *Pittsburgh Gazette*, as quoted in *Pa. Gazette*, Nov. 5, 1788.

CONCLUSION

1. Bogart, "Oration on Prejudice," *New York Mag., or Literary Repository* (New York, Mar. 1790), pp. 166–67 and 168. For a splendid (and, for the most part, unironic) account of "The Discovery of Prejudice," see Jordan, *White over Black*, chap. 7.

2. Benezet to Caspar Wister, 4 mo. 25, 1784, and to George Dillwyn, 7 mo. 1783, Benezet Papers.

3. *The Spirit of the Laws*, trans. and ed. Anne M. Cohler, Basia Carolyn Miller, and Harold Samuel Stone (New York, 1989; orig. pub. 1748), pt. 3, bk. 15, chap. 5, p. 250 (Franklin, of course, was influenced even by the Frenchman's going on to mockingly adduce against this view the case of the ancient Egyptians, who supposedly killed every red-haired person they could, since he stole it—Franklin, *A Narrative of the Late Massacres* . . . [Philadelphia, 1764], p. 13). For two other early assertions that the rioters failed to admit that "the Colour of the Skin can make no essential Difference," see Charles Read, *Copy of a Letter from Charles Read, Esq.,* . . . (Philadelphia, 1764), p. 4; and *A Dialogue Containing Some Reflections on the Late Declaration* . . . (Philadelphia, 1764), pp. 8–9. "Inward sin" is Jordan's phrase in *White over Black*, p. 311.

4. Benezet, *Some Observations on the Situation, Disposition, and Character of the Indian Natives* . . . (Philadelphia, 1784), p. iii (tawny); and to George Dillwyn, 7th mo. 1783 (well-disposed, lambs), Benezet Papers; *Indian Natives*, pp. 24 (ideas) and 36 (skins). For martyrdom to pacifism and European incitement, see *Indian Natives*, pp. 57n and 17–18. For Mass. reformers' similar views on Indian demoralization by prejudice in the 1790s, see John Wood Sweet, *Bodies Politic: Negotiating Race in the American North, 1730–1830* (Baltimore, Md., 2003), p. 307.

5. Benezet, *Indian Natives*, pp. 51 (intercourse, Indian neighbors), 52 (Providence), and 43 (reasonable); to Gen. Sir Jeffery Amherst, 7 mo. 1763, in Roberts Vaux, *Memoirs of the Life of Anthony Benezet* (Philadelphia, 1817), pp. 72–73. Benezet had it vaguely in mind to settle freed southern slaves "in that large extent of country, . . . [on] the west

side of the Allegany mountains" as well (Benezet to Dr. John Fothergill, 4th mo. 28, 1773, in Vaux, *Memoirs of the Life,* p. 30).

6. *Columbian Mag.* (Philadelphia, Feb. 1789), p. 109.

7. Gregory T. Knouff finds the same relative lack of concern with Indians' coloring ("Whiteness and Warfare on a Revolutionary Frontier," in *Friends and Enemies,* ed. Pencak and Richter, p. 242). The strongest contrary statement is Alden Vaughan, "From White Man to Redskin: Changing Anglo-American Perceptions of the American Indian" (1982), in *Roots of American Racism: Essays on the Colonial Experience* (New York, 1995), chap. 1—an essential early assessment, which I would suggest understates the evidence that Europeans, rather than starting out color-blind, described Indians as "tawny" very early, and then overstates the extent and earliness of a transition to seeing Indians as "red" (for which see Nancy Shoemaker, *A Strange Likeness: Becoming Red and White in Eighteenth-Century North America* [New York, 2004], chap. 6).

8. *Indian Natives,* pp. 52 (thoughtless); to Dr. John Fothergill, 4th mo. 28, 1773, in Vaux, *Memoirs of the Life,* p. 30 (danger); to George Dillwyn, 7th mo. 1783, Benezet Papers (prejudice); and see same to Caspar Wister, 4 mo. 25, 1784, Benezet Papers. For a review of northern antislavery's grudgingness, see Douglas R. Egerton, "Black Independence Struggles and the Tale of Two Revolutions: A Review Essay," *JSH* 64 (1998): 95–116.

9. See Daniel K. Richter, "'Believing That Many of the Red People Suffer Much for the Want of Food': Hunting, Agriculture, and a Quaker Construction of Indianness in the Early Republic," *JER* 19 (1999): 601–28, esp. p. 610; and *A Brief Account of the Proceedings of the Committee, Appointed in the Year 1795 by the Yearly Meeting of Friends of Pennsylvania . . .* (Philadelphia, 1805), and *A Brief Account of the Proceedings of the Committee, Appointed by the Yearly Meeting of Friends, Held in Baltimore . . .* (Baltimore, Md., 1805).

10. In the new republic, this arrangement ripped apart Indian lands and communities. First came Europeans' harassing encroachment; then, after squatting drove down the attractiveness for Indians of inhabiting a given tract and raised its value for farming, came official purchases, in what was increasingly a calculated two-part punch; see esp. Anthony F. C. Wallace, *Jefferson and the Indians: The Tragic Fate of the First Americans* (Cambridge, Mass., 1999), chap. 7. For borders and state monopsony power see Stuart Banner, *How the Indians Lost Their Land: Law and Power on the Frontier* (Cambridge, Mass., 2005), chap. 4, and Alan Taylor, *The Divided Ground: Indians, Settlers, and the Northern Borderland of the American Revolution* (New York, 2006), pp. 8–9 and 404–6.

11. Pa. constitution (1776), arts. 13–15, in *The Constitutions of the Several Independent States of America . . . ,* ed. Rev. William Jackson (London, 1783), pp. 192–93; Richard Alan Ryerson, *The Revolution Is Now Begun: The Radical Committees of Philadelphia, 1765–1776* (Philadelphia, 1978), pp. 234 and 252 n. 13 (voting); *Extracts from the Diary of Christopher Marshall . . . ,* ed. William Duane (Albany, N.Y., 1877), p. 68 (May 1, 1776).

12. *The Alarm, or An Address to the People of Pennsylvania . . .* (Philadelphia, 1776), pp. 4, 1, and 3; Pa. constitution (1776), preamble, in *Constitutions of the Several Independent States,* ed. Jackson, p. 181. For the revolutionaries' fiercely "cho[osing] to see their plu-

ralistic society as homogeneous" (p. 103), see Richard A. Ryerson, "Republican Theory and Partisan Reality in Revolutionary Pennsylvania: Toward a New View of the Constitutionalist Party," in *Sovereign States in an Age of Uncertainty,* ed. Ronald Hoffman and Peter J. Albert (Charlottesville, Va., 1981), pp. 95–133. For an improbable defense, on the grounds of religious toleration, of forcibly refounding the College of Philadelphia (packing the college corporation with non-Anglicans would actually "explode bigotry from among us"), see *Pa. Packet,* Nov. 25, 1779, p. 2; dissent in *Journals of the House of Representatives of the Commonwealth of Pennsylvania . . .* (Philadelphia, 1782), pp. 382–83 (Oct. 2, 1779).

13. *Pa. Packet,* Sept. 1, 1778, p. 3 (flesh, mercy); ibid., Sept. 26, 1778, p. 3 (further threatening); Robert F. Oaks, "Philadelphians in Exile: The Problem of Loyalty during the American Revolution," *PMHB* 96 (1972): 298–325; account to Meeting for Sufferings of Moses Roberts and Job Hughes, Apr. 9, 1780, Parrish-Pemberton Papers (under "Friends, Society of"). Though the exiles were not abused ("my companions and I increase in Fat or bulk," one wrote home; "Chocolate is generally my Breakfast & I believe contributes to this change"), two died; Henry to Elizabeth Drinker, Jan. 30, 1778, Drinker Correspondence, Q.C. For prosecution of speech, see, e.g., the case of Philip Lumbach, turned in by neighbors for "traiterously . . . [saying] the best News is that the Indians begin to murder on the Frontiers" (indictment, Dec. 1778 sessions, Northampton Co. Papers 3:283). For the ordinance defining treasonous speech (punishable, like a disloyal disposition, by indefinite detention), see *Journals of the House,* pp. 78–79 (Sept. 12, 1776); and, in general, Anne M. Ousterhout, *A State Divided: Opposition in Pennsylvania to the American Revolution* (Westport, Conn., 1987).

14. Wayne L. Bockelman and Owen S. Ireland, "The Internal Revolution in Pennsylvania: An Ethnic-Religious Interpretation," *Pa. History* 41 (1974): 156 (Quaker powerlessness); Brunhouse, *Counter-Revolution,* p. 180 (Byberry); Armstrong to John Harris, Mar. 25, 1784, Lamberton Scotch-Irish Papers 2:51. For fining and confiscation, see Arthur J. Mekeel, *The Relation of Quakers to the American Revolution* (Washington, D.C., 1979).

15. Militia privates' petition, Oct. 31, 1775, *Votes* 6:641; militia officers' petition, Oct. 31, 1775, *Votes* 6:640 and 639.

16. "Description of Gray's Gardens, Pennsylvania," *Massachusetts Mag., or Monthly Museum . . .* (Boston, July 1791), 3:413 and 415; Jasper Yeates to unknown, Aug. 21, 1776, *The Register of Pennsylvania,* Aug. 14, 1830, p. 105. For battlefield bones visible before, see *Pa. Gazette,* Dec. 14, 1758, and Oct. 21, 1756.

17. Coleridge to Southey, Sept. 1, 1794, *Collected Letters of Samuel Taylor Coleridge,* ed. Earl Leslie Griggs, 6 vols. (Oxford, 1956–1971), 1:99. For Priestley, and his involvement in a large-scale colonization scheme, see Robert E. Schofield, *The Enlightened Joseph Priestley: A Study of His Life and Work from 1773 to 1804* (University Park, Pa., 2004), chap. 15. For Asylum, see Alexander Graydon, *Memoirs of a Life Chiefly Passed in Pennsylvania within the Last Sixty Years* (Edinburgh, 1822), pp. 397–400; and Elsie Murray, "French Refugees of 1793 in Pennsylvania," *Proceedings of the A.P.S.* 87 (1944): 387–93.

18. John F. Watson, *Annals of Philadelphia and Pennsylvania in the Olden Time . . . ,* vol. 2 (Philadelphia, 1870), p. 529 (German farms); duc de la Rochefoucauld-Liancourt,

Travels through the United States of North America, the Country of the Iroquois, and Upper Canada..., 4 vols. (London, 1799), vol. 1, p. 187. For Indian land and American democracy, see esp. Alan Taylor, "Land and Liberty on the Post-Revolutionary Frontier," in *Devising Liberty: Preserving and Creating Freedom in the New American Republic*, ed. David T. Koenig (Stanford, Calif., 1995), pp. 81–108.

APPENDIX

1. Articles in the first, all-inclusive category came from places including the Caribbean, Fla., Bermuda, the Gulf Coast, coastal Africa, slave ships at sea, and, in one case, India; the second category, for mainland North American colonies alone, excludes all those places (Fla. and the Gulf Coast as well). The great height of the spike for 1760 in the mainland colonies as a whole, compared with its low level for the third category, the middle colonies alone, reflects the origin outside the mid-Atlantic (in the Carolinas) of nearly all that year's many stories about the Cherokee War. Systemic errors in the handling of apostrophes in the database used (maintained by Accessible Archives, Inc.) had to be corrected for, as did irrelevant uses of "white." My thanks to Helen Rogers for help with data entry and analysis.

2. As the chart shows, use of "white" to contrast Africans with Europeans had accounted for 70 percent of the more scattered cases from the middle colonies during the 20 years (1734–53) before the Seven Years' War, and the takeoff in talk of "white" people it brought. For the wartime years as a whole (1754–64), 77 percent of the uses of "white" recorded in the *Gazette* from the mainland colonies drew a contrast with Indians. Not shown separately on the chart (though also counted) are comparisons made with other non-European groups; or with no clear group at all. The rate of this last usage—"white" used absolutely—was vanishingly low before it started turning up in laws on militia duty, oath taking, and taxation in the Revolution.

3. Marie le Roy and Barbara Leininger, *Die Erzehlungen von Maria Le Roy und Barbara Leininger ... Aus ihrem eignen Munde ...* (Philadelphia, 1759), p. 10 ("sie hielten uns vor Indianer .... aber nachdem wir sie überzeugt hatten, daß wir Englische Gefangne wären ... so würden wir übergenommen"). "English" lost ground, then, for the same reason—a lack of coterminousness with the groups people saw as being really different and wanted to contrast—that, in the South, "Christian" had faded as a descriptor for nonslaves at the close of the preceding century (see Jordan, *White over Black*, pp. 95–96). Originally "white" was not a problem-free adjective, either. In trying out the language of skin color before the war, Franklin had excluded most Europeans (including Palatine Germans) from the class of "purely white People in the world," which was, he noted, "proportionably very small." His going on to call cheerfully for a brightening up of Pennsylvania ("why should we ... darken its People? ... where we have so fair an Opportunity, by excluding all Blacks and Tawneys, of increasing the lovely White and Red?") pointed up how problematic a source of unity the idea of skin-color kinship was for Europeans before the coming of Indian war and its rhetorical demands ("Observations concerning the Increase of Mankind ...," *Franklin Papers* 4:234; and note, too,

that when this essay became a political football in 1764, Franklin's having described Germans' skin color as nonwhite left no trace at all on public debates, while his having called them "Boors" set off a firestorm). A prevailing misinterpretation of the "red" in this passage (e.g., in Bruce Dain, *A Hideous Monster of the Mind: American Race Theory in the Early Republic* [Cambridge, Mass., 2002], p. 23) exactly reverses its intended sense: it referred in context not to Indians—whose color Franklin saw as tawny—but to one of the standard twin colors, the pallor and flush, of European beauty as described from Petrarch on, a usage conventional enough for Shakespeare to mock it in Sonnet 130. As Samuel Stanhope Smith noted, the typical complexion of northern Europe was "the mixture of red in white" (Smith, *Essay on Complexion*, p. 4).

ACKNOWLEDGMENTS

A BOOK is more things than it may seem to a reader. It is a simple machine for thinking, allowing an author to interlock ideas with greater clarity and depth than shorter bursts of speech or writing can sustain. It is a goal that organizes swaths of its writer's life, along the way giving "a value to every book, and an object to every inquiry" (as Gibbon observed). And when it is finished, it becomes an unmistakable connecting thread in one's personal past. As it unspooled it can be seen to have carried one first one way, then another—zigzagging to this place, this person, and to that, tracing a new constellation of friendships and debts.

For the resources that let me write the dissertation from which this book took shape, I am grateful to the Yale Graduate School, particularly in the person of former Dean Andrew Moore; the Pew Program in Religion and American History and its codirector, Harry S. Stout; the Mrs. Giles Whiting and Andrew W. Mellon foundations; and the staff of the Norwegian Nobel Institute and its hospitable director, Geir Lundestad. I have benefited since from support provided by Princeton University and the Princeton history department—especially funds or leave time supplied by the Richard Allen Lester University Preceptorship, the Committee on Research in the Humanities and Social Sciences (which supported the illustrations and map), the Class of '59 Junior Faculty Fund, and the Dean of the Faculty's office.

The staffs of Sterling Memorial Library and its Map Collection, the Beinecke Rare Book and Manuscript Library, and Firestone Library (including the late Lara Moore) were all important to this project's course. I am most grateful to the librarians and archivists of the American Philosophical Society, including Robert Cox and Roy Goodman; the Quaker Collection at Haverford College; the Library Company of Philadelphia; and the Friends Historical Library at Swarthmore College. Warren Wirebach of the Dauphin County Historical Society offered invaluable help on Susquehanna-side sources and personalities. And this book could not have been written, or even conceived, without the inexhaustible collections and staff, including Daniel Rolph, of the Historical Society of Pennsylvania.

For helping me try out ideas that proved central to the book I am grateful to Daniel Richter, and the collective brilliance of participants in the seminar of the McNeil Center for Early American Studies at the University of Pennsylvania; Jane Kamensky and her students at Brandeis University; participants in the Columbia University Seminar on Early American History and Culture; the works-in-progress series of the Shelby Cullom Davis Center for Historical Studies at Princeton; and Nancy Shoemaker, who offered insightful comments at a meeting of the Omohundro Institute of Early American History and Culture. My thoughts owe something more intangible but just as essential to each of the presenters and participants in the Colonial and Imperial Histories Colloquium at Princeton.

I am in the debt of James Merrell and Alan Taylor, who read and commented on parts of the manuscript at a pivotal point with insight, curiosity, and care, helping me see what I was trying to say, whether or not they agreed. Encouragement and careful readings of my work in an earlier incarnation by Robert Darnton, Anthony Grafton, Hendrik Hartog, Peter Lake, Susan Naquin, Robert Tignor (from whose administrative attentions I benefited immensely), and Sean Wilentz were especially heartening and helpful in setting this study's course, as were suggestions at its start by John Mack Faragher, Neal Salisbury, and Thomas Slaughter. Richard Beeman's enthusiasm helped me see what the book should be. And I continue to learn more from the scholarship of John Murrin, who truly has a mind forever voyaging, than seems quite plausible.

Tad and Lori Troilo have been steadfast friends and a source of relief, as have Hubertus Breuer and Cleo Godsey, Ernest Chung, Seth Harkness, Sterling Lambert, Andrew Lindholm, and Mark Wilson. Tonio Andrade, Anne Cross, and Unity Dienes, and latterly Liam Brockey, Nicholas Guyatt, Kevin Kruse, and Kenneth Norman have all offered their own welcome sorts of perspective. For their friendship and freely given help, thanks, too, to Peter and Letitia McPhedran, John Gillis, and my Philadelphia cousins Peter and Judith Rhoads Obbard, as well as to Robin and Benjamin Larsen and David Lane Fisher.

At Norton, Alane Mason's imagination and wonderful ability to cut through muddle have been essential, as has the help of Alex Cuadros. The job title of literary agent is helpless to convey what Jill Kneerim actually is: this book would not be half so good without her unflagging care, and it might not be at all. In recent years I profited from the preternaturally keen research assistance of Alicia Pittard and Helen Rogers. And the beauty and power of Stuart Allan's cartography has been a gift that shifted the way I see the stage-set of this book.

I am grateful to John Demos and Jon Butler for setting me, and the first version of this project, into motion, and for the extraordinary generosity with which they have overseen my doings since. I have learned a great deal not only from seeing how they think and write, but from the way they move through life. My parents, George and Jane Silver, have supported me, my family, and this book in every way they reasonably or unreasonably could. It is dedicated to them, in gratitude for how much I have learned from their love. My brother Mark, living a parallel life, has remained a hopeful reminder of how kind it is possible for a person to be. And the love and saving buoyancy of my wife Mona, and our daughter Celia, have not only helped to shape this book, but formed orbits of love that will long outlast it.

INDEX

Page numbers in *italics* refer to figures and charts;
page numbers beginning with 315 refer to endnotes.